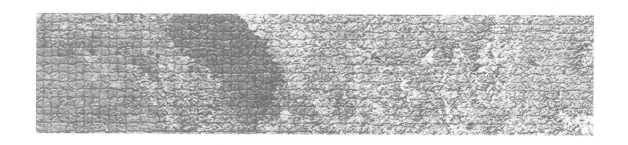

Microsoft®
Windows® 2000
Server

Teresa Smith

Kelly Smith

Front Range Community College

South-Western
Computer Education
an imprint of Course Technology

Thomson Learning™

Australia • Canada • Mexico • Singapore • Spain • United Kingdom • United States

Publisher: Kristen Duerr
Senior Product Manager: Dave Lafferty
Production Editor: Catherine DiMassa
Marketing Manager: Sue Ogar
Production Services: Shepherd, Inc.
Project Editor: Tricia Behnke
Technical Reviewers: Laura Schlegel, Jeff Beck

Copyright © 2001
by Course Technology, a Division of Thomson Learning
Cambridge, Massachusetts

South-Western Computer Education, an imprint of Course Technology, is a division of Thomson Learning. Thomson Learning is a trademark used herein under license.

ISBN: 0-538-68900-5
1 2 3 4 5 6 7   BM   03 02 01 00

Printed in the United States of America

Library of Congress Cataloging-in-Publication Data

Smith, Teresa (Teresa Irene), 1961–
   Microsoft Windows 2000 Server / Teresa Smith, Kelly Smith.
      p. cm.
   ISBN 0-538-68900-5 (perfect bound softcover)
      1. Microsoft Windows server. 2. Operating systems (Computers) I. Title: Windows
2000 Server. II. Smith, Kelly. III. Title.

   QA76.76.O63 .S589 2000
   005.7'13769—dc21

                                                                                        00-059490

For permission to use materials from this text or product, contact us by:
Web: www.thomsonrights.com
Phone: 1-800-730-2214
Fax: 1-800-730-2215

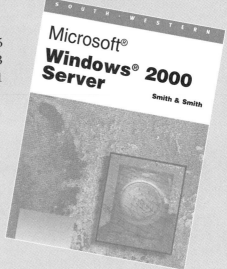
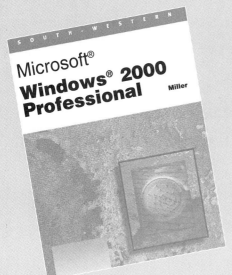

PREFACE

• • • • • • • • • • • • • • • • • •

South-Western's *Microsoft Windows 2000 Server* is a powerful tool for learning about Microsoft's newest desktop operating system, as well as for studying for MCSE or MCP certification. It is designed to be used in any class on business applications, technology, or computer applications. This textbook, along with the Instructor's Manual and Student Workbook, is all that is needed for a one-semester course. After completing these materials, the student should be able to install, configure, and troubleshoot Windows 2000 Server as well as understand the concepts of network management. The text contains information and exercises for each of the objectives in the Microsoft Exam 70-215, *Installing, Configuring, and Administering Microsoft® Windows® 2000 Server.*

It is assumed in this course that students have prior experience with graphical operating systems and are familiar with basic computing and networking concepts.

About the Materials

The full materials for this course include the student textbook, the student workbook, and the instructor's guide. Although advanced students may complete the course successfully in a self-guided manner, it is recommended that the course be taken in an instructor-guided, hands-on environment, especially for beginning or intermediate students.

Seventeen chapters are divided into five units that gradually introduce the skills necessary to manage a Windows 2000 Server-based network. Lessons divide each chapter into conceptual blocks and are accompanied by hands-on exercises that reinforce the presented information. Because the student provides the data used for the exercises, the text can serve as a roadmap for the configuration of an actual network. At the end of each chapter are review questions that are similar to the Microsoft exam questions, including multiple-answer multiple-choice scenarios. Each chapter is also accompanied by several tasks referred to as Performance Challenges. The challenges are designed to stretch students out of their comfort zone and encourage a quest for knowledge. Beyond defining the criteria and requirements, instructor input will be at a minimum.

The student workbook contains additional Performance Challenges as well as additional review questions. Definitions, short-answer, fill in the blank, and true/false questions are provided in the student workbook as a basis for study, chapter review, or test preparation.

About Microsoft Certification

An individual who is awarded Microsoft certification has successfully demonstrated the ability to perform specific tasks with Microsoft products. Because of this, companies in computer-related technical fields often use certification as a benchmark for hiring, promoting, and career planning. If a prospective employee has a Microsoft certification, the hiring company has an independent and reliable method of validating the claims on that person's resume.

Several degrees are available from Microsoft. The first degree is the Microsoft Certified Professional (MCP). To become an MCP, you must pass an exam that is designed to test your expertise on the single product for which you are testing. More advanced degrees, such as Microsoft Certified Systems Engineer (MCSE) and Microsoft Certified Developer (MCSD) require that you pass a series of core Microsoft Windows operating system and networking exams, including additional elective exams.

Questions on the newer Microsoft exams require not only recall of facts, but also the ability to perform network management tasks. The questions are challenging and often tricky in order to prove the person deserves the designation for which he or she is testing. In addition, the exams are not free. Some companies will invest in an employee's quest for certification, but usually funding is the responsibility of the employee. If you pass the exam (70% or better score), you get the certification. If you do not pass the exam, you lose the money you paid to take the exam. You can test again, but you pay the exam fee each time you take the test.

This course provides a foundation from which to continue your studies on Microsoft products and networking environments. After successfully completing the materials in this course, you may be ready to take Exam 70-215, *Installing, Configuring, and Administering Microsoft® Windows® 2000 Server.* However, additional exploration and assimilation will most likely be necessary, especially for topics covered in the later chapters of the text. An understanding of Windows NT Server 4.0 would also be beneficial.

To learn more about certification, visit Microsoft's Web site at the following address: *www.microsoft.com/trainingandservices* and then click on the **Certification** link. In addition to expanded opportunities in the computer industry, certification provides the added benefit of giving you access to exclusive Microsoft resources such as technical materials, secured Web sites, and product discounts.

You may take certification exams at Prometric and Virtual University Enterprises, independent testing organizations, which administer all Microsoft certification exams. To register for a Microsoft certification exam, decide which exam you want to take and note the exam number.

To Register with Prometric:

On-line: Visit Prometric's test registration site at *www.2test.com*.

Phone: Call (800) 755-EXAM (755-3926) in North America. Outside the United States and Canada, see the list of international contact numbers on the Prometric Web site.

To Register with VUE:

On-line: Visit VUE's Web site at *www.vue.com/ms/*.

Phone: Call the registration center nearest you. Registration centers are listed on the VUE Web site.

Acknowledgments

As Grammy winners can attest, no acknowledgement can fully express the feeling of gratitude one experiences upon the completion of a grand effort. The gratitude stems from the knowledge that success, in many ways, is dependent upon those who diligently work in the background or who have faithfully supported the one receiving recognition. It is with this realization that I thank the ones who have assisted me in producing this text. First, is my husband, Kelly, who both challenges and encourages me more than any human on earth. It was his amazing grasp of Windows NT 4.0 that caught the attention of John Wills at South-Western Publishing. All three of my South-Western Publishing editors, Jean Findley, Angela McDonald, and Dave Lafferty, were pleasant and helpful. In terms of producing the book, the project book team at Shepherd, Inc., is to be commended. Tricia Behnke, the project editor, is a jewel and helped me in so many ways including offering encouragement at precisely the right moment. My copy editor caught every oversight caused by late nights and long hours at the keyboard. I also need to thank my family for their understanding and patience when I could not attend every event or help them as I normally do. The names of the people in the review questions are an incomplete compilation of my many friends and family who have made me a better person. Lastly, and most of all, I thank God for giving me this wonderful life and these many talents that I can use to make a positive impact in this world. Where would I be without all of you? Thank you for everything.

Teresa Smith

Table of Contents

● ●

UNIT 1

IDENTIFICATION

UNIT 2

INSTALLATION AND CONFIGURATION

UNIT 3

CREATE THE USER ENVIRONMENT

UNIT 4

MANAGE THE SYSTEM

UNIT 5

DISASTER PROTECTION AND RECOVERY

UNIT

1

IDENTIFICATION

INTRODUCING WINDOWS 2000 SERVER

CHAPTER 1

OBJECTIVES

After completing this chapter, you should be able to:

- Understand basic network terminology

- Describe how a server functions within the network system

- Understand the purpose of a server operating system

- Identify the main features of Windows 2000 Server

- Understand the roles of the various operating systems in the Windows 2000 product line

OUTLINE

Introduction

History teaches us many things, not the least of which is how far we have come. Compared to the history of the world, the history of computers is very short. In a matter of decades, computers have gone from being basic calculators in the hands of a few to an innumerable conglomeration of interconnected devices that have infiltrated every part of our lives. Computers wake us up, brew our coffee, make our newspapers, monitor our car engines, open office doors, sit on our desks, and bring voices through our telephones.

From a business perspective, computers are an integral part of the modern free-enterprise system. This book approaches the subject of computers as they apply to the needs of a medium-sized business or corporation. Such a business might have as few as two computers connected together through a single network cable or as many as hundreds of computers connected through a complex networking system. As the next century unfolds, what does the future of computing hold?

Microsoft Corporation offers Windows 2000 Server as a server operating system to lead the way to that future. In order to understand how Windows 2000 Server will attain that lofty goal, you must first understand the basics of networks and how a server operating system functions. You will then be introduced to the newest features and capabilities of Windows 2000 Server as well as its relationship with companion products in the Windows 2000 family.

Lesson 1.1 Understand Networks and Servers

Fishing for Data

Without information a business would fail. Whether the goal of the endeavor is producing a product or providing a service, it is the collection and distribution of information that makes business profitable. We live in the Information Age, which means that information is a foundational element of our society. How is information collected and then distributed? For thousands of years, humans used word of mouth as their primary means of communication, which proved to be quite unreliable. The written word first appeared on cave walls and stones, but transporting written words in this manner proved impractical and necessitated the invention of paper and ink. Though handwriting was often slow and illegible, it sufficed for hundreds of years until the invention of typesetting machines, which brought an explosion of information creation and distribution. Finally, the invention of the telegraph, a simple invention that sent an electronic pulse down a wire, completes an ancestral family tree of modern networks.

The word **network** simply means "to connect." Every day, fishermen use nets of connected cords to catch fish. Just as a single cord could not catch as many fish as all the cords interconnected together, the amount of information that is gathered and distributed is far greater when computers are connected together. Fishermen have learned how to make fishing nets stronger and more effective. In the same manner, network engineers have found ways to make computer networks faster and more reliable. Similar to a hole in the net that reduces profit by allowing fish to escape, a computer network that is down reduces profit when the flow of information stops. One of the main objectives for this book is to teach you how to keep a network system up and running in the most efficient way possible. The first step is to understand the relationship between a network and a server.

Basic Description of a Computer Network

Networks are all about sharing. Without communication, there is not much opportunity for sharing. As an example of how networks function, consider what occurs when humans communicate. First, there must be a sender and a receiver; someone is talking, and someone else is listening. Next, a set of rules for communication must be established. If everyone talked at the same time, there would be noise but no communication. Once the rules are established, a common language must be determined. Communication cannot take place if one person is speaking English and the other Portuguese and neither knows the other language. Lastly, there must be a medium, which carries the signal; in this case, the medium is the air that carries the sound waves from one person to the other.

In a typical network, the sender and receiver are two computers. The rules for communication are defined by **standards,** and standards are implemented by the network hardware. Although *Ethernet* is a term that is commonly used, a networking standard such as 802.3 would be more precise. The language for the network is commonly referred to as a network **protocol** and includes TCP/IP or NetBEUI. The medium consists of cabling and other network equipment that carries the electromagnetic signal. If the standards are not followed, if the protocols do not match, or if the medium is not working, then there is no communication between the two computers.

Although the first networks were developed in the 1970s, protocols and standards were not agreed upon until the early 1980s. As programmers learned more about protocols and developed programs, they were able to make different computers and networks connect and exchange information. Their efforts paved the way for our modern Internet—a network of networks.

Even with protocols and standards in place, the process of moving large amounts of data over great distances is a challenge. If you had a birthday gift for your sister who was sitting in the kitchen of your house, for example, getting the package to her would be easy. If she lived in England, on the other hand, the amount of energy, time, and money expended to get the package to her would be much greater. Since the same is true for networks, most networks connect computers in the same office or building. Such a network is called a **Local Area Network (LAN).** If the distance the network spans is more than 1,000 feet—for example, across the street, across the city, across the country, or across the globe—the network will most likely be considered a **Wide Area Network (WAN).** The scope of this book is limited to LANs.

TIP

As a rule of thumb, if your company owns all of the equipment used in the network, the network is considered a LAN. If your network must pay for the use of equipment owned by other companies, such as a phone company or other service provider, the network is considered a WAN.

Components of a Network System

Network Cabling. Messages in modern networks are sent in the form of electrical pulses over copper cable, pulses of light over fiber optic cable, or through the air as radio or infrared light waves. Some networks even transmit data via satellites in orbit. Like the fishing nets in our example, the word *network* in reference to computer networks originated from the interconnected nature of the cabling. There are many different ways of connecting computers together with cables. The most common connection configurations, called **topologies,** include star, ring, and bus.

Network Operating System (NOS). The network operating system (NOS) is a collection of programs that work together to provide connectivity and sharing across the network cable. **Server programs** give some computers and peripherals the ability to accept requests for service across the network. **Client programs** give computers the ability to correctly request and use available services. The NOS packages requests from the keyboard and from applications in a succession of data envelopes for transmission across the network. Just as the post office has rules about packages being sent through the mail, networking protocols and standards govern how network data are packaged and sent.

Network Interface Card (NIC). The network cable attaches to a computer through the network interface card. The NIC changes the low-powered signals from the computer into more powerful signals that can cross the network cable. It also packages the data for transmission and controls access to the shared network cable. Characteristics that distinguish different types of NICs include the card's bus type, connectors, plug-and-play capability, and transmission speeds. Some servers can be **multi-homed,** which means that they have multiple NICs installed.

Network Connectivity Devices. In complex networks, the need to connect multiple cables together requires additional network devices specifically designed to make those connections. Table 1-1 lists common connectivity devices and their purpose.

Network Peripherals. Network peripherals are devices like modems and printers that can connect to the network cable directly. In order for users to gain access to a shared printer, the printer normally has to be connected to a networked computer. If that computer is down or powered off, the device will not be available on the network for others to access. Network peripherals are not dependent on a computer and, therefore, are more readily available.

NOTE: A thorough understanding of networking concepts is invaluable when administering a network with Windows 2000 Server. There are many sources of information on networking, including classes, textbooks, commercial books, and Internet Web sites. The scope of this book does not allow for in-depth coverage of the topic.

TABLE 1-1 NETWORK CONNECTIVITY DEVICES

DEVICE	DESCRIPTION
Hub	Organizes the cables and relays signals to other media segments. Some types of hubs can amplify the signal so it can travel farther. Intelligent hubs can even choose which path would be the quickest and send the signal that way.
Repeaters	Counteract the tendency for the electromagnetic waves to **attenuate** (or weaken) over distance by either amplifying the signal or regenerating the signal.
Multiplexers	Combine two or more separate signals and transmit them together. The signals are then extracted (demultiplexed) from each other when they reach their destination.
Routers	A combination of hardware and software that connects two or more networks together. A multi-homed Windows 2000 Server can be a router.

Designing a Network

Consider once again your sister's gift, her location in England, and your location in America. What decisions will have to made so that she can receive the gift unharmed and in a timely manner? One decision involves resources. If you have access to both an economy car and a jet airplane, which one would be best? Once your resources are chosen, you have to devise a route, keeping in mind that some routes are better than others (crossing the ocean as opposed to flying over the North Pole, for example). However, the one factor that will influence all of your decisions is cost. What delivery method can you afford? Similar considerations are required when designing a network.

Client Computers. The computers that are used to request access to network resources are called **client computers** or *nodes.* The number of client computers influences every area of network design. Table 1-2 describes the five major sizes of networks as they relate to the number of client computers.

Distance. Just as in human communications, when the distance between the participants increases, the medium becomes more complicated. The distance from the server to the farthest node will determine what protocol to use and what kind of cable will be required. Different cable types have varying specifications for distance; for example, Thinnet coax is limited to 185 meters, whereas optical fiber can reach as far as 2,000 meters.

TIP

Estimate how many client computers the network will have in the next three years, and include that growth in your network design. Because of rapid technology developments, evaluate all of your choices in terms of the near future.

TABLE 1-2 CATEGORIES OF NETWORKS BASED ON SIZE

NUMBER OF CLIENTS	NETWORK CATEGORY	DESCRIPTION
2 to 10	Peer-to-peer	Provides basic connectivity without a central computer (server) for file storage and security. Good for file sharing, printer sharing, e-mail, low budgets, and easy configuration.
10 to 50	Single-server	One computer is designated as the server and has control over security, resources, and services. Good for centralized file access, network printing, e-mail, security, backups, and Internet access.
50 to 250	Multiserver	More than one computer is designated as a server. Often the servers have specialized tasks such as file server, application server, messaging server, etc. Includes all of the benefits of single-server. Also good for large databases, application services, and WANs.
250 to 1,000	Multiserver high-speed backbone	A network with this number of nodes tends to be widely spread geographically. A high-speed cable called a **backbone** connects servers at multiple sites. The cost for these types of networks is very high, and management is more difficult.
1,000+	Enterprise	Enterprise networks are so large that they are not a single network, but a network of networks. Individual networks function locally and use the connection to other networks upon request.

Software and Data. Just like cars are the traffic on a highway, software and data cause traffic on a network. Some cities have highways with eight or more lanes so that the high volume of cars will not cause traffic jams. When designing a network, it is important to know how much information will be flowing through the system. A traffic jam on a network is called a **bottleneck,** and it has the same effect on people as a traffic jam on a highway. Users who have to wait get frustrated because they cannot get their work done in a timely manner. Freight trucks that take up more room on a highway can be compared to large software packages like computer-aided design and graphics packages that use large amounts of bandwidth as they traverse the network. **Bandwidth** is similar to the lanes on the highway; it measures the amount of

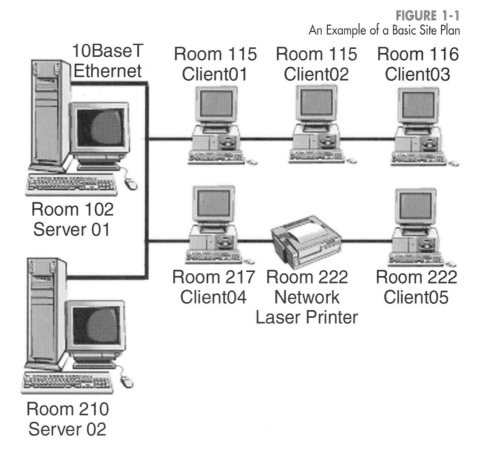

FIGURE 1-1
An Example of a Basic Site Plan

data that can flow at one time. Software packages such as word processors and spreadsheets that are installed on the client's hard drive do not require as much bandwidth.

Budget. Beyond the cost of the computers and software, determining the cost of a network includes NICs, cabling, other network devices, and labor for installation. Divide the total dollar amount by the number of clients to determine a per-client cost. Depending on industry conditions, the per-client cost of a medium-sized network can range from $150 to $250.

Site Plan. Every system administrator should create a **site plan,** which is a drawing of the physical characteristics of the network. The drawing includes the location of each computer and how the network cables connect the computers. It also details the locations of other networking devices such as hubs, routers, network printers, and so on. The site plan can be an invaluable document when expanding or troubleshooting the network. Figure 1-1 shows a simple site plan.

1.1

Create a Site Plan

To perform this exercise, you will need:

- A computer with a graphics program (such as Paint)
- Access to a computer lab
- A hard drive or floppy disk
- A printer

1. Use a graphics program to create a site plan for your computer lab.

2. Label the computers, network equipment, and network cable.

3. Save the file.

4. Print the file.

What Is a Server?

A computer that provides resources is called a **server,** and other computers that use those resources are called **clients.** The way servers and clients interact is similar to what happens in a drive-through lane at a fast-food restaurant. When you drive your car up to the speaker, there are mechanisms that inform the employee of your presence. The fuzzy voice says, "Order when you are ready." After you look over the menu and place your order, your request sets in motion a series of actions on the part of the employees, which includes the preparation and packaging of the food for delivery. As they work, you drive up to the window, pay the correct amount, and (if all is well) receive your food. If there is a problem, you can always call the manager to resolve the situation.

In the network world, the server is waiting for client requests. When a client is powered on, the server is made aware of the client's presence. The standards, protocols, and medium establish a means of communication and allow the information to flow between the client and server. Usually everything a client can request is stored on the server, but the server also stores a database of resources available on other computers. The site plan shown in Figure 1-1 demonstrates a network with two servers and several clients.

The hardware in a server computer cannot coordinate the network without an operating system. The **server operating system** is the collection of programs that make a server computer function as a server on the network. The programs include the graphical user interface, memory management, security, networking, performance tuning, error detection, administrative tools, and much more. Microsoft Windows 2000 Server is one of many server operating systems available on the market. To continue with our analogy, the methods of operation from one restaurant to another may be different, but the end result (getting some food) is the same. You most likely have a preference for one particular restaurant over another, and the same is true in server operating systems. We all know who the major fast-food chains are, and there are reasons why they are preferred. The same can be said for Windows 2000 Server, which commonly will be the server operating system of choice for many network administrators.

Lesson 1.2 Features and Benefits of Windows 2000 Server

What Is Windows 2000 Server?

Windows 2000 Server is the newest server operating system released by Microsoft Corporation. Previous versions of its predecessor, Windows NT 4.0, revolutionized the corporate computing standard by providing, among other things, a graphical user interface for system administrators who had grown weary of a command-line operating system. When the operating system was first released, Novell's server operating system was well entrenched in the industry. Undaunted, Windows NT 4.0 sales steadily grew until it outsold all competitors. It is from this foundation that Windows 2000 Server was launched.

Windows NT 4.0 was not a perfect server operating system, particularly in terms of handling very large networks. Because system administrators needed more flexibility, tighter security, and expanded features, Windows 2000 Server was designed to address those needs.

Windows 2000 Server Features

Having an understanding of Windows NT 4.0 would help you more fully appreciate the following list of improvements. Even if you are not familiar with Windows NT 4.0, this list is an impressive one. Do not despair if you do not recognize all of these terms, as this book will help you to understand them. For now, just think of them as "coming attractions." Table 1-3 summarizes the basic features of Windows 2000 Server.

Windows 2000 Server is an operating system that kept the strengths of Windows NT 4.0 and either eliminated or minimized the weakness. It is not perfect, and it will not be the ultimate operating system for the foreseeable future—for the future is ever changing. For the present, though, it should give administrators the tools required to successfully meet the needs of today's users. Mastery takes time and effort.

TABLE 1-3 WINDOWS 2000 SERVER FEATURES

FEATURE	DESCRIPTION
Lower total cost of ownership (TCO)*	Reduces the cost of running and administering a network by providing automatic installation and upgrading of applications and by simplifying the setup and configuration of client computers.
Security	Includes one of the strongest network security systems available today. Provides support for certification authorities and smart cards, as well as the **Kerberos** authentication protocol. Users are authenticated (proven to be who they say they are) before they gain access to resources or data on the computer or the network.
	The **New Technology File System (NTFS)** file system was expanded and given the new designation of 5.0. It provides expanded security for files, folders, printers, and other resources.
Active Directory	**Active Directory** is the name of the Windows 2000 Server directory service. The Directory is the database that stores information about network resources such as computers and printers. Users can access the database to find resources they need while allowing administrators to control access to those resources.
Performance and scalability	Supports up to four microprocessors with support for more from certain computer manufacturers.
	A server can be configured to be various types of servers, including a file server, print server, or applications server.
Disk management and backups	**IntelliMirror** copies data from desktop systems to servers, enabling users to move from one computer to another and still have the same desktop settings, applications, and documents available. If a connection to the server is lost, IntelliMirror can automatically use cached information from the local computer and, once the connection is restored, update the server.
	New backup utilities make backups and restores more reliable. The backup utility also supports a wider range of backup devices.
Networking services	Supports the most popular network protocols, including TCP/IP and network client utilities. The core TCP/IP network services all have been improved and updated.
	Can more fully facilitate interactions with other server operating systems like Novell NetWare, UNIX, and AppleTalk.
Communication services	Allows mobile users to connect to a computer running Windows 2000 through a service called **Dial-up networking.** Windows 2000 Server can support up to 256 simultaneous inbound dial-up sessions.
Internet integration	**Internet Information Server (IIS) 5.0** is included with Windows 2000 Server. Among other things, IIS allows the operating system to act as a Web-server platform to host Internet and intranet Web sites on network servers.
Integrated administrative tools	The **Microsoft Management Console (MMC)** provides a single interface for the efficient use of the many tools required for network administration. The tools can be combined to serve the needs of a particular administrator. New tools have been added, but even utilities purchased from other vendors can be implemented within the MMC.
Hardware support	Plug-and-Play compatible hardware is automatically detected, installed, and configured.
	Also supports the **universal serial bus (USB),** an external bus standard that eliminates earlier constraints of computer peripherals.

*Total cost of ownership (TCO) is the total amount of money and time associated with purchasing computer hardware and software. It also includes the costs involved in deploying the components (getting them ready for use) and then configuring and maintaining them. If a company can reduce these costs, it can use the money and resources elsewhere.

Lesson 1.3 All in the Windows 2000 Family

Most medium-sized businesses have more than one server, but the majority of the computers on a network will be used as clients. A person called a **user** normally uses a client computer to help with job-related tasks. Whether a client computer is used by a single user or shared by many users, the client operating system does not need the management capabilities of a server.

On the other hand, when a network grows and expands beyond the capabilities of a multiserver environment, a more powerful operating system is required. The Windows 2000 family is designed to meet all of these needs. Table 1-4 describes the family members.

Scalability is the key word when considering the migration from a small system of two or three computers to a large system of hundreds or even thousands of computers. By forming a family of products, Microsoft is assuring that the transition between levels will be smooth and cost effective. Of course, as you move up the line in power and capability, you also move up in cost. In the best scenario, the network system has helped your company grow and deserves the funding for expansion.

TABLE 1-4 PRODUCTS IN THE WINDOWS 2000 FAMILY

PRODUCT	DESCRIPTION
Windows 2000 Professional	High-performance, secure-network client computer operating system. Combines the features of Windows 98, while improving upon the features of Windows NT Workstation 4.0. This is the main desktop operating system for businesses of all sizes.
Windows 2000 Server	A file, print, and applications server, as well as a Web-server platform. Contains all the features of Windows 2000 Professional plus many server-specific functions. Ideal for small- to medium-sized enterprise applications.
Windows 2000 Advanced Server	A more powerful departmental and applications server. Provides rich NOS and Internet services.
Windows 2000 Datacenter Server	The most powerful operating system offered by Microsoft. Optimized for large data warehouses, econometric analysis, and server consolidation projects.

1.2

Document the Operating System

● ●

To perform this exercise, you will need:

■ A computer with a word processor

■ A copy of the site plan created in Exercise 1.1

■ A hard drive or floppy disk

■ A printer

1. Use a word processor to create a list of the operating system and software installed on each computer in the site plan. You will use this list later to record other software installations.

2. Save the file.

3. Print the file.

Summary

Computers are simply tools to help people get their work done. If connecting those computers together brings benefit, then a network is required. Making the connection is just the beginning of a functional networking system. In order for data to flow through the connection in a coherent manner, server operating systems must be capable of coordinating the individual functions of many parts into one more universal function. That function is to give users what they need when they need it.

Windows 2000 Server is the operating system Microsoft created for that purpose. Microsoft has listened to its customers and has attempted to meet the expressed needs by not only improving Windows NT 4.0 but also by pushing the limits of creativity to meet anticipated needs in the future. As an integrated whole, the Windows 2000 family of products is designed to expand in tandem with a growing company.

● ● ● ● ● ● ● ● ● ● ● ● ● ●

REVIEW EXERCISE

These questions will help you determine if you have learned enough to move on to the next chapter. If the graphic next to the option is a square (❑), there can be more than one answer for that question. If the graphic is a circle (○), there is only one correct answer. Color in the shape(s) to indicate your answer(s).

1. You have fifty client computers, two server computers, and a budget of $10,000 for creating a network environment. What sort of network would be best for the money you have to spend?

   a. ○ Peer-to-peer

   b. ○ Multiserver

   c. ○ Multiserver with a high-speed backbone

   d. ○ Enterprise

2. What are some of the responsibilities of a server operating system?

   a. ❑ Service client requests for data and applications

   b. ❑ Control access to files and resources

   c. ❑ Provide tools for administration

   d. ❑ Make sure the fries are not overcooked

3. Which of the following are parts of Windows 2000 Server security?

   a. ❑ NTFS 5.0

   b. ❑ IntelliMirror

   c. ❑ Kerberos Authentication Protocol

   d. ❑ UNIX

4. Active Directory is one of the most important additions to Windows 2000 Server. Which of the following statements accurately describe Active Directory?

   a. ❑ Active Directory is the name of the Windows 2000 Server directory service.

   b. ❑ The Active Directory is the database that stores information about network resources, such as computers and printers.

   c. ❑ Users can access the database to find resources they need.

   d. ❑ Administrators cannot control access to resources listed in the Active Directory.

5. You have been hired as the administrator of a small network. There are five computers. Four of them are about the same in processing power and hard drive space. Compared to the others, the fifth computer has almost four times as much hard drive space and three times the amount of memory. Which products from the Windows 2000 family will best fit the current needs of the company?

a. ❏ Windows 2000 Professional

b. ❏ Windows 2000 Server

c. ❏ Windows 2000 Advanced Server

d. ❏ Windows 2000 Datacenter Server

PERFORMANCE CHALLENGES

Performance Challenges can be performed for extra credit or to expand your knowledge. Beyond defining the criteria and requirements, instructor input will be at a minimum so that you can expand out of your comfort zone.

■ Research the cost of each of the products in the Windows 2000 family. Print a report detailing your findings. **Hint:** Check the Internet or call a local vendor.

■ Create a graphic for each of the star, ring, and bus networking topologies.

IDENTIFY HARDWARE AND SOFTWARE

CHAPTER

2

● ● ● ● ● ●

OBJECTIVES

After completing this chapter, you should be able to:

- Identify the basic hardware components in a PC

- Know the minimum hardware requirements for running Windows 2000 Server

- Search the Hardware Compatibility List for hardware and software testing information

- Make informed decisions about the implementation of application programs

- Understand the benefits of purchasing products with the Microsoft Logo

- Determine which licensing method is best for your network

OUTLINE

Introduction

One of the first things to understand about personal computers (PCs) is that they are constantly evolving; what is considered state of the art today may be outdated tomorrow. In order to be a good system administrator, you will need to stay current on changes in the PC market. There are several components of a PC that have an impact on how the unit integrates into the overall network and how well the users needs are serviced. Not every PC can function as a server, so the hardware components in a server are important.

Lesson 2.1 Understand Hardware Basics

The Motherboard

Most of the essential electronics for a PC are on a single printed circuit board called the motherboard. Many components, including memory chips, adapter cards, and hard drives, connect to the motherboard, which makes it one of the most important parts of the PC.

The Central Processing Unit

The brain of the PC is the **central processing unit (CPU),** which is a microprocessor chip created by companies such as Intel Corporation and AMD. Of the numbers issued by Intel to classify CPUs, the most famous designations are 8088, 80286, 80386, 80486, Pentium, Pentium II, Pentium III and Celeron.

The speed of a CPU is measured in **megahertz (MHz).** One megahertz is equal to one million ticks per second. Just like the inner workings of a clock, there is a certain amount of work that occurs between the ticks. Thus, a CPU running at 333 MHz will get more work done in the same amount of time than one running at 266 MHz.

In addition to speed, there are other specifications of the CPU that determine its capacity. Table 2-1 details these specs.

Taking Measurements

Do you know the difference between a bit and a byte? Just as we use ounces and pounds to measure liquids and food, the items within a computer

---

NOTE: You should already be familiar with the basics of hardware. This lesson provides a common foundation of terminology for the rest of the book.

TABLE 2-1 SPECIFICATIONS FOR RATING A CPU

ITEM	DESCRIPTION
Word size	Indicates the largest number that can be operated on in one operation and is currently in the range of 16 to 32 bits. Numbers are like coal to a steam engine—the more provided in one operation, the higher the energy output.
Numeric coprocessor	Modern CPUs can perform floating-point numerical computations. Older ones had an additional, separate chip. A numeric coprocessor is especially helpful with highly mathematical programs like graphics, spreadsheets, video games, and computer-aided design.
Memory	Each CPU has a maximum amount of memory that it can possibly use. The range at this time is between 1 megabyte and 4,096 megabytes. Memory is like workspace—the more, the better.
Internal cache RAM	Most CPUs have memory included in the chip. The closer the memory is to the CPU, the faster the access time will be. Therefore, any memory *inside* the CPU is very fast.
Data path	Indicates the largest number that can be transported into the chip in one operation and is currently in the range of 8 bits to 64 bits. This is like an 8-lane highway compared to a 64-lane highway; the one with the higher volume gets more work done.

TABLE 2-2 COMMON MEASUREMENTS FOR QUANTIFYING COMPUTER COMPONENTS

MEASUREMENT	QUANTITY
Byte (K)	Eight bits-approximately one character
Kilobyte (KB)	One thousand
Megabyte (MB)	One million
Gigabyte (GB)	One billion
Terabyte (TB)	One trillion

have measurements. These measurements, which are based on the metric system, are summarized in Table 2-2.

PC Memory

Memory in a PC is not so different from human memory; it is used as both a storage area and a work area. Although older PCs typically had only 640 K of memory to work with, many of today's PCs have hundreds of megabytes of available memory. This translates into a higher capacity for accomplishing tasks.

The full name of PC memory is **random access memory,** or **RAM** for short. If you take the words individually, you can see that the programs can randomly access the memory by reading data out of it or by writing data to it anytime they need to. (In computer terms, *read* means to retrieve and *write* means to store.) Every instruction of every program that runs on the computer must be loaded into RAM before it can execute (or run).

Although RAM is an important part of the PC, there is one drawback—it is dependent upon power to function. A technical term for this dependency is **volatility.** When you turn off (or reset) the computer, everything in RAM is lost.

The people who first invented PCs did not expect that programs would need more than 640 K of RAM, and they designed the PC operating system (DOS) and architecture to reflect that assumption. Subsequent designers had a difficult time breaking the "640 K barrier," as it has come to be known. Eventually, however, they did break the barrier and gradually increased the RAM capacity by establishing different areas of memory. For example, there was conventional memory, expanded memory, extended memory, plus upper-memory blocks, and high-memory blocks. Because of the incremental addition of memory blocks, memory access was slow and cumbersome for programs.

When Microsoft developers began work on Windows NT, they decided to redesign the memory management for the new operating system. Windows NT (and subsequently, Windows 2000) has a **flat memory model,** meaning that it can use all of the available memory; all of the old memory divisions are gone.

Physically, memory is contained within chips that are connected to the motherboard, and these memory chips are usually organized into what is called a **bank.** A typical motherboard has slots for four banks of memory. A bank contains eight or nine small chips or a mini-circuit board that has memory chips mounted on it. These mini-circuit boards, which are called **SIMMs,** come in several varieties; the two most common are 30-pin and 72-pin. The 72-pin SIMMs contain more chips and have more connector pins on the base of the board.

A newer type of memory board is **DIMMS,** which are physically longer and allow more room for connectors. More connectors translates into the potential for more memory on each board.

Another type of memory is **ROM,** which stands for **read-only memory.** Whereas RAM exists to help get work done, ROM's goal is to give instructions, rather than to take them. You learned that the instructions in RAM are lost when the computer is turned off, so how does a computer that will not function without instructions know what to do when it is turned back on? That is the function of ROM; the ROM instruction set exists whether the power is on or not because the instructions are actually *wired* into the circuitry. ROM is **nonvolatile** because it is not dependent on power to retain instructions. Part of ROM's function is to give the computer the instructions it needs to start running and *then* to initialize RAM. Therefore, RAM is dependent upon ROM to prepare the computer.

64-Bit Very Large Memory (VLM) Support

One of the newer developments in PC memory is **very large memory (VLM),** which allows 64-bit processors to access up to 32 GB of RAM. This is greatly improved from 32-bit computing, which limits addressable main memory and file sizes to 2 GB or less. VLM is especially useful with database programs where massive *amounts* of data need to be accessed quickly. With VLM, access times are up to 200 times faster than without it. Windows 2000 supports VLM.

Expansion Cards

The motherboard of the computer connects all of the components to each other. Motherboards also have **expansion slots** (usually between five and eight) that allow other circuit boards to plug into the motherboard. **Expansion boards** (also called **cards**) are used for video, sound, printing, mouse, modem communications, networks, and even for complicated software packages like computer-aided design programs. The expansion cards allow you to customize the particular capabilities of your system in addition to the configuration of the motherboard.

Ports and Connectors

If someone handed you a fan and asked you to make it work, you would probably go to an electrical outlet and plug the fan in. With a touch of the on-switch, the air is flowing. Just like an electrical device must connect to power to function, every peripheral device that needs to communicate with the computer must be connected to the computer. These connections are made through ports and connectors. With the fan, the port is the electrical socket and the connector is the plug head; both of these are standard in configuration for 110 power. With computers, there are many different types of ports and connectors. For example, the connector for a network cable is very different from the connector for a parallel printer.

Bus

Have you ever flown over a city in a helicopter? If you did, you would look down and see tiny vehicles traveling through an intricate system of connecting roads that lead to various buildings. This is similar to what happens inside the PC. Instead of roads, however, you would see silver metal traces on the printed circuit board of the motherboard. Instead of vehicles, the computer sends electrons along the traces. And instead of buildings, the electrons are traveling to and from various components on the motherboard, such as the CPU and memory chips.

If the electrons can only travel on the metal traces of the motherboard, how do they get up onto the expansion card? The answer is through a **bus.** This is not like a school bus; rather, it is more like a bus station. The electrons are sent to the station and then are connected to their destination. Some electrons are arriving and being sent to other locations on the motherboard, and the bus is very important in making these connections to and from the expansion cards.

TABLE 2-3 TYPES OF COMPUTER BUSES

BUS TYPE	PRONOUNCED	DESCRIPTION	DATA PATH	CLOCK RATE
AT (ISA)	Eye-sah	Accepted both 16- and 8-bit boards, difficult to install	16 bits	4.77 to 8 MHz
EISA	Eee-sah	Slow clock rate for backward compatibility, easier to install	32 bits	8 MHz
VESA local bus	Vee-sah	Invented for video cards, also called *VLB*, difficult to install	32 bits	33 MHz
PCI local bus	P C I	Plug-and-play installation, less interaction with CPU increases speed	64 bits	33 MHz (66 MHz in the works)
PC card (PCMCIA)	P C Card	Credit card size, hot swap (while computer is on), mostly used in laptops	16 bits	33 MHz
Universal serial bus (USB)	U S B	Plug and Play, one interrupt with multiple serial devices	1 bit, full-duplex	(Transfer rate) 1.5 Mb/s to 480 Mb/s depending on the peripheral

Like CPUs, buses also have data paths. If the data path for a bus is 16 bits, then the bus will have 16 data lines (that is, the bus is *16 bits wide*). If you had a Pentium CPU with a data path of 32 bits, a 16-bit bus would actually slow the system down; thus, the bus can either help or hinder performance.

Just like in the real world, we might have different companies running bus stations, so there are several different types of computer buses to consider. Table 2-3 summarizes the bus types.

Universal Serial Bus—The Newest Bus

The universal serial bus (USB) replaces all of the different kinds of serial and parallel port connectors with one standardized plug and port combination.

Using a feature known as **hot-swapping,** USB allows the user to attach or remove a peripheral without having to shut down and restart the PC. Once the peripheral is plugged in, the PC automatically detects the peripheral and configures the necessary software.

Most PCs on the market today, including many notebooks, are USB-ready. Some USB devices include scanners, digital cameras, computer telephony products, digital speakers, and digital gaming devices.

In addition, USB allows many peripherals to be connected at one time. Special USB peripherals—called USB hubs—have additional ports that let you "daisychain" multiple devices together. USB connections allow data to flow both ways between the PC and peripheral.

> **TIP**
>
> To learn more about USB, go to the Internet site *www.usb.org.*

Controllers

Any device connected to the motherboard is called a **peripheral.** The communication necessary between each peripheral and the motherboard occurs through **controllers.** For example, a hard disk needs a hard disk controller, a keyboard needs a keyboard controller, and so on. The functions of a controller include matching the transfer rate and amplifying the electronic signal between the peripheral and the CPU. Other names for controllers include **adapter, port,** and **interface.**

While controllers are on an expansion card (as in the case of a video controller), the controller occasionally is a chip on the motherboard (as in the case of the keyboard controller). Controllers are most often the topic of conversation in regard to storage devices like floppy disks and hard drives.

Floppy Disks

A floppy disk drive has an interface card with a controller. As a peripheral, a floppy drive is most often used to transport small amounts of data from one computer to another on floppy disks. The most common size of floppy disk used in earlier floppy drives measured 5 1/4 inches and held 360 K of data. Improvements in the technology led to more storage space on a smaller disk.

The most common floppy disk in use today measures 3 1/2 inches and stores 1.4 MB of data. Figure 2-1 shows the physical characteristics of the two common floppy sizes. The

FIGURE 2-1
Two Sizes of Floppy Disks: 5 1/4" and 3 1/2"

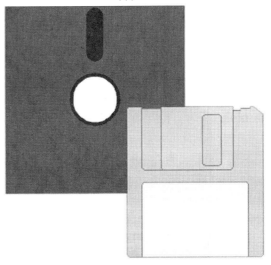

floppy drives themselves require periodic maintenance in the form of speed adjustment, head alignment, and head cleaning. The floppy disks are susceptible to temperature extremes, foreign particles, and eventual decay.

Even though they are unreliable and prone to failure, floppies are still a necessary part of a computer system. For example, some software vendors still distribute their software on floppy disks. Even Windows NT stores emergency repair information on floppies and also includes three floppy disks for optional use during installation.

Hard Disks

Hard drives are similar to floppy disks in how they store the data, but they differ from floppy drives physically. See Figure 2-2. For example, a floppy disk has one platter made of Mylar plastic that spins within a plastic casing. A hard disk usually has multiple platters made of metal that spin within a hermetically sealed metal casing. By its physical nature, metal can spin faster than plastic; therefore, the access and transfer rates of data to and from hard drives is much faster. Another difference is that floppies are meant to be portable, whereas hard drives are usually installed inside the case. In addition, the multiple platters of a hard disk and the fact that the hard drive is "fixed" within the case result in higher storage capacity. Finally, the read/write heads can be much more precise because they are held in a rigid position. For all of these reasons, hard drives are more reliable than floppies.

FIGURE 2-2
A Hard Disk Drive

Later in the book, you will discover the many options for using hard disks in a network environment. For example, you can use multiple disks to make a **stripe set.** If one hard drive in the stripe set fails, you can remove the bad drive; when you install a new one, the operating system will rebuild the data that were stored on the bad drive.

CD-ROM Drives

There were problems with the two data-storage options of floppies and hard drives: floppies did not hold enough information and died frequently; hard drives were reliable but not portable. The computer industry sought for alternative data-storage options, including removable hard drives and super floppies. These options were either too expensive or not sufficient to fill the need. The CD craze started in the music industry and was embraced by the computer industry as a medium for data storage that was small in size, resistant to damage, and able to hold a large quantity of information (approximately 680 MB) on one disk.

Since 1995, CDs have become a mainstay of the modern PC. The majority of vendors that previously distributed their software on floppy disks now use CDs instead. CD-ROMs have not replaced hard drives because current CDs do not store as much data as a hard drive and their access time is slower.

Tape Drives

Although hard drives are more reliable than floppies, they will not run forever. It is not a matter of *if* a hard drive will fail; it is a matter of *when*. Too many people and companies have valuable data on their hard drives that are not duplicated anywhere else. Tape drives are backup devices that duplicate the data from a hard drive to some type of tape media.

Drivers

Since hardware cannot function without instructions, **drivers** are programs that provide a software interface to the hardware device. Drivers are written for the specific device they control and for the specific operating system that governs the device. For example, if you have a printer driver for Windows 95, you will not be able to use that same driver for Windows NT. Even though the device is the same, the instructions are different because of the differences in the operating systems. Microsoft is moving toward counteracting this problem with the **Windows Driver Model (WDM),** which will contain the same drivers for both Windows 98 and Windows 2000. As more manufacturers adopt this model, more hardware installations will be immediately successful.

The following sources can be used to obtain the correct driver for a hardware device:

- The floppy disk or CD included in the device's original packaging

- The manufacturer (with a telephone call to customer service)

- The manufacturer's Internet site

- An Internet site specifically designed to provide hardware drivers

- The Windows 2000 Server installation CD (which includes many common drivers)

2.1 Documenting PC Hardware

• •

To perform this exercise, you will need:

■ A computer

■ A word processor

1. Using a word processor, document the hardware components for one PC.

   ■ Include specifications for the CPU, RAM, expansion cards,

number of slots, video, mouse, keyboard, hard drive space, floppy drive(s), CD-ROM(s), and so on.

   ■ If available, use Form 2.1 in the Student Workbook.

2. Print your results.

Lesson 2.2 Determine Hardware Requirements

Now that you have an overview of the basics of hardware, we will address the special needs of a server. Table 2-4 details the minimum hardware requirements for running Windows 2000 Server. As you read the table, keep in mind that depending on the individual situation of the company, changes may be necessary. Another determining factor is the purpose of the server. For example, a file server will need more hard drive space, whereas an application server will need more memory.

For maximum efficiency, the minimum hardware requirements should be exceeded whenever possible. For example, installing a faster hard drive can result in quicker response times when downloading a file from the server.

> ### MICROSOFT TEST OBJECTIVE
>
> Configure hardware devices. (On the exam, you may be required to know the minimum hardware requirements for a server. Memorize those numbers.)

IRQs

Interrupt request lines, or **IRQs,** are hardware lines that carry a signal from a device to the CPU. A hardware interrupt signals that an event has taken place that requires the processor's attention. The interrupt may come from the

TABLE 2-4 MINIMUM HARDWARE REQUIREMENTS FOR WINDOWS 2000 SERVER

HARDWARE ITEM	MINIMUM REQUIREMENT
CPU	Pentium 133 MHz or higher
Memory	128 MB for servers supporting one to five clients
Hard drive space	One or more hard disks with a minimum of approximately 685 MB (1 GB recommended) on the partition that will contain the system files
Networking	One or more network adapter cards
Display	Video display adapter and monitor with video graphics adapter (VGA) resolution or higher
Other drives	CD-ROM drive (12X or faster recommended) and floppy disk drive (1.4 MB)
Accessories	Keyboard and mouse (or other pointing device)

keyboard, the input/output ports, or the system's disk drives. In the PC, the main processor does not accept interrupts from hardware devices directly; instead, interrupts are routed to a chip that responds to each hardware interrupt, assigns it a priority, and then forwards it to the main processor.

Once the main processor has received the interrupt, it saves and suspends its current activity and then branches to an interrupt service routine. When the service routine is completed, the processor returns to the suspended activity. In the PC, interrupts are often divided into the following three classes:

- Internal hardware

- External hardware

- Software interrupts

Most of the interrupt lines in a PC are assigned to a particular device. For configuration purposes, each line is assigned a number. Table 2-5 lists the common settings for IRQ lines in a PC.

Sharing interrupts is not possible on many PC expansion boards, mostly because of the ISA bus. If you insert two boards and configure them to use the same interrupt line, you will have problems. The computer might crash, for example, when one board requests an interrupt that the other board is already using. When installing a new board, users usually had to choose an IRQ, set DIPswitches, install configuration software and drivers, and hope there were not any conflicts. Newer buses allow for IRQ sharing, as long as the boards support IRQ sharing.

Many headaches were caused by IRQ conflicts, and users were looking for an easier way. Microsoft introduced a solution with Plug and Play technology.

TABLE 2-5 COMMON IRQ LINES IN A PC

INTERRUPT LINE	DEVICE
0	Time
1	Keyboard
2	Cascade to IRQ9
3	COM2 or COM4 (not both)
4	COM1 or COM3 (not both)
5	XT hard disk controller, LPT2
6	Floppy disk controller
7	LPT1
8	Clock
9	Possible cascade to IRQ2
10	Available for other devices
11	Available for other devices
12	Motherboard InPort
13	Coprocessor
14	Hard disk
15	Available for other devices

Plug and Play

Hardware cannot function without instructions (drivers and other software instructions), so when a hardware device is inserted into the computer, its accompanying drivers need to be copied to the hard drive. The operating system must be made aware of the new addition, and the hardware configuration needs to complement other installed components without conflicts. Users in the past have had a difficult time with this process because all manufacturers used their own process for installing the drivers and software; thus, IRQ conflicts were common. **Plug and Play** was a concept created by Microsoft to counteract those problems. As its name suggests, the user could add or remove devices (plug) and the operating system would be able to adapt the hardware configuration without user intervention (play).

Microsoft's goal is to continue the evolution of Plug and Play by creating a comprehensive, system-wide approach to controlling system and device configuration. For example, Microsoft has created the *Advanced Configuration and Power Interface* (ACPI) *version 1.0* specification, which defines a new system board and BIOS interface that extends Plug and Play data to include power management and other new configuration capabilities—all under complete control of the operating system. The primary design goal of plug and play is to further the industry initiative to simplify personal computers for end users. Note, however, that not all hardware devices support Plug and Play. If this is the case, the user must perform the installation of drivers and software, resolve conflicts, and troubleshoot problems manually.

Lesson 2.3 Examine the Hardware Compatibility List

When Microsoft first released Windows 95, one of the main selling points was its ability to work with almost any hardware device in existence. Microsoft had worked long and hard to either create or procure drivers that were compatible with its operating system. The main objective for Windows 95's interaction with hardware was summed up in the word *compatibility*. Unfortunately, the architecture of the two operating systems is so different that the drivers created for use with Windows 95 will either not work or will cause major problems with Windows NT. To compensate for the lack of drivers for Windows NT, Microsoft created the **Hardware Compatibility List (HCL).** The HCL is a compilation of computers and computer hardware that have been extensively tested with Windows operating systems.

There two main sources for obtaining the HCL are:

■ The Windows 2000 Server installation CD (hcl.txt in the Support folder)

■ Microsoft's Web site (see Exercise 2.2)

CAUTION Microsoft only supports devices listed in the HCL. If you have a problem with a hardware device that is not on the HCL, do not expect anything more than "sorry" from Microsoft support. If you must use a device that is not on the HCL, call the manufacturer to obtain a compatible driver for your operating system.

EXERCISE

2.2   Browsing the HCL Web Site

To perform this exercise, you will need:

■ A computer with access to the Internet

1. Connect to the Internet.

2. Use your browser to go to *www.microsoft.com/hcl*.

■ You will see two text boxes (see Figure 2-3).

3. Click on the pull-down list button on the lower text box. You will see a list of devices.

FIGURE 2-3
HCL Search Text Boxes

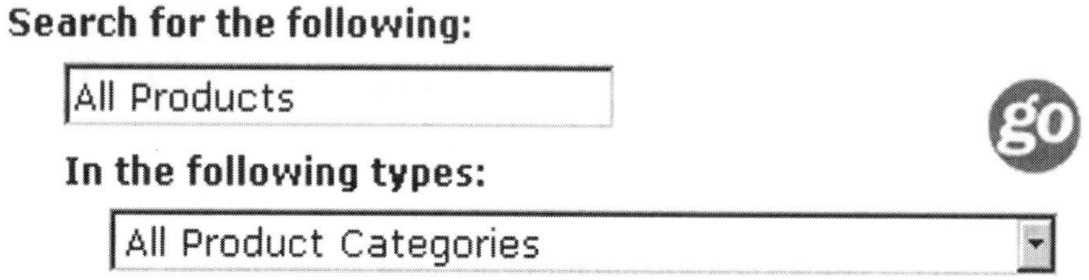

Search for the following:

All Products

In the following types:

All Product Categories

4. Scroll through the list, and click on **Printer.**

5. Click the **Go** graphic.

   ■ After the search is complete, you will see results similar to those shown in Figure 2-4. You can see the status of the device in the testing process for each of the Windows family products.

6. Click on the name of the first printer in the list.

   ■ You will see additional information about that printer and its status.

7. Close the details window by clicking the X button in the upper right corner of the window.

8. To understand the meaning of the compatibility graphics, click on the graphic labeled "The icons below mean . . .".

   ■ A window will open that gives a legend for the graphics and their meanings.

9. Close that window when you are finished reading.

10. To further refine your search, type **NEC** in the "Search for the following:" text box and click the **Go** button.

    ■ You will only see NEC printers. Notice some of those printers that have been proven to work with Windows 2000 Server.

11. Look at the details for one of the approved printers.

12. Spend some time initiating new searches and browsing through the HCL.

CAUTION: The information on this Web site will change as testing continues at Microsoft. Also, a manufacturer might change something about a device and not inform Microsoft, so it is a good idea to check with the manufacturer directly when in doubt about the compatibility of a device. If the product is not listed on the HCL, then it has not been tested and may not function under Windows 2000 Server. Using an untested device will likely cause problems.

FIGURE 2-4
Results of the Initial HCL Search Request

Product Type	Company Name	Product Name Please click below for more details.	Windows 95	Windows 98	Windows NT4 x86	Windows 2000 x86	Windows NT4 alpha
Printer	Abico	ABiCO CL-400KT [ ]				COMPATIBLE	
Printer	Abico	ABiCO CL-600BXII [ ]				COMPATIBLE	
Printer	Accel-A-Writer	8200 v2014.103 [N/A]			COMPATIBLE		COMPATIBLE
Printer	Adobe Systems	LaserJet II Cartridge v52.3 [N/A]			COMPATIBLE		COMPATIBLE
Printer	AGFA	1000[N/A]			COMPATIBLE	COMPATIBLE	COMPATIBLE
Printer	AGFA	1000SF v2013.108 [N/A]			COMPATIBLE		COMPATIBLE

The Microsoft "Designed for Windows" Logo

If you look on the packaging of some software programs or hardware devices, you will see Microsoft's flying Window logo, the words **Designed for,** and the name of one or more Microsoft operating systems. The logo can only be put on the box after the product has passed a rigorous set of tests. The logo also indicates that the product has been designed and tested to meet Microsoft's standard for compatibility. A product with this logo offers stable install and uninstall procedures, good interaction with other products containing the logo, and an assurance that full advantage has been taken of the latest Windows technologies.

Lesson 2.4 Determine Disk and File Configurations

The hard disk on the server is examined during a Windows 2000 Server installation. Before launching the setup program, it is important to know how the drive will be configured and how files will be stored.

Partitions

Hard drives will eventually fail and files can be corrupted, so separating the operating system files from the user data files and application programs is a good idea. If there is only one hard drive installed in a single server, you can **partition** the hard drive. Partitioning creates a logical separation on the disk. Rather than a directory listing showing a single C: drive, a partitioned disk would show a C: and a D: drive. You can create multiple partitions of different sizes, or you can leave part of the disk unpartitioned. In order for an operating system to be installed, at least one partition must exist.

Hard disks are now capable of storing gigabytes and even terabytes of information. Without partitioning, such massive storage areas can become a maze of nested folders. With this in mind, the following factors should be considered when determining the number of partitions and their sizes:

■ The Windows 2000 Server installation partition should be larger than 1 GB but does not need to be more than 2 GB.

■ Determine the amount of disk space required for storing user information.

■ Determine the size of the software application's program files and how much free space they need in order to function properly.

■ When a partition becomes full, a lengthy process is involved in expanding the space. It is best to overestimate rather than underestimate on partition sizes.

Most servers will have multiple hard drives that cause the above decision-making process to be even more interesting.

TIP

The setup program can be used to create multiple partitions; however, you should create only the installation partition with setup. Later, you will learn about an administrative tool called Disk Management that makes partition configuration much easier.

File Systems

Each partition must be **formatted** after it is created. Formatting arranges the magnetic particles on the hard disk platters into tracks, sectors, and cylinders so that data can be stored and retrieved. The format of the partition is determined by the file system. Windows 2000 supports the following three file systems:

1. Windows 2000 file system (NTFS)

2. File allocation table (FAT)

3. FAT32

Table 2-6 describes the features of NTFS. Because of these features, NTFS is usually the file system of choice. Windows 2000 or Windows NT are the only operating systems that can access data on a partition formatted as NTFS. If you need to use another operating system such as MS-DOS, for compatibility you could choose to format with FAT or FAT32.

Because FAT and FAT32 have limitations on how large a partition can be and do not offer file security, the only reason to use FAT or FAT32 is for **dual booting.** Dual booting allows the user to choose one of the installed operating

TABLE 2-6 NTFS FEATURES

FEATURE	DESCRIPTION
File- and folder-level security	Controls access to folders and files. Only users with the proper permissions can see or make changes to the folder or file.
Disk compression	Files can be compressed to allow for more data storage on a partition.
Encryption	Allows file data to be encrypted (logically scrambled in a manner that can only be deciphered by the user who encrypted the file or an administrator).
Disk quotas	Controls how much disk space an individual user can have.

systems during the boot (or startup) process and is only used if you have hardware or software that will not function under Windows 2000. During the boot process, a textual menu will appear that displays the options. If no option is chosen, the default operating system will be launched.

EXERCISE

2.3 Choosing Partitions and File Systems

To perform this exercise, you will need:

- A computer
- Access to a computer lab
- A hard drive

1. Select one of the computers in your computer lab.

2. Document the number of hard drives and their size.

3. Indicate which drive will hold the Windows 2000 Server files.

4. Decide if there should be additional partitions on the hard drive. Give the reason(s) why you made that choice.

5. Choose a file system for each partition, and write a paragraph detailing the choices you made.

6. Save the document for use during the installation phase.

7. Print the document.

Lesson 2.5 Determine Software Applications

Before computers became an integral part of the business world, people used multiple tools to get their work done. They would have a typewriter for creating letters, a calculator and a paper ledger for bookkeeping, pen and ink for graphics, and huge filing cabinets for data storage, just to name a few. Today, all of these functions can be performed with the help of one tool—the computer. (See Figure 2-5.)

FIGURE 2-5
The All-in-One Tool

What Is an Application?

People use the workstations (client computers) to run programs like word processors, spreadsheets, graphics programs, databases, and so on. These types of programs are called **applications** because they perform a specific function. In reality, however, one application is usually a collection of programs that work together.

There are many applications on the market for office productivity, including Microsoft's suite of programs called *Office 2000*. The most robust offering of Office 2000 includes applications for word processing, spreadsheets, databases, presentation graphics, Web development, graphics, messaging, and publications. All of these applications easily integrate with each other and present a common interface.

Modern applications need plenty of RAM and hard drive space to accommodate their user-friendly persona. Add to those needs the requirements of a network environment, and you will see why careful implementation planning is necessary. Because documentation lays a foundation of information from which a stable network can be built, thorough planning also requires extensive documentation.

Documenting Software Applications

When documenting applications, you will want to identify the following characteristics:

Name of the application: For example, the Office 2000 applications mentioned above are named Word, Excel, Access, PowerPoint, FrontPage, PhotoDraw, Outlook, and Publisher.

Manufacturer: This is the name of the company that produces the software. In the case of Office 2000, the manufacturer is Microsoft Corporation.

Version: Quality software is always in a state of transition from good to better. Newer versions of an application have changes that are intended to improve the product. Version designations vary from company to company. Microsoft ties its version designations to the operating system. For example, versions of FrontPage included FrontPage 95, FrontPage 98, and now FrontPage 2000.

Function of the application: This specifies what the application was designed to do. Examples include word processor, spreadsheet, database, and so on.

Compatibility with the operating system: A single application will usually not work under all operating systems. With Microsoft products, look for the "Designed for" logo on the box. If an application has the "Designed for Windows 95" logo, it should also work under Windows NT 4.0. If an application has the "Designed for Windows NT" logo, it will work under Windows 2000.

Network ready: Not all applications are intended for network usage. Network-ready applications have additional capabilities such as allowing multiple users to access the software at the same time and being able to run from the server instead of from the client. When applications are capable of being installed on a network, their installation can be either local or network.

NOTE: The word **local** refers to anything that occurs directly to or on the computer in question. The word **network** refers to anything that occurs remotely via the network cabling. As shown in Figure 2-6, if you are sitting at a client computer and the printer is local, then the printer is directly connected to a port on the computer, most likely by a parallel cable. If the operating system indicates you have access

FIGURE 2-6
A Local Printer Connected to a Client Computer

FIGURE 2-7
A Network Printer Connected to a Server Computer

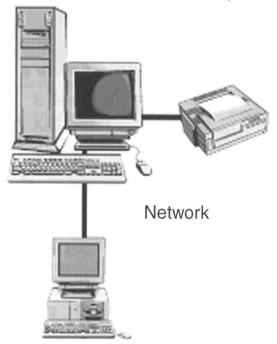

Network

to a network printer, then the printer is not directly attached to a port on the computer. Instead, the network printer may be connected to the server, another client, or directly to the network cable. (See Figure 2-7)

Depending on the hardware configuration, an application may be installed as either local or network. If a particular computer has the hard drive space and enough processing power, the applications are usually installed locally. Since most of the work is done on the client computer, this increases the response time. However, if the client computer is low on drive space or processing power, the application can be installed on the network (usually on a server) and can be run from there. The response time may be slower because the instructions have to travel back and forth across the network.

Hardware requirements: Determine what minimum hardware components are required in order for the application to function properly. These include CPU speed, hard disk space, RAM, and video specifications. Without sufficient hardware support, an application may run improperly, slowly, or not at all.

Installation considerations: One of the steps in any installation process is to indicate the drive and folder that will hold the application's program files. Knowing the answer to that question before installation protects against haphazard file placement. Most applications have a default directory (a predetermined folder name and placement in the hard drive structure), but the default may not conform to your network's specific needs.

Who needs to use the application: Know who the users are that need the application. This will help you when you start setting access permissions.

Licensing requirements: There are rules from the manufacturer about the legal use of the application. One rule that affects networks is the concurrent multiple-user agreement. In other words, how many users can simultaneously access the software? If the license is a "single-user" license, then the application can be loaded on only one computer. See Lesson 2.6 for more information on licensing.

EXERCISE

2.4 Documenting Software Applications

• •

To perform this exercise, you will need:

■ A computer

■ A word processor

■ A printer

1. Using a word processor, document the software installations on one PC.

2. Include all of the headings listed in this lesson (name, manufacturer, version, and so on)

■ If available, use Form 2.2 in the Student Workbook.

3. Print your results.

Lesson 2.6 Understand Software Licensing

Today's typical pirates do not rob sailing ships of their treasures, they rob software companies of their profits. Unauthorized use of software is called **software piracy,** and it happens every day.

Most of us would agree that if we want something that is for sale, we should pay for it before taking it and using it. However, many computer users have software that they have copied from someone else who made the original purchase. Most people feel that this is unfair to the creator of the software, and the government of the United States agrees—software piracy is a crime.

To use Windows 2000 Server legally, an individual or company must purchase **Client Access Licenses (CAL)** for the software. The two types of licenses available are **Per Server** and **Per Seat.**

Per Server licensing is where you agree to purchase a license that limits how many clients can be attached simultaneously to a particular server (See Figure 2-8) Thus, if

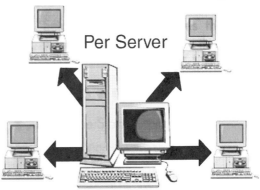

FIGURE 2-8
Per Server Configuration

Per Server

FIGURE 2-9
Per Seat Configuration

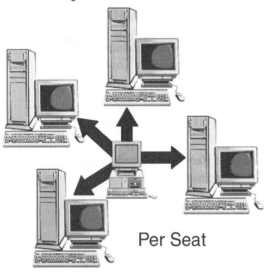

Per Seat

you purchased 50 client access licenses for one of your servers, only 50 clients could be attached to that server at the same time. When the 51st client wanted to connect, the system would not allow connection until one of the other clients disconnected. If you purchased another server, none of the CALs you bought would allow legal connection to the second server; you would have to buy more CALs for the second server. Therefore, Microsoft recommends Per Server only for small companies that have just one server.

Per Seat licensing is more flexible and is recommended for companies with more than one server. With this type of licensing, the company purchases one CAL for every computer on the network. There is no limit to the number of clients that can be simultaneously attached to any of the servers on the network. Thus, if you buy 200 CALs, all 200 computers could be attached to one, two, or all of your servers at the same time.

CAUTION: You can change from Per Server to Per Seat once for no additional cost and you do not have to notify Microsoft of this change. This is a one-way conversion; you cannot convert from Per Seat to Per Server. If you do not know which one to choose, then choose Per Server.

EXERCISE

2.5 Choosing a Licensing Method

● ●

To perform this exercise, you will need:

■ A computer

■ A word processor

■ A printer

1. Choose the licensing method (Per Server or Per Seat) for the installation of Windows 2000 Server on your server.

2. Using a word processor, document why you chose that method.

3. For your network, document how many CALs will need to be purchased and why.

4. Print your results.

Summary

The computer industry is in a constant state of change. Almost every day, innovations based on a previously laid foundation of knowledge and exploration are propelling us toward new discoveries in technology. Especially for system administrators, the learning process in computer technology is never complete. A thorough understanding of how hardware and software function and interact will be of great value when the time comes to actually manage a network with Windows 2000 Server. Most of the topics covered in this chapter will be covered in greater detail as you progress through the book. For example, you will see partitions, file systems, and licensing in the next chapter.

● ● ● ● ● ● ● ● ● ● ● ● ● ●

REVIEW EXERCISE

These questions will help you determine if you have learned enough to move on to the next chapter. If the graphic next to the option is a square (❑), there can be more than one answer for that question. If the graphic is a circle (○), there is only one correct answer. Color in the shape(s) to indicate your answer(s).

1. Which of the following are specifications for a CPU?

   a. ❑ Word Size

   b. ❑ USB

   c. ❑ VLM

   d. ❑ Data Path

2. How many bytes are in a gigabyte?

 a. ○ One thousand

 b. ○ One million

 c. ○ One billion

 d. ○ One trillion

3. Which of the following match the documented minimum hardware requirements for Windows 2000 Server?

 a. ❑ CPU: Pentium 166 MHz or higher

 b. ❑ 650 MB free disk space on the installation partition

 c. ❑ One or more network adapter cards

 d. ❑ 24X CD-ROM drive

4. A huge box is sitting next to your desk. Beside it stands your boss who is informing you of the fantastic deal he got on a new server for the network. He doesn't know a thing about computers, so as he talks, what concerns are running through your mind?

 a. ❑ Does the hardware meet the minimum specifications for Windows 2000 Server?

 b. ❑ What if there is a component that is not on the HCL?

 c. ❑ Since we have Per Seat licensing, will I have to change to Per Server?

 d. ❑ Is there any possible way I can be in Jamaica when this thing is added to the network?

5. A laser printer is attached to the server by a parallel cable. Client computers have access to the printer. From the server's perspective, is the printer a local printer or a network printer?

 a. ○ Local

 b. ○ Network

▼ PERFORMANCE CHALLENGES

These tasks can be performed for extra credit or to expand your knowledge. Beyond defining the criteria and requirements, instructor input will be at a minimum so that you can expand out of your comfort zone.

■ Search for entries in the Hardware Compatibility List for the hardware components you documented in Exercise 2.1. Print the details page for each component.

■ Write at least one paragraph detailing your opinion on software piracy and what could be done to prevent it.

IDENTIFY USERS AND RESOURCES

OBJECTIVES

After completing this chapter, you should be able to:

- Identify what makes users unique

- Create a coherent naming convention for both users and resources

- Describe the various ways resources can be connected to the network

- Check hard drive capacity and free space

- Identify the key characteristics of domains and workgroups

- Understand how users are authenticated for network access

- Document the physical elements of the network's location

OUTLINE

Introduction

People are important. That is a fact that can escape the rational thought process of a frazzled system administrator. People can be difficult to work with, prone to error, and demanding, but they are also the main motivation for having a network. People are the ones generating and using the massive amount of information that flows through network cabling around the globe. Without them, there would not be a need for many system administrators. This chapter explores the networking needs and concerns for users of computers. Understanding these concepts lays a foundation for managing users with the Active Directory.

Lesson 3.1 Characteristics of a User

To use means the application of something for some purpose, and the definition of a user is *one who uses.* If a person uses a computer, that person is a **user.** If you are the person responsible for ensuring that users can use the network for the purpose of completing their work, then you better know your users. When you know people, you know their personal characteristics, including their hair color, height, and sense of humor. The following questions will help you to identify the characteristics of a particular computer user:

- What is the full name of the user?

- How does this user fit into the organizational structure of the company?

- Where does the user do his or her work (city, building, office, cubicle, and so on)?

- Which computer does this user use?

- What applications does this user need in order to do his or her job?

- With whom does this user work (in a group, on a project, and so on)?

- To what network devices does this person need access?

- How can you contact the user (phone number/extension, e-mail, and so on)?

- What level of computer expertise and aptitude does this user have?

That last question may sound strange; however, you will find that there are varying levels of aptitude and expertise among users when they interact with a machine. Both of those factors influence whether or not their expectations are met in terms of getting what they need when they need it—even when

TABLE 3-1 DEFINING CHARACTERISTICS OF A USER

CHARACTERISTIC	DESCRIPTION
User	Employee's first name, middle initial, and last name
Username	According to your naming convention (see Lesson 3.2), this is the user's logon name (the name in the Active Directory database)
Position	The title the user holds within the company (also consider including the name of the user's supervisor)
Location	The city, building, office/cubicle where the user works
Contact info	The phone number and extension at which the user can be reached and his or her e-mail address
Computer name	The name of the computer assigned to the user
Software usage	The software this user needs in order to complete his or her work
Hardware usage	Network resources the user needs in order to complete his or her work
Group(s)	The group(s) of coworkers of which the user is a member
Expertise Rating	A numeric value (you determine the scale) indicating how proficient this user is with a computer
Notes	Miscellaneous information

the network is functioning well. An administrator's responsibilities include training the users, even if that training is simply a short conversation about how to avoid a particular problem in the future. Knowing users' aptitude and expertise will guide you in more effectively meeting their needs.

Table 3-1 provides a format for identifying users according to the characteristics discussed above.

EXERCISE

3.1 Identifying Users

To perform this exercise, you will need:

- A computer
- A word processor capable of making tables

1. Using a word processor and the format of Table 3-1, make a table that lists the characteristics for at least three users.

2. If you do not know information such as the computer name or username, just leave the box blank.

   ■ If available, use Form 3.1 in the Student Workbook.

3. Print your results.

Lesson 3.2 Naming Conventions for Users

Each user must have a unique user account name, called a **username.** Because other characteristics are dependent upon the username, the username must be unique. These characteristics include, for example, the user's password and permissions granted for accessing the network. The choices system administrators make to identify users are part of what is called a **naming convention.**

If the network is small and all of the users have different first names, you could deduce that using first names for the username is good. However, what happens when a new employee is hired and that person has the same name as another user? The username is no longer unique, and the naming convention must be revised. This time, you might add the last name to the first name. This will suffice until there are two people with the same first and last name, a common occurrence in large corporations.

One technique for developing a coherent, consistent naming convention is to test the proposed convention with actual data. Consider the pros and cons of each example in Table 3-2.

The proposed conventions under columns 1 and 2 have problems. Can you identify them? The problem in column 1 is that there could be any number of people with a last name of Jones and a first initial of C. The same problem

TABLE 3-2 EVALUATING NAMING CONVENTIONS

USER	PROPOSED CONVENTION 1	PROPOSED CONVENTION 2	PROPOSED CONVENTION 3
Charlie A. Jones	CharlieJ	JonesC	JonesCA
Charlene J. Jones	CharleneJ	JonesC	JonesCJ
Charlie A. Jantzen	CharlieJ	JantzenC	JantzenCA

occurs with the convention using the first name and last initial. The Active Directory lists usernames in alphabetical order, so there is some logic in putting the last name first; all of the users would be alphabetized by last name. Only the proposed convention in column 3 would work with this list of users. There is some prognosticating, or predicting the future, that needs to happen when developing naming conventions. Try to anticipate conflicts and circumvent them before they occur.

What if you needed to make some changes to a user account, but you did not know the username? Or what if you knew the person's name and needed the username? The best naming conventions are easily reconstructed from both ways. Using column 3 from Table 3-2 for an example, if you know Charlie's first and last name, you could construct his username (JonesCA). Conversely, if you know the username, you would have a pretty good idea of who JonesCA is.

Microsoft recommends using the person's last name and first initial. Although a less friendly way would be to use that person's insurance number, at least there is no danger of duplication. In the end, it is usually the system administrator who has to make the naming convention decisions and then live with them.

TIP

Usernames should be descriptive and concise. If there are too many letters in the username, the user will surely make a typo and will call you to say that he or she cannot get onto the network.

EXERCISE

3.2

Create a Naming Convention for Users

To perform this exercise, you will need:

- A computer
- A word processor

1. Using a word processor, create a two-column table.

2. In the first column, make a list of at least 30 users. The list can be actual users of your network or fictional users.

3. Create a naming convention that results in no duplicate usernames.

The names cannot be longer than 256 characters (less than 10 is ideal).

4. Type a description of your naming convention above the table (for example, First Name, Last Initial).

5. Prove your naming convention is valid by entering the usernames in the second column.

6. Print your results.

Lesson 3.3 Definition of a Resource

What Is a Resource?

A resource is anything that is connected to the network and made available to users through the network. Common resources include hard drive space (folders and files), printers, scanners, and CD-ROM drives. Figure 3-1 shows a printer connected to a workstation.

The network operating system must be aware of the resources in order to make them available to users. When a computer that is connected to the network boots, it announces what resources the user has decided can be accessed by other users via the network.

FIGURE 3-1
A Printer Connected to a Workstation

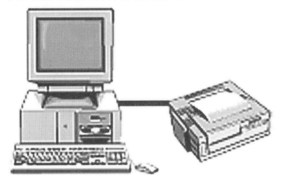

Identifying Resources

A fully identified list of resources on a network usually evolves over a period of time. However, there are some initial identification processes that can be performed.

If the network has been set up and computers are attached to the network, an inventory of what exists should be compiled. If the network has not been set up, a detailed list of available resources will assist the administrator in placing those resources within the network infrastructure.

Resources on a Workstation

Some resources such as hard drive space and CD-ROMs can be inside or connected to a workstation on the network. The person who uses the workstation is called the **owner** of the resources connected to his or her PC. Not only does that person get to decide what resources (if any) on the workstation are available to other users (called a **share**), but that person also decides what level of access (called **permissions**) the other users have. For example, an owner can create a share for a particular folder that makes the folder appear in other users' directories. The owner then sets the permissions on that folder. The owner might allow one group of users the permission to change documents in a particular folder, but users from another group can only read the documents. If an owner is either too restrictive or too lax in setting permissions, an administrator can **take ownership** of any resource and change the permissions.

FIGURE 3-2
Files Stored on a Server

When identifying resources on a workstation, document the computer name, location, and owner. In Chapter 10, you will learn how to make resources available on the network through sharing and how to set permissions for each resource.

Resources on a Server

One of the most common uses for a server is file storage. Rather than have folders on each workstation shared, the administrator may choose to have all the files centrally stored on a server, as shown in Figure 3-2. This approach to resource sharing has many benefits. The process of performing a **backup** gives a good example of how central storage is beneficial. A backup makes a copy of the folder contents in case the original folder is inaccessible because of hardware failure, file corruption, or accidental deletion. On even a small network there can be hundreds of shared folders. If those files are distributed throughout the network, the administrator must run a backup procedure on each workstation in order to back up the files. If all the files are on a server, the backup procedure is a one-step procedure. Setting permissions and other administrative tasks are also simplified in a centralized storage system.

When identifying resources on a server, document the server name, the available resources, and the resources' corresponding permissions. The administrator is the owner of resources on a server.

Resources Connected Directly to the Network

When a resource such as a printer or CD-ROM is connected to a workstation, the owner may see a drop in performance while network users are accessing the resource. If the resource is a printer, other users will have to physically enter the owner's office to get their printouts.

FIGURE 3-3
A Printer Connected to a Network Print Device

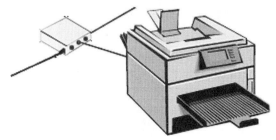

Network print devices can connect a printer directly to the network cabling, and some models have the capability of connecting to more than one device. These network print devices have their own **IP address** and ports for connecting to the network cable and the printer.

A variety of printers are being manufactured **network-ready,** which means that a network connection is built into the printer itself. Configurations like this keep the workstations and servers from being burdened by the device and also offer flexibility in the location of the resource.

Determine Disk Space

Users rely on disk space for storing huge amounts of data. Eventually, disk space becomes low and the computer's performance suffers. Because no computer works well (if at all) with a nearly full hard disk, administrators traditionally have asked users to be frugal and clean out unnecessary files (by deleting them). Deleting files is usually a low priority on a user's task list, so Windows 2000 Server has a solution in the form of **disk quotas.** Disk quotas are a part of the NTFS 5.0 file system and allow the administrator to set a predetermined limit on the amount of disk space a particular user can access for file storage. You will learn how to set a disk quota in Chapter 13.

TERMINOLOGY

An IP address is a unique number consisting of four numbers containing one to three digits connected by periods. 103.24.256.7 is an example of an IP address. Just as the numbers on a house uniquely identify that house on a street, the IP address uniquely identifies a network component on a network.

EXERCISE

3.3 View Hard Drive Properties

To perform this exercise, you will need:

■ A computer with a hard drive

1. Click on the **Start** button.

2. Select **Programs.**

3. Select **Accessories.**

FIGURE 3-4
The Properties Window of a Hard Drive

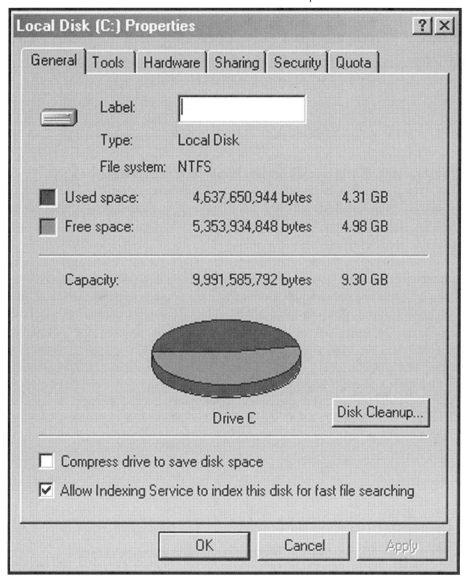

4. Click on **Windows Explorer.**

5. Right-click any hard drive icon.

6. From the Context menu, click on **Properties.**

7. Click the **Cancel button** when done viewing.

TABLE 3-3 EVALUATING RESOURCE NAMING CONVENTIONS

RESOURCE	PROPOSED CONVENTION 1	PROPOSED CONVENTION 2	PROPOSED CONVENTION 3
CD-ROM drive	CD-ROM	CD Bldg C	CD Station 4
Laser Printer	A-65	NJet4T	Laser3-102
Workstation	1	Lab-04	B7-R2-17

Naming Conventions for Resources

The naming convention for the entire network includes more than just usernames. Printers must have unique names, as do the computers, peripheral devices, and many elements in Active Directory. Almost every component of a network needs to have a unique name.

As with user naming conventions, one technique for developing a coherent, consistent naming convention is to test the proposed convention with actual data. Consider the pros and cons of each example given in Table 3-3.

Some of the entries in Table 3-3 do not give enough information about the resource. The user will be browsing the network, looking for a suitable resource, and the names given to the resource are his or her only clue about what the resource is and where it is located. The best resource names describe the resource and its location without being too wordy.

When documenting resources on the network, record the device name, a description of the device, its IP address (if necessary), and its physical location on the network.

EXERCISE

3.4 Create a Naming Convention for Resources

• •

To perform this exercise, you will need:

■ A computer with a word processor

1. Using a word processor, create a two-column table.

2. In the first column, make a list of at least ten different network devices.

The list can be actual devices on your network or fictional devices.

3. Create a naming convention that results in no duplicate device names and follows the guidelines in this lesson.

4. Type a description of your naming convention above the table.

5. Prove your naming convention is valid by entering the resource names in the second column.

6. Print your results.

3.5 Document Network Resources

To perform this exercise, you will need:

■ A computer with a word processor

■ To have read the rest of this chapter to complete all of the data

1. Using a word processor, create a two-column table.

2. Enter the following headings in the left column: Resource type, Resource description, Location, Resource name,

Resource owner, IP address (if necessary).

3. In the right column, enter data for a resource connected to your network.

4. Repeat steps 1–3 for each available resource.

5. Print your results.

Lesson 3.4 Security Concerns

When homeowners go on vacation, they often ask a trusted neighbor to watch over the house and take care of their animals. By giving the neighbor a key to the front door, the owners are allowing that person to enter the house. The owners know the person and know why the neighbor needs the key. There may be other locks within the house, but the caretaker probably does not need those keys. The owner only provides access to what the neighbor needs.

Domains and Workgroups

Like houses, a computer network system needs protection from unauthorized access. Rather than houses, a computer network has **domains.** A domain is a logical grouping of network computers that share a central **directory database.** A directory database contains user accounts and security information for the domain. In Windows 2000 Server, that list is known as the **Directory** and is the database portion of Active Directory. The information in the Directory includes information such as the groups to which the users belong and what files they are allowed to access. In our analogy, the directory database would be a list the owners use to keep track of who has keys to what.

A domain is not governed by geographical constraints. One domain can include computers in the same room or computers scattered all around the world. In some situations, a large network may have more than one domain. For right now, we will focus on a single-domain network. Later in your training, you will see how having multiple domains can be helpful in a very large network environment.

Each domain in the Windows 2000 Server network environment must have a unique name, and that name must conform to the **Domain Name System (DNS),** which is the domain naming system used on the Internet. DNS names are used to resolve computer names and to locate computers within their local networks and on the Internet. Rather than identifying computers solely with a string of numbers (IP addresses), DNS identifies computers with a string of characters. An example of a DNS-compatible domain name is *Microsoft.com,* where Microsoft is the name of the organization's DNS identity. When Microsoft wants to graphically illustrate a domain, it uses a triangle, You will learn more about DNS in Chapter 6 and Chapter 7.

Within the domain, there are special servers known as **domain controllers** that each have a copy of the Directory. There is one Directory, and all the domain controllers have a copy of it. This type of administration is called **centralized** because all user information is stored centrally (in one place).

Another model for connecting a small number of computers (usually less than ten) together for the sharing of network resources is known as a **workgroup.** In a workgroup, each computer has a **local security database** as opposed to one shared directory database on a server; it is referred to as local because the database is stored on the computer. A local security database is a list of user accounts and resource security information for one computer. Workgroups do not have a dedicated server and are therefore referred to as **peer-to-peer** workgroups. This type of administration is called **decentralized** because the information is not stored centrally; rather, it is distributed among multiple computers.

Workgroups are easier to configure than domains, but managing them is more challenging. For example, if the company hired a new user, the administrator of a workgroup would have to go to each computer and enter the new user's account information. The user would not be able use a computer that did not have his or her account information entered. In a domain, the administrator enters the new user's account information once on a domain controller and the user can log on to any computer in the domain. This is because all of the computers use the same Directory.

> ## TERMINOLOGY
>
> A computer running Windows 2000 Server in a workgroup is called a *stand-alone server.* A *member server* is a server that is not configured as a domain controller.

Authentication

After the homeowners have left on vacation, the neighbor comes to the house and puts a key in the deadbolt. If the neighbor has the right key, the lock will open. Instead of a dead bolt lock, Windows 2000 Server uses **authentication** and **permissions** to protect the contents of computer networks and to give users what they need to do their work. Authentication is the process by which users are verified to be who they say they are. Permissions are the specific actions the users can perform on objects in the computer or on the network.

The authentication process requires the user to enter a username and password during the **logon** process. When a computer is either shut down (totally powered off) and rebooted (turned back on) or has been locked by the previous user, a dialog box appears informing the user of the computer's state and the need for the logon process to be initiated. To log on to a Windows 2000 computer, the user must press Ctrl-Alt-Del (hold down the Ctrl and Alt keys, then press the Delete key). In response, the computer displays a Password Dialog box that has several options. Table 3-4 describes the options.

TABLE 3-4 OPTIONS FOR THE PASSWORD DIALOG BOX

OPTION	DESCRIPTION
Username	The unique name for the user as recorded in Active Directory. Usernames are not case-sensitive.
Password	A string of characters that proves the user's identity. Usually, only the user knows the password. When the user account is first set up, the administrator will enter a password. The next time the user logs on, he or she will be asked to assign a password. Administrators also have the option of making users change their passwords periodically. Passwords are case-sensitive. When the user types the password, the screen only shows asterisks (***). This is to protect the password from onlookers.
Log on to	A pull-down list that provides the choices for logging on to the local computer or to a domain. There may be multiple domains from which to choose. The user can only log on to a domain in which his or her account information has been entered.
Log on using dial-up connection	Allows a user to connect to a domain server by using dial-up networking from a remote location.
Shutdown	Closes all files, saves operating system data, and prepares the computer to be shut off. On Windows 2000 Server, the shutdown option is not available in order to prevent an unauthorized person from shutting down a server to which other users may be connected. The only way to shut down a server is to log on (probably as an administrator) and then press Ctrl-Alt-Del. Shutdown will then appear as an option in the Password Dialog Box.
Options (button)	Toggles on and off the Log On To option and the Log On Using Dial-up Connection option. This button only appears if the computer is a member of a domain.

The authentication process includes the following steps:

1. The user enters his or her logon information (detailed in Table 3-4).

   ■ If the user is logging on to the domain, Windows 2000 forwards this information to a domain controller.

   ■ If the user is logging on locally, Windows 2000 forwards this information to the local security database of that local computer.

2. Windows 2000 compares the logon information with the user information stored in the appropriate database.

   ■ If the user is logging on to a domain, the domain controller validates the logon information according to its copy of the domain's Directory.

   ■ If the user is logging on locally, the local security database of the local computer validates the logon information.

3. If the password goes with the username and the user account is entered in the Directory for the domain (or in the local security database if logging on locally), Windows 2000 generates an **access token** for the user. Figure 3-5 demonstrates this process.

An access token contains the user's security settings and is the user's identification for the computers in the domain or for that local computer (depending on the computer to which the user logged on). When a user requests access to a folder, for example, his or her access token is compared to the permissions set by the owner of that folder. One user's access token might let him or her change the files in that folder, while another user's access token would only let the user read the files.

FIGURE 3-5
The Logon Authentication Process When Logging on to a Domain

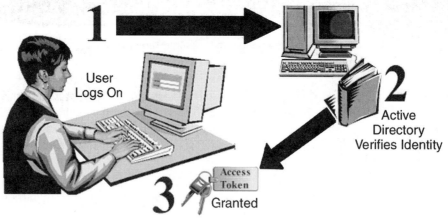

Lesson 3.5 Identify Physical Location of Users

In Microsoft terminology, a **location** is a place in which an organization has offices and users. Details about the buildings, including the city in which they are located, the number of floors, and where people are located within the buildings, helps in designing a networking system that meets the needs of the users. Administrators use location information when working with the physical parts of the network, such as cabling and routers, and it also helps identify where to go for on-location troubleshooting.

There are many questions to be answered in terms of location, including the following:

- What are the total numbers of physical locations, including remote sites, subsidiaries, and international offices?

- Where are offices located geographically (cities, counties, provinces)?

- How many buildings are there?

- How many floors are in each building?

- What is the square footage of each building?

- What business functions are performed at each location?

- Where are workstations located and who is using them?

- Where are the network devices located?

EXERCISE

3.6 Document the Location

To perform this exercise, you will need:

- A computer
- A word processor

1. Using a word processor, create a document that answers the previous location questions for the network system that includes your computer lab.

   - If available, use Form 3.2 in the Student Workbook.

2. Print your results.

Summary

The balancing act for a system administrator involves protecting the network from unauthorized access on the one side and providing for the needs of authorized users on the other. In order to balance the two, each user and resource must be uniquely identified. Naming conventions are important because everyone on the network will have to conform to those conventions. It is important to make them something logical.

The username and password together form the basis for identification (authentication). If the user tries to log on and is unable to correctly fill in the Password Dialog box, he or she is not going to gain access to the system. The domain and workgroup models govern whether administration is centralized or decentralized. Domains have at least one server with one Directory, whereas workgroups share resources and perform authentication on each computer without the use of a central server.

All the logical elements of a network must function within the physical characteristics of a location. In the day of calamity, you will be glad you know your location and how the network flows within it.

● ● ● ● ● ● ● ● ● ● ● ● ●

REVIEW EXERCISE

These questions will help you determine if you have learned enough to move on to the next chapter. If the graphic next to the option is a square (❑), there can be more than one answer for that question. If the graphic is a circle (○), there is only one correct answer. Color in the shape(s) to indicate your answer(s).

1. John and Joan Steffen are married, and your company hired both of them this week. Which of the following naming conventions will result in a unique username for each of them?

   a. ❑ Last Name, First Initial

   b. ❑ First Name, Last Initial

   c. ❑ Last Name, First Name

   d. ❑ Last Name, First two letters of First Name

2. Who can change the permissions for resources on the local computer?

    a. ❑ The user who wants access

    b. ❑ The owner of the resources

    c. ❑ The administrator

    d. ❑ No one

3. How many databases hold authentication information for a Windows 2000 domain?

    a. ○ One

    b. ○ Two

    c. ○ Three

    d. ○ As many as there are computers

4. How many databases hold authentication information for a Windows 2000 workgroup?

    a. ○ One

    b. ○ Two

    c. ○ Three

    d. ○ As many as there are computers

5. A user powers up her Windows 2000 workstation and prints a graph on a color printer that is not attached to her computer. Which of the following occurred during the authentication process?

    a. ❑ Logon information was entered by the user

    b. ❑ The user pressed Ctrl-Insert-Delete

    c. ❑ The user gave one drop of blood

    d. ❑ An access token was generated

▼PERFORMANCE CHALLENGES

■ Using one page from your local phone book, create a naming convention that would result in unique names. As an extra challenge, make the username be less than 10 characters. For the ultimate challenge, make it less than 6 characters.

■ Create the following two scenarios and write at least two paragraphs on each:

    1. A network without any security

    2. A network with too much security

INSTALLATION AND CONFIGURATION

PREPARE FOR INSTALLATION

OBJECTIVES

After completing this chapter, you should be able to:

- Check hardware components for compatibility and functionality

- Describe how dual booting affects the boot process

- Understand the differences between a new installation and an upgrade

- Know the two media types available for installation and choose between them

- Understand the difference between joining a domain or joining a workgroup

- Compile a series of documents detailing information required for installation of Windows 2000 Server

OUTLINE

Introduction

When presented with the opportunity to install a new and improved operating system, most people would rip open the package, find the first installation CD, slam it in the drive, and launch the setup program. The excitement soon fades, however, when they are asked for configuration information and do not know the answers. To save yourself some trouble, you must be prepared. This chapter will make the installation process easier by helping you define the answers to configuration questions, so take a deep breath and keep the shrinkwrap on the box for one more chapter.

Lesson 4.1 Prepare the Hardware

Hardware and software depend on each other. If one is bad, it does not matter how good the other one is—performance will suffer. This is especially true with operating systems such as Windows 2000 Server, which is a powerful operating system with specific needs. In Chapter 2, you learned about minimum hardware requirements, disk partitions, and file systems. Now is the time to make sure you have met those requirements.

Exceeding Minimum Hardware Requirements

Refer to Table 2-7 for the minimum hardware requirements of Windows 2000 Server. You will notice that the minimum requirement for hard disk space is 685 MB, but the recommended hard disk space is at least 1 GB. Windows 2000 Server uses the open disk space on the installation partition for memory management and file handling. If there is insufficient space, system performance will suffer, response times will increase, and users will be unhappy. The same is true of memory. There is a logical limit where massive amounts of disk space or memory are no longer beneficial, but exceeding the minimum requirements in all respects is usually a good idea.

With the peripheral devices on a server, common sense will determine the best choices. For example, while the fastest CD-ROM you can afford would be great because installations would go faster, getting a state-of-the-art video card would not be a wise purchase. This is because the server generally does not have a designated user; it simply sits in a corner and runs.

Verify Minimum Hardware Requirements Are Met

To perform this exercise, you will need:

- Access to the server on which installation will occur

- Documentation for that server's components

- A word processor

1. Using a word processor, document the hardware components for the server.

2. Create a two-column table that lists the minimum hardware components in the left-hand column and the actual components of the server in the right-hand column.

3. Print your results.

Determine Hardware Compatibility

Microsoft has worked diligently to test drivers created by hardware vendors to assure compatibility with the Windows 2000 Server operating system. However, considering the thousands of hardware devices in existence since the dawn of the computing age, it is easy to understand what a giant undertaking it has been to test every single component. While there have been instances where Microsoft has written the drivers, usually Microsoft depends on hardware vendors for this task. The **Hardware Compatibility List (HCL)** is designed to inform users of the status of compatibility testing of existing drivers. To avoid non-functional equipment or intermittent problems, assure that every component in the server is designated *compatible* on the HCL.

Figure 4-1 illustrates the icons on the HCL, which indicate the testing status of the component.

FIGURE 4-1

Meanings of the Icons on the HCL

 Indicates that this product has met all of the Microsoft Requirements for the logo program.

 Indicates that this product has met all of the Microsoft Requirements for the logo program and there is a driver available for download.

 Indicates that this product does not meet all of the Microsoft Requirements for the logo program but has been deemed compatible with Windows.

4.2

Check the HCL for Server Components

To perform this exercise, you will need:

- A computer with access to the Internet
- Documentation for the server's components
- A word processor

1. Browse the HCL site (refer to Exercise 2.2 for steps) for each component in the server.

2. Create a two-column table that lists the hardware components and peripherals in the left-hand column and the results of the HCL search in the right-hand column.

- If available, use Form 4.1 in the Student Workbook.

3. Print your results.

If a component is not listed on the HCL or is untested, you have the following two choices:

1. Replace the component with a tested component (recommended).

2. Leave the component in and monitor the results.

Lesson 4.2 Upgrading vs. New Installation

To upgrade is to *improve,* or to take an already good product such as Windows NT Server and make it better. Many companies that have had Windows NT as their server operating system for years have invested both time and money in implementation, configuration, and performance enhancements. Fortunately, to take advantage of the improvements in Windows 2000 Server, administrators do not have to sacrifice all of the work they have devoted to the old operating system.

Reasons to Upgrade

Though there may be many reasons to choose an upgrade over a new installation, the following are the most common:

- The old operating system allows upgrading.

- Configuration is simpler because existing user accounts, settings, groups, rights, and permissions are retained.

- Files and applications do not need to be recopied to the disk after the upgrade process.

These three reasons make upgrading sound simple, but moving from one operating system to another can be quite complicated. This process of transition is called **migration.**

Migration

When Microsoft released Windows 2000 Server as an improvement for Windows NT, it also included mechanisms for helping administrators transition to the new product. Whereas migration in nature means moving from one region and settling in another, the meaning in computer terms is the process of moving from one program to another. For example, Windows NT administrators create a user account for each of their users. Rather than reenter each of those names for the new operating system, Windows 2000 Server has a utility that migrates the names from windows NT's account database into the Active Directory. Table 4-1 suggests some steps for a successful migration.

The following Microsoft products can upgrade directly to Windows 2000:

- Windows 95

- Windows 98

- Windows NT 3.51 SP5

- Windows NT 4.0

To migrate from older Microsoft operating systems (like Windows for Workgroups), you would have to upgrade to one of the operating systems on the list and then upgrade to Windows 2000.

MICROSOFT TEST OBJECTIVE

Upgrade a server from Microsoft Windows NT 4.0.

TIP

Migration from one operating system to a newer operating system created by the same vendor (Microsoft, for example) is usually easier than switching to an operating system created by a different vendor (Novell, for example).

TABLE 4-1 SUGGESTIONS FOR SUCCESSFUL MIGRATION TO WINDOWS 2000 SERVER

STEP	DESCRIPTION
Clear out the deadwood	Delete unnecessary files from the hard drive. Delete any user accounts that are not active. Remove applications that are no longer in use. Make sure there is plenty of free disk space.
Upgrade hardware	Legacy (outdated) hardware may not be compatible with the new operating system. Upgrade the hardware before installation.
Remove network protocols besides TCP/IP	TCP/IP is improved in Windows 2000 Server (covered in Chapter 13) and should be the protocol of choice.
DNS	Implement a DNS structure (covered in Chapter 13), and have all client computers use DNS.
Map out the system architecture	The architecture in Windows 2000 is different from Windows NT. You might need fewer domain controllers, for example.
Create a budget	Determine funding for potential hardware upgrades, software upgrades, and overtime for workers.
Perform project management actions	Create task lists and time lines for completing the tasks. Assign workers to the tasks.
Back up files	Before upgrading, make a complete backup of your current files. You can back up files to a disk, a tape drive, or another computer on the network.
Disabling disk mirroring	Before upgrading, if you have disk mirroring installed on the target computer, disable it before running setup. It can be reenabled after completion of the installation. Disk mirroring is discussed in Chapter 16.
Disconnect UPS devices	An **Uninterruptible Power Supply (UPS)** is a device that uses a battery as an alternate power source if the main power goes out. Disconnect the connecting serial cable before running Setup (assuming the UPS is connected to the target computer). Windows 2000 Server Setup attempts to automatically detect devices connected to serial ports; UPS equipment can cause problems with the detection process.
Review applications	Before starting the Setup program, read **relnotes.doc** (in the root directory of the Windows 2000 Server CD-ROM). This document has a section titled *Application Notes* that lists applications that need to be disabled or removed before Setup is run.
Testing	Test the new system before implementation by installing on a separate computer, and then add in network components and applications. Test after each addition.
Deployment	Consider migrating servers in small numbers and allowing them to function for a while with the nonupdated servers, rather than bringing all of them on-line in one step. If there is a problem, only one section of the network will be affected.
Performance	Evaluate the success of the deployment and work on problems as they arise.
Rollback	If problems after migration are so severe that they cannot be overcome quickly, restore all of the systems from backups and return to the testing phase.

New Installation

A new installation occurs when one of the following conditions exists:

- There is no previous operating system installed on the computer.

- The hard drive has multiple partitions and the new operating system will be installed on a partition with no previous operating systems.

- There is no need to keep configurations and data from a previous operating system. In this case, the new operating system *replaces* the previous operating system.

Procedurally, the initiation of the installation process is the same whether you are upgrading or performing a new installation. However, the decision to totally replace an existing operating system should not be taken lightly. If the migration does not go smoothly, your users do not have a network. One option, which is explored in the next section, is to configure the system to **dual boot** both operating systems until the new system is tested and stable.

EXERCISE

4.3 Choose an Installation Type

To perform this exercise, you will need:

- A computer
- A word processor

1. Choose if the installation of Windows 2000 Server in your lab should be a new installation or an upgrade.

2. Write at least one paragraph detailing why you chose that option.

3. Write at least one paragraph detailing why you did not choose the other option.

4. Print your document.

Lesson 4.3 Understand Multiple OS Booting Options

Dual booting is a feature of Windows 2000 Server that allows an administrator to choose between more than one operating system during the boot process. When a server configured for dual booting is powered up, a list of previously installed operating systems appears. The administrator selects the desired operating system, and the computer continues with the boot process.

Dual Booting Advantages

Dual booting offers more flexibility in configuration of a server, especially during a migration process. For example, you could leave Windows NT Server on the computer and create another partition for installing Windows 2000 Server. When the new configuration is stable, you could delete the Windows NT files and return to a single boot configuration.

It is important to keep in mind that some legacy software and hardware might not function under Windows 2000 Server. The best way to solve this dilemma is to find another program or device that is compatible and to replace the one that is not. Most software vendors know that Windows 2000 is the operating system of choice for many of their clients and are either in the process of adapting their product or already have a Windows 2000-compatible version. There are, however, vendors that are not progressive, and their product is truly legacy. If the incompatible product must be used "as is," dual booting with an older operating system like MS-DOS or Windows 95/98 may be the only alternative.

Dual Booting Disadvantages

The following disadvantages to dual booting must also be considered:

- A security loophole can occur when using operating systems based on the FAT file system. Unlike NTFS, FAT does not have file-level security and is not as immune to viruses.

- Valuable disk space is used by each additional operating system.

- Tasks that are performed under one operating system are not recorded on the other operating system. For example, a user account created under the Windows NT operating system would have to be reentered under Windows 2000.

- Dual booting makes the entire system more complex,which can lead to future problems.

Configuring a Dual Boot

During the installation process, the Setup program will scan the hard drive for previously installed operating systems. If any are found, a boot menu is automatically created that includes Windows 2000 and the other operating system(s). When the computer is restarted, the boot menu will appear early in the boot process and the user can select which operating system is to be launched for that session. If the user does not select an option, the default option automatically will be selected after 30 seconds.

CAUTION: If you are dual booting between Windows 2000 Server and any other operating system, Windows 2000 Server must be placed in a separate partition on the computer. Windows 2000 Server could overwrite crucial files used by the other operating system.

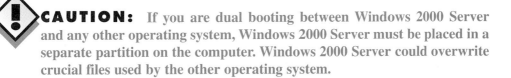

EXERCISE

4.4 Determine Dual Boot Requirements

To perform this exercise, you will need:

- A computer with access to the Internet
- A word processor

1. Determine if there is another server operating system installed on the lab server, and answer the following questions:

    - If the server has another operating system installed, will it be necessary to dual boot that operating system with Windows 2000 Server? Why or why not?

    - If the server does not have another operating system installed, are there hardware devices or software programs that need a different operating system than Windows 2000 Server? If so, list the products and the operating system they require. If not, search the HCL to locate one device that has been proven compatible with another operating system but is not tested or has been proven incompatible with Windows 2000 Server. Print the screen that shows the details of the device.

2. Print your document.

Lesson 4.4 Installation Media Options

The Setup program is designed to work in multiple stages. You will be prompted for information, files will be copied, and the computer might be restarted several times. The Setup program can be launched from two different locations: the Windows 2000 Server CD-ROM and over the network. Of course, installing from a CD-ROM requires that the computer have a CD-ROM drive. Installing over the network is usually performed when an additional server is being added to the network.

You should install from a CD-ROM if:

- The network has not been configured
- This is the first server to have Windows 2000 Server installed
- The servers are in the same location
- The network bandwidth is not sufficient to support network installation

Install over the network if:

- The server does not have a fast CD-ROM (or if the drive is not functional)
- The server to be added is at a remote location
- Network bandwidth is sufficient to support network installation

EXERCISE

4.5 Choose an Installation Media

To perform this exercise, you will need:

- A computer
- A word processor

1. Choose if the installation of Windows 2000 Server in your lab should be from a CD-ROM or over the network.

2. Write at least one paragraph detailing why you chose that option.

3. Write at least one paragraph detailing why you did not choose the other option.

4. Print your document.

Lesson 4.5 Joining a Domain or Workgroup

Chapter 3 introduced you to workgroups and domains. One of the installation tasks is the adding or **joining** of the computer to either a domain or a workgroup.

Joining an Existing Domain

When joining a domain during installation, the following information must be provided:

- **A domain name:** This is the DNS name for the domain that will be joined.

- **A computer account:** Before a computer can join a domain, an administrator must create a computer account in the domain. If your user account is the member of an administrator group, you can create the computer account during installation. If you are not an administrator, you will need to have an administrator create the account before starting the installation.

- **An available domain controller and a server running the DNS service (called the *DNS server*):** When you join the computer to the domain, at least one domain controller and one DNS server must be on-line.

Joining a Workgroup

You would only join a workgroup if the network does not have a domain controller or in order to prepare for joining a domain at a later time. When a Windows 2000 Server computer joins a workgroup, it is referred to as a **stand-alone server** because it is not a member of a domain. To join a workgroup, you simply supply the name of the existing workgroup during the installation process. If the workgroup name you enter does not exist, the Setup program will create the workgroup.

EXERCISE

4.6 Determine Domain Details

To perform this exercise, you will need:

- A computer
- A word processor

1. Answer the following questions about the domain the server will be joining:

    - Does a domain to be joined currently exist?

      If the answer is yes: What is the name of the domain?

      If the answer is no: What will be the name of the new domain?

    - Has the computer account been created?

      If the answer is yes: Who created it?

      If the answer is no: Will it be created during installation?

2. Print your document.

TABLE 4-2 PRE-INSTALLATION CHECKLIST

TASK	DONE
Verify that the computer components meet the minimum hardware requirements.	✓
Verify that all of the hardware is listed on the HCL.	✓
Determine how the hard drive will be partitioned and in what partition Windows 2000 server will be installed.	✓
Select the file system for the Windows 2000 partition (the best choice is NTFS).	✓
Choose a licensing mode for the server that will be running Windows 2000 (per server or per seat).	✓
Identify whether the computer will join a domain or a workgroup.	✓
Determine the name of the computer.	✓
Create a computer account in the domain to be joined.	✓
Create a password for the Administrator account.	✓
Determine if dual booting is required.	✓
Decide how you will launch the Setup program (CD-ROM or network).	✓

Lesson 4.6 Pre-Installation Checklist

Table 4-2 presents a pre-installation checklist that should be completed before launching the Setup program.

EXERCISE

Compile Pre-Installation Information

To perform this exercise, you will need:

■ A computer

■ A word processor

1. Create a two-column table similar to Table 4-2.

2. Add a column to the right of the *Done* column. Title the new column *Description*.

3. Enter specific information discovered during this chapter's exercises into the description column.

   ■ For example, beside the entry *Determine whether the computer will join a domain or work-group,* enter the name of the domain or workgroup under the *Description* column.

   ■ If available, use Form 4.2 in the Student Workbook as an example.

4. Print your document.

Summary

Preparation contributes to success. Having collected the information required for installation and knowing that the hardware meets the specifications will contribute to a smooth installation procedure. Imagine how much more time and mental effort would have to be expended if you had launched the Setup program without knowing the information discussed in this chapter. Undoubtedly, it would have been necessary to abandon and restart the Setup process several times. Many of the steps listed in Table 4-1 should also be considered when performing a new installation.

● ● ● ● ● ● ● ● ● ● ● ● ● ●

REVIEW EXERCISE

These questions will help you determine if you have learned enough to move on to the next chapter. If the graphic next to the option is a square (❑), there can be more than one answer for that question. If the graphic is a circle (○), there is only one correct answer. Color in the shape(s) to indicate your answer(s).

1. While preparing for a Windows 2000 Server installation, you discover that the software product used most frequently by your company will not run under the new operating system. What are your options?

   a. ❑ Purchase a Windows 2000-compatible program that performs the same function.

   b. ❑ Request a compatible version from the vendor.

   c. ❑ Configure a dual boot with the operating system the software requires.

   d. ❑ Kick, scream, pull your hair out, calm down, accept your fate, and then do one of the above.

2. You hold in your hand the Windows 2000 Server installation CD-ROM. Which of the following conditions would prompt you to insert the CD in the server's drive?

   a. ❑ Windows 2000 Server has not been installed on any computer on the network.

   b. ❑ A domain controller located in another building already has Windows 2000 Server installed. Your network has plenty of bandwidth to handle the installation process.

   c. ❑ All of the servers, including the one to which you are about to install, are in the same room. The CD-ROM drive door is open.

   d. ❑ Your network is already overloaded with handling user traffic.

3. To which naming system must a Windows 2000 domain name conform?

   a. ○ CAL

   b. ○ DNS

   c. ○ NTFS

   d. ○ UPS

4. When preparing for a migration to Windows 2000 Server, which of the following statements are valid?

   a. ❑ Connect the UPS through the serial cable before running Setup (assuming the UPS is connected to the target computer).

   b. ❑ Consider migrating servers in small numbers and allowing them to function for a while with the nonupdated servers rather than bringing all of them on-line in one step.

    c. ❏ Delete all of the files from the hard drive and then perform a backup of the entire system.

    d. ❏ If problems after migration are so severe that they cannot be overcome quickly, restore all of the systems from backups and return to the testing phase.

5. Which of the following steps should be done before installation of Windows 2000 Server?

    a. ❏ Verify that the computer components meet the minimum hardware requirements.

    b. ❏ Create a domain account in the computer to be joined.

    c. ❏ Select the file system for the Windows 2000 partition.

    d. ❏ Choose a licensing mode for the server that will be running Windows 2000.

▼PERFORMANCE CHALLENGES

■ Search the HCL for a device that is not yet certified as compatible with Windows 2000 Server. Contact the vendor and inquire as to when they expect to have a compatible driver available. Document the vendor information and the vendor's response to your inquiry.

■ Contrast and compare the following: domain controller, stand-alone server, and member server.

INSTALL WINDOWS 2000 SERVER

OBJECTIVES

After completing this chapter, you should be able to:

■ Install Windows 2000 Server from a CD-ROM drive on a clean hard drive

■ Install Windows 2000 Server from a CD-ROM drive already running various Windows operating systems

■ Understand the concepts of network installation

■ Describe the functions of each screen in the Setup wizard

■ Use the Setup wizard to install and configure Windows 2000 Server

■ Understand the sequence for installing Service Packs

■ Describe how to automate installations of Windows 2000 by using the Setup Manager wizard

■ Troubleshoot common installation problems

OUTLINE

Introduction

Now that you have completed your research and have gathered your information, it is time to put all of your hard work to task and actually perform the installation. Microsoft has attempted to make the installation process as painless as possible. User-friendly screens and dialog boxes ask the necessary questions and help the person using the Setup program answer those questions correctly. The installation of Windows 2000 Server to a clean hard disk involves the following four-stage process:

1. Run the Setup Program

   ■ Prepares the hard disk for later stages

   ■ Copies files necessary for the Setup wizard to run

2. Run the Setup wizard

   ■ Requests information like names, passwords, licensing, and so on

3. Install Windows NT networking

   ■ Requests networking information

   ■ Installs networking components

TERMINOLOGY

A **wizard** is a program that presents a series of screens and dialog boxes designed to help the user complete a specific task. There are many wizards in Windows 2000 Server. One, for example, helps the user to configure a printer for use over the network.

4. Complete the Setup program

■ Copies additional files to the hard disk

■ Configures the computer

■ Restarts the computer after installation is complete

You might breathe a sigh of relief after installation is complete, but your job is not over; in truth, it has just begun. The remainder of this chapter describes additional options for installation and also describes activities that should be performed after installation. Lastly, this chapter discusses steps to take when an installation is not successful. Your first choice is to decide whether you will install from a CD-ROM (Lesson 5.1) or over the network (Lesson 5.2). Although you should read both lessons, you will most likely perform one or the other.

Lesson 5.1 Start Setup from a CD-ROM

Several options are available for running Setup from a CD-ROM. Each of the following exercises details the steps required for installing from a computer running a preexisting operating system. This means that the computer has been booted to the other operating system and then the Setup program is launched from the CD-ROM.

Exercise 5.4 provides the steps for installing to a clean hard drive on a computer configured to boot from the CD-ROM drive. If a computer is not configured to boot from the CD-ROM, you will have to use **Setup Boot Disks** (included in the Windows 2000 Server box) to copy minimal

> **MICROSOFT TEST OBJECTIVE**
>
> Perform an attended installation of Windows 2000 Server.

CD-ROM drivers to the hard drive. Once the drivers are copied, the CD-ROM drive will be accessible and you can follow the steps in Exercise 5.4. Read all of the exercises before deciding which exercise would work best for your situation.

5.1 Start Setup from a CD-ROM on a Computer Running MS-DOS

To perform this exercise, you will need:

■ Access to the server on which installation will occur

■ The Windows 2000 Server CD-ROM

1. Insert the Windows 2000 Server CD-ROM in the drive.

2. At the command prompt, type **cd i386.**

3. Press **Enter.**

4. Type **winnt.**

5. Press **Enter.**

    ■ Setup will launch.

5.2 Start Setup from a CD-ROM on a Computer Running Windows 3.x

To perform this exercise, you will need:

■ Access to the server on which installation will occur

■ The Windows 2000 Server CD-ROM

1. Insert the Windows 2000 Server CD-ROM in the drive.

2. Using File Manager, click on the button for the CD-ROM drive.

3. Double-click the **i386** directory.

4. Double-click the file **winnt.exe.**

    ■ Setup will launch.

EXERCISE

5.3

Start Setup from a CD-ROM on a Computer Running Windows 95, Windows NT 3.51, Windows 4.0, or Windows 2000 Server

To perform this exercise, you will need:

■ Access to the server on which installation will occur

■ The Windows 2000 Server CD-ROM

1. Insert the Windows 2000 Server CD-ROM in the drive.

■ Setup will automatically launch.

EXERCISE

5.4

Start Setup and Perform a New Installation by Starting the Computer from a Bootable CD-ROM

To perform this exercise, you will need:

■ Access to the server on which installation will occur

■ The Windows 2000 Server CD-ROM

1. Shut down the computer.

2. Insert the Windows 2000 Server CD-ROM in the drive.

3. Start the computer.

■ Setup will automatically launch.

EXERCISE

5.5

Start Setup Using the Setup Boot Disks

To perform this exercise, you will need:

■ Access to the server on which installation will occur

■ The four Setup disks included in the Windows 2000 Server box

■ The Windows 2000 Server CD-ROM

1. Insert Setup Disk 1 in the floppy disk drive (A:).

2. Start (or restart) the computer.
   - A brief message is displayed about the system configuration being checked.
   - A gray bar at the bottom of the screen indicates that Setup is loading Windows 2000 Executive, a minimal version of the Windows NT kernel.

3. When prompted, insert Setup Disk 2 into the floppy drive, and press Enter.
   - Setup loads software components to support the computer's motherboard, bus, and mass media hardware.
   - Setup loads the Setup program files.

4. When prompted, insert Setup Disk 3 into the floppy drive, and press Enter.
   - Setup loads additional software components.
   - Setup initializes Windows 2000 Executive.
   - The Windows 2000 Server Setup screen is displayed.

5. When prompted, insert Setup Disk 4 into the floppy drive, and press Enter.

6. Read the Setup Notification message, and press Enter.

7. Read the Welcome To screen, and press Enter.

8. When prompted, insert the Windows 2000 Server CD-ROM in the drive.
   - Setup will launch.

Lesson 5.2 Install over the Network

To install Windows 2000 Server from a network, the files must be shared directly from the CD-ROM or copied to a shared folder; the Setup program then is run from that location. You will learn how to share network resources such as CD-ROM drives and folders in Chapter 13. If a network installation is required for your situation, you will need the assistance of your instructor to complete these steps.

EXERCISE

5.6

Start Setup and Install over the Network

● ●

To perform this exercise, you will need:

■ Access to the server on which installation will occur

■ Access to the computer with a shared CD-ROM drive or a shared folder that contains a copy of the files on the Windows 2000 Server installation CD

■ The Windows 2000 Server CD-ROM (unless the files are in a shared folder)

1. On a server on the network, share the installation files either by inserting the CD-ROM and sharing the CD-ROM drive or by copying the files from the **\i386** directory on the CD-ROM to a shared folder.

2. On the computer on which you want to install Windows 2000 Server, connect to the shared CD-ROM or shared folder.

3. Find and run the appropriate file in the **\i386** directory of the CD-ROM or in the shared folder by completing one of the following steps:

■ From a computer running MS-DOS or Windows 3.x, run **winnt.exe.**

■ From a computer running Windows 95, Windows 98, Windows NT 3.51, Windows NT 4.0, or a version of Windows 2000 Server, run **winnt32.exe.**

■ Setup will launch.

Lesson 5.3 Using the Setup Wizard

Using the Setup wizard involves selecting options from a series of screens and dialog boxes. In this lesson, you will be guided through a Setup procedure on a clean (empty) hard drive.

Getting Started

After the Setup program has been started, the screen turns bright blue. At the bottom of the screen is a white bar that displays information. The Setup program is inspecting the hardware and installing files and drivers needed to begin the installation of Windows 2000 Server. The message *Setup is starting Windows 2000* will appear on your screen.

After a brief wait, the screen refreshes and displays *Welcome to Setup* at the top. On this screen, the following three choices are available:

- To set up Windows 2000 now, press ENTER.

- To repair a Windows 2000 installation, press R.

- To quit Setup without installing Windows 2000, press F3.

Before you press Enter, consider why the other two options exist. When would you need to repair a Windows 2000 installation? An example would be a situation in which you installed a program that changed files in the operating system and caused a negative result. One recourse would be to boot to the CD and choose the R option to return the operating system files to their original configuration. The Repair option can also repair the Registry, which is an important database within Windows 2000. It also can recopy the files needed for booting to the boot sector. The result of the third option is the termination of the Setup program.

Licensing Agreement

The next screen contains the Windows 2000 Licensing Agreement, and the frame in the middle of the screen is filled with legalese. The following three options are listed at the bottom of the screen:

- F8 = I agree

- ESC = I don't agree

- PAGE DOWN = Next page

You should read every word in a license agreement. If you do not agree with the terms of the agreement, press the Escape key, and the installation will be aborted. To accept the terms of the license agreement, press F8.

Searching for Other Operating Systems

After you press F8, the white bar at the bottom of the screen says that Setup is searching for previous versions. If Setup finds another version, most likely a Windows NT operating system, the installation path would ask if you want to upgrade or perform a new installation. If the hard disk is clean (empty), this search is going to be brief. If the hard disk does have another operating system, a dual boot menu will be created.

FIGURE 5-1
Hard Disk Status Frame

```
9537 MB Disk 0 at Id 0 on bus 0 on atapi
C:   NTFS            9529 MB (8922 MB free)
     Unpartitioned space    8   MB
```

Disk Partitions

The next screen displays a list of existing partitions and unpartitioned space on the computer. Figure 5-1 shows an example of the status of a computer's hard disk. Above the hard disk status frame are the following three options:

■ To set up Windows 2000 on the selected item, press Enter.

■ To create a partition in the unpartitioned space, press C.

■ To delete the selected partition, press D.

You could choose to leave the drive as one large partition or use the other options for changing the current partition configuration. Most administrators would not use the entire 9 GB for the operating system. A common configuration would include two partitions—one for the operating system and one for data. The individual situation determines the size of each partition.

Notice that the second option only allows a partition to be created from *unpartitioned* space. Since the system does not have a way at this point to alter partitions, the existing partition must be deleted before a new one of a different size can be created.

EXERCISE

5.7

Partition a Hard Drive during Setup

• •

To perform this exercise, you will need:

■ To have started Setup and performed the steps to this point

■ A hard drive large enough to sustain two partitions

1. Press D to delete the current partition.

   ■ The screen refreshes.

   ■ The frame displays that the original partition is now in unpartitioned space.

   ■ The same three choices are available.

2. Press C to create a new partition in unpartitioned space.

   ■ A box with a cursor appears.

   ■ Enter the size of the new partition in megabytes. For example, if you want the new partition to be 4 GB, you would enter 4000.

3. Press Enter.

   ■ The screen refreshes.

   ■ The frame now displays the size of the new partition and how much of the disk is occupied by unpartitioned space.

4. Repeat step 2 and step 3 if you need to create more partitions.

   ■ The first partition is labeled C:.

   ■ The second partition is D:.

   ■ The third partition would be E:, and so on.

5. Use the arrow keys to highlight the C: drive.

6. Press Enter.

File Systems

The next screen indicates that Setup will install Windows 2000 on partition C. Although you have the option to press the Escape key if that is not the partition you want, the real purpose of this screen is to have you select which file system you want to use on the partition. The following two choices are available:

■ Format the partition using the NTFS file system.

■ Format the partition using the FAT file system.

EXERCISE

5.8 Formatting a Partition with NTFS

● ●

To perform this exercise, you will need:

■ To have started Setup and performed the steps to this point

1. Use the arrow keys to highlight the NTFS option.

2. Press Enter.

   ■ Setup displays the following warning: *CAUTION: Formatting this drive will delete all files on it.*

- Setup displays the status of the C: drive and offers two options:

  - To format the drive, press F.

  - To select a different partition for Windows 2000, press ESC.

3. Press F.

   - The screen then displays the message *Setup is formatting,* which is accompanied by a yellow bar that graphically represents the percentage of completion for the format process.

Entering Server Settings

The screen welcomes you and asks if you want to upgrade to Windows 2000 or install a new copy of Windows 2000. To select *Install a new copy,* click once in the circle next to that option.

At the bottom of the screen, three buttons provide the options of *Back, Next,* and *Cancel.*

The Back button is designed to display the previous screen; since there is not a previous screen to return to, the word on the button is gray. In Windows an option that appears in gray is unavailable at that time. The Next button takes you to the next screen in the sequence of screens, and the Cancel button will terminate the installation process. After completing all of the sections of a screen, you would normally click the Next button. Note that the rest of this section, the text will not give specific directions to click the Next button. To see the new topic, you should click the Next button.

> **TERMINOLOGY**
>
> A **radio button** indicates that only one of the available options in that section of the dialog box can be selected at one time.

CHOOSING OR CREATING PARTITIONS

The next dialog box gives you the opportunity to create or specify a partition on which Windows 2000 Server will be installed. The following three choices are available:

1. Create a partition from unpartitioned space available.

2. Specify an existing partition (if another operating system is in this partition, the operating system will be erased).

3. Delete an existing partition to create more unpartitioned disk space for the Windows 2000 Server partition (requires confirmation because all of the information in the existing partition will be erased).

This interface should be easier to work with than the nongraphical one at the beginning of the installation process. You now have the option to change the partition choices you made originally, if necessary. Windows 2000 Server also has a **Disk Management** utility that lets you change these settings; it has an interface similar to what you see on the screen.

SELECTING REGIONAL SETTINGS

Next, a dialog box appears for customizing the language, locale, and currency settings. Click on the various tabs to see the options. You would normally accept the defaults for all of these options if you live in the United States. For now leave the time and date settings at their defaults, for a better interface is available later in the installation process for these settings.

FIGURE 5-2
Regional Options

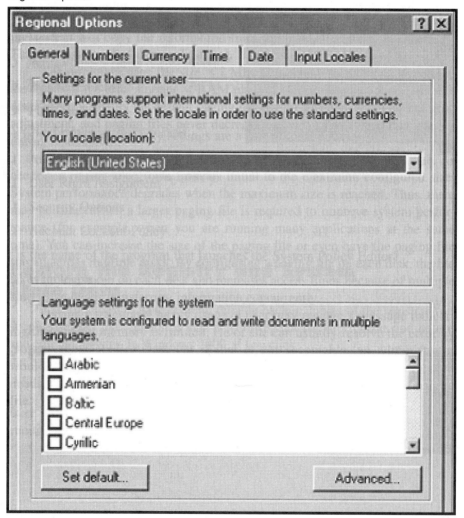

PERSONALIZATION

The next dialog box asks for the user's name and the organization, which will be used for product registration by applications installed later. Setup uses the organization name to create the default computer name. Type the appropriate name in the Name box, and type the name of your organization or company in the Organization box.

CHOOSING LICENSING MODE

By default, the Per Server licensing mode is selected. Select the licensing mode for your situation, and enter the number of licenses that have been purchased. Remember that you can later change *once* from Per Server to Per Seat at no cost. After that, you no longer have the option to change.

ENTERING THE COMPUTER NAME

This is one of the areas that you need to know and conform to your organization's naming conventions. The following rules apply to computer names within Windows 2000 Server:

- The name must be unique within the domain. No other computers or installations of server operating systems on another partition can have the same name.

- The name can be no longer than 63 characters.

- If the name is longer than 15 characters, pre-Windows 2000 Server computers will recognize the computer by the first 15 characters of the name only.

- It is recommended that only Internet-standard characters be used in the computer name. The standard characters are the numbers 0 to 9, uppercase and lowercase letters from A to Z, and the hyphen (-) character.

Consider the following example of a company with five servers at a Denver site and four at a Bismark site. The naming convention for company's computers includes the following:

- All letters are to be capitalized.

- The first three letters designate the company (BDW).

- A hyphen (-) follows the first three letters.

- The fourth letter designates the site (*D* for Denver or *B* for Bismarck).

- The fifth letter designates the type of computer (*S* for Server or *W* for Workstation).

- The last two digits are a sequential numbering system (starting with 01 for the first installation and 02, 03, and so on for subsequent installations).

Given this convention, the first server at the Denver site would have the name BDW-DS01.

Enter the appropriate computer name for your server.

TABLE 5-1 WINDOWS 2000 SYSTEM COMPONENTS

COMPONENT	DESCRIPTION
Indexing Service	Enables fast, full-text searching of files
Internet Information Service	IIS Services (Web and FTP support) along with support for FrontPage transactions, ASPs, database connections, and receiving of posts
Management and Monitoring Tools	Includes tools for monitoring and improving network performance
Message Queuing Services	Message Queuing provides loosely coupled and reliable network communication services
Networking Services	Contains a variety of specialized, network-related services and protocols
Other Network File and Print Services	Shares files and printers on this computer with others on the network
Script Debugger	Identifies errors in script programs running on your computer

SETTING THE ADMINISTRATIVE PASSWORD

The next two entries are highly sought pieces of information by those who either want to gain power or to destroy property. The administrative password belongs to a special user account called the **Administrator.** Just like administrators of an organization, the Administrator account in Windows 2000 has the most power to affect the system. Since anyone with access to the password for the Administrator account can log in and do *anything* to the system (good or bad), it is critical that the Administrator account has a strong password.

Microsoft recommends that the password contain at least seven characters. Although you can have up to fourteen characters, it would be time-consuming for the administrator to enter each time. The strongest passwords are a combination of letters, numbers, and other characters like @,?, or $ that you can remember. Usernames are not case-sensitive, but passwords are, so you can even add some capital letters to make the password even more difficult to guess. The password text box should not be left blank, for this means there is no password on the Administrator's account.

Enter your administrator account password now.

CHOOSING SERVER COMPONENTS

A new dialog box with the word **Components** at the top should appear. Windows 2000 Server has components that can be chosen within this screen; they then can be mixed and matched to fit your particular *computing* needs. Table 5-1 gives a brief description of each of the components. Although you might not understand all of the terminology in the table now, you will by the time you finish the book.

Before you leave this screen, it is important to note that, you can add or edit components to the operating system after installation. Later chapters in the

TABLE 5-2 DESKTOP AREA AND COLORS PAGE SETTINGS

SETTING	DESCRIPTION
Color Palette	Changes the number of colors. Usually higher color depths will result in better graphics.
Desktop Area	Changes the resolution of the images. The higher the number, the more pixels there are in the screen grid. Drag the slider to see a graphic representation of how the setting will affect the size of the desktop. Some users will have a hard time reading the smaller print on higher settings. 800 by 600 is most common.
Refresh Frequency	At regular intervals, the image on a monitor is redrawn (refreshed) one line at a time. The refresh frequency rate determines the speed at which the screen image will be redrawn. Higher refresh frequencies usually result in crisper displays. You must select a frequency supported by your monitor because too high a frequency could damage the device.

text will give details on how to customize these settings, so consider using the defaults at this time.

ADJUST THE DISPLAY

During the initial installation procedures, Setup detected the video adapter installed in the computer. The Desktop Area and Colors page allows you to alter the default settings for your monitor and video adapter. Table 5-2 describes the items you can change using this screen.

If you decided to change the settings on this screen, use the Test button to make sure the changes you made will result in a readable image. During the testing of the display settings, a colorful bitmap is displayed. A dialog box appears asking if the bitmap displayed properly. If it did, click the **Yes** button and continue to the next screen. If it did not, change the settings and test them again, repeating this process until the bitmap displays properly.

SET THE DATE, TIME, AND TIME ZONE

As shown in Figure 5-3, a dialog box for setting the date and time appears. Exercise 5.9 will help you to establish these settings.

FIGURE 5-3
Setting the Date and Time

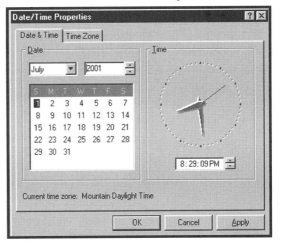

5.9

Setting the Date and Time

To perform this exercise, you will need:

■ To have started Setup and performed the steps to this point

1. Set the month by clicking on the down arrow near the displayed month and selecting the appropriate month from the list.

2. Set the year by using the up and down arrows by the year text box.

3. Click directly on the calendar for the number that corresponds to today's date.

4. Set the time by clicking on the number for the hour and then using the up and down arrows. Click on the minutes, and use the arrows again to set the correct time.

5. Click on the Time Zone tab at the top of the dialog box. A colorful screen appears with a green map of the world.

6. If available, click the box at the bottom of the dialog box to have the computer automatically adjust for daylight savings time.

7. Click OK.

SPECIFYING NETWORKING SETTINGS

Setup is now ready to begin the process of configuring the server to function as a part of the network. Exercise 5.10 demonstrates how to use these screens to make a stand-alone server in a workgroup. You will learn how to create and join a new Windows 2000 domain in the next chapter.

EXERCISE

5.10   **Installing Network Components**

To perform this exercise, you will need:

■ To have started Setup and performed the steps to this point

■ To be viewing the *Networking Settings* screen

1. Click on the text **Typical Settings.**

2. Click Next.

    ■ Setup installs networking components used for accessing shared resources.

    ■ Setup configures TCP/IP to automatically obtain an IP address from a DHCP server on the network.

3. On the *Domain Membership* screen, select **No, This Computer Is Not On A Network, Or Is On A Network Without A Domain.**

4. Enter the name of the workgroup as **WORKGROUP.**

5. Click Next.

COMPLETING THE INSTALLATION PROCESS

Setup displays the *Completing Setup* screen and gives the status of the process that includes copying files, saving configuration changes, and deleting temporary files. This process could take several minutes.

When the process is complete, Setup displays the *Completing the Windows 2000 Setup Wizard* screen. Before you click the Finish button on this screen, remove the Windows 2000 Server CD-ROM from the CD-ROM drive.

CAUTION: If you neglect to remove the Windows 2000 Server CD-ROM before rebooting, the Setup process could start all over again (if the CD-ROM drive is bootable). If this happens, remove the CD-ROM and restart the computer again.

Shortly after you click Finish, the computer will restart.

If a dialog box appears at this time indicating that one or more errors were encountered during setup, click Yes to view the **System Setup log.** Write down the information displayed in the log. Normally, these are errors that can be corrected later using configuration programs in Windows 2000 Server. Lesson 5.7 lists common problems that might occur during installation and what you might do to resolve those problems. Click Close after documenting the errors. Setup will then continue the installation process and will finish by restarting the computer.

When the computer reboots, a newly installed version of Windows 2000 Server appears. Every time Windows 2000 Server boots, the operating system will run a hardware-detection routine to see if there were any hardware components added when the computer was shut down. If a particular hardware device was not detected during the Setup process, the Found New Hardware wizard is displayed after the user logs on. Exercise 5.11 describes how to use the wizard, but keep in mind that you may or may not see these screens when your server boots.

5.11

Using the Found New Hardware Wizard

To perform this exercise, you will need:

- To have started Setup and performed the steps to this point

1. Log on by pressing Ctrl-Alt-Delete.

- The Enter Password dialog box is displayed.

2. In the User Name box, type **Administrator.**

3. In the Password box, type the password you assigned to the Administrator account during Setup.

4. Click OK.

- If new hardware is detected, the Found New Hardware wizard is displayed.

- Windows 2000 Server will install the appropriate drivers for the hardware.

5. Verify that the **Restart the Computer When I Click Finish** checkbox is cleared.

6. Click **Finish** to complete the wizard.

FINAL STEPS

When installation is complete, Windows 2000 Server displays the Configure Server dialog box. You will use this dialog box throughout this book to change configurations. For now, just minimize the Configure Server dialog box. You have completed the basic installation of Windows 2000 Server and are logged on as Administrator.

Lesson 5.4 Deploy Service Packs

A **service pack** is a collection of programs created by a software manufacturer after the release of a software product. The programs in the service pack might fix errors and/or incorporate new features. Normally, service packs are sequentially numbered. At the time of this writing, Service Pack 1 (SP1) provides the latest updates to the Windows 2000 family of operating systems. These updates are a collection of fixes in the following areas: setup, application compatibility, operating system reliability, and security. You can access the service pack files through the Microsoft Web site. If the service pack is not listed on the Windows 2000 page, perform a search for "service pack." When a service pack is released, carefully review how the service pack will affect your system and then decide if the service pack should be installed. Microsoft offers documentation in the form of a readme file on the service pack Web page to help you determine whether to install a particular service pack. In most cases, the product will greatly benefit from the service pack installation. You can procure the service pack files from the Web site by either ordering a CD or downloading. Exercise 5.12 describes how to deploy Service Pack 1 from the Web.

> **MICROSOFT TEST OBJECTIVE**
>
> Deploy service packs.

> **TIP**
>
> Before installing a service pack, perform a full backup of the operating system. If something goes wrong, you can always restore the backup and then reevaluate the service pack.

CAUTION: Service packs must be installed in sequence since they build on each other. Installing a service pack out of order would most likely cause problems with the entire system.

EXERCISE 5.12

Deploy Service Pack 1 from the Web

To perform this exercise you will need:

- To have installed Windows 2000 Server
- To log on as an administrator
- Access to the Microsoft Windows 2000 Service Pack Web site: http://www.microsoft.com/windows2000/downloads/recommended/sp1/default.asp

There are two installation options for Service Pack 1 available from the Web:

- The express installation
- The network download

To download the express installation:

1. Using your browser, go to the Microsoft Windows 2000 Service Pack Web site.

2. Click **Install Service Pack 1.**
   - The express installation automatically detects which files need to be updates and then copies those file to a temporary file on the computer. It then installs the files and updates the computer.

To download and extract the network download:

1. Using your browser, go to the Microsoft Windows 2000 Service Pack Web site.

2. Click **Install Service Pack 1.**
   - During the download, the compressed Service Pack executable file (SP1network.exe) is saved on the computer.

3. At the command prompt, type **SP1network.exe,** and press Enter.

To distribute the Service Pack over the network:

1. Connect to the network drive that contains the Service Pack 1 files.

2. Change to the drive letter of the network drive.

3. Change the folder to \i386\update.

4. Double-click **Update.exe.**

5. Follow the instructions on the screen.

Lesson 5.5 Perform an Unattended Installation

The tasks that must be performed on a small network can multiply in a large networking environment to the point that there is not enough time to accomplish all of the tasks. Whenever

MICROSOFT TEST OBJECTIVE

Perform an unattended installation of Windows 2000 Server. Create unattended answer files by using Setup Manager to automate the installation of Windows 2000 Server. Create and configure automated methods for installation of Windows 2000.

possible, administrators will automate their tasks, or, in other words, make the computer do part of their work. Installations of both Windows 2000 Server and Windows 2000 Professional can be automated in various ways to varying degrees of automation.

Understanding Disk Duplication

If two computers have identical hardware configurations, you can use **disk duplication** to speed up the installation process. Disk duplication involves the use of third-party image-copying software to create a master disk image from the original Windows 2000 operating system computer. The disk image is saved on a shared folder or CD-ROM and is then copied to the multiple-destination computers. When the user starts the destination computer, the **Mini-Setup wizard** will launch and will ask the user for computer-specific information, such as the computer name and the administrator's password for the local computer. What if the user does not know the answers to the questions? You can use the **Setup Manager** to create a file named **Sysprep.inf** that can answer the questions for the Mini-Setup wizard, thus bypassing the user altogether.

TERMINOLOGY

Third-party software means that a company other than Microsoft is the manufacturer of the software or utility. Microsoft has cooperated with the manufacturer to integrate the enhancement with the Windows 2000 programs.

Using the Windows 2000 Setup Manager Wizard

The **Windows 2000 Setup Manager Wizard** assists in automating installations on computers that do not have identical hardware configurations. The Setup Manager is used to create an installation **script,** which is a file that provides information about the variations in hardware configurations for the computer that will receive an installation. During an unattended installation, the Setup program uses the information in the script instead of prompting the user for information with dialog boxes. The unattended installation script is created once and contains the configuration information common to all of the computers on which the installation will occur.

UNIQUENESS DATABASE FILE (UDF)

When installing to a large number of computers, one unattended installation file will not be sufficient, for the information is too generic. For example, you already know that each computer has to have a unique computer name. Another file called the **Uniqueness Database File (UDF)** can be used to identify the differences among installations, such as the computer name and the username for that installation. Without a UDF, all of the computers would have the same name. Thus, the UDF alters the results of the unattended installation by providing information for a specific computer. The following is an example of a UDF that customizes the installation for two different computers (the square brackets [ ] indicate a section heading):

[UniqueIds]

comp1 = UserData

comp2 = UserData

[comp1:UserData]

FullName = "Rusty Scalpel"

OrgName = "One Hour Surgery Center"

ComputerName = ST-A07

[comp2:UserData]

FullName = "Roy Rogers"

OrgName = "Spurs R Us"

ComputerName = ST-B19

Note that in order to perform an unattended installation with Windows NT 4.0, administrators had to create a script called an **answer file.** The answer file was a simple text document with specific entries for answering the installation questions. The way the file was written (syntax) had to be exact or the answer file would not function properly. The name of the file was **unattend.txt.** Even though Windows 2000 Server can use unattend text files, Setup Manager provides a graphical user interface and reduces errors in syntax.

FEATURES OF SETUP MANAGER

Setup Manager contains the following features:

- Provides an easy-to-use graphical user interface for creating and modifying answer files

- Makes UDFs for specifying computer-specific or user-specific information

- Simplifies the inclusion of application setup scripts in the answer file

- Creates the distribution folder used for the installation files

Before you can access Setup Manager, you uncompress some files from the Windows 2000 Server CD-ROM. To uncompress (also called *unzip*) files, you need to have installed a utility called WinZip, which can be downloaded from the WinZip homepage—www.winzip.com. Exercise 5.13 describes the steps for accessing Setup Manager.

EXERCISE

5.13 Installing and Running the Setup Manager

To perform this exercise, you will need:

■ To have installed Windows 2000 Server

■ The Windows 2000 Server CD-ROM

■ An installed copy of WinZip

1. Log on as the Administrator.

2. Insert the Windows 2000 Server CD-ROM into a CD-ROM drive.

3. Launch Windows Explorer.

   ■ Click the Start button.

   ■ Select Programs.

   ■ Select Accessories.

   ■ Select Windows Explorer.

4. Click on the CD-ROM drive that contains the Windows 2000 Server CD-ROM.

5. Double-click the **Support** folder.

6. Double-click the **Tools** folder.

7. Double-click **deploy.cab.**

8. Using WinZip, indicate a folder to which the files will be unizipped.

9. Open the folder to which you unzipped the files from **deploy.cab.**

10. Double-click the file named **Setupmgr.exe.**

EXERCISE

5.14 Using Setup Manager to Create an Answer File

To perform this exercise, you will need:

■ To have installed Windows 2000 Server

■ To have performed Exercise 5.13

1. The following three options are available from the initial Setup Manager screen:

   ■ Create a new answer file (default).

NOTE: Not all beta versions of Windows 2000 Server have the Resource Kit on the distribution CD. If you are using a beta version, you will need to search the disks of either earlier or later versions.

- Create an answer file that duplicates this computer's configuration.

- Modify an existing answer file.

2. Select **Create a new answer file,** and click Next.

   - The next screen asks what product the answer file will install. The choices are as follows:

     - Windows 2000 Unattended Installation

     - Sysprep Install

     - Remote Installation Services

3. Select **Windows 2000 Unattended Installation,** and click Next.

   - The next screen asks to which platform does this answer file install. The choices are as follows:

     - Windows 2000 Professional

     - Windows 2000 Server

4. Select **Windows 2000 Server,** and click Next.

   - The next screen asks what level of interaction you want from the user during the installation. The choices are as follows:

     - Provide defaults

     - Fully automated

     - Hide pages

     - Read only

     - GUI attended

   - Notice that as you click on each item, the description box below the choices describes the results of selecting the item.

5. Select **Fully automated,** and click Next.

6. Click the checkbox to indicate that you accept the terms of the License Agreement for Windows 2000 (if you do), and click Next.

7. Enter your name in the "Name:" text box.

8. Enter your organization's name in the "Organization:" text box.

9. From the *Licensing Mode* screen, select the licensing mode that your organization is using (Per Server or Per Seat).

10. Enter the name of a computer (using your organization's naming convention for computer names), and click Add.

11. Repeat step 10 for each computer on which the product will be installed using this answer file. When finished entering computer names, click Next.

12. Enter the password for the "Administrator in the Password:" text box.

13. Enter the password again in the "Confirm Password:" text box.

14. Click the checkbox to automatically log on as Administrator when the computer starts, and leave the **Number of times to auto logon** as 1. Click Next.

15. On the *Display Settings* screen, leave each of the boxes as **Use Windows default** unless you know the specific settings for colors, screen area, and refresh frequency. Click Next.

16. On the *Network Settings* screen, click the **Typical settings** option unless you know you need custom settings. Click Next.

- The next screen is for entering whether the computer will be a member of a workgroup or a domain.

- If you select workgroup, enter the name of the workgroup (or use the default name of WORK-GROUP).

- If you select domain, enter the name of the domain.

- If you select domain and a computer account will not have been previously created for the computer, you will have to enter a username and corresponding password for a user account that has permission to create a computer account. This would normally be an administrator.

17. When you have filled out the *Workgroup* or *Domain* screen, click Next.

18. On the *Time Zone* screen, click the pull-down list button and select the appropriate time zone.

- The next screen indicates that you have completed a basic installation and provides the option to edit additional settings. The additional settings include regional settings, area code, languages, browser settings, installation folder, installing printers, and running a command after setup completes.

19. Click **No, do not edit the additional settings.**

- On the *Distribution Folder* screen, you indicate whether the Windows source files will be stored on a network drive (in a distribution folder) or will come from a Windows 2000 Server CD-ROM. If you select **Yes, create or modify a distribution folder,** the next screen will ask you to provide the path for the folder.

20. Select **No, this answer file will be used to install from a CD,** and click Next.

21. On the *Answer File Name* screen, accept the default location and filename (make note of the path and that a UDF file was automatically created when you entered more than one computer). Click Next.

22. Setup Manager indicates that files were created and where those files are stored. Click the Finish button.

USING THE ANSWER FILE

Winnt32.exe is the program that actually runs Setup during installation. You can change the way **winnt32.exe** functions by using **switches** on the command line. A switch is a string of characters preceded by a slash (/) at the end of a command line that alters the way the command is executed. For example, the following command lines will have different results:

- Winnt32 /syspart:F
- Winnt32 /tempdrive:D
- Winnt32

Switches are optional. If no switch is used, a default set of parameters will be applied. You can use more than one switch on a command line. Table 5-3 lists the switches for Winnt32.exe that can be used to initiate and alter an unattended installation.

TABLE 5-3 SWITCHES FOR THE *WINNT32.EXE* COMMAND THAT ARE USED IN UNATTENDED INSTALLATIONS

SWITCH	DESCRIPTION
/unattend[num]: [answer_file]	Performs an installation in unattended Setup mode. *Num* is the number of seconds between the time that Setup finishes copying the files and when it restarts the computer. *Answer_file* is the name of the answer file.
/udf:id [,*UDF_file*]	Indicates an identifier (id) that Setup uses to specify how a Uniqueness Database File (UDF) modifies an answer file. The UDF file overrides values in the answer file, and the identifier determines which values in the .UDF file are used. For example, /udf:User7,company.udf will cause Setup to use the information specified in the User7 section of the company.udf file. If no UDF file is specified, Setup prompts the user to insert a disk that contains the $Unique$.udf file.
/s:sourcepath	Specifies the source location of the Windows 2000 files. To simultaneously copy files from up to eight multiple servers, specify multiple /s sources. If you use multiple /s switches, the first specified server must be available or Setup will fail.
/tempdrive: drive_letter	Directs Setup to place temporary files on the specified partition and to install Windows 2000 on that partition.
/copydir: folder_name	Creates an additional folder within the folder in which the Windows 2000 files are installed. For example, if the source folder contains a folder called Our_drivers that has modifications just for your site, you can type /copydir:Our_drivers to have Setup copy that folder to the installed Windows 2000 folder. So then the new folder location would be C:\Winnt\Private_drivers. You can use /copydir to create as many additional folders as is necessary.
/copysource: folder_name	As with /copydir, /copysource creates a temporary additional folder within the folder in which the Windows 2000 files are installed. Unlike the folders /copydir creates, /copysource folders are deleted after Setup completes.

TABLE 5-3 CONTINUED

SWITCH	DESCRIPTION
/cmd: *command_line*	Instructs Setup to carry out a specific command before the final phase of Setup. This would occur after the computer has restarted twice and after Setup has collected the necessary configuration information, but before Setup is complete.
/syspart: *drive_letter*	Specifies that Setup startup files can be copied to a hard disk. You would mark the disk as active, and then install the disk into another computer. When the computer boots, it automatically starts with the next phase of the Setup. You must always use the /tempdrive parameter with the /syspart parameter.
/checkup gradeonly	Checks the computer for upgrade compatibility with Windows 2000. For Windows 95 or Windows 98 upgrades, Setup creates a report named Upgrade.txt in the Windows installation folder. For Windows NT 3.51 or 4.0 upgrades, the report is saved to the Winnt32.log in the installation folder.
/cmdcons	Adds to the operating system selection screen a Recovery Console option for repairing a failed installation. It is only used post-Setup.
/m:*folder_name*	Specifies that Setup copies replacement files from an alternate location. Instructs Setup to look in the alternate location first and if files are present, use them instead of the files from the default location.
/makelocalsource	Instructs Setup to copy all installation source files to the local hard disk. Use /makelocalsource when installing from a CD to provide installation files when the CD is not available later in the installation.
/noreboot	Instructs Setup to not restart (boot) the computer after the file copy phase of winnt32 is completed so that you can execute another command.

To perform an unattended installation of Windows 2000 Server, you must specify the answer file when Setup begins, either by using the bootable CD method, or by running Winnt32.exe. To use the answer file you created in Exercise 5.14, you would need to run winnt32.exe from a command line and use the appropriate switch(es). Below is an example command line—you would need to adjust the entries according to your situation.

EXERCISE

5.15 Manually Launch an Answer File

• •

To perform this exercise you will need:

■ To have created an answer file

■ To have installed Windows 2000 Server

1. Click **Start.**

2. Point to **Programs.**

3. Point to **Accessories.**

4. Select **Command Prompt.**

5. Type the following command line (substitute your filenames for the ones below):
   Winnt32 /unattend1:stan-dard.txt /udf:computer27, workstation.udf

6. Press Enter.

   ■ The setup program will launch and use the information in the answer file.

UNATTEND.BAT

When you click Finish on the final screen of the Setup Manager wizard, a file named *Unattend.bat* is created. If you double-click that file, the installation will launch and the answer file will be used without having to enter the command and switches shown above.

EXERCISE

5.16 Automatically Launch an Answer File

● ●

To perform this exercise you will need:

■ To have installed Windows 2000 Server

■ To have created an answer file using Setup Manager

1. Launch Windows Explorer.

2. Browse to the folder to which you unzipped the files from deploy.cab (see Exercise 5.13).

3. Double-click on **unattend.bat**

   ■ The setup program will launch and use the information in the answer file.

Lesson 5.6 Troubleshoot Failed Installations

An installation of Windows 2000 Server should complete without any errors, especially if you planned for the installation adequately. Errors are rare, but they can occur. Table 5-4 lists some of the common installation problems and how you might solve them.

TABLE 5-4 COMMON INSTALLATION PROBLEMS AND SOLUTIONS

PROBLEM	POSSIBLE SOLUTION
Media errors	There is a problem with either the device or the media. If installing from a CD-ROM, use a different CD. If you only have one Windows 2000 Server CD-ROM, contact Microsoft or your vendor for another copy.
Nonsupported CD-ROM device	This problem should be averted when you checked the HCL. Replace the CD-ROM drive with a supported drive. If this is not possible, you may have to find another source for installation, such as a network installation.
Insufficient disk space	Delete and create partitions as needed to create a partition that is large enough for installation.
Failure of dependency service to start	Make sure you installed the correct protocol and network adapter in the Network Settings dialog box during Setup. Verify that the adapter is configured correctly and that the local computer name is unique on the network.
Inability to connect to the domain controller	Verify the name of the domain is correct.
	Verify that the server running the DNS Service and the domain controller are both running and online. Consider installing into a workgroup and then joining the domain later.
	If you are reinstalling Windows 2000 and using the same computer name, delete and then recreate the computer account.
Failure of Windows 2000 to install or start	Verify that all of the hardware is on the HCL and that Windows 2000 is detecting all of the hardware.

Summary

The Setup program is designed to make installation of Windows 2000 Server as painless as possible. Careful collection of information and the application of that information within the Setup screens contributes to a successful installation. The Setup program can be launched from a variety of media, depending on the individual situation of the computer and network. For large organizations, installations can be automated using the Setup Manager wizard. If an installation does fail, solve the problem through troubleshooting and then start the installation again. Remember to make backups of the existing operating system before performing an upgrade.

• • • • • • • • • • • • • •

REVIEW EXERCISE

These questions will help you determine if you have learned enough to move on to the next chapter. If the graphic next to the option is a square (❑), there can be more than one answer for that question. If the graphic is a circle (○), there is only one correct answer. Color in the shape(s) to indicate your answer(s).

1. You already have Windows 2000 Server installed on several domain controllers. Now you need to install Windows 2000 Server on a computer that does not support booting from the CD-ROM. What other options do you have for installation?

   a. ❑ Use the Setup boot disks included with Windows 2000 Server.

   b. ❑ Install a bootable CD-ROM drive.

   c. ❑ Perform a network installation.

   d. ❑ Create a new partition, copy the contents of the CD-ROM to the partition, then boot from the new partition.

2. The components of a computer have been upgraded so it can be a Windows 2000 server. The 3 GB hard drive has Windows 95 installed on a 400 MB partition. Which of the following will prepare the disk for a Windows 2000 Server installation?

   a. ○ Reformat the hard drive and use the existing partition for the Windows 2000 Server files.

   b. ○ Delete existing partitions and create a 600 MB partition for the Windows 2000 Server files.

    c. ○ Delete existing partitions and create a 2 GB partition for the Windows 2000 Server files.

    d. ○ The disk does not need changed in any way. Simply upgrade directly from Windows 95 to Windows 2000 Server.

3. How many characters are allowed in a Windows 2000 computer name?

    a. ○ 15

    b. ○ 25

    c. ○ 37

    d. ○ 63

4. When devising a password for the Administrator account, what should you keep in mind?

    a. ❑ Passwords should be longer than 15 characters in length.

    b. ❑ Passwords are case-sensitive.

    c. ❑ Passwords can be blank.

    d. ❑ The Administrator password should be easy to guess.

5. What do you need in order for a computer to join a domain during the installation process?

    a. ❑ The DNS domain name of the domain to be joined.

    b. ❑ A computer account that exists in the domain.

    c. ❑ A server running the DNS service.

    d. ❑ An available domain controller in the domain to be joined.

6. What two types of installations are available after downloading Service Pack 1 from the Web?

    a. ❑ QuickFix

    b. ❑ Express

    c. ❑ Network

    d. ❑ Unintended

▼ PERFORMANCE CHALLENGES

- Launch the Setup program in at least two different ways. Use a word processor to document the steps you performed for each way.

- If the Setup boot disks were either lost or damaged, what program would you use in order to create a new set?

CHAPTER 6

CONFIGURE THE DNS SERVICE

OBJECTIVES

After completing this chapter, you should be able to:

- Explain the purpose of DNS and how it functions

- Define name resolution

- Configure TCP/IP for DNS

- Install the DNS Service on a server

- Create different types of zones

- Configure a client to use the DNS Service

OUTLINE

Introduction

If you were asked to describe a tree from the ground up you would probably say that the tree starts with a root that is attached to a trunk. The trunk supports large branches that support smaller branches that in turn support even smaller branches. Eventually each branch ends in a leaf.

Now imagine that tree upside down, with the root at the top and the branches at the bottom. This is what we call a **hierarchical** structure. As shown in Figure 6.1, a hierarchical structure helps to define the position of objects in the structure and their relation to other objects.

FIGURE 6-1

Hierarchical Structure of an Upside-down Tree

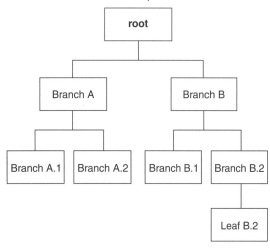

If you needed to examine Leaf B.2, you could not simply jump into that part of the tree. Instead, you would have to climb the tree, moving to the appropriate branches until you reached the leaf. It is the same in a hierarchical structure. In order to describe the location and relationships associated with the object named Leaf B.2, we include the root and all of the branches between the root and the leaf. The description would look something like this:

root\BranchB\BranchB.2\LeafB.2

If you were to substitute directory names for branches and leaves, you would have a description that looks like this:

C:\WINNT\system32\Repl\import\scripts

C:\ is the root node; WINNT, system32, Repl, and imports are intermediate nodes; and scripts is a leaf node.

Understanding the **directory tree** concept will help you understand the **Domain Name Service (DNS).** The DNS was introduced as a standard in 1983 in order to provide an index of host names on the Internet. Unlike earlier host-naming mechanisms, DNS uses a hierarchical database to resolve host names into IP addresses.

It is important to understand DNS because Windows 2000 Active Directory directory services uses DNS as a location service to identify domains and domain host computers during processes such as logging onto the network. Therefore, this chapter provides a solid foundation for learning about Active Directory.

Lesson 6.1 Understand DNS Concepts

DNS is a distributed database that is used in TCP/IP networks to resolve computer names to IP addresses. DNS is the Internet's name space standard. For example, www.microsoft.com is a name space for Microsoft Corporation that is registered with DNS. When you enter that name in a browser, DNS finds the IP address that corresponds to that name. Without DNS you would have to enter 207.47.131.137 in your browser to go to Microsoft's home page.

DNS performs the following functions:

- Internet name space standard
- Name registration
- Name-to-address resolution
- Hierarchical structured host names
- Locator service for Windows 2000

TIP

If you want to know the IP address for an Internet Web site, launch a command prompt window and type in **ping x** (where x represents the name of the site). For example, for Microsoft you would type **ping microsoft. com.** You will need a connection to the Internet in order for this utility to work.

Domain Name Space

The **Domain Name Space** provides the hierarchical structure for the DNS database. Each partition of the DNS database is referred to as a **domain.** The DNS database is indexed by names with the domain name, which indicates its position in the structure. Figure 6-2 shows the domain name compared to the structure.

ROOT DOMAIN

The root domain is represented by a period (.) and is at the top of the hierarchy. This domain is managed by several organizations, including Network Solutions, Inc.

TOP-LEVEL DOMAINS

The top-level domains are represented by two- or three-character name codes and are organized by either their organization type or their geographic location. Table 6-1 lists examples of top-level domain names.

The last two entries in Table 6-1 list the domains for two countries; each country has a top-level domain code name.

TERMINOLOGY

The term **domain** in reference to DNS is not the same as a domain in Windows 2000. A domain in Windows 2000 Server is a grouping of computers and devices that are administered as a unit. A domain in DNS is a name for the levels in the hierarchy. Also, do not confuse Domain Name Service with Domain Name Space.

FIGURE 6-2
Hierarchical Structure of a Domain Name Space

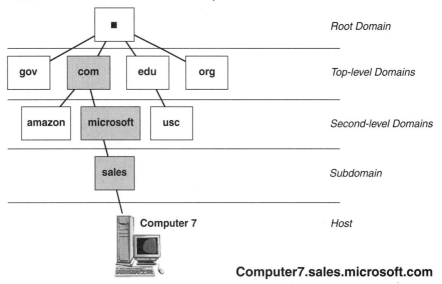

	■		Root Domain
gov	com	edu	org	Top-level Domains
amazon	microsoft	usc		Second-level Domains
	sales			Subdomain
	Computer 7			Host

Computer7.sales.microsoft.com

TABLE 6-1 DNS TOP-LEVEL DOMAIN CODE NAME EXAMPLES

DOMAIN NAME	DESCRIPTION	USED BY
gov	Government Organizations	United States
mil	Military	United States
com	Identifies commercial organizations (very large)	Worldwide
edu	Educational Institutions—limited to 4-year colleges and universities	Worldwide
org	Noncommercial organizations or those that do not fit into the other categories	Worldwide
net	Includes network providers and Internet administrative computers	Worldwide
int	Organizations established by international treaties	Worldwide
au	Country code of Australia	Country
us	Country code of the United States	Country

SECOND-LEVEL DOMAINS

Organizations such as Network Solutions, Inc., assign and register second-level domains to individuals and organizations for the Internet. The name has two parts: a top-level name and a unique second-level name. Table 6-2 lists some second-level domain names.

TABLE 6-2 DNS SECOND-LEVEL DOMAIN NAME EXAMPLES	
DOMAIN NAME	**DESCRIPTION**
ed.gov	United States Department of Education
microsoft.com	Microsoft Corporation
stanford.edu	Stanford University
w3.org	World Wide Web Consortium
pm.gov.au	Prime Minister of Australia

SUBDOMAINS

Organizations can extend their second-level domain name to include departments, divisions, or other geographic locations. Subdomains have three parts: a top-level name, a unique second-level name, and a unique name representing the department or location. In the example **sales.microsoft.com,** sales is the subdomain.

Host Name

A host name refers to a specific computer on the Internet or a private network. It is the left-most portion of a **fully qualified domain name (FQDN).** An FQDN describes where the host is located in the hierarchical structure and is used to resolve a name to an IP address. In Figure 6-2, for example, **Computer7** would be the host name, and **Computer7.sales.microsoft.com.** would be the FQDN (note that the FQDN includes the last period because that period represents the root domain).

Guidelines for Creating Domain Names

The following guidelines are used to create domain names:

- Limit the number of domain levels to no more than five levels because too many levels increases administrative tasks.

- Use unique names to ensure that the name has no duplicates in the DNS name space.

- Use simple names because they are easier for users to remember and also simplify administration.

- Avoid lengthy domain names. Domain names can be up to 63 characters, including periods. If the domain name is too long, it may interfere with the total allowed for a FQDN (255 characters).

- Use standard DNS characters and Unicode characters.
  - Windows 2000 supports following standard DNS characters: A–Z, a–z, 0–9, and the hyphen (-).
  - The DNS Service also supports the Unicode character set that contains characters not found in the ASCII character set. These characters include entries required for languages like Spanish, French, and German.

Zones

Perhaps you have seen "No Parking Zone," or "No Passing Zone" signs along the roadside. When you see the word *zone,* you know that the area near the sign is governed by a special rule. Once you are out of the zone, the rule is no longer in effect. A **zone** in DNS is similar in that the zone represents a certain portion of the domain name space. Zones are used to partition the domain name space into manageable sections.

Each zone in a DNS name space has its own database file that contains the name-to-IP-address mappings. Any subdomain in the zone will have entries in the zone database. Each zone is anchored to a specific domain, referred to as the zone's **root domain.** In Figure 6-3, the root domain for Zone1 is *sales* and the root domain for Zone2 is *HR* (human resources). Zone1's database contains mappings for the sales domain but does not have entries for the human resources domain.

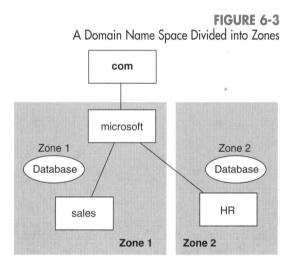

FIGURE 6-3
A Domain Name Space Divided into Zones

Name Servers

The zone database file is stored on a DNS name server. A name server can store the database for one zone or multiple zones, but only one name server contains the master zone database file. The master zone database file is referred to as the **primary zone database file** for the zone. When changes such as adding domains or hosts are made to a zone, those changes are performed on the name server (called the **primary master name server**) that contains the primary zone database file.

There are several advantages to having more than one name server. Multiple name servers act as backups to the server that contains the primary zone database file. Multiple name servers, also called **secondary master domain servers,** do the following:

- **Perform zone transfers.** A **zone transfer** occurs when the additional name servers obtain a copy of the zone database file from the primary master name server.

- **Provide redundancy.** If the primary master name server fails, there are secondary master domain name servers to take its place.

- **Improve access speed for remote locations.** Additional name servers reduce query traffic across slow WAN links.

- **Reduce the load on the primary master name server.**

Lesson 6.2 Resolving Names

If you did not know the phone number of someone you needed to call, you would most likely use a phone book. Once you found the person's name, you would see the phone number that corresponds to that name. In other words, the name was *resolved* into a phone number.

Instead of resolving names to phone numbers, DNS resolves names into IP addresses. This process is called **name resolution.** The mapping of names to IP addresses is stored in the DNS distributed database.

DNS name servers can resolve names using forward and reverse lookup queries. A **forward lookup query** resolves a name to an IP address, and a **reverse lookup query** resolves an IP address to a name.

When a zone encompasses a domain name space, it is said to have **authority** for the domain name space. A name server can only resolve a query for a zone for which it has authority. If a name server cannot resolve the query, it passes the query to other name servers that can. The name server stores (caches) the query results to reduce the DNS traffic on the network.

Lesson 6.3 Install the DNS Service

You are now ready to install the Microsoft DNS Server Service on a computer running Windows 2000 Server.

Preparing for Installation

By default, computers running Windows 2000 are configured as **Dynamic Host Configuration Protocol (DHCP)** clients. When a DHCP client needs an

IP address, it sends a message to a server requesting an IP address. The server has a table of available IP addresses, but in a routed environment, it has to know the appropriate IP address for the particular subnet on which the client is located. Because the IP address can change from one session to another, you must configure TCP/IP with a **static IP address** before installing the DNS Server Service. A static IP address does not change from one session to another.

EXERCISE

6.1 Configure TCP/IP for DNS

This exercise should be performed if:

■ You have one computer that will be the DNS server

This exercise should *not* be performed if:

■ A DNS server already exists on your network.

1. Log on as Administrator.

2. Right-click on **My Network Places.**

3. Select **Properties** from the Context menu.

■ The Network and Dial-Up Connections window appears.

4. Right-click **Local Area Connection.**

5. Select **Properties** from the Context menu.

■ The Local Area Connections Properties dialog box appears.

6. Click the **Internet Protocol (TCP/IP).**

■ Make sure the checkbox to the left of TCP/IP is checked.

7. Click the Properties button.

■ The Internet Protocol (TCP/IP) Properties dialog box appears (see Figure 6-4).

8. Select **Use the Following IP Address.**

9. Type an appropriate IP address in the IP Address box.

■ The IP address used for this textbook will be 192.168.0.1.

■ The subnet mask should be 255.255.255.0.

■ The Default Gateway box should be empty.

10. Check the **Use the Following DNS Server Addresses** option.

11. Type the IP address (same as step 9) in the Preferred DNS Server box.

■ If you are on a network, you may use the address of an available DNS server instead of your computer's address. If you

FIGURE 6-4
The TCP/IP Properties Dialog Box

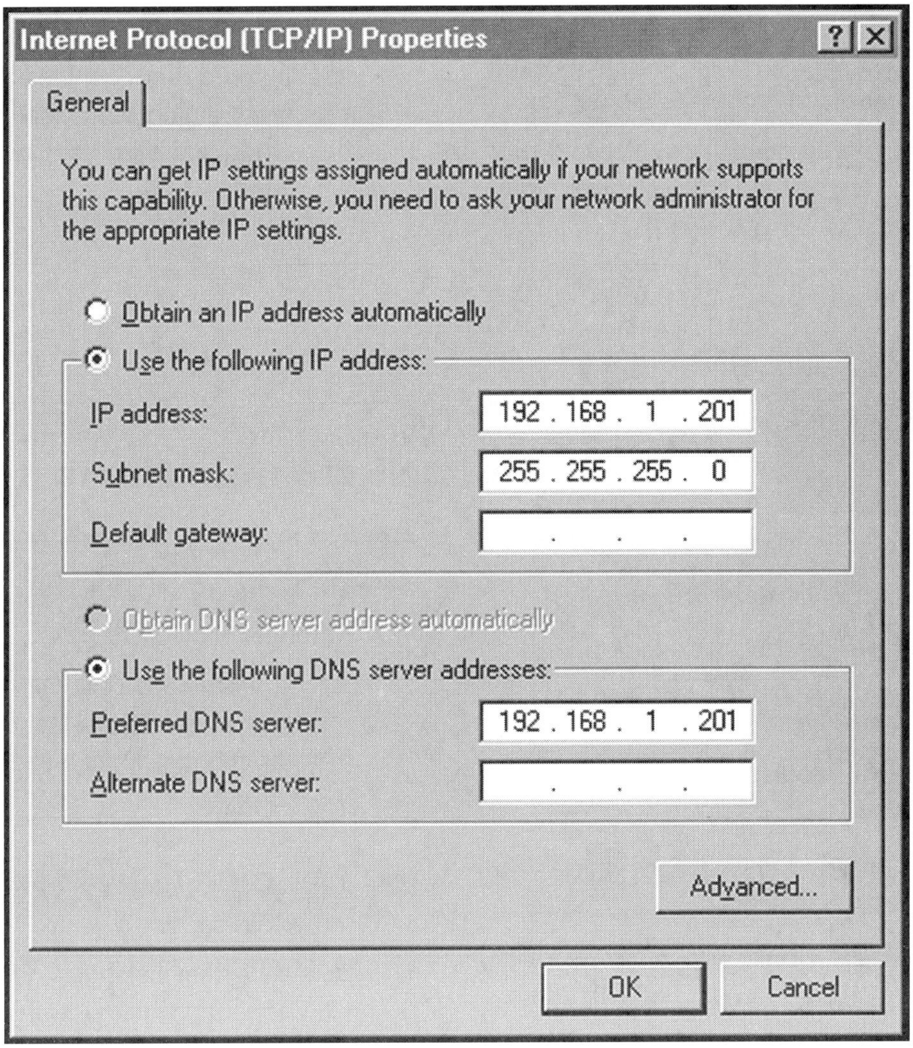

Internet Protocol (TCP/IP) Properties [?] [X]

General

You can get IP settings assigned automatically if your network supports this capability. Otherwise, you need to ask your network administrator for the appropriate IP settings.

○ Obtain an IP address automatically

● Use the following IP address:

IP address: `192 . 168 . 1 . 201`

Subnet mask: `255 . 255 . 255 . 0`

Default gateway: `.   .   .`

○ Obtain DNS server address automatically

● Use the following DNS server addresses:

Preferred DNS server: `192 . 168 . 1 . 201`

Alternate DNS server: `.   .   .`

Advanced...

OK   Cancel

are using an existing DNS server, you do not have to install the DNS Service on your computer.

12. Click **Advanced.**

- The Advanced TCP/IP Settings dialog box appears.

13. Click the **DNS** tab.

14. In the DNS Suffix For This Connection box, type **domain.com.**

- If you are on a network, check with your instructor to make sure it is okay to use **domain.com** as your DNS domain name.

- If your instructor requires you to use another name, substitute that name whenever you see **domain.com** in the textbook.

15. Click **OK** to close the Internet Protocol (TCP/IP) Properties dialog box.

16. Click **OK** to close the Local Area Connection Properties dialog box.

 ■ If you get a Local Network dialog box indicating that you must shut down and restart the computer, click **Yes.** Log back on as Administrator.

 ■ If you did not get the Local Network dialog box, close the Network and Dial-Up Connections window.

6.2

Configure the DNS Domain Name

This exercise should be performed if:

■ You have completed Exercise 6.1.

1. Right-click **My Computer.**

2. Select **Properties** from the Context menu.

 ■ The System Properties dialog box appears.

3. Click the **Network Identification** tab.

4. Click **Properties.**

 ■ The Identification Changes dialog box appears.

5. Click **More.**

 ■ The DNS Suffix and NetBIOS Computer Name dialog box appears.

6. In the Primary DNS Suffix Of This Computer box, type **domain.com** (or the appropriate alternative as discussed in step 14 of Exercise 6.1).

7. Click **OK** to close the Identification Changes dialog box.

 ■ A warning box appears stating you must restart the computer for changes to take effect.

8. Click **OK.**

9. Click **OK** to close the System Properties dialog box.

 ■ A System Settings Change box appears, which asks if you want to restart your computer.

10. Click **Yes** to restart the computer.

 ■ After the computer reboots, you might get another message indicating the need for a second restart. If this happens, click **Yes** to restart the computer.

EXERCISE

6.3

Install the DNS Service

To complete this exercise, you will need:

- To have completed Exercise 6.2
- The Windows 2000 Server CD-ROM

1. Log on as Administrator.

2. Open the Control Panel (Choose **Start,** than **Settings,** then **Control Panel**).

3. Double-click **Add/Remove Programs.**

   - The Add/Remove Programs window appears.

4. Click **Add/Remove Windows Components.**

   - The Windows Components wizard appears (see Figure 6-5).

5. Scroll through the list and click on the name **Networking Services,** but do not alter the checkbox to the left of the component.

6. Click **Details.**

7. In the Subcomponents Of Networking Services list box, select the checkbox to the left of **Domain Name Service (DNS).**

FIGURE 6-5

Click Here to Add or Remove Windows Components Such as DNS

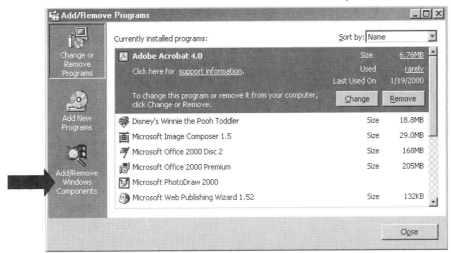

8. Click **OK.**

   ■ You are returned to the Windows Components page.

9. Click **Next.**

   ■ The Configuring Components page appears, and a status indicator begins tracking the configuration process.

   ■ After a few moments, the Insert Disk dialog box appears.

10. Insert the Windows 2000 Server CD-ROM.

11. Click **OK.**

    ■ Setup copies the required files to the hard disk.

12. Click **Finish** to close the Windows Components wizard.

13. Close the Add/Remove Programs windows.

14. Close the Control Panel.

15. Remove the CD-ROM.

Lesson 6.4 Configure the DNS Service

Y ou configure DNS in Windows 2000 by using the **DNS snap-in.** A snap-in is the term used to describe a utility program that is usually accessed through the Microsoft Management Console. When the DNS snap-in is run for the first time, a wizard guides you through the configuration process. The wizard assists in configuring the following items:

■ A root name server

■ A forward lookup zone

■ A reverse lookup zone

Configure a DNS Name Server

The first item the DNS wizard offers is the option to make one of your servers into a **root name server.** Root name servers store the location of name servers with authority for all of the top-level domains in the domain name space (for example, com). Top-level name servers provide a list of name servers with authority for the second-level domains (microsoft.com, for example).

The two reasons why you would choose to designate a root name server for your intranet are as follows:

1. There is no connection to the Internet. Because of this, the root level domain is for your intranet only.

2. You are using a proxy service to gain access to the Internet. This would mean you are creating the root of your local DNS domain name space, and the proxy service does the translation for access to the Internet.

TERMINOLOGY

A **proxy server** is the only server on a network with a connection to the Internet. Because the proxy server is the only computer with an IP address that is valid on the Internet, all of the other computers go through the proxy server to gain access to the Internet. When a client makes a request from the Internet, the proxy server sends out the request on behalf of the client. When the proxy server receives the results of the request, it relays those results back to the client.

EXERCISE

Launch the DNS Manager

To complete this exercise, you will need:

■ Access to a server running Windows 2000

1. Log on as Administrator.

2. Click **Start.**

3. Point to **Programs.**

4. Point to **Administrative Tools.**

5. Select **DNS.**

   ■ The DNS console appears (see Figure 6-6).

6. Select your server in the console tree.

   ■ Information about configuring DNS appears in the details pane.

7. From the Action menu, select **Configure The Server.**

   ■ The *Configure DNS Server* wizard welcome screen appears.

FIGURE 6-6
DNS Manager Window

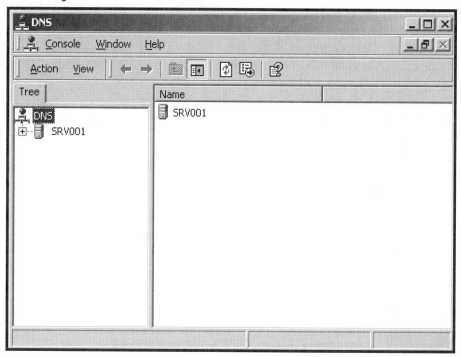

Creating Zones

You must create at least one forward lookup zone in order for the DNS service to function. When you right-click on the **Forward Lookup Zone** folder, the wizard will present the following three configuration options:

1. Zone Type

2. Zone Name

3. Zone Database

ZONE TYPE

Table 6-3 describes the three types of zones that can be configured with the DNS wizard.

ZONE NAME

A zone is typically named after the highest domain in the hierarchy that the zone encompasses (the root domain for the zone). For example, for a zone that encompasses microsoft.com and sales.microsoft.com, the zone name would be microsoft.com.

TABLE 6-3 DNS ZONE TYPES FOR CONFIGURATION

ZONE TYPE	DESCRIPTION
Standard Primary	The master copy of a new zone. The zone is administered and maintained on the computer on which it was created.
Standard Secondary	A read-only replica of an existing zone for the purpose of redundancy and to reduce the load on the name server holding the primary zone database file. A primary zone must exist before a secondary zone can be created. During creation, you must specify a DNS server (called the **master server**) that will transfer zone information to the name server containing the standard secondary zone.
Active Directory-Integrated	The master copy of a new zone that uses directory services based on Active Directory technology. If the zone database is stored in Active Directory directory services, it is said to be an Active Directory-integrated zone. (You will learn more about Active Directory in the next chapter.)

ZONE DATABASE FILENAME

The zone database filename defaults to the zone name with a .DNS extension. For example, if the zone name is microsoft.com, the default zone database filename is microsoft.com.dns.

EXERCISE

6.5 Creating Forward and Reverse Lookup Zones

• •

To complete this exercise, you will need:

■ To have completed Exercise 6.4

1. In the Configure DNS Server wizard, click **Next.**

   ■ The wizard collects setup information.

   ■ The Root Server page appears.

2. Ensure that the **This Is The First DNS Server On This Network** option is selected, and then click **Next.**

   ■ The Create Forward Lookup Zone page appears.

3. Verify that **Yes, Create A Forward Lookup Zone** is selected, and then click **Next.**

   ■ The Zone Type page appears.

4. Verify that the **Standard Primary** option is selected, and click **Next.**

5. The Zone Name page appears.

6. Type **domain.com** (or the DNS domain name you entered in Exercise 6.1), and click **Next.**

   ■ The Zone File page appears.

7. Ensure that the **Create A New File With This File Name** option is selected and that the name of the file to be created is **domain.com.dns.** (If you are not using domain.com, substitute your DNS domain name.) Click **Next.**

   ■ The Create Reverse Lookup Zone page appears.

8. Ensure that **Yes, Create A Reverse Lookup Zone** is selected, and click **Next.**

9. The Zone Type page appears.

10. Ensure that the **Standard Primary** option is selected, and click **Next.**

11. Ensure that the **Network ID and Subnet Mask** option is selected, and type in the first three octets of your static IP address. (Your IP address was entered in step 9 of Exercise 6.1.) For example, if you used 192.168.0.1, you would enter **192.168.0** in the Network ID box.

12. Click **Next.**

   ■ The Zone File page appears.

13. Ensure that the **Create A New File With This File Name** option is selected, and click **Next.**

   ■ The Completing the Configure DNS Server wizard page appears.

14. Review the summary information, and then click **Finish.**

   ■ The Forward and Reverse Lookup Zones appear in the DNS console (see Figure 6-7).

FIGURE 6-7
After DNS Configuration the Lookup Zones for the Domain Are Displayed

ADDING RESOURCE RECORDS

The DNS Manager also can be used to add resource records to the zone database. A resource record is an entry in the database that provides additional information about the events that occur while using DNS. There are many different types of resource records, including those described in Table 6-4.

DNS automatically creates the SOA and NS resource records. To add other resource records, right-click the zone to which you want to add the record, click **New,** and then select the type of record you want to add.

TABLE 6-4 DNS RESOURCE RECORDS

RESOURCE RECORD	DNS MANAGER NAME	DESCRIPTION
SOA	Start of Authority	Identifies which name server is the authoritative source of information for data within this domain.
NS	Name Server	Lists the name servers that are assigned to a particular domain.
A	Host	Lists the host name-to-IP-address mappings for a forward lookup zone.
PTR	Pointer	Points to another part of the domain name space. For example, in a reverse lookup zone, it lists the IP-address-to-name mapping.
HINFO	Host Information	Identifies the CPU and operating system used by the host. Use this record as a low-cost resource-tracking tool.

Dynamic DNS

When changes are made to the domain over which a name server has authority, the zone database file on the server has to be manually updated to reflect those changes. The DNS Service includes a dynamic update capability called **Dynamic DNS (DDNS).** With DDNS, name servers and clients within a network automatically update the zone database files. DDNS interacts with DHCP to maintain synchronized name-to-IP-address mappings for network hosts. Anytime you can have the computer do work for you, let it. Exercise 6.6 provides the steps for enabling DDNS.

EXERCISE

6.6 Configuring the Dynamic DNS Service

• •

To complete this exercise, you will need:

■ To have completed Exercise 6.5

1. Log on as Administrator.

2. Click **Start.**

3. Point to **Programs.**

4. Point to **Administrative Tools.**

5. Select **DNS.**

6. Expand your server in the console tree.

7. Expand Forward Lookup Zones.

8. Expand **domain.com** (or your DNS domain name).

9. Select **domain.com** (click on it to highlight it).

10. Right-click **domain.com.**

11. Select **Properties** from the Context menu.

   ■ The domain.com Properties dialog box appears.

12. Click the **General** tab.

13. In the **Allow Dynamic Updates?** drop-down list, click **Yes.**

   ■ DDNS is now configured for forward lookup zones.

14. Click **OK.**

15. Expand Reverse Lookup Zones.

16. Expand the **192.168.1.x** subnet (or the appropriate one for your network).

17. Right-click the **192.168.1.x** subnet.

18. Select **Properties** from the Context menu.

19. In the **Allow Dynamic Updates?** drop-down list, click **Yes.**

   ■ DDNS is now configured for reverse lookup zones.

20. Click **OK.**

Lesson 6.5 Configure a DNS Client

Now that you have completed the necessary steps to configure a server to use the DNS service, each client that will use DNS must also be configured. Exercise 6.7 details the necessary steps to configure a client to use the DNS service.

EXERCISE

6.7

Configuring a DNS Client

To complete this exercise, you will need:

■ To have completed Exercise 6.5

■ Access to a client computer that will use the DNS service

1. Right-click **My Network Places.**

2. Select **Properties** from the Context menu.

   ■ The Network and Dial-Up Connections window appears.

3. Right-click **Local Area Connection.**

4. Select **Properties** from the context-menu.

   ■ The Local Area Connections dialog box appears.

5. Leaving the checkboxes as they are, click on **Internet Protocol (TCP/IP).**

6. Click the Properties button.

   ■ The Internet Protocol (TCP/IP) Properties dialog box appears (see Figure 6-4).

7. Select **Use The Following DNS Server Addresses.**

8. Verify or type in the IP address of the Preferred DNS server; if there is an Alternate DNS server, type in that address as well.

9. Click the Advanced button.

   ■ The Advanced TCP/IP Settings page appears.

10. Click the **DNS** tab (see Figure 6-8).

11. Using the up and down arrows beside the In Order Of Use box, you can set the search order the client will use when sending queries to a name server.

    ■ The client will send its query requests to the name server at the top of the list.

    ■ If that name server is not responding, the client will send the query to the next name server on the list.

    ■ Configuring some of the clients to use a secondary name server will reduce the load on the primary name server.

12. In the DNS Suffix For This Connection box, type the name of the DNS domain name (**domain.com** or your DNS domain name).

FIGURE 6-8
The DNS Tab of the Advanced TCP/IP Settings Page

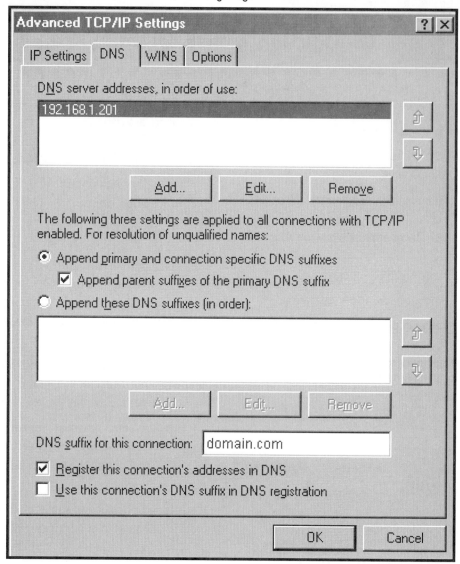

13. Click **OK** to close the Advanced TCP/IP Settings page.

14. Click **OK** to close the Internet Protocol (TCP/IP) Properties dialog box.

15. Click **OK** to close the Local Area Connections dialog box.

16. Click the **X** to close the Network and Dial-Up Connections window.

Summary

The hierarchical structure of DNS organizes the contents of the distributed database used to resolve names to IP addresses. When configuring DNS, you need to know the IP address of the DNS server and the DNS domain name.

Name servers resolve both forward and reverse lookup queries. A forward lookup query resolves a name to an IP address, whereas a reverse lookup resolves the IP address to a name. In order for the lookup queries to function, you must configure the lookup zones. Zones have authority over the domain name space they encompass and are used to reduce administrative tasks. A primary master name server must service each zone. Secondary name servers have a copy of the primary database and perform zone transfers to synchronize the contents of the original database with the copied versions. Windows 2000 Server has the capability of making updates to the DNS database automatic. This feature is known as Dynamic DNS, or DDNS.

● ● ● ● ● ● ● ● ● ● ● ● ● ●

R EVIEW EXERCISE

These questions will help you determine if you have learned enough to move on to the next chapter. If the graphic next to the option is a square (❏), there can be more than one answer for that question. If the graphic is a circle (○), there is only one correct answer. Color in the shape(s) to indicate your answer(s).

1. Which of the following are types of domains in the DNS structure?

    a. ❏ Top-level domains

    b. ❏ Sub-level domains

    c. ❏ Subdomains

    d. ❏ Second-level domains

2. When would you configure a server as a root server?

    a. ❏ Your network is not connected to the Internet.

    b. ❏ Your server will be the root server for the Internet.

    c. ❏ You are using a proxy service to gain access to the Internet.

    d. ❏ You want to serve root beer to your clients.

3. Dynamic DNS differs from DNS because

   a. ❑ DDNS requires that changes to the zone database files be done manually.

   b. ❑ Name servers and clients within a network automatically update the zone database files.

   c. ❑ DDNS interacts with DHCP to maintain synchronized name-to-IP address mappings for network hosts.

   d. ❑ It does not. They are the same thing.

4. A forward lookup query resolves

   a. ○ IP addresses to names

   b. ○ Names to IP addresses

   c. ○ IP addresses to IP addresses

   d. ○ Names to Names

5. Which of the following statements are true regarding zones?

   a. ❑ Zones are used to partition the domain name space into manageable sections.

   b. ❑ A zone transfer occurs when the primary master name server obtains a copy of the zone database file from the secondary name servers.

   c. ❑ Each zone in a DNS namespace has its own database file that contains the name-to-IP-address mappings.

   d. ❑ Any subdomain in the zone will have entries in the zone database.

PERFORMANCE CHALLENGES

- Compile a list of the current top-level domains on the Internet.

- DNS has an option for monitoring the DNS Service. Using the DNS Manager, right-click on the name server to monitor, and select **Properties.** Click on the **Monitoring** tab, and then try both types of queries listed there. Write a paragraph stating the purpose and actual results of each query option.

UNDERSTANDING ACTIVE DIRECTORY

OBJECTIVES

After completing this chapter, you should be able to:

■ Explain the purpose and function of Active Directory directory services

■ Identify the logical structures within Active Directory, including domains, Organizational Units, Trees, Forests, and Objects

■ Describe how Active Directory interacts with DNS

■ Determine a domain namespace for your organization

■ Install Active Directory

■ Create the first domain controller in a forest

■ Describe the interrelationships between components in a multiple domain environment

OUTLINE

Introduction

O f all the changes and enhancements made to Windows NT Server 4.0 through the release of Windows 2000 Server, Active Directory Services was one of the most significant. Active Directory provides a single location from which network management can occur. This means that administrative tasks such as adding, removing, and relocating users and resources are easier, more flexible, and more efficient.

An architect would not disturb one shovelful of dirt without first planning the entire building. The architect's job is to determine the needs of the client, prioritize those needs, and then develop the blueprints that fit those needs. Before installing Active Directory, you need to understand what a directory service is and how the Active Directory directory service functions as a part of a Windows 2000 network. Then you will be ready to design and build an Active Directory structure that will fit the needs of your organization.

Lesson 7.1 Active Directory Concepts

Directory Services

In Windows 2000 Server, information and resources are organized *logically* rather than physically, which means that they are organized by their meaning and how an organization uses them. In other words, by grouping resources logically, you can find them by their names—regardless of where they are physically stored. This would be similar to speaking a person's name into a telephone and having the phone look up the person's name from its internal list, dial the appropriate number, make the connection, and allow you to talk to that person—no matter where that person is in the world.

Telephone companies use a **database** to track all of the names, addresses, and phone numbers of the people and businesses in their area. A database holds pieces of information. The foundation of Active Directory is a **distributed**

database that makes the logical organization of users and resources possible. A distributed database does not have to be stored on one server but can be distributed amongst several servers.

To make the database more useful, **directory services** for the database allow the information to be organized, queried (or searched), and reported upon. A directory service is a network service that identifies all resources on a network and makes them accessible to users and applications. In Windows 2000, the directory services are called **Active Directory.** Other operating systems use directory services as well. Novell's directory service, for example, is called NDS.

Ease of Administration

Rather than having to use several programs to manage resources, Active Directory provides a single point of administration. An administrator can log on to one computer and administer objects on any computer in the network. Changes made to the directory are automatically replicated to all the domain controllers. (Replication will be discussed in greater detail in Lesson 7.4.) Because network resources are organized in a hierarchy (levels of objects), managing those resources is simplified.

Scalability

The hierarchical structure of objects enhances the ability of the Active Directory to grow in proportion to the growth of the company, which was one of the concerns with Windows NT Server 4.0. In computer terms, to **scale** means to increase in size. For example, Active Directory is able to scale from a small company with 300 objects to a very large company with thousands or even millions of objects. (Lesson 7.2 defines Windows 2000 objects.)

Lesson 7.2 Logical Structure and Organization

Objects

As shown in Figure 7-1, the pieces of information in the database of Active Directory are called **objects.** Objects represent the individual elements of a network environment, including users, groups, resources, folders, computers, applications, and even security policies. Each object is distinct and has a name. Object **attributes** are characteristics of objects in the directory; for example, the attributes of a user account include the user's first and last name, e-mail

FIGURE 7-1
Resources Are Called Objects

account, department, and so on. The attributes for a computer object would include the computer name and a description. Active Directory can contain more than one million objects.

Because managing a million objects can be a challenge, Active Directory allows system administrators to create **object classes,** which are also known as **object types.** Object classes are logical groupings of objects, such as users, computers, and printers. This is especially useful when searching for available resources. For example, you would be able to see a list of all printers without having to know where they are located.

EXERCISE

7.1

Identify Objects

To perform this exercise, you will need:

■ Access to the computer lab

■ A list of potential users

■ A word processor

1. Using a word processor, list the following objects that will exist on your lab network:

    ■ Users (include first and last names)

    ■ Computers (list by computer name)

    ■ Printers (include model and type)

2. Print your results.

FIGURE 7-2
Circles Represent Organizational Units

Organizational Units

Objects are organized into **Organizational Units (OUs),** which help with managing objects by logically grouping objects according to their related function or for ease of administration (see Figure 7-2). Because OUs can be nested inside other OUs, an OU is considered to be a **container object;** that is, it can contain other objects within itself. Microsoft uses the shape of a circle to represent OUs.

Domains

As shown in Figure 7-3, the OU structure is contained within a **domain,** which is represented by a triangle. A domain is a logical container of objects that share common security and user account information. All of the OUs within the domain are controlled by the domain policies, including partitioning, authentication, and security policies.

Domains have special computers called **domain controllers (DCs),** which run the server operating system and provide services necessary to have a functioning domain. For example, each domain controller stores a complete copy of the domains's Active Directory database.

Trees and Forests

Although a domain is a self-contained unit, it may also need to be connected to other domains. For example, a user may need to access a resource that is not contained in his or her domain. In Active Directory, domains can be connected together into what is called a **tree.** In large enterprise environments, multiple trees can be connected by a **forest,** which is a grouping or hierarchical arrangement of one or more trees (see Figure 7-4). Lesson 7.5 covers the relationship between trees and forests in more detail.

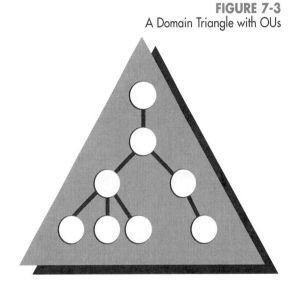

FIGURE 7-3
A Domain Triangle with OUs

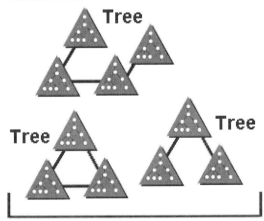

FIGURE 7-4
Trees in a Forest

7.2

Construct an Active Directory Structure

● ●

To perform this exercise, you will need:

■ A graphics program

■ Access to graphics on the Instructor CD or the ability to recreate them

1. Create a graphical representation of the Active Directory structure that includes the following:

■ Four domains demonstrating hierarchical relationships

■ Three to seven organizational units within each domain that are connected in a hierarchical relationship

■ At least two valid objects in each organizational unit

2. Print your results.

The Schema

Even in a small domain there can be hundreds or thousands of objects. As those objects are created and managed, rules are needed in order for the objects to be most useful. The **schema** provides those rules by defining all of the objects, classes, and attributes that can be stored in Active Directory (see Figure 7-5). You could think of the schema as a set of definitions for Active Directory objects.

One of the ways the schema affects an object is by defining whether attributes for an object require a value. For example, a rule in the schema could say that the *First Name* attribute must have an entry (value) but *Telephone Number* and *Address* are optional.

FIGURE 7-5
The Schema Defines Objects in the Active Directory

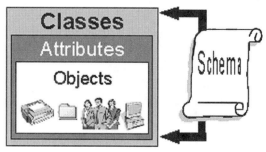

The schema is **dynamically extensible.** *Extensible* means that the schema can be modified. Those modifications include defining new object classes and their attributes and defining new attributes for existing objects. *Dynamically* means that the update to the schema happens immediately and, therefore, the new objects are available for use immediately. Members of the *Schema Admins group* can modify the schema by using the **Active Directory Schema Manager.**

Lesson 7.3 Names in Active Directory

All in The Family

The relationships of objects in a hierarchical system are often referred to in terms of *parent* and *child.* If one domain is directly above another in the structure, the higher-level domain is referred to as the parent, and the lower-level domain is referred to as the child. As with human family trees, children can also become parents. Figure 7-6 illustrates this concept.

FIGURE 7-6
Parent and Child Relationships in a Hierarchical Structure

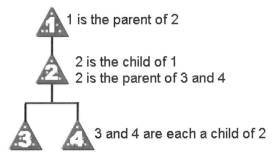

1 is the parent of 2

2 is the child of 1
2 is the parent of 3 and 4

3 and 4 are each a child of 2

Names in human family trees identify who the person is and can also indicate that person's relationship to other people in the family tree. Names are important in Windows 2000 as well. Some names are shared, and others are unique, but each name represents a portion of the network environment. If you have the full name, you can find any item on the network—no matter where it is located.

Name Resolution

Name Resolution is the process that translates a name into the object it represents. To apply an analogy, let's say that you are a boy who wants to go to a movie with a girl named Lucy Anderson. You do not know her phone number, so you look in the phone book. The phone book is the directory you used to resolve her name into a phone number, and the phone number is the object that her name represented.

When a user requests the use of a printer, the user will refer to that printer by name. Active Directory will resolve the name into the actual device.

Namespace

Each Active Directory has a name that represents all of the objects within the database (like the phone book for a city represents all of the people and businesses in its proximity). Examples of names include joycity.com, jazzy.com, and globaltech.msft. **Namespace,** which is the technical word that describes the name, is a bounded area in which a name is translated into the objects it contains. For example, joycity.com represents all of the objects contained within it, and you would have to go through joycity.com to access the objects it holds. To return our dating analogy, assume that you find Lucy's phone number only to discover that Lucy Anderson lives with her parent, John Anderson. Before you can see Lucy, you have to go through her father first. Her father would be the namespace, or the bounded area with a name and objects within it, and his namespace could be Anderson.com.

EXERCISE

7.3

Create a DNS Namespace

To perform this exercise, you will need:

■ A word processor

1. Produce a list of at least five possibilities for your organization's DNS namespace.

2. Print your results.

As described in Table 7-1, there are two types of namespaces: contiguous and disjointed. As you can see, the Active Directory does not refer to objects in the same way we refer to people. We know people by their first name and last

TABLE 7-1 NAMESPACE TYPES

NAMESPACE TYPE	DESCRIPTION	ANALOGY
Contiguous	The name of the child object always contains the name of the parent domain. A tree is a contiguous namespace because the name of any child object in a tree always contains the name of the parent tree.	Lucy could have a namespace of her own, but it would also include her father's name: Lucy.Anderson.com.
Disjointed	The names of a parent object and of a child of the same parent object are not directly related to each other. A forest is a disjointed namespace because all of the trees in a forest do not share a common naming structure.	Lucy might have a stepsister named Jessica. They are not related to each other, but they are contained in the same family unit. They have different names. Example: Jessica.Parker.com

name, and we might add a middle initial if two people have the same first and last name. Because of the interconnectivity of modern networking environments across the country and the world, Active Directory supports several common naming conventions. These conventions enable users and applications to gain access to Active Directory through familiar formats.

Domain Name System

The namespace concept used by the Active Directory actually comes from the **Domain Name System (DNS).** As illustrated in Figure 7-7, Active Directory uses DNS as a location service to identify domains and domain host computers during processes such as logging onto the network. A user at a client computer enters information on the Password dialog box and clicks OK. The NetLogon Service requests a domain controller, and DNS locates the domain controller. The domain controller authenticates the user and creates an access token.

FIGURE 7-7
DNS Server Assisting a Client During Logon

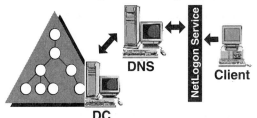

Active Directory Name Types

The following three different types of names for objects in Active Directory are especially helpful when performing queries:

■ Distinguished Name

■ Relative Distinguished Name

■ User Principle Name

Figure 7-8 demonstrates how these three name types relate to each other.

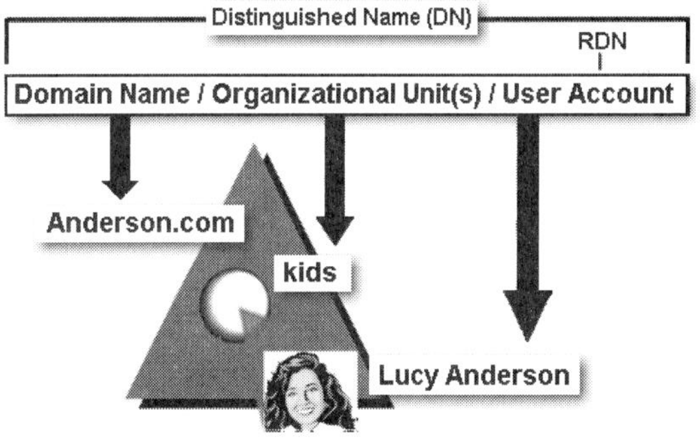

DISTINGUISHED NAME

The first type of name for objects in Active Directory is the **Distinguished Name (DN).** The DN identifies the container that holds the object as well as the complete path of container objects by which the object is reached. The DN is used when searching for an object and is guaranteed to be unique.

For example, Lucy Anderson is one of the kids in her father's house. Her DN would be Lucy Anderson@kids.anderson.com. If this were a company, *Lucy Anderson* would be the user, *kids* is the division, *anderson* is the company, and *com* is the container of commercial organizations in the United States on the Internet.

FIGURE 7-8
DNs and RDNs

RELATIVE DISTINGUISHED NAME

The next type of name is the **Relative Distinguished Name (RDN),** which is the part of the name that is an **attribute** of the object. An attribute is a quality or characteristic of a person or thing, and objects have attributes as well. The attributes of objects are categories of information that define the characteristics of all objects. An example of a user object attribute is the username.

The **values** of the attributes make the objects unique. The value in a username attribute is the actual data (Lucy Anderson, for example). You can search for an object if you know one or more of the object's attributes, which means that you do not have to know the entire DN (Lucy Anderson@kids.anderson.com) to find Lucy; you would just need to know one or more of her attributes. The RDN is the portion of the DN that is needed to find an object after a search context (the Users container, for example) has been established.

In order to facilitate accurate searches, you cannot have two RDNs by the same name in an OU. For example, there can only be one Lucy Anderson in the kids OU. If Lucy's mother is also named Lucy but is located in the parents OU, their DNs are still unique.

USER PRINCIPAL NAME

The last type of name is the **User Principal Name (UPN).** The UPN in Active Directory is the name with which the user logs on in Windows 2000. It is a "shorthand" name for the user object. For example, Lucy's UPN might be Lucy@anderson.com. Because it identifies Lucy without having to know exactly where she is in the structure, the UPN is a more user-friendly name than the DN or RDN. Since you will use these name types when you perform actual searches on the Active Directory, knowing them will make those searches more successful.

GLOBALLY UNIQUE IDENTIFIER

The **Globally Unique Identifier (GUID)** is a 128-bit number that is guaranteed to be unique. GUIDs are assigned to objects when they are created and are mostly used by applications for object retrieval. The GUID never changes, even if the object is renamed.

Lightweight Directory Access Protocol

Another common naming convention used by Active Directory is the **Lightweight Directory Access Protocol (LDAP).** LDAP is the core protocol used by Windows 2000 between directories and applications. The DNs and RDNs discussed previously are LDAP standards for referring to objects. Let's return again to our example of Lucy Anderson to see how LDAP is used in Windows 2000. Assume that Lucy Anderson is the object. Her DN in LDAP would be *DC=com, DC=anderson, OU=kids, CN=Lucy Anderson,* where *DC* is Domain Component, *OU* is Organizational Unit, and *CN* is Common Name.

Lesson 7.4 Replication and Sites

Replication of Active Directory Entries

As mentioned earlier, each of the domain controllers store a replica of the Active Directory. Any changes made to the database on one domain controller must be distributed to all of the other domain controllers. The distribution of changes is called **replication.** The goal of replication is to make sure each domain controller has an accurate and up-to-date version of the Active Directory contents.

Active Directory uses **multi-master** replication, which means that no single domain controller is the master domain controller. The domain controllers in Windows 2000 Server are peers. Each of the domain controllers has a writable copy of the Active Directory. It is possible that domain controllers may have different information for a short period of time until all of the domain controllers have synchronized their changes. Therefore, creating an environment where replication can occur efficiently is important.

Sites

One of the ways to optimize replication is through the definition of **sites.** A site is a combination of one or more Internet Protocol (IP) subnets that are connected by a high-speed link. By defining a site, you can configure the access and replication topology of the Active Directory so that Windows 2000 uses the most efficient links for replication and logon traffic. Sites are graphically represented by an oval.

Whereas domains define the logical structure of the organization, a site defines the physical structure of the network. You use the logical structure to organize your network resources, and you use the physical structure to configure and manage your network traffic. The logical structure and the physical structure are independent of each other, which has the following consequences:

> **TERMINOLOGY**
>
> If a network has more than one site, the sites are connected through a **site link.** Sites and site links are created during the replication configuration process.

- The network's physical structure does not have to correlate to the logical structure.

- There can be multiple domains in one site as well as multiple sites in one domain (see Figure 7-9).

- The namespaces of the site and the domain do not necessarily have to correlate to each other.

FIGURE 7-9

Multiple Domains in a Site and Multiple Sites in a Domain

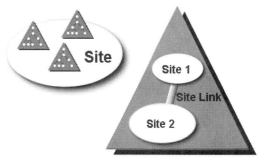

DOMAIN CONTROLLER PLACEMENT

Sites and domain controllers together comprise the physical network. Therefore, the first step in planning a site structure is to determine where a domain controller is needed. Remember that users access the domain controller when they need to interact with the Active Directory entries. If the connection to the domain controller is slow, users will become frustrated. For the best performance, have at least one domain controller at each site so that users' requests are being serviced within their own LAN connection rather than over a slower WAN connection.

CONNECTIVITY AND BANDWIDTH

When grouping subnets into Windows 2000 sites, you need to examine **connectivity** and available **bandwidth.** Connectivity refers to the speed of the connection, while bandwidth refers to how much information can flow through the connection at one time. Sites should only have subnets that are connected by fast and reliable links. Together connectivity and bandwidth have a dramatic effect on response time for the user. A connection that is fast and reliable may be heavily used for other network purposes such as file transfers. If 70 percent of the connection's bandwidth is used without any Active Directory traffic, you might consider creating sites on both sides of the connection instead of having one site that incorporates the connection.

REPLICATION TRAFFIC

Replication does generate traffic on a network as the domain controllers are updating each other's directory entries. The more changes that are made to the Active Directory, the more replication traffic will be generated. In addition, less information is replicated between domain controllers from different domains than between domain controllers in the same domain.

CONFIGURING A REPLICATION TOPOLOGY

You configure sites in order to optimize replication traffic and enable users to connect to a domain controller using a reliable, high-speed connection. Active Directory directory services automatically constructs a default topology to enable replication within one domain. For a network with multiple locations, you would configure the replication topology to minimize the impact of replication traffic on the network.

When you create sites and site links, you are actually mapping the physical network to the Active Directory. Part of the mapping process includes providing information about the available connections, preferred connection times, and available bandwidth. Active Directory uses this information to determine the time and connections for replication that will provide the best performance for the users of the network. **Active Directory Sites and Services** is the name of the utility used to configure sites and site links.

Lesson 7.5 Plan for Implementation

To plan for implementation, you must think like an architect and let the needs of the users determine the design rather than the technology. Technology may make business more efficient, but the needs of the users should prevail. This lesson will help you provide a foundation for the overall structure. The best design strategy is to make a simple design, test it to make sure it works, and then increase the complexity if necessary.

Design a Naming Strategy

Before installing Windows 2000 Active Directory directory services, you must decide what the organization's namespace will be. Because you and your users will be tied to this name for a very long time, this is an important decision. The name should be descriptive, easy to remember, and easy to enter. Many companies use their company name for a namespace.

If your company intends to have a presence on the Internet, it is important to register the name with the Internet DNS registration authority prior to implementation. This will save the disappointment of choosing a name that is already taken. Each namespace must be unique, and unless your company has the financial resources to buy the existing name from the entity that already registered it (assuming that entity is willing to sell), you will have to choose another name.

EXERCISE

7.4 How to Register a Name with the DNS Naming Authority

To perform this exercise, you will need:

■ Access to the Internet

1. Access the following Web site: www.networksolutions.com

   ■ The first screen displays a textbox for entering a desired name.

2. After you enter the name you would like to register, the program searches the database for that name. If it is available, you continue with step 3. If it is not available, you can search for a different name until one you enter is unique.

3. The next screen requests the type of name you would like to purchase.

4. Exit the Web page (unless you have the means to purchase the appropriate package).

If your organization does not plan to have a presence on the Internet, the namespace options are practically limitless. However, you may want to plan for the future and choose a unique name in case your organization chooses to be on the Internet at a later date.

When planning the implementation of Active Directory, keep the following in mind:

■ Where the offices are located. Do you need to create a site or sites? If yes, what are the replication ramifications?

■ The potential for future growth and reorganization. An Active Directory structure has a lifespan of three to five years. What will the company needs be like then?

■ How users will gain access to network resources. Remember their need for speed.

EXTENDING AN EXISTING NAMESPACE

If your organization already has a presence on the Internet, you can extend that presence to include Windows 2000 Advanced Server domains. When you use the same namespace for both internal and external resources, you must create two separate DNS zones. One zone is for internal name resolutions, and the other provides name resolutions for external resources such as Web servers, FTP servers, and mail servers.

CREATING A NEW INTERNAL NAMESPACE

Another option is to have a completely different namespace for internal resources than the namespace already in use on the Internet. This requires you to reserve two namespaces with the Internet DNS registration authority. Consider this option when a clear distinction between external and internal resources is required.

Planning Organizational Units

If you only have one domain, user accounts and resources can be organized in a hierarchy of OUs similar to the structure of the organization. Consider the following when planning OUs:

■ There are two ways for organizing the OU structure:

■ **Organizational structure:** Make the OU structure similar in design to the company's organizational structure. For example, if the company has four divisions—sales, marketing, production, and support—you could have four OUs by the same names.

FIGURE 7-10
Structuring an OU Based on Organization or Network Administration

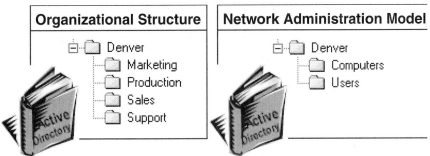

- **Network administrative model:** Make the OU structure conform to the tasks to be performed by network administrators. For example, if one administrator manages user accounts and the other manages computer accounts, you would make two OUs: one for users and one for computers (see Figure 7-10).

- Whenever possible, create new OUs as opposed to creating new domains. A multiple domain environment is more difficult to manage. For example, it is easier to move a user account between organizational units than it is between domains.

- Administrative tasks are more easily performed when similar network resources are in the same OU.

DESIGNING FOR DELEGATION OF ADMINISTRATIVE AUTHORITY

An administrator assigned most of the resource permissions in a Windows NT 4.0 environment. The owner of the resource also had some control. When even the smallest setting on the most insignificant file needed a change, the administrator would have to make time to change the permission. When there were thousands of users, this list of changes on their many files was an administrative nightmare. Windows 2000 Server relieves part of this burden by allowing an administrator to **delegate authority,** which means that trusted users are granted the authority to have control over designated objects—usually an OU—in Active Directory. Figure 7-11 illustrates how delegation of authority could be configured. The administrator could choose a manager in the HR (Human Resources) department and give that

FIGURE 7-11
Delegating Authority Reduces the Workload of a Centralized Administrator

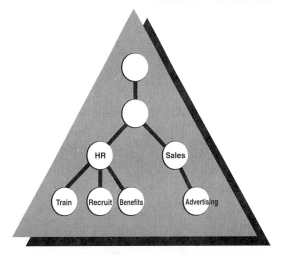

person the authority to change permissions on resources in the HR OU, the Training OU, and the Recruiting OU. This does not give the HR manager the authority to make changes to the Sales OU structure. This delegation of authority frees the administrator to do more important work.

Planning Domains

A well-planned OU structure within a domain simplifies administrative tasks. The first domain created in Active Directory is very important for the following reasons:

- The first domain created is the root domain of the entire forest (also referred to as the **forest root**).

- The forest root contains the configuration and schema information for the forest.

- The first domain cannot be renamed (choose a good name, in other words).

- Additional domains are added to the root domain to form the tree structure.

SINGLE DOMAIN MODEL

Because Active Directory can hold more than a million objects, most organizations that used a multiple domain configuration in Windows NT 4.0 will be able to use a single domain model in Windows 2000 Server. Having one domain simplifies administration, especially in terms of security. Moving objects around in OUs is also easier than moving them between domains. The hierarchical structure of OUs allows more flexibility in conforming the structure to the needs of the organization.

MULTIPLE DOMAIN MODEL

Reasons to create multiple domains include the following:

- Different password requirements between organizations

- Large numbers of objects

- Different Internet domain names

- Better control of replication

- The need for decentralized network administration

    Lesson 7.7 discusses the multiple domain model in more detail.

Planning a Site

The domain structure and the site structure are maintained separately in Active Directory. As you plan sites, consider the following:

- Check the availability of bandwidth for replication traffic.

■ Combine only those subnets that share fast and reliable network connections of at least 512 Kbps.

■ Configure sites so that replication occurs at times that do not hinder network performance.

7.5

Identify Elements in an Active Directory Structure

To perform this exercise, you will need:

■ A graphics program

■ A word processor

■ The list created in Exercise 7.1

1. Using a word processor, insert the list from Exercise 7.1 into a three-column table.

   ■ Label the first column **Object.**

   ■ Label the second column **OU.**

■ Label the third column **Domain.**

2. For each object, identify the name of the OU(s) to which that object will belong.

3. For each OU, identify the name of the domain to which that object will belong.

4. Print your results.

7.6

Create a Graphical Active Directory Structure

To perform this exercise, you will need:

■ A graphics program

■ The list created in Exercise 7.3

1. Using a graphics program, create a graphical representation of the Active

Directory structure you identified in Exercise 7.3. Include the following:

■ Domain(s)

■ OUs

2. Print your results.

Lesson 7.6 Install Active Directory

Installation Requirements

Before you can install Active Directory, the server and the network must meet the following requirements:

- A computer running Windows 2000 Server or Windows 2000 Advanced Server or Window 2000 Datacenter Server

- A partition or volume that is formatted with the NTFS file system

- Adequate disk space (1 GB recommended)

- TCP/IP installed and configured to use DNS

- A DNS server that supports service (SRV) resource records and the DNS dynamic update protocol (optional)

If you are installing Active Directory and if you are creating a domain or domain controller in an existing Windows 2000 network, you must have the following network credentials for creating a domain:

- The logon name of a user account that can create a domain controller

- A valid password for the user account

- The name of the domain

Installation Options

The Active Directory Installation wizard will require that you make several choices during the installation process. Depending on the answers you give, you may be led through additional choices. The decision tree is represented in Figure 7-12. You will answer these questions each time you add a domain controller to the network. Additional information about the specific domain controller is required after all of the questions are answered. The next section will demonstrate the installation process.

FIGURE 7-12
Active Directory Installation Choices

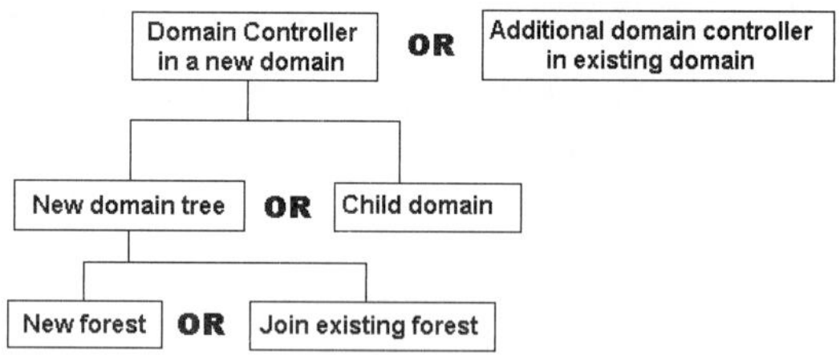

Installing Active Directory

During the installation process, Active Directory keeps a **log,** which is a file or set of files that list actions or events in a chronological order. The log for the Active Directory installation will list the results of each installation step. The log files, which are saved in the *systemroot*\Debug folder, are especially helpful when troubleshooting.

LAUNCHING THE ACTIVE DIRECTORY INSTALLATION WIZARD
The name of the program that launches the Active Directory Installation wizard is **Dcpromo.exe.** Exercise 7.7 demonstrates how to launch this program.

EXERCISE

7.7 Launch the Active Directory Installation Wizard

To perform this exercise, you will need:

■ Access to the server

1. Click the Start button.

2. Select Run. . . .

3. Type **dcpromo.exe** in the "Open:" text box.

4. Click OK (or press Enter).

■ The welcome screen of the Active Directory Installation wizard is displayed.

EXERCISE

7.8 Establishing a Root Domain

To perform this exercise, you will need:

■ To have access to the server that will be the first domain controller

■ To have launched the Active Directory Installation wizard (by completing the steps in Exercise 7.7)

1. From the Active Directory Installation wizard welcome screen, click **Next.**

■ The Domain Controller Type page appears.

2. Select **Domain Controller For A New Domain.**

3. Click **Next.**

   ■ The Create Tree Or Child Domain page appears.

4. Select **Create A New Domain Tree.**

5. Click **Next.**

   ■ The Create Or Join Forest page appears.

6. Select **Create A New Forest Of Domain Trees.**

7. Click **Next.**

   ■ The New Domain Name page appears.

8. Type **domain.com** in the "Full DNS Name For New Domain" box (or substitute your system's DNS name).

   ■ The NetBIOS Domain Name page appears.

9. Ensure that **DOMAIN** appears in the Domain NetBIOS Name box.

10. Click **Next.**

    ■ The Database And Log Locations page appears.

11. Ensure that **C:\Winnt\Ntds** is the location of both the database and the log files.

12. Click **Next.**

    ■ The Shared System Volume page appears.

13. Ensure that the Sysvol folder location is **C:\Winnt\sysvol.**

14. Click **Next.**

    ■ The Windows NT 4.0 RAS Servers page appears.

15. Click **Next** to accept the default option.

16. Type in the administrative password (created in Chapter 5 during installation of Windows 2000 Server), and confirm that password.

17. Click **Next.**

    ■ The Summary page appears detailing the options you selected.

18. Review the contents, and then click **Next.**

    ■ The Configuring Active Directory progress indicator appears.

19. When the Completing The Active Directory Installation Wizard page appears, click **Finish.**

    ■ The installation wizard displays a status window that describes the progress of the installation process (see Figure 7-13).

    ■ When the installation is complete, a dialog box will ask if you want to restart the computer now or wait until later.

20. Click **Restart Now** to restart the computer.

FIGURE 7-13
Summary of Active Directory Installation Choices

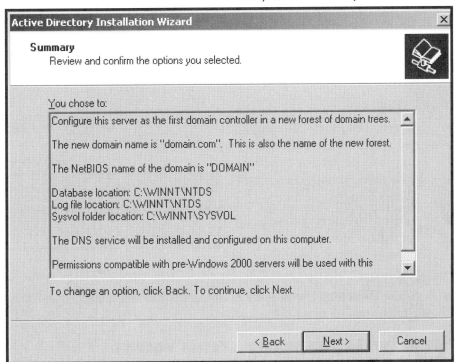

EXERCISE

7.9

Viewing the Domain

To perform this exercise, you will need:

- To have completed Exercise 7.8

1. Log on as Administrator.

2. Double-click **My Network Places.**

3. Double-click **Entire Network.**

4. Click the **Entire Contents** link.

   - The Microsoft Windows Network icon appears.

5. Double-click **Microsoft Windows Network.**

   - The Microsoft Windows Network window appears.

   - The Domain icon should be shown.

6. Close the Microsoft Windows Network window.

After Installation

There are several events that take place after an installation of Active Directory directory services is completed. Knowing these events will assist you later when you need to maintain and/or troubleshoot the system.

MENUS

As shown in Figure 7-14, the Administrative Tools menu will have the following entries added:

- **Active Directory Domains and Trusts** is used to administer domain trusts and user principal name suffixes and to change the domain mode.

FIGURE 7-14
Active Directory Options Are Added to the Administrative Tools Menu

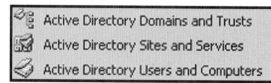

- **Active Directory Sites and Services** is used to administer the replication of Active Directory data.

- **Active Directory Users and Computers** is used to administer and publish information in the directory.

THE DATABASE AND SHARED SYSTEM VOLUME

After installation, Active Directory creates the following three files:

- The **Active Directory database** is the directory for the new domain.

- The **database log file** temporarily stores changes made to the Active Directory database.

- The **shared system volume** is a folder structure that stores scripts and other information needed for file replication between domain controllers. The default location for the shared system volume is **systemroot\Sysvol.**

CAUTION: Running **dcpromo.exe** on a domain controller allows you to remove Active Directory from the domain constroller and demotes it to a stand-alone server. If you remove Active Directory from all domain controllers in a domain, the directory database is also deleted and the domain no longer exists.

DOMAIN MODES

Most networks will have multiple domain controllers. The type of operating system installed on those domain controllers affects under which domain mode the domain will function. There are two domain modes—mixed and native.

- **Mixed mode** allows a Windows 2000 Server domain controller to interact with any domain controllers in the domain that are running previous versions of Windows NT Server. This usually occurs when a network is in the migration process. Domain controllers running previous versions of Windows NT Server are called **down-level domain controllers.**

- **Native mode** occurs when all of the domain controllers in the domain are running Windows 2000 Server. Running in native mode has several advantages, including less overhead for backward compatibility and the ability to take full advantage of the new features of Windows 2000 Server.

To change from mixed to native mode, you use the Active Directory Domains and Trusts snap-in. Once you change to native mode, support for down-level domain controllers is no longer available and you cannot add a down-level domain controller to the system. The reason for this is that the change from mixed mode to native mode is one way only; you cannot change from native back to mixed.

Other Installation Options

ADDING A DOMAIN CONTROLLER TO AN EXISTING DOMAIN

After the first domain controller is created, you should make another computer a domain controller as well. This will provide fault tolerance in case the first domain controller fails, and it will help balance the load for Active Directory tasks.

To add a domain to an existing domain, launch the Active Directory Installation wizard (see Exercise 7.7). Table 7-2 details the choices you would make on each installation wizard page.

After you click the Finish button, Active Directory will make the computer into a domain controller, will replicate the Active Directory database from the existing domain controller, and will add the three options to the Administrative Tools menu.

TABLE 7-2 INSTALLATION ANSWERS FOR ADDING A DOMAIN TO AN EXISTING DOMAIN

ON THIS PAGE	DO THIS
Domain Controller Type	Click **Additional domain controller for an existing domain.**
Network Credentials	Specify the username, password, and domain name of a user account that has permission to create domain controllers in Active Directory (usually the administrator account).
Additional Domain Controller	Specify the DNS name of the existing domain.
Database and Log Locations	Either specify locations or accept the defaults.
Shared System Volume	Either specify the location or accept the default.

TABLE 7-3 INSTALLATION ANSWERS
FOR CREATING A CHILD DOMAIN

ON THIS PAGE	DO THIS
Domain Controller Type	Click **Domain Controller for a new domain.**
Create tree or child domain	Click **Create a new child domain in an existing domain tree.**
Network Credentials	Specify the username, password, and domain name of a user account that has permission to create domain controllers in Active Directory (usually the administrator account).
Child Domain Installation	Specify the DNS name of the parent domain and the name of the new child domain.
Domain NetBIOS Name	Specify the NetBIOS name for the new domain.
Database and Log Locations	Either specify locations or accept the defaults.
Shared System Volume	Either specify the location or accept the default.
Windows NT 4.0 RAS Servers	Specify if you will weaken permissions to support users who access the network through remote access servers running Windows NT 4.0.

CREATING A CHILD DOMAIN

After the root domain is established, you can create additional domains in the tree. Each new domain within the tree can either be a child of the root domain or a child of another child domain.

To create a child domain, launch the Active Directory Installation wizard (see Exercise 7.7). Table 7-3 details the choices you would make on each installation wizard page.

After you click the Finish button, Active Directory will make the computer into a domain controller, will replicate the Active Directory database from the existing domain controller, and will add the three options to the Administrative Tools menu.

Lesson 7.7 Introduction to a Multiple Domain Environment

Domains, Trees, and Forests

The following analogy will help you understand the multiple domain environment. In Figure 7-15, you see three houses that are labeled A, B, and C; the houses are located in a small development on the same street.

FIGURE 7-15
Three Houses on a Street in a Development

Each house represents a domain. The people (users) within the house use things (objects) to accomplish their work around the house. Each user is governed by policies and rules that apply only to that house. There is someone who decides the various permissions each family member has for each object. For example, the kids in House A do not get to use the lawn mower, but in House B they do (they are future landscape architects).

The street would translate into the tree to which each domain belongs. All of the houses on the street have a unique number, but they also have the name of the street in their address: 2513 Riverside Street, 2511 Riverside Street, and 2509 Riverside Street. Likewise, all of the domains in a tree have a **contiguous namespace:** sales.microsoft.com, hr.microsoft.com, advertising.microsoft.com.

Each house is a separate entity from the others. Neighbors do not usually walk into each other's houses and take objects without first requesting access; in fact, people today lock their houses to prevent such occurrences. Information does not necessarily flow freely between domains in a tree either. Security—how to allow access to objects according to who needs the objects and for what purpose—is an issue. To facilitate controlled access, domains set up a **trust.** A **trust relationship** is a link between domains such that the *trusting* domain honors logon authentications of the *trusted* domain.

Using our houses for an example, let's say that the lawn mower used by the people in House B stops working. The man from House B goes to his neighbor in House A and asks if he can use her lawn mower. She says, "Sure, use it anytime you need to." The woman in House A is *trusting* the man in House B to go into her garage, get the lawn mower, use it, and return it. The man in House B is the one being *trusted.* He has been authenticated (proven to be who he says he is) and has been given the appropriate permission to gain access to her house (but only to the garage where the lawn mower is stored). Once the connection between domains is established through trusts, information can be exchanged between domains despite the differences in domain policies.

The small development in which the houses are located would translate into a **forest.** A development has many streets with different names. Likewise, trees and the forest that contains them do not have a contiguous namespace, but trusts are established that allow information to be exchanged.

Types of Trusts

Active Directory supports the following two different kinds of trusts:

- One-way, nontransitive
- Two-way, transitive

ONE-WAY, NONTRANSITIVE TRUSTS

Let's return to the scenario with the three houses to explain the terms *one-way* and *nontransitive*. The man in House B has just finished using House A's lawn mower and has put it away in House A's garage. Later that day, the woman in House A is using her hedge-trimmer when it stops working. She asks the man in House B if she can borrow his hedge-trimmer. He thinks about it but decides not to let her because his hedge-trimmer is brand new and he does not know if she is able to take care of it according to his standards.

Translating the houses into domains, we can make the following correlation: In a **one-way trust relationship,** if DomainA trusts DomainB, DomainB does not automatically trust DomainA.

Our analogy can be continued to explain nontransitive trust relationships. The man in House B is friendly with both of his neighbors. Suddenly, the lawn mower at House C stops working. The neighbor in House C notices that the man in House B has been using a nice lawn mower and asks if he can use it. Thus, the man in House B returns to his neighbor in House A to ask if she will let the lawn mower be used by someone else. She does not know the man in House C and does not really trust him, so she says "No."

Again, translate the houses into domains. In a **nontransitive trust relationship,** if DomainA trusts DomainB and DomainB trusts DomainC, then DomainA does not automatically trust DomainC (see Figure 7-16).

You can see that a one-way, nontransitive trust is restrictive and does not promote sharing. Windows NT 4.0 and earlier versions of NT used these types of trusts. The trusts had to be manually created, so a network with several domains required the creation of many trusts and left administrators searching for an easier way.

FIGURE 7-16
One-way, Nontransitive Trust Relationship

TWO-WAY, TRANSITIVE TRUSTS

A two-way, transitive trust is the relationship between parent and child domains within a tree and between the top-level domains in a forest. With Windows 2000, by default, the trust relationships among domains in a tree are established and maintained *automatically.*

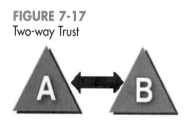

FIGURE 7-17
Two-way Trust

Let's return to our house analogy to demonstrate. The man in House B can use the lawn mower from House A. Because of his neighbor's generosity, he lets her use his brand new hedge-trimmer. They trust each other; that is, they have a two-way trust. If DomainA trusts DomainB, then DomainB trusts DomainA (see Figure 7-17).

With this basis of trust, if the man in House C asked to use the lawn mower, the woman in House A would let him. Why?

FIGURE 7-18
Two-way Transitive Trust

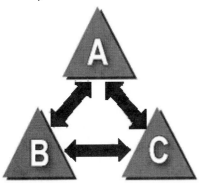

Because she trusts her neighbor in House B and he trusts the man in House C. When one person's trust is transferred to another person there is a transitive trust. If DomainA trusts DomainB and DomainB trusts DomainC, then DomainA trusts DomainC (see Figure 7-18).

In a world with two-way, transitive trusts, sharing is maximized. If DomainA trusts DomainB and DomainB trusts DomainC, then DomainA trusts DomainC and DomainC trusts DomainA. The people in the three houses all trust each other.

By default, Windows 2000 uses two-way, transitive trusts. When a child domain is created, a trust relationship is established automatically with its parent domain. The parent imparts a trust relationship with every other domain in the tree. As a result, users in one domain can access resources (to which they have been granted permission) in all other domains in the tree.

Global Catalog Server

Most developments have a homeowner's association that helps everyone live peaceably in the same area. The association often sets standards for the development, facilitates maintenance, and generally tries to help the residents be happy. One of the helpful items they might create is a phone directory of the people who live in the development. Even though there is a phone book for the city, having a list of only the people in the development helps everyone communicate with their neighbors more efficiently.

Microsoft created a similar subset or index of information for a forest called the **global catalog.** The global catalog provides a complete view of the entire directory so that both users and administrators can find objects by identifying one or more of an object's attributes. It stores a partial replica of each object and its attributes to conserve space and speed searches. For example, for a user account, the global catalog may only have the user's first name, last name, and logon name (see Figure 7-19). Searching for information in a subset of the forest-wide database is faster because there is less information to search.

FIGURE 7-19
The Global Catalog Server Holds a Subset of Information in the Active Directory

A **Global Catalog Server** is a domain controller that stores a copy of the global catalog and processes queries to the global catalog. By default, the first domain controller in a new forest is a global catalog server.

The global catalog is created each time the Active Directory is replicated (or copied) to all of the Domain Controllers. It is both a service and a physical storage location, so it is part of both the logical and physical structures.

TABLE 7-4 INSTALLATION ANSWERS FOR CREATING A NEW TREE

ON THIS PAGE	DO THIS
Domain Controller Type	Click **Domain Controller for a new domain.**
Create tree or child domain	Click **Create a new domain tree.**
Create or join forest	Click **Place this new domain tree in an existing forest.**
Network Credentials	Specify the username, password, and domain name of a user account in the Enterprise Admins group, which exists in the root domain of the forest.
New Domain Tree	Specify the DNS name for the new tree.
Domain NetBIOS Name	Specify the NetBIOS name for the new domain.
Database and Log Locations	Either specify locations or accept the defaults.
Shared System Volume	Either specify the location or accept the default.
Windows NT 4.0 RAS Servers	Specify if you will weaken permissions to support users who access the network through remote access servers running Windows NT 4.0.

CREATING A TREE IN AN EXISTING FOREST

After the root domain is established, you can create additional trees in the forest (if your network requires multiple trees).

To create a new tree in an existing forest, launch the Active Directory Installation wizard (see Exercise 7.7). Table 7-4 details the choices you would make on each installation wizard page.

After you click the Finish button, Active Directory will make the computer into a domain controller, will replicate the Active Directory database from the existing domain controller, and will add the three options to the Administrative Tools menu.

Summary

Being an architect takes a lot of studying, memorizing, theorizing, and practicing. Without thorough planning, the building will not be structurally sound. The same applies to the construction of an Active Directory structure. Launching the Active Directory Installation wizard without adequate preparation will result in a network that is unable to service the users adequately. Representing the structure graphically can help check your logic and will act as a foundation when expansion is necessary.

In this chapter you were introduced to a large amount of terminology that will be necessary to know as new topics are introduced in later chapters. Among those terms, you should become most familiar with the following: forest, tree, domain, organizational unit, and object. You also need to understand how those terms interrelate with each other in both descending and ascending order. In later chapters, you will see how important the namespace and name types are when managing the Active Directory contents.

Even though this chapter introduced the multiple domain environment, it is best to use as few domains as possible. Whenever feasible, you should use organizational units. Multiple domain environments are complicated and more difficult to administer. For example, it is in this environment that sites, replication, and trusts enter the picture. Configuring the Active Directory structure to maximize efficiency will be a challenge, and most networks require some level of complexity. Practice on a single domain environment before tackling multiple domains. There are entire books on this topic alone.

● ● ● ● ● ● ● ● ● ● ● ● ●

REVIEW EXERCISE

These questions will help you determine if you have learned enough to move on to the next chapter. If the graphic next to the option is a square (❑), there can be more than one answer for that question. If the graphic is a circle (○), there is only one correct answer. Color in the shape(s) to indicate your answer(s).

1. DomainA trusts DomainB and DomainB trusts DomainC. In which of the following trust relationships would DomainA trust DomainC?

   a. ❑ One-way, nontransitive

   b. ❑ Two-way

   c. ❑ Transitive

   d. ❑ Two-way, transitive

2. Your company has one remote office connected by a slow WAN link. You are receiving calls from users in the remote office who say that it can take over five minutes to log on. There is a domain controller and a global catalog server at the remote office. What could be the source of the problem?

   a. ❏ You don't have enough organizational units in the network.

   b. ❏ You haven't configured sites for your network.

   c. ❏ The client computers' date and time settings are incorrect.

   d. ❏ Domain controllers that are located across the slow link are occasionally authenticating users.

3. What is the name of the program that launches the Active Directory Installation wizard?

   a. ○ Adinstall.exe

   b. ○ dcpromo.bat

   c. ○ dcpromo.exe

   d. ○ setup.exe

4. Before running the Active Directory Installation wizard, what should you check on the server?

   a. ❏ That you have a partition and volume formatted with NTFS.

   b. ❏ That you have enough disk space to store the directory.

   c. ❏ That Windows 2000 Server has been installed.

   d. ❏ That TCP/IP is configured to use DNS.

5. Which of the following statements are true regarding a multiple domain environment?

   a. ❏ All of the domains in a tree have a contiguous namespace.

   b. ❏ In a trust relationship the *trusted* domain honors logon authentications of the *trusting* domain.

   c. ❏ A tree and the forest it belongs to are not required to have a contiguous namespace.

   d. ❏ The global catalog is a huge book with a list of everything that is for sale on planet earth.

PERFORMANCE CHALLENGES

- Make a list of the DNs for the following persons. Use the structure described in the chapter examples. Invent names where necessary.
  - Lucy Anderson
  - Lucy's father
  - Lucy's mother
  - Lucy's brother
  - Lucy's stepsister, Jessica Parker
- Graphically represent a domain structure that includes the following:
  - One forest
  - Two trees
  - At least three domains in each tree
  - At least four organizational units in each domain
  - At least five objects in each organizational unit

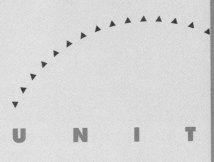

CREATE THE USER ENVIRONMENT

CREATE OBJECTS

OBJECTIVES

After completing this chapter, you should be able to:

■ Design a hierarchical structure of organizational units within a domain

■ Create and manage organizational units

■ Create user accounts and place them appropriately in the hierarchical structure

■ Name the two built-in user accounts installed automatically by Windows 2000 Server and describe their function

■ Use the Add a Printer wizard to install a printer on a computer

■ Make a CD-ROM drive available to other users on the network

■ Create a folder using Windows Explorer

■ Make a folder available to other users on the network

OUTLINE

Introduction

Would you like to shop at a store that carried more than a million different products from which to choose? Would you still shop at that store if it had no shelves, no racks, and no storage containers of any kind? Imagine a million objects in one big pile in the middle of a warehouse; that is what a domain would be like without organizational units. In this chapter, you will learn how to create organizational units and other objects, including user accounts, computer accounts, and resources. In order for computers and users to be recognized by the network, they must have an account.

Lesson 8.1 Create Organizational Units

Organizational units (OUs) are container objects that can hold other objects such as users, printers, groups, computer accounts, and other OUs. Their main purpose is to organize network resources for the domain.

Designing a Hierarchy of OUs

An OU can be contained within another OU that is within another OU, and so on. Because of this capability, planning the position of each OU within the domain's hierarchical structure is important. Several approaches are available for creating an efficient OU structure.

The Company's Organizational Structure

A company's organizational structure reflects the way people interact with each other in terms of who has authority over whom. You can create an OU structure that reflects those interactions. For example, you could create an OU for each department (sales, human resources, customer service, and so on), or if the company has several geographic locations, you could create a separate OU for each location. As shown in Figure 8-1, many companies have an organizational chart that lists the people in the organization and identifies each person's supervisor. Such documents are especially helpful when designing an OU structure.

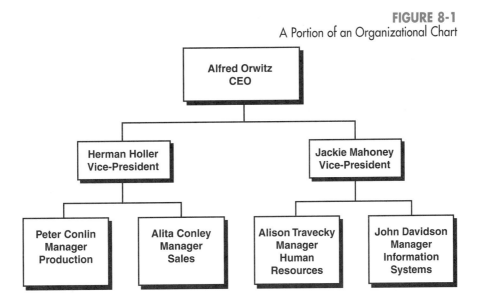

FIGURE 8-1
A Portion of an Organizational Chart

THE COMPANY'S NETWORK ADMINISTRATION MODEL

Often a large network is managed not by one administrator but by a team of administrators. The various tasks for network management would be distributed amongst the administrators. One administrator might be responsible for managing the user accounts, another might be in charge of maintenance on the server, and another might take care of hardware. In this case, you could create an OU for users, an OU for servers, and another OU for hardware.

DELEGATION OF AUTHORITY

Windows 2000 allows administrators to delegate administrative control over OUs. Rather than a network administrator having to change permissions on every folder, a manager or other responsible person can be given the authority to change permissions. This can save an administrator many hours of detail work and can allow him or her to perform more vital functions.

Checking Permissions

Not everyone who can log on to the network has the permission to create OUs. You must have **Read, List Contents,** and **Create Organizational Unit Objects** permissions on the parent container (domain or OU) to create OUs within that container. List Contents permissions are necessary in order to view the newly created OU. Since members of the Administrators group have these permissions by default, if you log on as an administrator, you will be able to create OUs. You will learn how to set permissions in Chapter 10.

Creating an OU

Exercise 8.1 details how to create an OU that is the child of the domain.

Create Organizational Units

To perform this exercise, you will need:

- Access to a domain controller
- Printed results of Exercise 7.5 and Exercise 7.6

1. Log on as administrator.

2. Click the Start button.

3. Point to **Programs.**

4. Point to **Administrative Tools.**

5. Click **Active Directory Users and Computers.**

6. In the console tree, right-click **domain.com.**

7. Point to **New** from the Context menu.

8. Select **Organizational Unit** (see Figure 8-2).

- The New Object—Organizational Unit dialog box appears.

9. In the "Name" box, type the name of your first Organizational Unit as listed in Exercise 7.5. (Refer to the graphical representation created in Exercise 7.6.)

10. Click **OK.**

11. Expand **domain.com** to view the new OUs (see Figure 8-3).

12. Repeat step 6 through step 10 for each additional OU that will be a child of the root.

13. Exit the Active Directory Users and Computers window when finished.

FIGURE 8-2
Viewing the Active Directory Structure with Newly Created OUs

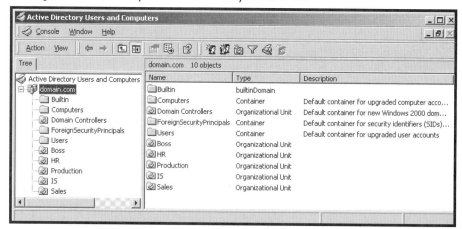

In Figure 8-2 Windows 2000 has automatically created some of the child objects for **domain.com.** An icon showing a folder with a book represents an OU, and the description to the right of the folder reveals that the Domain Controllers OU was automatically created. In this example, an administrator has created an OU structure that reflects the organizational chart shown in Figure 8-1. The new OUs are Boss, HR, Production, IS, and Sales. You can enter a description for an OU by right-clicking the OU name in the tree pane and selecting Properties. Click the General tab to enter a description, then click OK to finish.

Managing OUs

Organizational units can be moved and renamed in the same way you work with files and folders in Windows Explorer. To rename an OU, highlight the name and then click the name again to open the Rename-Editing box. Type the new name, and press Enter. To move an OU, simply drag and drop. To make a new OU, right-click on the container object that will be the parent of the new OU; for example, to add a new OU under the Sales OU, right-click on Sales. As in Exercise 8.1, select New, Organizational Unit, then type the name and click OK. Because of its hierarchical nature, you can expand and collapse the OU structure in the same way you expand and collapse the folder structure in Windows Explorer.

Lesson 8.2 Create User Accounts

Plan User Accounts

The preparation work you completed in Chapter 3 will serve you well in this chapter. One of the steps in planning user accounts is to identify the people who use the network. Each user must have a user account in order to log on to the network and also to gain appropriate access to network resources. Another step involves deciding in which OU the user account will be created. If a user works in the sales department, for example, it would make sense to create the user account in the Sales OU.

Predefined User Accounts

Two user accounts—the guest account and the administrator account—are predefined, or "built-in," by the Windows 2000 installation program. These two accounts are primarily

---

TIP

The Active Directory console has a toolbar with buttons that perform common Active Directory actions with one click. You can learn the function of each button by resting your mouse on the button (without clicking). A "tool tip" will appear telling you the function of the button. Using these buttons can increase your efficiency.

TABLE 8-1 BUILT-IN USER ACCOUNTS

ACCOUNT NAME	PURPOSE
Administrator	The administrator account has extensive rights and permissions on the system. This account cannot be deleted, but it can and should be renamed. If you keep the name "Administrator," a hacker only needs to work on the password to break into the system.
Guest	The guest account has restricted rights and permissions on the system. This account is often used to allow users who do not need a permanent account to log on. For example, visitors who need to use a word processor and printer would log on using the guest account.

involved in the initial logon process for a computer. Table 8-1 lists the accounts and their purpose.

Both accounts have default settings that control what the user can and cannot do. It is advisable to check those settings and change them as necessary for your organization's security needs. Chapter 12 explains how to change user account properties.

Create a User Account

You can use the Active Directory Users and Computers administrative tool on any available domain controller to create a user account.

CHECK YOUR PERMISSIONS

To add a user account to an OU, you must have the permission to add new objects to the OU. By default, members of the Administrators group can add objects anywhere in the domain.

EXERCISE

Create a User Account

● ●

To perform this exercise, you will need:

■ Access to a domain controller

■ Printed results of Exercise 7.5 and Exercise 7.6

1. Log on as administrator.

2. Click the Start button.

FIGURE 8-3
The First Screen in the New Object—User Dialog Box

New Object - User		☒
	Create in: domain.com/Boss	
First name:	Alfred	Initials: P
Last name:	Orwitz	
Full name:	Alfred P. Orwitz	
User logon name:		
orwitza	@domain.com ▼	
User logon name (pre-Windows 2000):		
DOMAIN\	orwitza	
	< Back Next > Cancel	

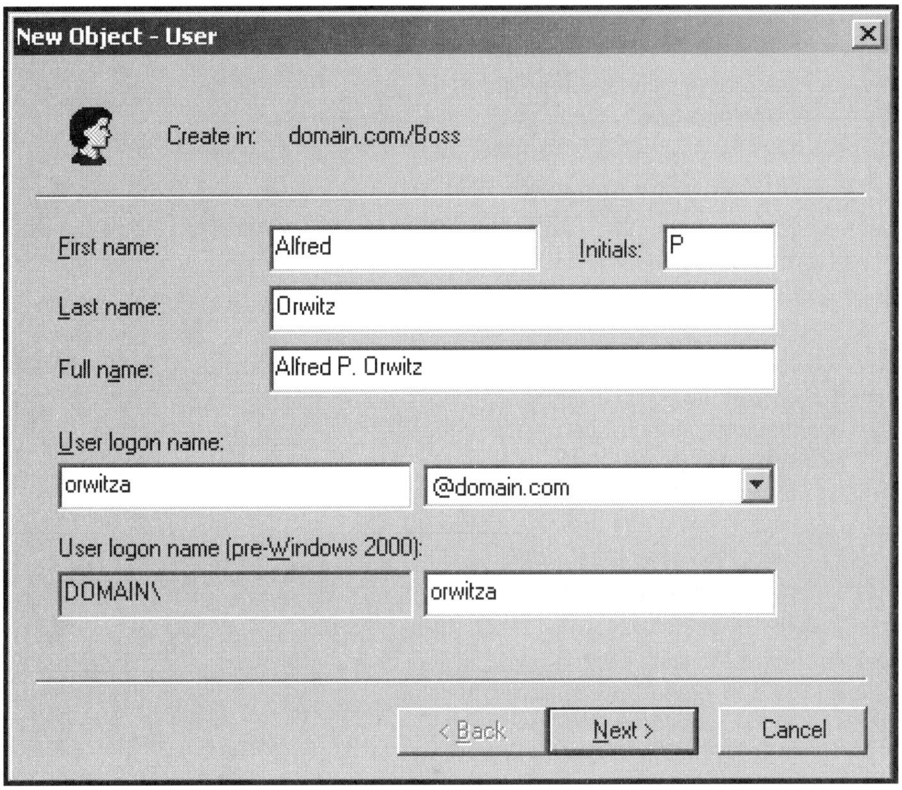

3. Point to **Programs.**

4. Point to **Administrative Tools.**

5. Click **Active Directory Users and Computers.**

6. In the console tree, right-click the OU that will contain the new user account. (Note that you can create a user account directly in the domain, but doing so limits delegation options and increases complexity. It is best to create user accounts within an OU.)

7. Point to **New.**

8. Select **User.**

■ The New Object—User dialog box appears.

9. **Enter** the appropriate information in the text boxes (see Figure 8-3 and Table 8-2 for a description of these fields).

10. Click **Next.**

TABLE 8-2 USER ACCOUNT DIALOG BOX ENTRIES

FIELD	DESCRIPTION	EXAMPLE
First Name	The user's first name. This field or the Last Name field is required.	Lucy
Last Name	The user's last name. This field or the First Name field is required.	Anderson
Full Name	The user's complete name. This name must be unique in the OU. Active Directory displays this name in the OU.	Lucy Anderson
User Logon Name	The user's unique logon name based on your naming convention. This is required and must be unique in the enterprise (forest). Note that the @domain.com is displayed in the next field. It has a pull-down list button in order to display other domain options. Together these two fields form the UPN.	AndersonLucy@ kids.anderson.com
User Logon Name (pre-Windows 2000)	The user's unique logon name that is used to log on from computers running earlier versions of Windows (NT 4.0, 3.51, etc.). This is required and must be unique in the domain.	AndersonL

11. Enter the appropriate information in the text boxes of the Password page (see Figure 8-4 and Table 8-3 for a description of these fields).

12. Click **Next.**

13. Verify that the user account options are correct, and then click **Finish.**

14. Click on the OU to view the new user account (see Figure 8-5).

FIGURE 8-4
The New Object—User Password-Requirements Page

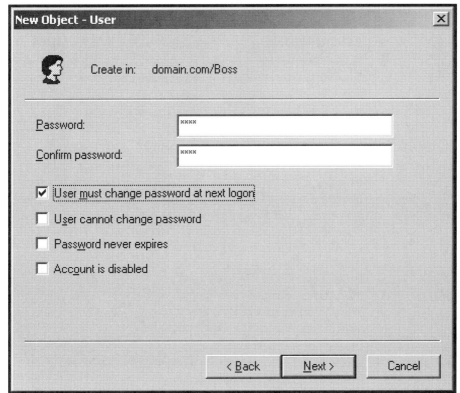

After the User Account Is Created

After the account is created, it is replicated to all other domain controllers in the domain and the account name is displayed in the parent OU. You also have the option of configuring other properties for the account, such as logon hours, telephone number, address, group memberships, and more. You will learn all about configuring user account properties in Chapter 12.

TABLE 8-3 USER ACCOUNT PASSWORD-REQUIREMENTS PAGE ENTRIES

FIELD	DESCRIPTION	EXAMPLE
Password	The password that is used to authenticate the user. For greater security, you should always assign a password (rather than leave it blank).Remember that passwords are case-sensitive.	toeJam
Confirm Password	Type the password a second time to make sure you typed it correctly in the previous field.	toeJam
User Must Change Password At Next Logon	To allow users to designate their own passwords, select this checkbox. They would enter and confirm the new password as part of their next logon process. Only the user knows his or her own password. If a user forgets the password, you will need to assign a new one and have the user log on. With this option checked, the user then will have to choose and enter a new password.	Checked = enabled
User Cannot Change Password	Check this box if you want more than one person to use the account (such as guests) or to maintain control over user account passwords. Only administrators can change the password.	Checked = enabled
Password Never Expires	If you never want the password to be changed, check this box. Passwords can be set to expire, forcing the user to create a new password. This tightens security.	Checked = enabled
Account Disabled	When checked, the account will not be available for use. You might disable an account if someone is on vacation or if a new employee is not on the job yet.	Checked = the account is disabled

FIGURE 8-5
The New User Account Is Displayed

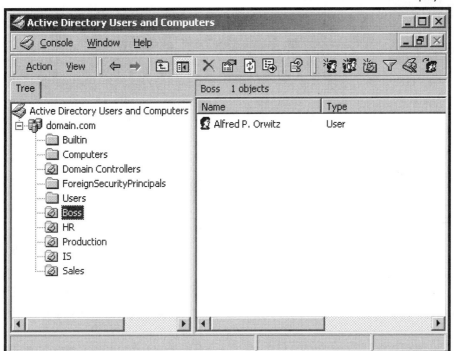

Lesson 8.3 Create Computer Accounts

Computer accounts are similar to user accounts except that they represent nodes (computers) on the network rather than people. Every computer connected to the network must have a computer account in order to participate on the network. The account is used to authenticate and audit the computer and is also used when assigning permissions for access to network resources.

Create a Computer Account

As demonstrated in Exercise 8.3, you can create a computer account on any domain controller.

8.3 Create a Computer Account

To perform this exercise, you will need:

- Access to a domain controller

- To know the naming convention for computers on your network

1. Log on as administrator.

2. Click the Start button.

3. Point to **Programs.**

4. Point to **Administrative Tools.**

5. Click **Active Directory Users and Computers.**

6. In the console tree, right-click the OU that will contain the new computer account.

   - Create the account in the OU that contains users to whom you may want to delegate authority over computer accounts.

   - In Figure 8-6, for example, the computer accounts were created in the IS (Information Systems) OU because that OU also has the users who administrate the network.

7. Point to **New.**

8. Select **Computer.**

   - The New Object—Computer dialog box appears (see Figure 8-6).

9. Enter the name of the computer (must be unique in the enterprise/forest).

10. Enter the name of a User or Group that has permission to join the computer to a domain (or accept the default).

11. Click **Finish.**

12. Click on the OU to view the new computer account (see Figure 8-7).

13. Repeat steps 6–11 for each computer account to be created.

AFTER THE ACCOUNT IS CREATED

After the account is created, Active Directory will replicate the information to all of the other domain controllers in the domain.

FIGURE 8-6

The New Object—Computer Dialog Box

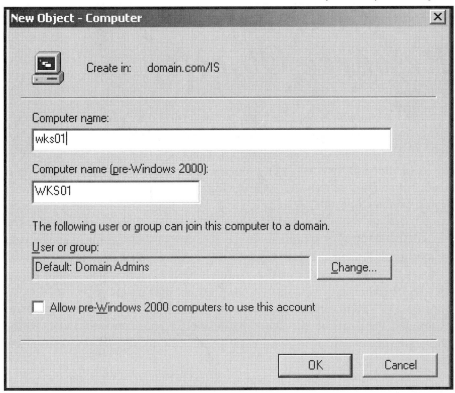

FIGURE 8-7

New Computer Accounts

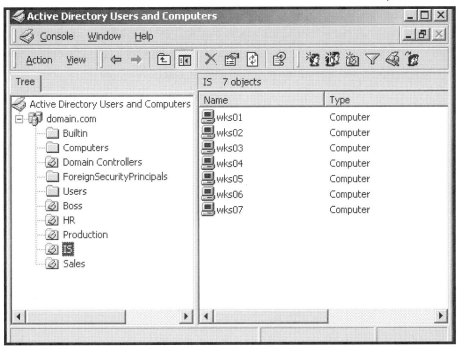

Lesson 8.4 Create Resource Objects

People who access the network are referred to as *users* because they *use* the network resources to help them get their work done. Network resources include files, printers, CD-ROM drives, scanners, and many other types of devices. After a device has been properly installed and configured, you must make Active Directory aware of the device's presence on the network. In other words, you must post the device.

There are various ways to post a network resource depending on the type of resource. For example, to post a printer you would use the Add Printer wizard in the **Printers** folder (choose Start, Settings, Printer, and Add Printer). To make a folder or file available as a resource, you would create the file or folder and then set the permissions that allow or restrict access. Sharing a CD-ROM would involve right-clicking on the drive in **My Computer** and then setting the share permissions. The exercises listed in the remainder of this chapter give examples of how to add the most common types of resources.

Add a Printer

Before launching the Printer Installation wizard, be sure that the print device is functional and properly connected to the network. If the drivers are not available on the Windows 2000 Server CD, you may need to have access to printer drivers. When you add a printer, you will be asked for the name of the printer. Refer to your organization's naming conventions.

EXERCISE

8.4 Add a Printer

To perform this exercise, you will need:

■ Access to a networked computer with a printer attached

■ The Windows 2000 Server CD or the media (CD or floppy) from the manufacturer that has the appropriate drivers for the print device

1. Log on as administrator.

2. Click the Start button.

3. Point to **Settings.**

4. Select **Printers. . . .**

■ The Printers window is opened.

5. Double-click the **Add Printer** icon.

■ The Add Printers wizard is launched and the welcome screen displayed.

6. Click **Next.**

■ The Local or Network Printer screen appears.

7. Indicate if the printer is **local** (connected to the computer you are using) or **network** (not directly connected to your computer).

■ Notice that if you select Local, Windows 2000 can automatically detect the printer.

8. Click **Next.**

■ The Locate Your Printer screen appears.

9. If you know the name of the printer, you can enter the name in the "Name:" text box.

■ If you know the URL of the printer, you can enter the URL in the "URL:" text box (an URL is a naming convention used on the Internet and on intranets).

■ If you do not know the name or the URL, you can click **Next** to browse for the printer.

10. To demonstrate how browsing works, make both text boxes blank and click **Next.**

■ The Browse For Printer screen appears (see Figure 8-8).

■ Double-click the domain in which the printer is located.

■ Double-click the computer to which the printer is attached.

■ Click on the name of the printer.

11. Click **Next.**

■ The Default Printer screen appears.

12. Click **Yes** if you want applications to use this printer as the default. This means that when the user clicks on a printer button, the output will go to the default printer. It will also be the first printer in a list when the user selects File, Print. Click **No** if you want a different printer to be the default.

■ The final screen of the Add Printer wizard is displayed and includes a summary of the options you selected.

13. Click **Finish.**

14. The Printers window should now display an icon for the printer. The black checkmark indicates which printer is set as the default.

FIGURE 8-8
The Browse for Printer Screen with a Printer Selected

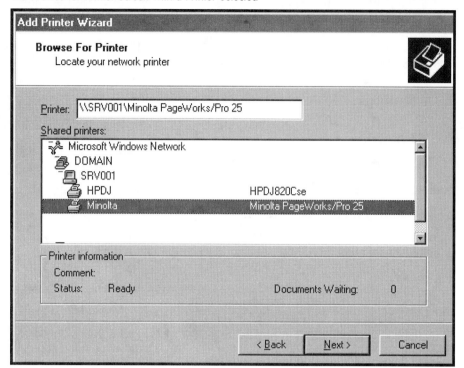

Share a CD-ROM

A shared device appears on the network when users are browsing. If a device is not shared, it will not be listed.

While some networks have a bank of CD-ROM drives, the drive normally is attached to a workstation. The media in the drive is removable, so even though the drive is available after being shared, its contents may vary.

EXERCISE

8.5   Share a CD-ROM

To perform this exercise, you will need:

■ Access to a networked computer with a CD-ROM drive

1. Log on as administrator.

2. Open **My Computer.**

3. Right-click on the **CD-ROM drive icon.**

4. Select **Sharing . . .** from the Context menu.

   ■ The CD-ROM Properties dialog box is displayed with the Sharing tab in front (see Figure 8-9).

5. Click **Share this folder.**

6. Enter the appropriate information (see Table 8-4).

7. Click **OK.**

   ■ A hand appears under the CD-ROM drive icon in **My Computer** indicating that the device is shared.

TABLE 8-4 SHARING DIALOG BOX FIELDS

FIELD NAME	DESCRIPTION
Share name	When other users are browsing the network, the share name is the name they will see listed.
Comment	Gives additional information and can be more user-friendly than the share name alone.
User Limit	You can limit the number of users that are allowed to be connected to the object at one time. Use the spin boxes to enter numbers, or just type in the number. Usually it is fine to leave the setting at **maximum allowed.** Do not alter this setting at this time.
Permissions button	When clicked, the Permissions dialog box is displayed. Permissions allow you to determine what groups or users are allowed access and what they are allowed to do with the object. You will learn more about permissions in Chapter 10. Do not alter these settings at this time.
Caching	When clicked, the Caching dialog box is displayed. Caching is the process of copying data from memory to the hard drive. When the data that were stored are requested again, they are pulled from the hard drive. Do not alter these settings at this time.

FIGURE 8-9
Sharing Dialog Box

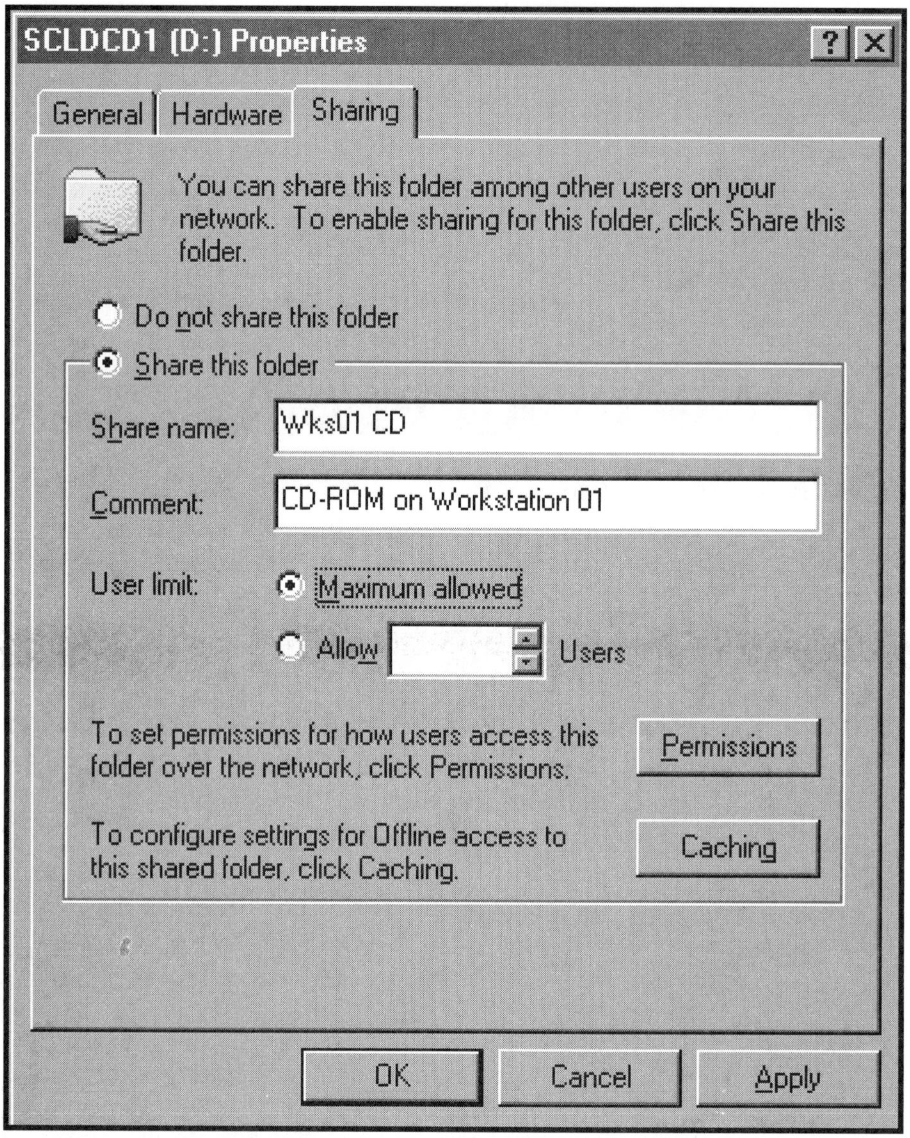

Create a Folder

Whereas folders in a filing cabinet hold pieces of paper, folders in a subdirectory structure on a hard disk hold files. Folders can be created and then made available to other users on the network. Exercise 8.8 demonstrates how to create a folder and then share it. Chapter 10 will cover how to set permissions for folders.

EXERCISE

8.6

Create and Share a Folder

• •

To perform this exercise, you will need:

■ Access to a Windows 2000 computer

1. Log on as administrator.

2. Click the Start button.

3. Point to **Programs.**

4. Point to **Accessories.**

5. Select **Windows Explorer.**

■ The Windows Explorer window opens.

6. Double-click on the **My Documents** folder.

7. Right-click on a blank area of the left-hand pane.

8. Point to **New** on the Context menu.

9. Select **Folder** from the cascading menu.

■ An editable text box appears beneath a new folder icon.

10. Type the name of the new folder in the text box under the icon (replacing the words "New Folder").

11. Press the **Enter** key, or click on another area of the screen.

■ The new folder is created.

12. Right-click on the new folder.

13. Select **Sharing. . .** from the Context menu.

■ The New Folder Properties dialog box is displayed with the **Sharing** tab in front.

14. Click **Share this folder.**

15. Enter the appropriate information (see Table 8-4).

16. Click **OK.**

■ A hand appears under the folder icon indicating that the folder is shared.

17. Exit the Windows Explorer window.

Summary

Active Directory can hold millions of objects. With proper planning and a strategy for organizing those objects, users will have access to the resources they need. In this chapter, you learned how to create several different kinds of objects. The first object was a container object known as an organizational unit, or OU. Organizational units provide a logical structure for organizing objects. One of the objects in the Active Directory is a user account. Every user must have an account in order to log on to the network. You learned how to use the **Active Directory Users and Computers** console to create user accounts. That same console is used to create computer accounts. When it comes to creating resource objects, there are various methods depending on the resource being created. You learned how to add a printer using a wizard and how to share a CD-ROM drive and create a shared folder using Windows Explorer. Remember to use your organization's naming convention when creating objects.

• • • • • • • • • • • • •

REVIEW EXERCISE

These questions will help you determine if you have learned enough to move on to the next chapter. If the graphic next to the option is a square (❑), there can be more than one answer for that question. If the graphic is a circle (○), there is only one correct answer. Color in the shape(s) to indicate your answer(s).

1. What types of objects can an OU hold?

   a. ❑ User accounts

   b. ❑ Domains

   c. ❑ Groups

   d. ❑ OUs

2. One day, while creating user accounts, you receive a phone call from a user who says he has forgotten his password. What can you do to help him?

   a. ❑ Open the user account properties, read his password, and then tell him what it is.

   b. ❑ Assign a new password and check the box that requires him to change the password the next time he logs on.

   c. ❑ Assign a new password and do not check the box that requires him to change the password the next time he logs on.

   d. ❑ There is nothing you can do. He will not be able to log on ever again. He might as well join the circus.

3. What console is used to create a computer account?

   a. ○ Add a Printer wizard

   b. ○ Active Directory Users and Computers

   c. ○ Active Directory Computers and Users

   d. ○ Windows Explorer

4. You have finished creating a user account. What changes occurred because of your action?

   a. ❑ The Active Directory contains one more object than it did before.

   b. ❑ The user account will be replicated to all of the other domain controllers in the domain.

   c. ❑ When you click on the parent OU in the Active Directory Users and Computers console, you will see the user account name.

   d. ❑ No changes occurred.

5. Debi is in charge of producing the company newsletter. She discovers that a fellow employee named Lee has a CD-ROM disk full of graphics she would like to use. Because he had spent a lot of time compiling the graphics from various sources, Lee does not want to loan her the disk. What is the most effective solution Debi could suggest so that they can both access the graphics while the CD-ROM disk stays in his office?

   a. ○ Lee could share his cubicle and his computer with Debi.

   b. ○ Debi could use his computer when he was on coffee break or at lunch, as long as she changed her hours to do so.

   c. ○ Lee could use the **Sharing** tab on the Properties of his CD-ROM drive to make the drive available over the network.

   d. ○ Lee could purchase a CD-R drive, install it on his computer, buy a blank CD disk, learn the CD-R software, duplicate the disk, and give a copy to Debi.

■ Answer the following questions about passwords:

- ■ Should a password ever be left blank? Why or why not?

- ■ What makes the strongest passwords?

- ■ What are the advantages of letting users determine their passwords?

- ■ What would be the disadvantage of an administrator setting the passwords for all of the users?

- ■ When a password expires, the user is prompted to enter a new and different password. Why would this be an advantage?

■ Using Windows Explorer, create a hierarchy of folders on a floppy disk that shows the relationships between your grandparents and their offspring. Include your uncles and aunts, your parents, yourself, and your siblings. You can include your cousins (although it is not required). You can do both your mother's side and your father's side, but only one is required. An example of what such a folder structure might look like follows in Figure 8-10:

FIGURE 8-10

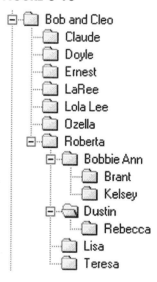

CREATE GROUPS

OBJECTIVES

After completing this chapter, you should be able to:

■ Describe what a group is and why groups are necessary in a domain

■ Know the difference between a security group and a distribution group

■ Name the three group scopes and their differences

■ Explain what local groups are and which computers use them

■ Understand the recommended method for creating groups

■ Create a group

OUTLINE

Introduction

In a small organization with only a few users, managing each user independent of the other users would not be difficult. However, in a large organization with thousands of users, managing them individually would be practically impossible. By putting users together in logical groupings, an administrator can make changes that affect everyone in the group. If a group has 100 users, a change translates into one action versus 100 actions on the part of the administrator. In this chapter, you will learn the different types of groups and how to create them.

Lesson 9.1 Understand Groups

Groups are usually formed around common tasks or projects that the users are working on cooperatively. For example, for a group of people who are in the accounting department, you could create a group for accounting. To assist a group of people who work in many different departments but who are working on a company-wide project together, you could form a temporary group that could be deleted when the project is completed. Not only can many people belong to one group, but also one user with a diversified job description may belong to more than one group. Consider the following when planning groups:

- **What groups are needed?** The more groups you create, the more work there is in administering them.

- **Which user accounts will be members of each group?** Permissions for access to resources are usually granted to a group as opposed to an individual user. You should think carefully about who really needs access to the objects and to what level. For example, you would not want to add every user to the administrators group. Since the administrator is the only person who is allowed to perform certain activities, there would be no security if everyone belonged to the administrators group.

- **In what OU will the group reside?** If your OU structure is based on the organizational structure of the company, placing groups within that structure should be fairly easy.

- **How far reaching should the group's influence be?** The next section describes the scope of a group. When you create a group, you must designate its scope.

Group Types

The two types of groups in Windows 2000 are Security groups and Distribution groups. Table 9-1 explains their differences.

Understanding Group Scope

A group is a container object, which means that it can hold other objects. By assigning each group a **scope,** you are able to either expand or

TABLE 9-1 TYPES OF GROUPS

GROUP TYPE	DESCRIPTION
Security Groups	Used to assign or deny rights and permissions to groups of users and computers so that they can gain access to resources. Security groups are the only groups that Windows 2000 uses.
Distribution Groups	Used by applications as lists for nonsecurity-related functions. An example would be the need to regularly send e-mail messages to a certain group of users. Logon performance is better because the access token is smaller. If you do not have plans to use a group for security issues, create a distribution group.

limit the influence the group has on the network. The scope of the group is one of the group's attributes, and both security and distribution groups have a scope attribute. The scope attribute determines which user accounts can be members of the group and where the group can be used in the network. Windows 2000 has a slightly different approach to group scope than previous versions of Windows NT. Because of these differences, a network running in native mode (all domain controllers are Windows 2000 Servers) will have more flexibility than one running in mixed mode (some Windows NT domain controllers exist on the network). There are three different scopes in a Windows 2000 network:

- Universal
- Global
- Domain local

UNIVERSAL GROUPS

Universal groups can contain user accounts, global groups, and other universal groups from any Windows 2000 domain in the forest. A security group with a universal scope can only be created in a native mode domain. Permissions can be granted to universal groups for all domains in the forest, regardless of where the universal group is actually located.

GLOBAL GROUPS

In native mode domain, global groups can contain user accounts and global groups from the *domain* in which the group exists. In a mixed mode domain, a global group can only have *user accounts* from the domain in which the group exists. Permissions can be granted to global groups for all domains in the forest, regardless of where the global group is actually located.

DOMAIN LOCAL GROUPS

In a native mode domain, domain local groups can contain user accounts, global groups, and universal groups from any domain in the forest. They can also hold domain local groups from the same domain. In a mixed mode domain, they can only contain user accounts and global groups from any domain.

Study Table 9-2 for a summary of group scopes.

GROUP SCOPE	IN NATIVE MODE, CAN CONTAIN	IN MIXED MODE, CAN CONTAIN	CAN BE A MEMBER OF	PERMISSIONS CAN BE GRANTED FOR
TABLE 9-2 GROUP SCOPES FOR SECURITY GROUP MEMBERSHIP				
Universal	From any domain in the forest: • User accounts • Global groups • Other universal groups	Not applicable	In any domain: • Domain local • Universal groups	All domains in the forest
Global	From the same domain: • User accounts • Global groups	From the same domain: • User accounts	In any domain: • Universal • Domain local groups In the same domain: • Global groups	All domains in the forest
Domain local	From any domain in the forest: • User accounts • Global groups • Universal groups From the same domain: • Domain local groups	From any domain: • User accounts • Global groups	In the same domain: • Domain local groups	The domain in which the domain local group exists

THE PURPOSE OF SCOPES

Even though it seems complicated, group scope is designed to simplify network management. Remember that groups are formed in order to keep the administrator from having to edit user account information for each user when a change occurs that affects multiple users. You can use one step to change the permissions for a group of thirty users, or you can use thirty steps to make one change to thirty user accounts. You can see which of those two scenarios would be more time consuming. Why have different kinds of groups? The answer includes the need for flexibility, simplified administration, and control over resource access.

For an example of meeting those needs, imagine that we have a large, native mode domain with five domains. Look at the rules for global groups in Table 9-2. If the only scope available for a forest were global groups, an administrator would not be able to create a group that affects users in the entire forest. Since there can be hundreds of groups in a forest, one change could translate into hundreds of steps. Conversely, with the universal group scope, an administrator can put global groups from each domain into the universal group. One change to the universal group affects all of the global groups, no matter where they are in the forest. Consider the following example: There are 20 administrative assistants in the company, and each person has a user account. The user accounts of the administrative assistants are added to a global group in their respective domains. Each domain in the forest has one global group for the administrative assistants. If there are changes that only affect the administrative assistants in a single domain, the global group membership is sufficient.

Consider what would have to be done in order to give all of the administrative assistants in the whole company access to a new folder that holds company-wide forms. Rather than having to go to the global group in each domain, the administrator simply adds the global groups to a universal group. He or she then edits the permissions for the folder and gives everyone in the universal group access to the folder. From now on, any other changes that affect all of the administrative assistants will be simplified into a single step. Compare the administrative burden for each change to the network:

■ User accounts only = 20 steps

■ Global groups only = 5 steps

■ Universal groups = 1 step

DETERMINING THE BEST SCOPE

Scope must be determined for each group and depends on how the users need to be affected. After all, the goal of determining the best scope is to give users access to the resources they need. Networks are all about connectivity, and group scopes either increase or limit the level of interaction. One way to look at connectivity is to shrink the focus to a single user with a shared resource. For example, assume that there is a user named Tammy in our forest who has a color printer attached to her workstation. Tammy would not want everyone in the entire company to be able to print documents on her color printer, for the printer would be running all day (running out of ink and paper), and people would be coming from every building to Tammy's cubicle to get their printouts. However, Tammy may want to let four people from her domain use the printer because they are working on a presentation project with her. The administrator puts Tammy in a global group with the other project participants and then gives that group access to the printer. The administrator does not put that global group into a universal group at this time.

Months later the project is complete, and Tammy's presentation is so spectacular that the CEO wants her to expand the project to include the entire company. There are now ten people working on the project, and they are located in different domains. What group scope is needed now? Global groups will not suffice because you cannot include members from other domains. You could use a universal group, but that might be overkill. Universal groups give access to resources in any domain to members from any domain in the forest. The resource is located in one domain as opposed to being scattered across many domains. Thus, in this case, the administrator could use a domain local group because a domain local group gives access to resources in one domain to members from any domain in the forest. Figures 9-1 illustrates these concepts.

TIP

If you desire to pass the Microsoft Exam, you must not only memorize but also understand the contents of Table 9-2. Scenario-type questions like the one presented in this lesson (only more vague in nature) will challenge your understanding of group scopes.

Lesson 9.2 Learn about Local Groups

All of the groups discussed previously are replicated to all of the domain controllers, which have a copy of the Active Directory. If a computer is a member server, it does not maintain a copy of the directory. These computers can be members of a domain local group, but individual users may choose to create a local group to provide access to resources on the member server when a domain local group is not created for that purpose. You can use local groups to give permissions only to resources on the local computer. Local groups can also be created for computers running Windows 2000 Professional.

Rules for Local Groups

Keep in mind the following rules for local groups:

- Local groups can contain local user accounts from the computer where the local group is created.

- Local groups can contain global and universal groups from any domain.

- Local groups cannot be members of any other group.

FIGURE 9-1
Group Scopes

Domain Local Group

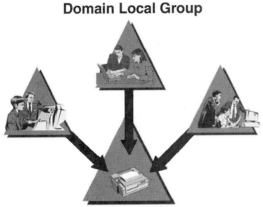

**Members from any domain in the forest.
Use for access to resources in one domain**

Global Group

**Members from own domain only
Use for access to resources in any domain**

Universal Group

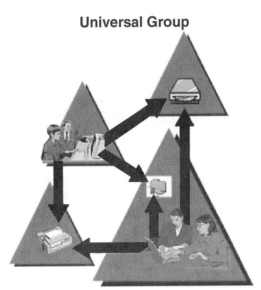

**Members from any domain in forest
Use for access to resources in any domain**

Built-in Local Groups

All member servers, stand-alone servers, and computers running Windows 2000 Professional have built-in local groups. These groups have the right to perform tasks on a *single* computer, which include performing backups and restores, changing the time, and administering system resources. Table 9-3 briefly describes who belongs to the built-in groups and what they can do.

TIP

The term *built-in* means that the item being referred to was created as a part of the installation process.

TABLE 9-3 LOCAL GROUP MEMBERSHIP PRIVILEGES

LOCAL GROUP NAME	DESCRIPTION
Administrators	Members can perform any administrative tasks on the computer.
Backup Operators	Members can use Windows 2000 Backup to back up and restore the computer.
Guests	Members can only perform tasks that the administrator has predefined. This account is usually very restrictive.
Power Users	Members can create and modify local user accounts and share resources.
Replicator	Used for file replication in a domain.
Users	Members can perform only tasks the administrator has predefined and can only access resources for which the administrator has assigned permissions.

Lesson 9.3 Strategy for Creating Groups

The preparation activities you performed in Chapter 3 will help you as you begin to create groups, for you now know who your users are and to what resources they need access. If multiple users need access to a particular resource, you would create a group for that purpose. The location of the users and the location of the resource will help determine which scope the group should have. You can see from Table 9-2 that groups can be nested within groups. Because of this, your logic for how the groups relate to each other is important. Consider making a mapping of the groups during your planning.

Keep the following strategy in mind when creating groups of varying scopes: *Put user accounts into global groups, and then put global groups into domain local groups and assign permissions to the domain local groups.* To help you remember this process, use the acronym AGDLP:

■   A = Accounts: Put user accounts into

■   G = Global groups and then put global groups into

■ DL = Domain local groups and assign

■ P = Permissions to domain local groups

Figure 9-2 demonstrates the flow of the strategy.

The AGDLP strategy provides the most flexibility and reduces the complexity of assigning network resources because you start with the smallest element (users) and put them into a limited scope group (global) and then you put them into a larger scope group (domain local). This is similar in concept to nesting dolls, where the smallest doll fits inside a slightly larger doll, then that doll fits into a larger doll, and so on. Once the dolls are nested within each other, whatever happens to the largest doll happens to the others. If you shake the largest doll, for example, all of the dolls are shaken. It is the same with groups; when you assign a permission to the domain local group, all of the other groups or user accounts that are within (members of) the domain local group are affected by the permission.

FIGURE 9-2
Flow of AGDLP Strategy

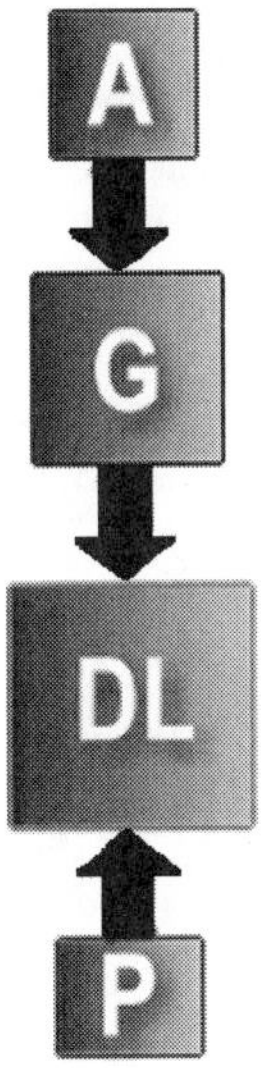

Lesson 9.4 Create Groups

EXERCISE

9.1

Create a Group

To perform this exercise, you will need:

■ Access to a domain controller

■ To know the naming convention for groups on your network

1. Log on as administrator.

2. Click the Start button.

3. Point to **Administrative Tools.**

4. Click **Active Directory Users and Computers.**

5. In the console tree, right-click the container object (OU or group) that will contain the new group.

FIGURE 9-3
New Object—Group Dialog Box

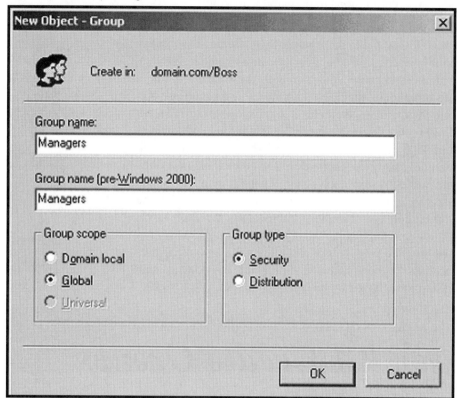

6. Point to **New.**

7. Select **Group.**

   ■ The New Object—Group dialog box appears (see Figure 9-3).

8. Enter the name of the group (must be unique in the container).

9. Click **Finish.**

10. Click on the container object to view the new group account.

11. Repeat steps 5–9 for each group to be created.

ADD MEMBERS TO A GROUP

Once your groups are created, you are ready to start adding objects to the group.

FIGURE 9-4

The Select Users, Contacts, or Computers Dialog Box for the Managers Group

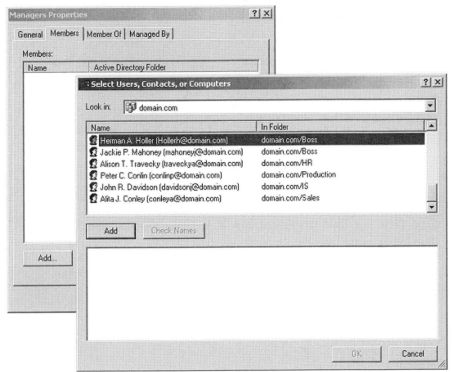

EXERCISE

9.2

Add Members to a Group

To perform this exercise, you will need:

■ Access to a domain controller

■ Existing groups and user accounts

1. Log on as administrator.

2. Click the Start button.

3. Point to **Administrative Tools.**

4. Click **Active Directory Users and Computers.**

5. In the console tree, right-click the group to which you want to add members.

6. Select **Properties.**

■ The Group Properties dialog box is displayed.

7. Click the **Members** tab.

8. Click the **Add** button.

■ The Select Users, Contacts, or Computers dialog box appears (see Figure 9-4).

9. Using the Look in: pull-down list button, select the domain from which to display user accounts and groups.

   ■ The **Entire Directory** option in this list allows you to view user accounts and groups from anywhere in Active Directory.

10. Click on the object that you want to be a member of the group.

11. Click the **Add** button.

   ■ The object is then displayed in the lower pane (see Figure 9-5).

12. Repeat steps 9–11 for additional accounts or groups to be added to this group.

13. Click **OK** to add the members.

   ■ The Managers group properties window now displays the new members.

14. Click **OK** to close the Properties dialog box.

TIP

You can perform the process described in Exercise 9.2 by starting with the user account or group to be added. Right-click on the object to be added, and select **Properties.** Click on the **Member Of** tab, and select the group(s) of which you want the object to be a member. This is the most efficient method when adding a single user account or group to multiple groups.

FIGURE 9-5
User Accounts Being Added to a Group

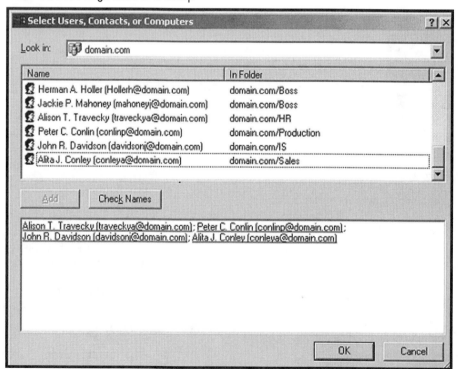

Lesson 9.5 Identify Built-in Groups

Built-in groups are created during installation and are designed to save an administrator time in creating commonly used groups. Even though the user rights and group membership are predetermined in built-in groups, the administrator has the option of changing the properties of any built-in group. Some built-in groups may never be used, depending on the particular situation. Three additional categories of built-in groups—global, domain local, and system—are created when Windows 2000 Server installs.

Built-in Global Groups

In addition to creating a group, Windows 2000 may also add members to the group. Global groups put common types of users together. These predetermined user accounts could be removed from a built-in global group, or additional user accounts can be added to a built-in global group. Although these built-in groups do not have any inherent rights, rights and permissions can be granted by adding the global group to a local domain group or by assigning specific rights to the global group. Table 9-4 describes the most commonly used built-in global groups.

TABLE 9-4 MEMBERSHIPS IN COMMONLY USED BUILT-IN GLOBAL GROUPS

GLOBAL GROUP NAME	DESCRIPTION
Domain Users	Each new domain user account is a member, as is the administrator. This group is automatically added to the Users domain local group.
Domain Admins	The administrator account is a member. This group is automatically added to the Administrators domain local group.
Domain Guests	The guest account is a member. This group is automatically added to the Guests domain local group.
Enterprise Admins	Add user accounts to this group for users who should have administrative control for the entire network. Then add this group to the Administrators domain local group in each domain. The administrator account is a member.

TABLE 9-5 COMMONLY USED BUILT-IN DOMAIN LOCAL GROUPS

DOMAIN LOCAL GROUP NAME	DESCRIPTION
Account Operators	Members can create, delete, and modify user accounts and groups. Members cannot modify the Administrators group or any other operators groups.
Server Operators	Members can share disk resources and can back up and restore files on a domain controller.
Print Operators	Members can set up and manage network printers on domain controller.
Administrators	Members can perform all administrative tasks on all domain controllers and the domain itself. The Administrator account and the Domain Admins global group are members.
Guests	Members can only perform tasks for which they have been granted rights. Members cannot make permanent changes to their desktop (colors, wallpaper, shortcuts, etc.). The Guest user account and the Domain Guests global group are members.
Backup Operators	Members can back up and restore all domain controller's using Windows Backup.
Users	Members can only perform tasks for which they have been granted rights and can gain access to only those resources to which they have been assigned permissions. This group should be used to assign permissions that apply to every user with a user account in your domain.

Built-in Domain Local Groups

Domain local groups provide users with user rights and permissions to perform tasks on domain controllers and in Active Directory. You add user accounts or global groups to domain local groups in order to give predefined rights and permissions to those accounts. Table 9-5 describes domain local groups and the capabilities they give their members. As you read through the descriptions, consider how these groups could be beneficial to a busy administrator.

Built-in System Groups

Every computer running Windows 2000 has built-in system groups. You cannot modify the specific membership in built-in system groups, but they can represent different users at different times. Windows 2000 bases system group membership on how the computer is accessed, not on who uses the computer. Table 9-6 describes the most commonly used built-in system groups.

TABLE 9-6 COMMONLY USED BUILT-IN SYSTEM GROUPS

SYSTEM GROUP NAME	DESCRIPTION
Everyone	Includes all users who access the computer.
Authenticated Users	Includes all users with a valid user account on the computer or in Active Directory. Use the Authenticated Users group instead of the Everyone group to prevent anonymous access to a resource.
Creator Owner	Includes the user account for the user who created or took ownership of a resource. If a member of the Administrators group creates a resource, the Administrators group is owner of the resource.
Network	Includes any user with a current connection from another computer on the network to a shared resource on the computer.
Interactive	Includes the user account for the user who is logged on at the computer.
Anonymous Logon	Includes any user account that Windows 2000 did not authenticate (for example, it may have been authenticated by a Windows NT machine).
Dialup	Includes any user who currently has a dial-up connection.

Summary

Groups simplify administration of resources by placing together users who perform similar tasks or who are working on a shared project. The administrator can make adjustments to permissions and can apply those changes to the group, as opposed to having to apply the change to each user account individually. Group scope provides for maximum flexibility in how groups are allowed to have (or are restricted from having) access to network resources. Group scope is particularly important in large organizations where forest-wide interactions occur. Groups are created using the **Active Directory Users and Computers** console. When creating a group, you choose the container object that will hold the group. When a user account becomes a member of a group, the account is given the permissions that are applied to the group. Built-in groups are created during installation and save an administrator time in setting up commonly used groups.

REVIEW EXERCISE

These questions will help you determine if you have learned enough to move on to the next chapter. If the graphic next to the option is a square (❏), there can be more than one answer for that question. If the graphic is a circle (○), there is only one correct answer. Color in the shape(s) to indicate your answer(s).

1. What is the name of the strategy that provides the most flexibility and reduces the complexity of assigning network resources?

   a. ○ AGDLP

   b. ○ ADLPG

   c. ○ APGDL

   d. ○ DLGPA

2. Wendy is a member of the administrators local group on her computer. What does this allow her to do?

   a. ❏ Become a member of the domain admins group

   b. ❏ Set permissions for access to resources on her computer

   c. ❏ Create domain local groups

   d. ❏ Perform backups and restores on her computer

3. Which console is used to create groups?

   a. ○ Active Directory Accounts and Groups

   b. ○ Active Directory Sites and Replication

   c. ○ Active Directory Users and Computers

   d. ○ Active Directory Management Resource

4. Andrew is an administrator who is responsible for creating groups for the domain. On one particularly stressful day, he was in such a rush that he used the following process: He put the user accounts into global group, then he set permissions on the global group. Lastly, he added the global group to a domain local group. Where did he go wrong?

   a. ❏ He should have added the global group to the user account.

   b. ❏ He should have set permissions on the domain local group, not the global group.

   c. ❏ He should have put the domain local group into the global group after the permissions were set.

   d. ❏ He should have taken a break and, when he returned refreshed, used the AGDLP strategy.

5. Which scope is not available in a mixed mode domain?

   a. ○ universal

   b. ○ Global

   c. ○ Domain Local

PERFORMANCE CHALLENGES

......

Without looking at Table 9-2, fill in the missing elements of the following table:

GROUP SCOPES FOR SECURITY GROUP MEMBERSHIP

GROUP SCOPE	IN NATIVE MODE, CAN CONTAIN	IN MIXED MODE, CAN CONTAIN	CAN BE A MEMBER OF	PERMISSIONS CAN BE GRANTED FOR
Universal	From any domain in the forest: • _____ • Global groups • _____ _____ _____	Not applicable	In any domain: • Domain local • _____ groups	All domains in the forest
Global	From the same domain: • _____ • Global groups	From the same domain: • User accounts	In any domain: • Universal • Domain local groups In the same domain: • _____ _____	_____ _____
Domain local	From any domain in the forest: • User accounts • Global groups • _____ _____ From the same domain: • _____ groups	From any domain: • _____ • Global groups	In the same domain: • Domain local groups	The domain in which the _____ _____ group exists

IMPLEMENT SECURITY

OBJECTIVES

After completing this chapter, you should be able to:

- Define standard NTFS folder and file permissions

- Understand the results of setting conflicting permissions

- Assign file permissions on a folder or file

- Assign share permissions on a network resource

- Understand how to take ownership of a file

- Explain how permissions are affected by copying and moving files

- Describe the differences between the various security policies in Windows 2000 Server

- Use the Security Settings/Account Policies console

- Launch the System Policy Editor

OUTLINE

Introduction

What would happen if everyone in town knew your PIN number for access to your bank account through ATM machines? In a perfect world, your money would still be safe. In the real world, we must protect our valuables from unauthorized access. Just as keeping your PIN number a secret protects your money, the security mechanisms in an operating system protect network resources. Security is a growing concern among computerized companies, and there are two different approaches to security: optimistic and pessimistic. The optimistic approach assumes a high trust level for network users and only restricts access to information they do not need or should not have. The pessimistic approach assumes a lower level of trust and restricts access to *everything* except what the users specifically need to do their work. Knowing which approach is best for your situation helps to define a security implementation strategy. Users probably prefer the optimistic approach, while administrators lean towards the pessimistic. This chapter provides information on how to implement security on a network.

TABLE 10-1 FOUR SECURITY ELEMENTS IN WINDOWS 2000

SECURITY ELEMENT	DESCRIPTION
NTFS Permissions	Specify which users and groups can have access to files and folders. Also determines what the user can do with the contents of the file or folder.
Share Permissions	Used to make folders available to network users by allowing them to connect to the folder and gain access to the folder's contents. Permissions control what level of access they are given.
Policies	Policies are methods for defining the user's environment. For example, the *group policy* can control what programs are available to the user and what appears on their desktop. *Software policies* can enable or disable options in an application's menus. There are even *security policies* that allow you to configure security settings for particular computers and groups.
Auditing	The process of monitoring both user activities and operating system activities on a computer.

Lesson 10.1 Elements of Windows 2000 Security

Security settings define the security-relevant behavior of the system. The term *security setting* is interchangeable with security configuration. Security settings include security policies (account and local policies), access control (services, files, and registry), event log, group membership (restricted groups), Internet protocol security policies, and public key policies.

Windows 2000 provides a variety of security configuration options from which the network administrator can choose. You already have been introduced to the gatekeeper—the logon process. Once a user is logged on, there are additional security settings that control what resources a user has access to and what actions the user can perform. The security elements you will study in this chapter are listed in Table 10-1.

Lesson 10.2 Understand NTFS Permissions

New *Technology File System,* or **NTFS,** was a file system created specifically for Windows NT. Compared to previous file systems such as the FAT (File Allocation Table) file system, NTFS offered the following protective features to ensure the reliable storage and retrieval of data:

- **Fault Tolerance:** NTFS logs all changes that are made to the file system and can redo or undo every file or directory update to correct discrepancies from system failures or power losses. NTFS can also repair hard disk problems "on the fly" with a process called **hot fixing.** After every write to a hard disk, the sector is reread to verify its integrity. If the data are different, the sector is flagged as bad and the write is performed again to a different place. This occurs without the application ever being informed of a hard drive problem, so the user will not see an error message.

- **Security:** Permission to use a file or directory can be maintained for each file, if necessary. Auditing capabilities assist the administrator in tracking the files.

- **File and Partition Sizes:** NTFS can store files up to 16 exabytes (2^{64} power) in length.

- **File Compression:** NTFS provides real-time file compression. File compression removes redundancy from files, thereby decreasing their physical size, and compresses on a file-by-file basis (if corruption occurs, it only affects one file). File compression can compress or decompress individual files or all files in a directory.

- **Performance:** To decrease fragmentation, NTFS always attempts to save files in contiguous blocks. It also implements a B-tree directory structure (rather than the linked list directory structure used by the FAT system), which speeds file access and reduces the possibility of a missing link resulting in data loss.

- **Disk Quotas:** The newest version of NTFS (included in Windows 2000) also includes disk quotas that can be used to limit the amount of hard disk space a user is allowed to use for storage.

NTFS permissions are used to specify which users and groups can have access to files and folders. Once they have access, NTFS can also control what actions they are allowed to perform on the contents of the file or folder. There are some differences between permissions for folders and permissions for files. In addition, NTFS permissions are only available on volumes formatted for NTFS. If you access a file or folder on a different file system (FAT or FAT32, for example), the Permissions options on the dialog boxes will be grayed-out.

TABLE 10-2 NTFS FOLDER PERMISSIONS

PERMISSION	USERS CAN
Read	See a list of files and subfolders in the folder. They can view folder ownership, permissions, and attributes.
Write	Create new files and subfolders within the folder. They can change folder attributes and view folder ownership and permissions.
List Folder Contents	See the names of files and subfolders in the folder.
Read & Execute	Move through folders to open other files and folders, even if they do not have permission to use those folders. They can perform actions permitted by the Read and List Folder Contents permissions.
Modify	Delete the folder plus perform actions permitted by the Write and Read & Execute permissions.
Full Control	Change permissions, take ownership, and delete subfolders and files. They can also perform actions permitted by all other folder permissions.

Folder Permissions

Permissions assigned to folders control the access that users have to the folder and to the files and subfolders contained within the folder. Table 10-2 lists the permissions that can be assigned to a folder.

Giving a user account or group Full Control permissions over a folder is an act of bravery and is rarely done, for most users do not need that level of control over the folder. For example, consider the following scenario: Christy is the project manager for an important project that required the creation of an elaborate structure of folders. Within the folders there are hundreds of files that were created by various members of the project team. One evening after having worked for 10 hours, Christy inadvertently right-clicks on the top folder of the structure and selects "Delete." Windows 2000 asks if she is sure, and she confirms her request (thinking she is deleting just one folder). The entire structure and all of its files are sent to the Recycle Bin. You know that it is fairly easy to recover items from the Recycle Bin only if the user has not emptied the Recycle Bin before the restore can occur. If the user has emptied the Recycle Bin, you might then have to go to the backup tape archives to retrieve the files. If the files were not backed up within the last 10 hours, Christy will have lost that work. With Full Control, the user can change the permissions so that not even an administrator can view the contents (fortunately, administrators can take ownership and change the permission back to something more reasonable). Thus, you should carefully consider folder permissions, and you should have a very good reason for granting Full Control.

TABLE 10-3 NTFS FILE PERMISSIONS

PERMISSION	USERS CAN
Read	Open the file and read it and view file attributes, ownership, and permissions
Write	Overwrite the file (save changes), change file attributes, view file ownership and permissions
Read & Execute	Run applications and perform actions permitted by the Read permission
Modify	Make changes to the file, delete the file, and perform the actions permitted by the Write and the Read & Execute permissions
Full Control	Change permissions, take ownership, delete the file, and perform actions permitted by all other file permissions

There are times when you do not want a particular user account or group to have any access whatsoever to a folder or file. To deny all access to a folder, deny the Full Control permission for that user account or group. If these users try to access the folder, the system will deliver an "Access Denied" message.

File Permissions

File permissions control the access users have to files and folders. Table 10-3 lists the NTFS file permissions.

Lesson 10.3 Assign Permissions

Administrators, the owners of the file or folder, and users with Full Control permission are allowed to assign NTFS permissions. Remember that administrators can take either an optimistic or a pessimistic approach to security when assigning permissions. Although users may become frustrated and unable to do their work if the permissions are too restrictive or improperly assigned, too many users setting permissions can also present problems.

Access Control List

Every file and folder has an **Access Control List (ACL)** that contains a list of all of the user accounts and groups that have been given the permission to access the file or folder. The ACL also lists what type of access each user account or group has been given. The individual entries in the ACL are called **Access Control Entries (ACE).** When a user attempts to access a file or folder,

NTFS checks the ACL for an ACE that shows either the user's user account or a group to which that user account belongs. If no ACE exists, the user is not allowed access. If there is an ACE, the action the user is trying to perform (Write, for example) must also be listed.

Multiple Permissions

Permissions can be set for a single user account and for each group to which the user account belongs. Sometimes these permissions are different. The user account, for example, may be only allowed to Read the file, but one of the groups to which the user account belongs also may be able to Write to the file. Which permission should the user receive: Read or Write, neither or both? Rules and priorities govern decisions about whether the user should receive Read permission, Write permission, neither, or both.

PERMISSIONS ARE CUMULATIVE

In the previous paragraph's scenario, the user would have both Read and Write permission on the file because varying permissions are cumulative, or added together. The user's *effective permissions* for a file or folder are the sum of the NTFS permissions that were assigned to the user account and to all of the groups to which the user belongs.

FILE PERMISSIONS OVERRIDE FOLDER PERMISSIONS

File permissions have a higher priority than folder permissions. A user with permissions to access a file will be able to access the file even if he or she does not have the permission to access the folder containing the file.

DENY OVERRIDES OTHER PERMISSIONS

If a user account has Full Control but one of the groups to which the user belongs has a Deny permission assigned, the user will not have access. Because the Deny permission overrides all other permissions, it is not a favorable way of controlling access to resources and should be used with care. For example, deny could be used if an employee is fired and you want to protect the network from intentional sabotage or if the file is extremely sensitive in nature (containing employee salaries, for example).

Inheritance of Permissions

Just like you inherited your physical attributes from your ancestors through your parents, files and subfolders inherit permissions from their parent folder. The permissions that are assigned to a parent folder are automatically given to both existing files and newly created files or subfolders within the parent folder.

Prevent inheritance of permissions by deselecting a checkbox on the Security tab of the Properties dialog box (see Figure 10-1). The folder at which you prevent permissions inheritance becomes the new parent folder, and permissions

MICROSOFT EXAM OBJECTIVE

Monitor, configure, troubleshoot, and control access to files, folders, and shared folders.

assigned to that folder are passed on to the files and subfolders contained within the new parent folder.

Assigning NTFS Permissions

You use Windows Explorer to assign permissions to a folder or file.

FIGURE 10-1
Setting Inheritance on the Security Tab of a Folder's Properties Dialog Box

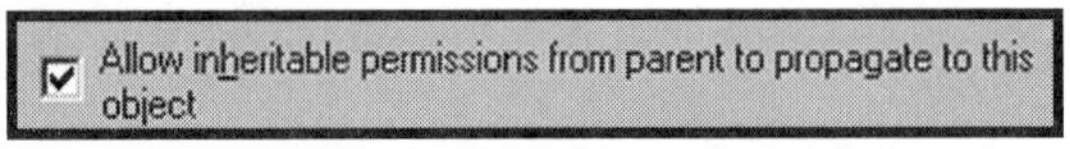

☑ Allow inheritable permissions from parent to propagate to this object

EXERCISE

10.1 Assigning NTFS Permissions to a Folder

● ●

To perform this exercise, you will need:

■ Access to a domain controller

■ An existing folder

1. Log on as an administrator.

2. Click the Start button.

3. Point to **Programs.**

4. Point to **Accessories.**

5. Click **Windows Explorer.**

6. Right-click on the folder to which permissions will be assigned.

7. Select **Properties.**

■ The folder's Properties dialog box is displayed.

8. Click the **Security** tab (see Figure 10-2).

■ The existing security settings are displayed.

■ Notice that you cannot change the permissions for an adminis-

trator's account, except to deny permission to the administrator (which is not a good idea).

9. Click the **Add** button.

■ The Select Users, Computers, or Groups dialog box is displayed.

10. Click on the name of the user account or group that will be given permission to access this folder.

11. Click the **Add** button.

■ The name of the user account or group appears in the lower pane.

12. Click **OK** to exit the Select Users, Computers, or Groups dialog box.

■ The name you selected in step 10 appears in the upper window of the **Security** tab.

13. Click on the name of the user account or group you added in step 10.

■ Notice the lower pane displays the permissions given to the parent folder (see Figure 10-3).

FIGURE 10-2
Security Tab for Setting Permissions on a Folder

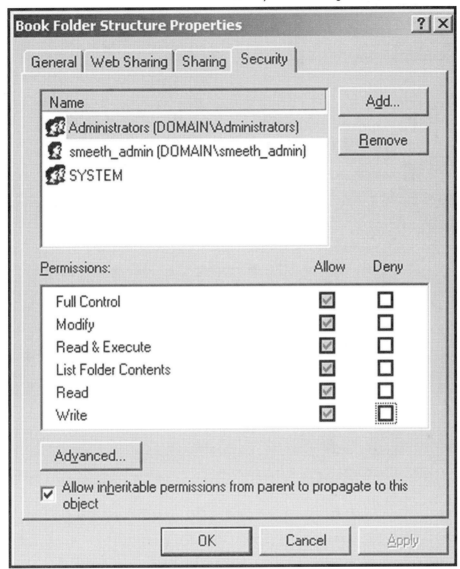

14. Adjust the permissions settings according to security needs.

15. Click **OK** to close the Properties dialog box.

Whenever possible, you should set permissions on a folder and let the inheritance take care of setting the permissions. Sometimes, though, it is necessary to assign permissions for a single file.

FIGURE 10-3
Security Tab with Newly Added User Account

Book Folder Structure Properties　　　　　? X

General | Web Sharing | Sharing | Security

Name　　　　　　　　　　　　　　　　　Add...
  Administrators (DOMAIN\Administrators)
  Peter C. Conlin (conlinp@domain.com)　　Remove
  smeeth_admin (DOMAIN\smeeth_admin)
  SYSTEM

Permissions:　　　　　　　　　　　Allow　　Deny

	Allow	Deny
Full Control	☐	☐
Modify	☐	☐
Read & Execute	☑	☐
List Folder Contents	☑	☐
Read	☑	☐
Write	☐	☐

Advanced...

☑ Allow inheritable permissions from parent to propagate to this object

OK　　　Cancel　　　Apply

EXERCISE

10.2 Assigning NTFS Permissions to a File

• •

To perform this exercise, you will need:　　■ An existing file

■ Access to a domain controller　　　**1.** Log on as an administrator.

2. Click the Start button.

3. Point to **Programs.**

4. Point to **Accessories.**

5. Click **Windows Explorer.**

6. Right-click on the folder to which permissions will be assigned.

7. Select **Properties.**

- The file's Properties dialog box is displayed.

8. Click the **Security** tab.

- The existing security settings are displayed.
- Notice the difference in the available permissions as compared to the permissions on a folder.

9. Click the **Add** button.

- The Select Users, Computers, or Groups dialog box is displayed.

10. Click on the name of the user account or group that will be given permission to access this folder.

11. Click the **Add** button.

- The name of the user account or group appears in the lower pane.

12. Click **OK** to exit the Select Users, Computers, or Groups dialog box.

- The name you selected in step 10 appears in the upper window of the Security tab.

13. Click on the name of the user account or group you added in step 10.

- Notice the lower pane displays the permissions given to the parent folder.

14. Adjust the permissions settings according to security needs.

15. Click **OK** to close the Properties dialog box.

Taking Ownership

The owner of a folder or file has Full Control permission and also has the ability to change permissions. Ownership of folders and files can be transferred from one user account or group to another user account or group. An administrator can take ownership of any file or folder, regardless of the set permissions. If an administrator takes ownership, the administrator's group owns the file or folder.

The current owner or any user with Full Control permissions can assign the Full Control permission or the Take Ownership **special access permission.** Special access permissions enable users to change permissions and take ownership of folders and files. Exercise 10.3 demonstrates how to set the Take Ownership permission, and Exercise 10.4 shows you how to take ownership. You must do this in two steps because ownership cannot be assigned; instead, the file must be set to allow a user account or group to take ownership and then the user or group member must take ownership.

> **MICROSOFT EXAM OBJECTIVE**
>
> Monitor, configure, troubleshoot, and control local security on files and folders.

10.3

Setting the Take Ownership Special Access Permission

• •

To perform this exercise, you will need:

■ Access to a domain controller

■ An existing file

1. Log on as an administrator.

2. Click the Start button.

3. Point to **Programs.**

4. Point to **Accessories.**

5. Click **Windows Explorer.**

6. Right-click on the file to which permissions will be assigned.

7. Select **Properties.**

   ■ The file's Properties dialog box is displayed.

8. Click the **Security** tab.

   ■ The existing security settings are displayed.

9. Click the **Advanced** button.

   ■ The Access Control Settings dialog box is displayed.

10. Click on the user account or group that will be granted the Take Ownership permission.

11. Click the **View/Edit** button.

   ■ The Permission Entry dialog box appears.

12. Click in the checkbox for **Take Ownership** at the bottom of the list in the Allow column.

   ■ A checkmark appears in the checkbox.

13. Click **OK** to close the Permission Entry dialog box.

14. Click **OK** to close the Access Control Settings dialog box.

15. Click **OK** to close the Properties dialog box.

10.4

Taking Ownership of a File

• •

To perform this exercise, you will need:

■ Access to a domain controller

■ The file used in Exercise 10.3

1. Log on as the user you designated to take ownership (step 10 of Exercise 10.3).

2. Click the Start button.

3. Point to **Programs.**

4. Point to **Accessories.**

5. Click **Windows Explorer.**

6. Right-click on the file to which permissions will be assigned.

7. Select **Properties.**

   ■ The file's Properties dialog box is displayed.

8. Click the **Security** tab.

   ■ The existing security settings are displayed.

9. Click the **Advanced** button.

   ■ The Access Control Settings dialog box is displayed.

10. Click on the **Owner** tab.

    ■ The Owner dialog box appears.

11. In the **Change Owner To** list, click on the name of the user account or group that will take ownership of the file (see Figure 10-4).

12. Click **OK** to close the Owner dialog box.

FIGURE 10-4
Taking Ownership in the Access Control Settings Dialog Box

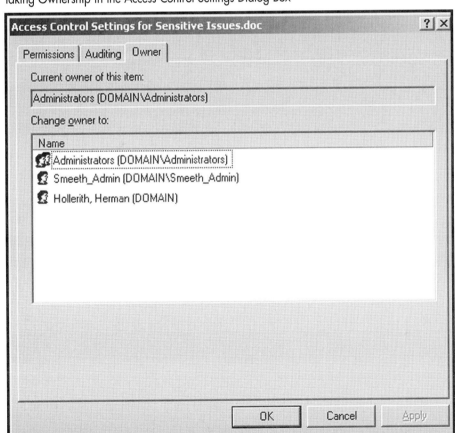

13. Click **OK** to close the Access Control Settings dialog box.

14. Click **OK** to close the Properties dialog box.

Lesson 10.4 How Copy and Move Affect Permissions

The process of copying and moving files and folders is a very common task for administrators. Although it seems logical that the permissions you set on a file would stay the same when you copy the file to another location, sometimes they stay the same and sometimes they change. Initially this may seem to be a disadvantage, but if you understand the rules that control permission transfers, you can use them to your advantage. The most important detail to keep in mind when you copy or move files is the original location of the file and the destination location (to which the file will be copied or moved). Table 10-4 and Table 10-5 along with Figure 10-5 and Figure 10-6 demonstrate the rules. The file used as an example in these tables is contained in a folder named "Q" on the C: drive. Drives C: and D: are formatted as NTFS, and drive E: is formatted as FAT. In all of the cases listed in Table 10-4 and Table 10-5, you must have the Write permission for the destination folder and you must have the Modify permission for the source folder or file.

TABLE 10-4 HOW COPYING A FILE AFFECTS ITS PERMISSIONS

ORIGINAL LOCATION	NEW LOCATION	RESULTS
Folder Q on drive C:	Folder U on drive C:	Permissions are changed to match the permissions for Folder U.
Folder Q on drive C:	Folder V on Drive D:	Permissions are changed to match the permissions for Folder V.
Folder Q on drive C:	Folder W on Drive E:	Permissions are lost. There are no NTFS permissions on a FAT file system.

TABLE 10-5 HOW MOVING A FILE AFFECTS ITS PERMISSIONS

ORIGINAL LOCATION	NEW LOCATION	RESULTS
Folder Q on drive C:	Folder U on drive C:	Permissions do not change.
Folder Q on drive C:	Folder V on Drive D:	Permissions are changed to match the permissions for Folder V.
Folder Q on drive C:	Folder W on Drive E:	Permissions are lost. There are no NTFS permissions on a FAT file system.

FIGURE 10-5
How Copying Affects Permissions

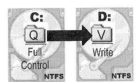
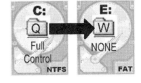

Copy

FIGURE 10-6
How Moving Affects Permissions

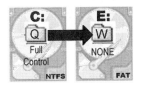
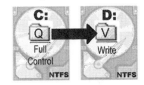

Move

Lesson 10.5 Understand Shared Folder Permissions

When a folder is configured as shared, other users can connect to the folder over the network and gain access to the contents of the folder. What they are able to do with the contents of the folder is controlled by permissions, as listed in Table 10-6.

Shared folder permissions have the following characteristics:

- Shared folder permissions apply only to a parent folder and not to the files or subfolders contained within it. Because of this, shared folder permissions provide less detailed security than NTFS permissions.

- Shared folder permissions are only effective when accessed across the network. They do not restrict access to users who gain access from the local computer.

TABLE 10-6 SHARED FOLDER PERMISSIONS

PERMISSION	USERS CAN
Read	Display folder names, file names, file data, and attributes; run program files; and change folders within the shared folder
Change	Create folders, add files to folders, change data in files, append data to files, change file attributes, delete folders and files, and perform the actions permitted by the Read permission
Full Control	Change permissions, take ownership, delete the file, and perform actions permitted by the Change permission

■ Shared folder permissions are the only way to secure network resources on a FAT volume.

■ The default shared folder permission is Full Control, and it is assigned to the Everyone group when the folder is shared. (You can change this, of course.)

Multiple Shared Folder Permissions

One user can be a member of multiple groups, with each group having various share permissions. When one user is a member of two groups with differing share permissions, the user's *effective permissions* are cumulative; that is, they are added together. For example, if Josva belongs to a group with Read access and also belongs to a group with Change access, Josva gets Change (Change includes Read). The exception to this addition is the Deny permission. Deny overrides all other permissions, even Full Control. If any group to which the user belongs has a Deny permission, the user will not have access.

NTFS Permissions and Shared Folder Permissions

Shared folder permissions secure resources on a FAT file system. However, when shared folders are used on an NTFS volume, they must also have the appropriate NTFS permissions applied. When a shared folder permission and an NTFS permission are different, the *most restrictive* permission is applied.

When Shared Folders Are Copied or Moved

When a shared folder is copied, the original folder is still shared but the copied folder is not shared. When a shared folder is moved, the folder is no longer shared.

EXERCISE

10.5   Sharing a Folder

• •

To perform this exercise, you will need:

■ Access to a domain controller

■ An existing folder

1. Log on as an administrator.

2. Click the Start button.

3. Point to **Programs.**

4. Point to **Accessories.**

5. Click **Windows Explorer.**

6. Right-click on the folder to be shared.

7. From the Context menu, select **Sharing. . . .**

■ The **Sharing** tab of the folder's Properties dialog box is displayed.

8. Click on the **Share this folder** radio button.

9. Enter a name for the share (make it user-friendly and less than 12 characters in length).

10. Enter a comment if additional information is needed.

11. Decide the number of users that can be connected to the share simultaneously or accept the maximum.

12. Click the **Permissions** button.

■ The Share Permissions dialog box appears (see Figure 10-7).

■ Notice the default settings for a shared folder.

13. Click the **Add** button to add user accounts or groups to the list of who can access the shared folder.

14. Click on the user account or group you added in step 13.

15. Adjust the permissions in the lower pane as necessary for security.

16. Repeat steps 14 and 15 for each user account or group you added in step 13.

17. Click **OK** to close the Permissions dialog box.

18. Click **OK** to close the Properties dialog box.

MICROSOFT EXAM OBJECTIVE

Monitor, configure, troubleshoot, and control access to files and folders in a shared folder.

FIGURE 10-7
Share Permissions for a Folder

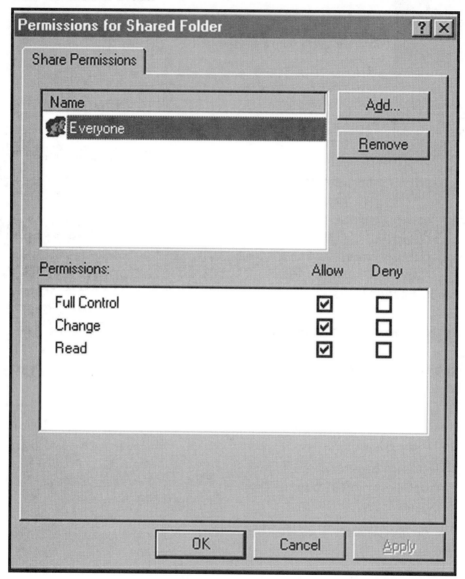

Lesson 10.6 Configure Policies

Policies are often defined by companies when they need to control how their processes function. For example, a company might have a hiring policy that includes such entries as not hiring on the basis of race or sex.

Their equal opportunity employment policy helps define how hiring will be done. Policies are more than rules; they are definitions of how something will function, and they provide boundaries and control interactions. In the Windows 2000 environment, most of the policies address security concerns. This lesson gives an overview of the most common policies. Exercise 10.6 helps you launch one of the consoles necessary for setting policies.

MICROSOFT EXAM OBJECTIVE

Implement, configure, manage, and troubleshoot policies in a Windows 2000 environment, including Local policy, System policy, and Account Policy.

EXERCISE

10.6 Launching the Security Settings/Account Policies Console

To perform this exercise, you will need:

■ Access to a domain controller

1. Log on as an administrator.

2. Click the Start button.

3. Point to **Programs.**

4. Point to **Administrative Tools.**

5. Click **Local Security Policy.**

■ The secpol (Security Settings/Account Policies) window appears.

Account Policies

Account policies apply to user accounts, and this security area contains attributes for the following:

■ **Password policy:** For domain or local user accounts, this policy determines settings for passwords such as how long a password is valid.

■ **Account lockout policy:** For domain or local user accounts, this policy determines when and for whom an account will be locked out of the system. For example, if a user is unsuccessful in logging on after three attempts, that user is locked out of the system and would have to contact the administrator for assistance.

- **Kerberos policy:** For domain user accounts, this policy determines Kerberos-related settings, such as ticket lifetimes and enforcement.

Account policies should not be configured for organizational units that do not contain any computers, since organizational units that contain only users will always receive an account policy from the domain.

Windows 2000 only allows one domain account policy, and that account policy is applied to the root domain of the domain tree. Any Windows 2000 workstation or server that is a member of the domain will use the domain account policy by default. The only exception to this rule is when another account policy is defined for an organizational unit. The account policy settings for the organizational unit have an effect on the local policy on any computers contained in the organizational unit.

Exercise 10.7 will demonstrate how to change one of the settings for an account policy. One of the security concerns during the logon process is someone attempting to enter the system without knowing a valid username and password. The Account Lockout Policy allows you to set how many attempts a user will have before the user is locked out of the system. If a user is locked out, a call to an administrator will remedy the situation.

> **TERMINOLOGY**
>
> **Kerberos** is an Internet security standard protocol for handling authentication of user or system identity. The latest version of Kerberos is V5. With Kerberos V5, passwords sent across network lines are not just plain text; they are encrypted. There are other security features as well. Windows 2000 uses Kerberos to enhance security. A **ticket** is given to a user who wants to authenticate to a specific service in the domain.

EXERCISE

10.7 Setting an Account Lockout Policy

● ●

To perform this exercise, you will need:

- Access to a domain controller
- To complete the steps in Exercise 10.6

1. Double-click **Account Policies** in the tree pane.

   - The tree expands to show the three subfolders.

2. Click on **Account Lockout Policy.**

   - The right pane shows the settings for lockouts.

3. Double-click on **Account lockout threshold.**

   - The Local Security Policy for Account lockout threshold appears (see Figure 10-8).

FIGURE 10-8
Setting the Account Lockout Policy

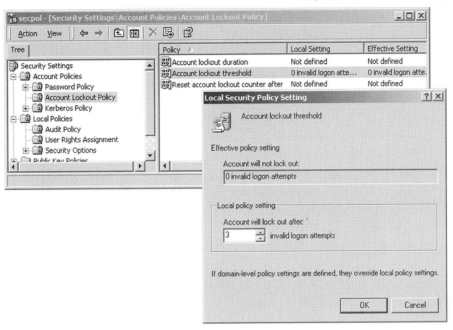

- Notice that the default setting is 0, which means that the user would not be locked out regardless of the number of times he or she tried to log on.

4. Either type **3** in the "Account will lockout:" text box or use the spin box arrows.

5. Click **OK.**

   This process of expanding the tree, selecting the policy heading, double-clicking the desired policy, and adjusting the settings in the dialog box is the same process you would use to modify any policy. The scope of this book does not allow for in-depth coverage of every policy option.

CAUTION: Modifying policies without a full knowledge of how the change will affect the system is dangerous. Policies can be far-reaching and challenging to troubleshoot should they cause problems. As a student in this course, you can browse through the individual policies, but you should not make any changes unless your instructor allows you to do so.

Local Policies

Local policies apply to the local computer and are based on the computer the user is logged into and the rights the user has on that particular computer. This security area contains attributes for the following:

- **Audit policy:** This policy determines which security events are logged into the Security log on the computer (successful attempts, failed attempts, or both). The Security log is a part of **Event Viewer** (which will be discussed in Chapter 11).

- **User rights assignment:** This policy determines which users or groups have logon or task privileges on the computer.

- **Security options:** This policy enables or disables security settings for the computer, such as Administrator and Guest account names, floppy drive and CD ROM access, driver installation, and logon prompts.

AUDITING

In the course of a day, users on an average-sized network can perform thousands of actions. Most of those actions are mundane, but some have an adverse effect on the network. Auditing is a way to record and evaluate specific actions the users are performing. For example, if a user is unsuccessful at logging in, that action can be recorded in an audit log file. Upon examination of the log, you could determine who was trying to log on, at what computer the user's attempt was made, and even the time of the user's attempt. You can audit both successful and failed attempts at actions.

> **MICROSOFT EXAM OBJECTIVE**
>
> Implement, configure, manage, and troubleshoot auditing.

You would not want to audit *every* action performed on the network, for reviewing all of the log entries would be very time-consuming. Actions are not audited by default, and you must be logged on as an administrator or as a member of the Administrators group to set up auditing of files and folders. If you have the appropriate administrative permissions, you can specify what types of actions are audited. In order to enable auditing, you first establish a local audit policy on the computer where the actions occur, then you choose the actions to audit.

EXERCISE

10.8 Establishing an Audit Policy for Account Logon Events

To perform this exercise, you will need:

- Access to a domain controller

- To complete the steps in Exercise 10.6 (Launching the Security Settings/Account Policies console)

1. Double-click **Account Policies** in the tree pane.

  - The tree expands to show the three subfolders.

2. Click on **Audit Policy.**

  - The right pane shows the settings for audits.

3. Double-click on **Audit account logon events.**

  - The Local Security Policy for Audit account logon events appears (see Figure 10-9).

  - Notice that the default setting is to have neither success nor failure audited.

4. Click in the **Failure** checkbox to audit failed logon attempts.

  - In a large network, you would probably not want to have a log entry made every time a user was successful in logging on.

5. Click **OK.**

FIGURE 10-9
Setting the Audit Policy for Account Logon Attempts

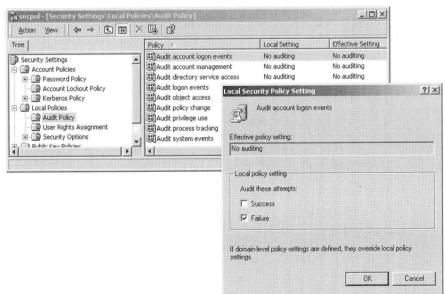

Depending on whether you want to audit Active Directory objects or local objects, you would use one of the following auditing tools.

■ For Active Directory objects, use **Active Directory Users and Computers.**

■ For files and folders, registry keys, and network printers, use the **Security** tab in the object's Properties dialog box. This allows you to specify which types of access to those objects you would like to audit.

Exercise 10.9 demonstrates how to establish an audit for the actions performed on a particular folder by either the Users group or the Domain Users group. You would track the actions on an object anytime you want to know who is accessing the object or trying to access it inappropriately.

EXERCISE

10.9   Establishing an Audit of Actions on a Folder

To perform this exercise, you will need:

■ Access to a Windows 2000 computer (domain controller preferred)

1. Right-click on the folder to be audited.

2. Select **Properties.**

   ■ The folder's Properties dialog box is displayed.

3. Click on the **Security** tab.

   ■ The Security dialog box is displayed.

4. Click the **Advanced** button.

   ■ The Access Control Settings dialog box is displayed.

5. Click on the **Audit** tab.

6. Click on the **Add** button.

■ The Select User, Computer, or Group dialog box appears.

7. Click on the Users group if you are on a workstation, or click on the Domain Users group if you are on a domain controller.

8. Click the **OK** button to close the User, Computer, or Group dialog box.

   ■ The Auditing Entry dialog box appears (see Figure 10-10).

9. Click the appropriate columns (successful or failed) for the access actions you would like to audit.

   ■ By default, the actions are not selected.

   ■ The three actions checked in Figure 10-10 are simply examples of options an administrator could choose.

FIGURE 10-10
The Auditing Entry Dialog Box

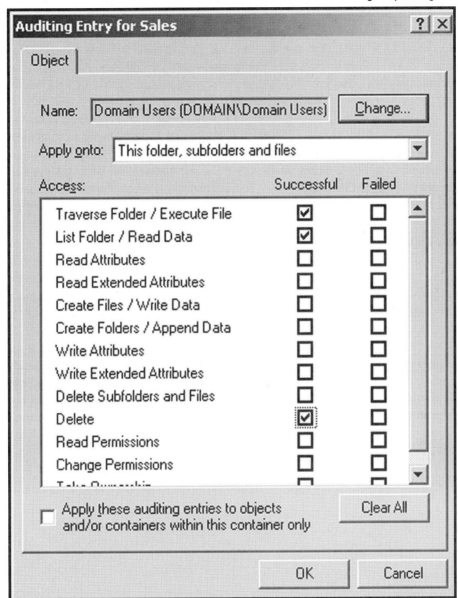

10. Click **OK** to close the Auditing Entry dialog box.

11. Click **OK** to close the Access Control Settings dialog box.

12. Click **OK** to close the folder's Properties dialog box.

USER RIGHTS ASSIGNMENT

User rights give users the authority to perform specific actions at the local level, including logging on to a system interactively or backing up files. Administrators can assign specific rights to group accounts or to individual user accounts. User rights are not the same as permissions because User Rights apply to *user accounts,* whereas permissions apply to *objects.* Assigning user rights is one way that you can delegate or restrict administrative control within a domain.

Although user rights can be given to individual user accounts, it is best to administer them by groups. This ensures that a user logging on as a member of a group automatically inherits the rights associated with that group. If a user is a member of multiple groups, the user's rights are cumulative, which means that the user has more than one set of rights. There are two types of user rights: **privileges** and **logon rights.**

Privileges

When you were a small child, you probably did not have any responsibilities. As you grew in size and understanding, you were given more and more responsibility, and if you proved yourself worthy, you were also given more privileges. You were allowed to do certain things that were usually reserved for an older person. **Privileges** in a Windows 2000 environment can be assigned to users or groups and allow the recipient to perform certain actions on the local computer that would normally be the responsibility of an administrator. Exercise 10.10 will demonstrate how to give the Domain Users group the privilege of changing the system time on the local computer. (You normally would not let users change the system time on the local computer. Most networks are configured to have the workstations get their time setting directly from the domain controllers, which can be configured to get their time directly from an atomic clock facility. This way, all of the computers are on exactly the same time—a very valuable setting when replication occurs.)

EXERCISE

10.10   Assigning Privileges to a Group

To perform this exercise, you will need:

- Access to a domain controller

- To complete the steps in Exercise 10.6 (Launching the Security Settings/Account Policies console)

1. Double-click **Local Policies** in the tree pane.

- The tree expands to show the three subfolders.

2. Click on **User Rights Assignment.**

- The right pane shows all of the user rights that are available.

- Look through the list.

3. Double-click on **Change the system time.**

- The local security policy for **Change the system time** appears.

- The Assigned to: box shows the default groups that can change the system time.

4. Click the **Add** button.

- The Select User, Computer, or Group dialog box appears.

5. Click on the Domain Users group.

6. Click **OK** to exit the Select User, Computer, or Group dialog box.

- The Domain Users group is shown in the Assigned to: box.

- Members of the Domain Users group can now log on to the local computer.

7. Click **OK** to exit the Local Security Policy dialog box.

Some of these privileges can override permissions set on an object. For example, a user logged on to a domain account as a member of the Backup Operators group has the right to perform backup operations for all domain controllers. However, this requires the ability to read all files on those servers, even files on which their owners have set permissions that explicitly deny access to all users. A user right (in this case, the right to perform a backup) takes precedence over all file permissions.

LOGON RIGHTS

Logon rights apply to a user account or group during the logon process. The following list shows the logon rights in the list of the User Rights Assignment policy that can be assigned to a user:

- Access This Computer from Network

- Log On Locally

- Log On as a Batch Job

- Log On as a Service

- Deny Access to This Computer from the Network

- Deny Logon as a Batch Job

- Deny Logon as a Service

- Deny Local Logon

SECURITY OPTIONS

The final entry in the local policies section is security options, which is a list of settings that affect the security of the local computer. Since the best way to understand them is to review the list, Exercise 10.11 demonstrates how to view these Security Options.

EXERCISE

10.11 Viewing Security Options

To perform this exercise, you will need:

■ Access to a domain controller

■ To complete the steps in Exercise 10.6 (Launching the Security Settings/Account Policies console)

1. Double-click **Local Policies** in the tree pane.

■ The tree expands to show the three subfolders.

2. Click on **Security Options.**

■ The right pane shows all of the security options that are available.

■ Look through the list.

3. Exit the Security Settings/Account Policies Console.

Introduction to Group Policy

Users like to decorate their computer desktop almost as much as they like to decorate their offices. While their choice of wallpaper or colors is not significant, there are some settings that are best controlled by an administrator so that the user's system can remain functional and optimized. For example, the options that users have on the Start menu should be those programs that are most beneficial for helping them get their work done. **Group Policy** settings define the contents of the user's desktop environment that an administrator needs to manage. Some of the contents include the programs that are available to users, the programs that appear on the user's desktop, and Start menu options.

To create a specific desktop configuration for a particular group of users, you use the **Group Policy snap-in** in the Microsoft Management Console (covered in Chapter 11). When Group Policy settings are specified, they are contained in a Group Policy object. The Group Policy object is associated with selected Active Directory objects—sites, domains, or organizational units.

Group Policy includes settings for **User Configuration,** which affect users, and settings for **Computer Configuration,** which affect computers.

USER CONFIGURATION

The User Configuration node in Group Policy is used to set policies applying to users, regardless of the computer to which they log on.

User Configuration typically contains subnodes for Software Settings, Windows Settings, and Administrative Templates, but because Group Policy can have snap-in extensions added to or removed from it, the exact set of subnodes you see may be different. User policy (settings located under the **User Configuration** node in Group Policy) is obtained when a user logs on.

COMPUTER CONFIGURATION

Administrators use the Computer Configuration node in Group Policy to set policies that are applied to computers, regardless of who logs onto them.

The Computer Configuration usually contains the subnodes Software Settings, Windows Settings, and Administrative Templates. However, because Group Policy can have extensions added to or removed from it, the exact set of subnodes you see may be different. Computer policy settings are located under **Computer Configuration** and are obtained when a computer boots.

System Policy

Windows NT 4.0 introduced the System Policy Editor, which was used to create a system policy to control user work environment and actions, and to enforce system configuration settings for all computers running Windows NT 4.0. Policies define the various components of the desktop environment, including the applications available to users, the applications that appear on users' desktops, and the entries displayed on the Start menu.

A Windows 2000 version of System Policy Editor (poledit.exe) is available. Whenever possible, it is best to use **Group Policy** instead of System Policy for Windows 2000 clients. Although the functions of the System Policy Editor is largely replaced by Group Policy, it is still useful under the following circumstances:

- **Management of computers running Windows 95 or Windows 98.** The Windows 2000 version of the System Policy Editor must be run locally on computers running Windows 98 or Windows 95 to create Config.pol files compatible with the local operating system.

- **Management of computers running Windows NT 4.0 Workstation and Windows NT 4.0 Server.** These computers also need their own style of .pol file: NTConfig.pol.

- **Management of stand-alone computers running Windows 2000.** A Windows 2000 computer that is not joined to any domain is therefore not subject to non-local Group Policy by way of Active Directory. The only Group Policy that applies to such a computer is local Group Policy, which contains settings for only one user. Only the Windows 2000 version of System Policy Editor is compatible with Windows 2000.

10.12 Exploring the System Policy Editor

• •

To perform this exercise, you will need:

■ Access to a domain controller

1. Log on as administrator.

2. Click the Start button.

3. Select **Run. . . .**

■ The Run dialog box appears.

4. In the "Open" textbox, type **poledit.exe.**

5. Press Enter, or click **OK.**

■ The System Policy Editor window appears.

■ There are two icons: Local Computer and Local User.

6. Double-click on **Local User.**

■ The Local User Properties dialog box appears (see Figure 10-11).

7. Use your mouse to expand and collapse the structure of policy settings.

8. Click the **Cancel** button (this will ensure that no changes are saved).

9. Exit the System Policy Editor window.

10.13 Create a New System Policy for a Domain

• •

To perform this exercise you will need:

■ Access to a domain controller

■ To consider making a backup before performing this exercise because it alters entries in the registry

1. Log on as administrator.

2. Launch the **System Policy Editor** (see Exercise 10.12).

3. From the **File** menu, select **New Policy.**

4. Specify what the registry-setting changes apply to, do either of the following:

■ Double-click **Default User** to change **HKEY_CURRENT_USER** registry settings for all users on the domain.

FIGURE 10-11
Policy Settings in the Local User of the Security Policy Editor

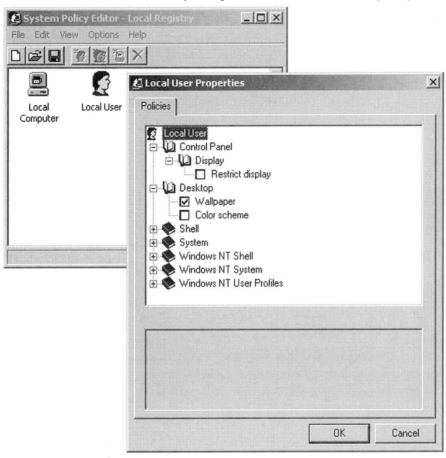

■ Double-click **Default Computer** to change **HKEY_ LOCAL_MACHINE** registry settings for all computers on the domain.

5. To add to the registry settings, from the **Edit** menu, select **Commands** to do the following:

■ To change **HKEY_CURRENT_ USER** for specific users, select **Add User.**

■ To change **HKEY_LOCAL_ MACHINE** for specific computers, select **Add Computer.**

■ To change **HKEY_CURRENT_ USER** for specific groups, select **Add Group.**

6. If necessary, finish configuring policy settings for any other policy files you have added.

7. From the **File** menu, select **Save As.**

8. In **Save in,** specify the Netlogon folder on the primary domain controller (PDC), such as \\Server-Name\netlogon.

9. In **File name,** type **NTconfig.pol** (for Windows 98 and Windows 95 clients, type **Config.pol**).

10. Click **Save.**

   ■ The policy is enforced on each computer running Windows NT 4.0, Windows 98 or Windows 95 when users log on.

   ■ Incorrectly editing the registry may severely damage the system. Before making changes to the registry, back up any valued data on the computer.

10.14 Create a New System Policy for an Individual Computer

To perform this exercise you will need:

■ Access to a client computer

■ To consider making a backup before performing this exercise because it alters entries in the registry

1. Log on as administrator.

2. Launch the **System Policy Editor** (see Exercise 10.12).

3. From the **File** menu, select **Open Registry.**

4. Double-click **Local Computer.**

5. Expand the **Network** branch.

6. Expand **System policies update.**

7. Select **Remote update.**

8. To have the registry process error messages displayed on client computers, click **Display error messages.**

9. To download the policy file from a server other than a domain controller, in **Update mode,** select **Manual (use specific path),** and then provide the specific path.

10. If necessary, finish configuring policy settings for any other policy files on the computer, and then save the policy files in the appropriate folder.

   ■ Make sure the policy file has a .pol extension.

   ■ Incorrectly editing the registry may severely damage your system. Before making changes to the registry, you should back up any valued data on the computer.

Security Configuration Tool Set

Windows 2000 predecessor, Windows NT 4.0, provided a number of graphical tools that could be used individually to configure various aspects of system security. However, these tools are not centralized – an administrator had to open three or four applications to configure security for one computer. Windows NT 4.0 also lacked comprehensive tools for security analysis. Windows 2000 improved this situation with the creation of the **Security Configuration Tool Set** that provides a central location where the entire system's security can be viewed, analyzed, and adjusted, as necessary. Table 10-7 describes the security areas that can be configured using the Security Configuration Tool Set.

Administrators can use the following components of the Security Configuration Tool Set to configure some or all of the security areas described above:

- **Security Templates snap-in** allows the creation of a text-based template file that contains security settings for all security areas.

- **Security Configuration and Analysis snap-in** can configure or analyze Windows 2000 operating system security. Its operation is based on the contents of a security template that was created using the Security Templates snap-in.

- **Secedit.exe** is a command-line version of the Security Configuration and Analysis snap-in. It allows security configuration and analysis to be performed without a graphical user interface.

- **Security Settings extension to Group Policy** is used to configure local security policies as well as security policies for domains or organizational units (OUs). Local security policies only include the Account Policy and Local Policy security areas described above. Security policies defined for domains or OUs can include all security areas.

TABLE 10-7 SECURITY CONFIGURATION TOOL SET CONFIGURATION AREAS

AREA	CONFIGURABLE ITEMS
Account Policies	Password, lockout, and Kerberos settings
Local Policies	Audit, user rights, and security options
Event Log	Settings for system, application, security and directory service logs
Restricted Groups	Policy regarding group membership
System Services	Startup modes and access control for system services
Registry	Access control for registry keys
File System	Access control for folders and files

Working with Security Templates

The Security Templates snap-in is used to create a text-based template file that can contain security settings for all of the security areas supported by the Security Configuration Tool Set. These template files can then be used to configure or analyze system security using other tools. Exercise 10.15 demonstrates how to load the Security Template snap-in.

EXERCISE

10.15 Load the Security Template Snap-in

To perform this exercise you will need:

■ Access to a Windows 2000 Server

1. Log on as an administrator.

2. Click **Start.**

3. Click **Run.**

4. Type **MMC /s.**

5. From the Console menu, select **Add/Remove Snap-in.**

6. Click the **Add** button.

7. From the list of available stand-alone snap-ins, select **Security Templates.**

8. Click the **Add** button.

9. Click the **Close** button.

10. Click **OK.**

Modifying a Security Template

To create a custom security template, you would right-click the default templates folder (C:\WINNT\security\templates) and select New Template. As with other consoles, several templates are pre-configured. Customizing a pre-configured template can save time over creating a template from scratch. Exercise 10.16 demonstrates how to modify the secure workstation or server template (securews.inf).

EXERCISE

10.16

View Settings in Securews.inf

To perform this exercise you will need:

- Access to a Windows 2000 Server
- To have performed Exercise 10.15

1. From within the Security Templates snap-in, expand the Security Templates branch.

2. Expand the C:\WINNT\security\ templates branch (where C:\WINNT

is the folder into which you installed Windows 2000).

3. Scroll down within the C:\WINNT\ security\templates branch and expand the securews.inf branch (see Figure 10-12).

4. Browse the **Account Policies** and **Local Policies** defined by

FIGURE 10-12

Viewing entries in the Securews.inf template

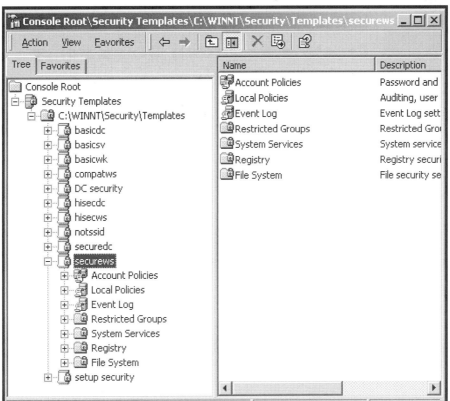

Securews by expanding those folders, selecting the different areas and viewing the **Stored Template** settings in the right pane.

5. If the template needed to be altered to fit your situation, you would make the alterations at this point and save the changes.

Create a Restricted Group Policy

A Restricted Group Policy defines who should and should not belong to a specific group. When a template that defines a restricted group is applied to a system, the Security Configuration Tool Set adds members to the group and removes members from the group to ensure that the actual group membership coincides with the settings defined in the template. Exercise 10.17 demonstrates how to define a restricted group policy for the Local Administrators group in addition to the restricted group policy that is already defined for the local Power Users group in Securews.inf.

EXERCISE

Create a Restricted Group Policy

To perform this exercise you will need:

- Access to a Windows 2000 Server
- To have performed Exercise 10.15

1. Expand the **securews** branch.

2. Right-click **Restricted Groups.**

3. Select **Add Group.**

4. Type **NewAdmins** as a group name.

5. Click **OK.**

 ■ The local Administrators group is added as a restricted group in the right pane of the Security Templates snap-in.

6. Double-click **Administrators** in the right pane.

7. Click **Add.**

8. Click **Browse.**

 ■ The **Select Users or Groups** dialog box appears.

9. Select **Administrator.**

10. Click **Add.**

11. Click **OK.**

12. Click **OK.**

13. Click **OK.**

This restricted group policy now states that only the local administrator user can belong to the Administrators local group when the Securews template is used to configure a Windows 2000 system. During configuration, the tool set removes all other users that belong to the Administrators group at the time of configuration. Similarly, if the Administrator user does not belong to the Administrators group, the Security Configuration Tool Set adds the Administrator user to the Administrators group.

Troubleshooting Policies

PERFORM A SECURITY ANALYSIS

Even the tightest security configurations should be analyzed periodically to identify security breaches that may exist or that have developed. You can analyze current system settings against a baseline template at anytime. The first step in analyzing security is to load the Security Configuration and Analysis snap-in. Follow the steps in Exercise 10.15, substituting Security Configuration and Analysis for Security Templates in step 7.

All configurations and analyses are database-driven. Therefore, you must get the baseline analysis template into a database prior to performing the analysis operation. Exercise 10.18 demonstrates how to create a database for analysis.

EXERCISE

10.18 Create a Database for Security Analysis

To perform this exercise you will need:

■ Access to a Windows 2000 Server

■ To have performed Exercise 10.15

1. From within the Security Configuration and Analysis console, right-click **Security Configuration and Analysis** in the left pane.

2. Select **Open Database** from the context-menu.

3. Type **analysis.sdb** as the name of the database.

4. Click **Open.**

5. Select **securews.inf** as the security template to import into the database.

6. Click **Open.**

   ■ The name of the database is displayed in the right pane and more options appear on the context-menu for Security Configuration and Analysis.

Now that the database has been created, you are ready to perform the security analysis that will compare the template against existing policy settings. Exercise 10.19 demonstrates how to perform a security analysis.

10.19 Perform a Security Analysis

● ●

To perform this exercise you will need:

■ Access to a Windows 2000 Server

■ To have performed Exercise 10.18

1. Right-click **Security Configuration and Analysis.**

2. Select **Analyze Computer Now** from the context-menu.

3. Specify the log file for the analysis operation by typing **C:\WINNT\ security\logs\secure.log.**

4. Click **Open.**

5. Click **OK.**

■ A progress dialog box is displayed as the analysis occurs.

Once the analysis process is complete, you will want to view the results. Exercise 10.20 demonstrates how to view and interpret the results of a security analysis.

10.20 Viewing Security Analysis Results

● ●

To perform this exercise you will need:

■ Access to a Windows 2000 Server

■ To have performed Exercise 10.19

1. From the **Security Configuration and Analysis** node, click **View.**

2. Select the **Description Bar** to expose the database you are working with.

3. Expand **Security Configuration and Analysis** in the left pane.

4. Expand **Local Policies.**

5. Select **Security Options.**

- In the right pane, both database and actual system settings are displayed for each object.

- Any discrepancies are highlighted with a red flag.

- Consistencies are highlighted with a green check mark.

- If there is no flag or check mark, the security setting was not configured in the template that was imported.

After the initial analysis process is complete, you may wish to either edit the baseline template or edit the actual security settings. After editing the settings, consider running the analysis again. This process assists the administrator in locating holes in security settings.

Group Policy Troubleshooting

An important part of troubleshooting Group Policy problems is to understand how various components depend upon each other. For example, Software Installation relies on Group Policy, and Group Policy relies on Active Directory. Active Directory relies on proper configuration of network services. When trying to fix problems that appear in one component, it is generally helpful to check whether components, services, and resources on which it relies are also working correctly. Because of this hierarchical dependency, Event logs are useful for tracking down problems.

Other considerations include:

- Group Policy affects only users and computers contained in sites, domains, and organizational units. Group Policy objects are not applied to security groups. Link Group Policy objects to sites, domains, and organizational units only. Keep in mind that the location of a security group in Active Directory is unrelated to whether Group Policy applies to the users and computers in that security group.

- Group Policy settings can be prevented, intentionally or inadvertently, from taking effect on users and computers in several ways. A Group Policy object can be disabled from affecting users, computers, or both. It also needs to be linked either directly to an organizational unit containing the users and computers, or linked to a parent domain or organizational unit so that the Group Policy settings apply through inheritance.

- Group Policy objects cannot be linked to Active Directory containers other than sites, domains, and organizational units.

- When multiple Group Policy objects apply, they are processed in this order: local, site, domain, organizational unit. By default, settings applied later have precedence.

- Group Policy can be blocked at the level of any organizational unit, or enforced through a setting of **No Override** applied to a particular Group Policy object link.

- Local policies are the weakest. Any Active Directory–based policy can overwrite them. Check to see what Group Policy objects are being applied through Active Directory, and if those Group Policy objects have settings that are in conflict with the local settings.

- An administrator must have Full Control of the Group Policy object to open it in the Group Policy console and also be a member of a security group with Full Control on the Group Policy object. For example, a domain administrator can manage Active Directory–based Group Policy. An administrator on a computer can edit the local Group Policy object on that computer.

Lesson 10.7 Configure Local Users and Groups

By default, newly created user accounts in a domain will be global accounts and are listed as such in the Active Directory. If a computer is running Windows 2000 Professional or is a member server running Windows 2000 Server, you can also create local user accounts on that computer. A local user account can be granted permissions and rights from the local computer, whereas domain or global user accounts are managed by the network administrator. The local computer authenticates local accounts according to its own security database. Global accounts are authenticated by central security database (the Active Directory) stored on a domain controller.

MICROSOFT EXAM OBJECTIVE

Implement, configure, manage, and troubleshoot local accounts.

Local Users and Groups is a tool that can be used to manage local users and groups. You can create new users and groups, add users to groups, remove users from groups, disable user and group accounts, and reset passwords. This tool is only available on computers running Windows 2000 Professional and member servers running Windows 2000 Server. The **Local Users and Groups** tool is not available on domain controllers. **Active Directory Users and Computers** is the tool used to manage global users and groups.

Users and Passwords in Control Panel is another tool that allows you to add local users to a client computer and to add a local user to a group. Users and Passwords can be used to create or change the password for a local user account, which is useful when creating a new user account or if a user forgets a password.

EXERCISE

10.21 Create a Local Account

To perform this exercise you will need:

- Access to a member server running Windows 2000 Server or a computer running Windows 2000 Professional

1. Log on as an administrator.

2. Launch **Control Panel.**

3. Open **Users and Passwords.**

4. Click the **Advanced** tab.

5. Click the **Advanced** button.

   - The **Local Users and Groups** tool is launched.

6. Click on **Users** in the tree pane.

7. From the **Action** menu, select **New User.**

8. Fill in the appropriate information about the new user.

9. Click the **Create** button.

10. Click the **Close** button.

    - The new user account appears in the content pane.

11. **Exit** the Local Users and Groups tool.

10.22

Change a Local Account Password

To perform this exercise you will need:

- Access to a member server running Windows 2000 Server or a computer running Windows 2000 Professional

- To have performed Exercise 10.21

1. Log on as an administrator.

2. Launch **Control Panel.**

3. Double-click **Users and Passwords.**

4. From the **Users** tab, click on the desired user account.

5. Click the Set Password button.

   - The Password dialog box appears.

6. Enter a new password.

7. Confirm the new password by typing it again.

8. Click **OK.**

9. **Exit** the Users and Passwords tool.

Troubleshooting

The Users and Passwords tool is not used for managing groups. Groups are managed within the Local User and Groups tool. You can, however, use Users and Passwords to place a user in only one group. If you need to add a user to more than one group, use Local Users and Groups. If you want to set up other password requirements such as minimum length, expiration time, or uniqueness, open Group Policy and go to Password Policy.

If the computer is part of a network, you can add network user accounts to groups on the computer, and those users can use their network passwords to log on. A local user cannot change the password of network user. For management purposes, local users, global users, and global groups can be added to local groups. However, you cannot add local users and groups to global groups.

When Active Directory is available, using local accounts should be avoided because changes to local account settings must be performed at each local computer. Decentralized administration is less efficient than managing user accounts from a central location like the Active Directory.

Summary

Windows 2000 Server has a variety of security mechanisms used to protect network resources from both intentional and unintentional damage. From the logon process to the setting of permissions on an individual file, the security in Windows 2000 is wide-ranging in its ability to control the network environment. NTFS file permissions protect folders and files, while share permissions protect resources accessed over the network. There are rules that govern how files are affected when one user is a member of two groups with conflicting permissions. Permissions can be altered when a file is copied from one folder to another folder on a different volume. Lastly, you learned that policies provide control and boundaries for users and computers on the network. Account policies apply to user accounts, and local policies apply to the local computer. Group Policy is a program for Active Directory object control. System Policy is a program that was used in Windows NT 4.0 but is mostly replaced by Group Policy. Security issues are a main concern of any network administrator.

● ● ● ● ● ● ● ● ● ● ● ● ● ●

▼ R EVIEW E XERCISE

These questions will help you determine if you have learned enough to move on to the next chapter. If the graphic next to the option is a square (❏), there can be more than one answer for that question. If the graphic is a circle (○), there is only one correct answer. Color in the shape(s) to indicate your answer(s).

1. Kirk needs to access a file that is in a subfolder on the file server. He does not have permission to access the folder that is above the subfolder. What NTFS file permission would allow him to move through folders to open other files and folders, even if he does not have permission to use those folders?

   a. ○ Read

   b. ○ Write

   c. ○ Read & Execute

   d. ○ Modify

2. Kate is a member of the sales group and a member of the marketing group. She is about to open a file to which the sales group has Write file access, but the marketing group only has Read file access. What will she be able to do with the file?

   a. ❑ She can open the file, but she cannot save changes.

   b. ❑ She can open the file, make changes, and save the file in the same folder.

   c. ❑ She can take ownership of the file and change the permission to Read & Execute.

   d. ❑ She can save the changes to a new file in the same folder.

3. Kathy calls Ron and asks for a copy of last week's sales report because she wants to reformat the structure of the document. The original document needs to be kept for record-keeping purposes. Ron, who is the owner of the sales report, makes a copy from his folder and pastes the sales report into Kathy's folder. Kathy's folder has Read & Execute permission. If Kathy had Write permissions on the original document, what permission will she have on the duplicate file?

   a. ○ Read

   b. ○ Write

   c. ○ Read & Execute

   d. ○ Full Control

4. Which of the following security settings are a part of local policies?

   a. ❑ Audit Policy

   b. ❑ User Right Assignment

   c. ❑ Security Options

   d. ❑ Account Lockout Policy

5. What is the name of the program that launches the System Policy Editor?

   a. ○ syspole.exe

   b. ○ sysedit.exe

   c. ○ poledit.exe

   d. ○ polesys.exe

PERFORMANCE CHALLENGES

- Based on the folder structure you created for your family tree in the Chapter 8 Performance Challenge, create a user account for each family member. Give each person varying levels of permissions to access the folders in the structure. Use screen shots of the folders' properties and a word processor to document your actions.

- What would be the worst possible approach to security in a Windows 2000 environment? List at least two scenarios describing security breaches caused by a lack of planning.

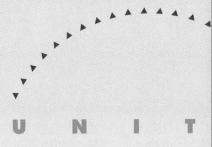

MANAGE THE SYSTEM

USE ADMINISTRATIVE TOOLS

CHAPTER

11

OBJECTIVES

After completing this chapter, you should be able to:

- Describe the relationships between the MMC, an MMC Console, and its associated snap-ins

- Use the Event Viewer administrative tool

- Create a custom MMC console and add snap-ins to that console

- Schedule tasks to start automatically

- Describe the purpose of each Control Panel utility

OUTLINE

Introduction

What tools would you need to paint a house? At the very least, you would need a ladder, a paintbrush, and a bucket of paint. What tools would you need to administer a Windows 2000 network? You already have used one of the tools, the Active Directory Users and Computers console, but many other administrative tools are available. A good painter is familiar with his or her tools, chooses the ones that best fit the job, and knows how to use them to an advantage. The same approach will ensure success in network administration. Although an in-depth understanding of each tool could be valuable to you, the scope of this text can only give you an introduction to the most commonly used tools. The three primary administrative tools are the **Microsoft Management Console (MMC),** the **Task Scheduler,** and the **Control Panel.**

Lesson 11.1 Explore the Microsoft Management Console Interface

The **Microsoft Management Console (MMC)** provides one location for creating, saving, and opening administrative tools, which are called **MMC consoles.** Before the MMC, administrators would have to remember where the administrative tools were located; some were on the Start menu, some were launched from a command prompt, and some were launched from within other applications. MMC consoles contain one or more **snap-ins,** which are the actual tools used to perform tasks. Consoles are saved as files, have an .MSC extension, and contain all of the settings for a snap-in. An administrator can choose which snap-ins to use and can create a custom MMC console. MMC consoles can even be created for other administrators or users who have specific administrative tasks to perform.

The MMC has the following benefits:

- **One management interface:** Most of the administrative tasks can be performed from within the MMC, which is more efficient than navigating menus and launching various applications.

- **Centralized administration:** Most of the administrative tasks can be performed from one computer. The administrator can stay in his or her chair and can perform tasks without having to go to a different domain controller or workstation.

- **Remote administration:** Many snap-ins offer remote administration, which allows the administrator to perform actions on a computer other than the one he or she is using.

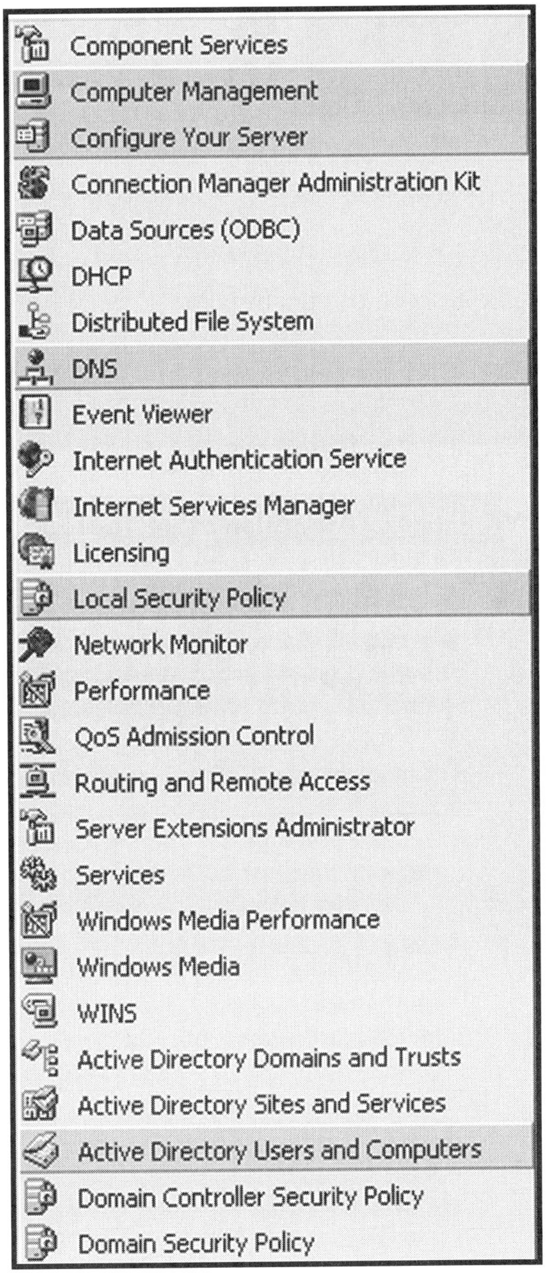

Types of MMC Consoles

The two types of MMC consoles are **preconfigured** and **custom.** Preconfigured MMC consoles have commonly used snap-ins, and you can see them by opening Programs then Administrative Tools from the Start menu (see Figure 11-1). The Administrative Tools on your computer may differ from the one displayed in Figure 11-1 depending on the applications you have installed or features you have configured. For example, the Active Directory menu items would not appear if Active Directory were not installed. Custom MMC consoles are created by launching an empty MMC console and configuring the various snap-ins.

FIGURE 11-1
The Administrative Tools Menu

- Component Services
- Computer Management
- Configure Your Server
- Connection Manager Administration Kit
- Data Sources (ODBC)
- DHCP
- Distributed File System
- DNS
- Event Viewer
- Internet Authentication Service
- Internet Services Manager
- Licensing
- Local Security Policy
- Network Monitor
- Performance
- QoS Admission Control
- Routing and Remote Access
- Server Extensions Administrator
- Services
- Windows Media Performance
- Windows Media
- WINS
- Active Directory Domains and Trusts
- Active Directory Sites and Services
- Active Directory Users and Computers
- Domain Controller Security Policy
- Domain Security Policy

Use a Preconfigured MMC Console (Event Viewer)

To perform this exercise, you will need:

■ Access to a domain controller

1. Log on as administrator.

2. Click the Start button.

3. Point to **Programs.**

4. Point to **Administrative Tools.**

5. Select **Event Viewer.**

   ■ The Event Viewer window is opened (see Figure 11-2).

   ■ Notice the available logs (your choices may differ depending on what you have installed on your system).

6. Click on **System Log** in the tree pane.

7. Scroll through the list in the content pane.

8. Double-click on an entry to view the properties of that event.

9. Click **OK** to close the Properties dialog box.

10. Close the Event Viewer.

Although many of the Administrative Tools use the console interface shown in Figure 11-2, the options and their functions will differ. Becoming familiar with each tool is the goal of every administrator.

FIGURE 11-2
The Event Viewer Window

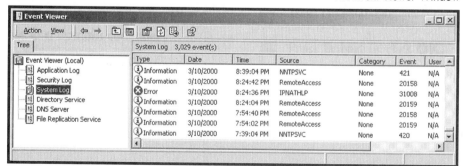

Windows 2000 saves custom MMC console files in the **My Administrative Tools** folder. This folder does not exist until you create your first custom MMC console. The My Administrative Tools folder is user-specific, which means that the contents of that folder are directly related to the user account that created the custom MMC consoles. Exercise 11.2 will demonstrate how to create a custom MMC.

Types of Snap-Ins

The two types of snap-ins are **stand-alone snap-ins** and **extension snap-ins.** Stand-alone snap-ins are usually referred to simply as *snap-ins* and are used to perform Windows 2000 administrative tasks. Each snap-in provides one function or a related set of functions.

Extension snap-ins, which usually are referred to as *extensions,* provide additional functionality to another snap-in. An analogy of this relationship is a teacher's assistant helping a teacher. Extensions have the following characteristics:

■ Extensions can work for one snap-in or several snap-ins, based on the function of the snap-in. In our teacher analogy, the teacher's assistant may be studying biology and, therefore, could assist any biology teacher. However, he or she would not be much help to a physics teacher.

■ When you want to add an extension, Windows 2000 will only display the extensions that are compatible with the snap-in.

■ When you add a snap-in to a console, MMC adds all available extensions by default. You can then remove any extensions that you do not want.

Console Modes

The console mode determines what actions a user will be able to perform when he or she uses an MMC console. The two available console modes are **author mode** and **user mode.**

When an MMC console is saved in author mode, the user has full access to all MMC functionality, which includes modifying the MMC console. When the user has this type of access, he or she can:

■ Add or remove snap-ins

■ Create new windows

■ View all portions of the console tree

■ Save MMC consoles

User mode restricts what the user is able to do to the MMC console. When an MMC console is saved in user mode, the user cannot add snap-ins to, remove snap-ins from, or save the MMC console. There are three types of user modes:

■ **Full access:** Users are allowed to navigate between snap-ins, open new windows, and gain access to all portions of the console tree.

- **Delegated Access, Multiple Windows:** Users are not allowed to open new windows or gain access to a portion of the console tree. Users can view multiple windows in the console.

- **Delegated Access, Single Window:** Users are not allowed to open new windows or gain access to a portion of the console tree. Users can only view one window in the console.

Lesson 11.2 Create a Customized MMC Console

While most people who purchase a new car do not make any changes to the car, some people choose to customize it by adding window tinting, new wheels, better tires, a chrome gearshift, a spoiler, and so on. Where one person might lower a car so that it is closer to the ground, another person might take that same car type and raise it; that is the joy of customization. You have the same customization ability in the MMC. By customizing an MMC console, you make the interface for performing your administrative tasks fit your personal needs. You might even create several different consoles for different areas of responsibility. This is no different than a car owner having several different kinds of cars such as a commuter car, a sports car, and a utility vehicle. Before you can begin the customization process, you need to launch an empty console by following the steps in Exercise 11.2.

EXERCISE

11.2 Launch the MMC with an Empty Console

To perform this exercise, you will need:

- Access to a domain controller

1. Log on as administrator.

2. Click the Start button.

3. Point to **Run. . . .**

4. In the "Open" text box, type **mmc.**

5. Press Enter, or click **OK.**
   - An MMC console window titled *Console1* opens.
   - A window titled *Console Root* appears inside the Console1 window (see Figure 11-3).

FIGURE 11-3
The MMC with an Empty Console Open

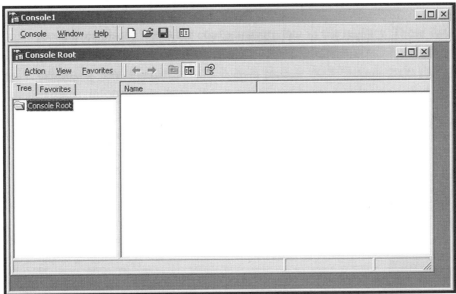

TABLE 11-1 CONSOLE MENU OPTIONS

MENU OPTION	USED TO
New	Create a new custom MMC console
Open	Open an existing MMC console
Save or Save As	Save the current MMC console for later use
Add/Remove Snap-in	Add or remove one or more snap-ins and their associated extensions to or from an MMC console
Options	Configure the console mode and create a custom MMC console

Once you open an empty console, you must decide which action(s) you want to perform. Table 11-1 describes the options on the Console menu and their functions.

11.3

Create a Custom MMC Console

To perform this exercise, you will need:

■ Access to a domain controller

■ To perform Exercise 11.2

1. Maximize the Console1 window.

2. Maximize the Console Root window.

3. Click on the Console menu.

   ■ The Console menu options are displayed.

4. Select the Options menu choice.

   ■ The Options dialog box is displayed (see Figure 11-4).

   ■ Notice the default settings.

5. Click **OK.**

6. From the Console menu, select **Save As.**

   ■ The Save As dialog box appears.

   ■ Notice the default settings, including where the new console is going to be stored on the Start menu and the extension for MMC consoles.

7. In the filename box, type in a name that describes the purpose of the console (for example, *Computer Management*).

8. Press Enter, or click **OK.**

9. From the Console menu, select **Exit.**

Now that you have created a custom console, you will want to launch the console so that you can configure snap-ins. Exercise 11.4 explains how to launch a custom console.

FIGURE 11-4
MMC Console Options Dialog Box

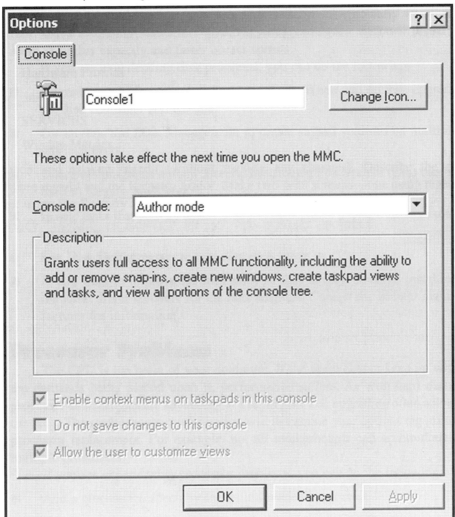

EXERCISE

11.4 Open a Custom MMC Console

To perform this exercise, you will need:

- Access to a domain controller
- To have performed Exercise 11.3

1. Click the Start button.

2. Point to **Programs.**

3. Point to **Administrative Tools** (or **My Administrative Tools,** whichever location you chose when you saved the console in step 6 of Exercise 11.3).

4. Select the console name you entered in step 7 of Exercise 11.3.

- Notice the name of the console on the menu includes the .msc extension.

- The custom console is launched.

EXERCISE

Add a Snap-in to a Custom MMC Console

To perform this exercise, you will need:

- Access to a domain controller

- To have performed Exercise 11.4

1. Click the Console menu.

2. Select **Add/Remove Snap-in.**

- The Add/Remove Snap-in dialog box appears with the **Stand-alone** tab selected.

3. Click the **Add** button.

- The Add Stand-alone Snap-in dialog box appears (see Figure 11-5).

- This is a list of all of the available snap-ins.

- If you click on each option, the description section of the dialog box will describe the snap-in.

4. Click on the snap-in you want to add to this console (for example, *Computer Management,* as shown in Figure 11-5).

5. Click the **Add** button.

- MMC displays the Select Computer dialog box.

- You can add this snap-in for the local computer or select a computer that is on the network by browsing for the other computer.

6. After selecting which computer will be administered (for example, local) with this snap-in, click the **Finish** button.

7. Repeat steps 5 and 6 for each additional snap-in you want to incorporate into this console.

FIGURE 11-5
Adding a Snap-in to an MMC Console

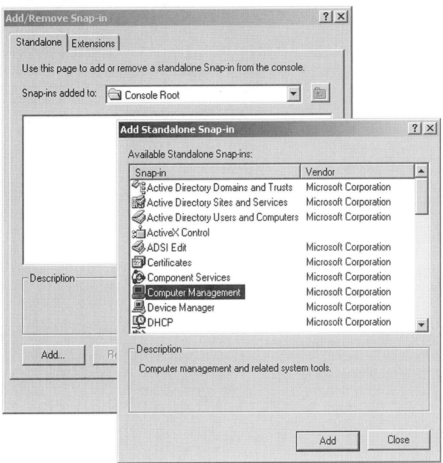

8. Click the **Close** button to exit the Add Standalone Snap-in dialog box.

   ■ The name of the snap-in appears in the Add/Remove Snap-in dialog box.

9. Click **OK** to close the Add/Remove Snap-in dialog box.

   ■ The snap-in appears in the Console tree pane (see Figure 11-6).

   ■ If the snap-in can be expanded (you will see a plus sign next to the name), double-click the snap-in to expand it.

FIGURE 11-6

The Computer Management Snap-in in an MMC Console

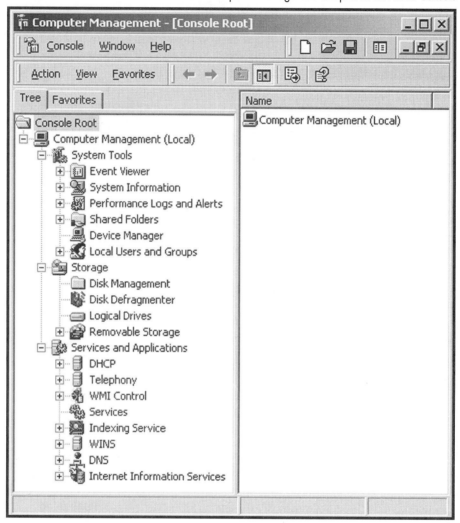

Each of the snap-ins displayed in Figure 11-6 could have been added individually. The computer management snap-in is a collection of snap-ins compiled by Microsoft since these are the most commonly required snap-ins for managing computers. You can remove any of the snap-ins or their associated extensions that you do not need to use. Exercise 11.6 describes how to remove extensions from snap-ins.

EXERCISE

11.6

Remove a Snap-in from a Custom MMC Console

To perform this exercise, you will need:

■ Access to a domain controller

■ To have performed Exercise 11.5

1. Click the Console menu.

2. Select **Add/Remove Snap-in.**

   ■ The Add/Remove Snap-in dialog box appears with the **Stand-alone** tab selected.

3. Click the **Extensions** tab.

   ■ The Extensions dialog box is displayed.

4. Use the pull-down list of Snap-ins that can be extended and select the snap-in to be edited.

5. Remove the checkmark from the Add all extensions checkbox.

   ■ The checkboxes in the Available extensions: list become editable (black instead of grayed-out).

6. Remove checkmarks from any extensions that you want to be removed from the snap-in.

7. Click **OK.**

8. Expand the affected snap-in to ensure the change was made.

9. Exit the console.

10. When prompted for confirmation to save console settings, click **Yes.**

Lesson 11.3 Use Task Scheduler

Anything an administrator can get the computer to do on its own without human intervention frees the administrator to do other tasks. **Task Scheduler** is a Windows 2000 Server utility that can cause a program, script, or document to launch at a specified time and interval or when certain operating system events occur. Some examples of tasks that are helpful when automated include performing backups, deleting temporary files, and launching network utilities.

Scheduled tasks are saved in the **Scheduled Tasks** folder. You can view the contents of this folder by opening the Control Panel. (The next lesson covers the use of Control Panel.)

Schedule a Task to Start Automatically

● ●

To perform this exercise, you will need:

■ Access to a domain controller

1. Click the Start button.

2. Point to **Settings.**

3. Select **Control Panel.**

■ The Control Panel window opens.

4. Double-click the **Scheduled Tasks** folder.

■ The Scheduled Tasks window opens.

5. Double-click **Add Scheduled Task.**

■ The opening screen of the Scheduled Task Wizard is displayed.

6. Click **Next.**

■ A list of available programs for automated launch is displayed (see Figure 11-7).

■ If the program you want is not listed, you can browse the system for the program by clicking the **Browse** button.

FIGURE 11-7
List of Programs in the Scheduled Task Wizard

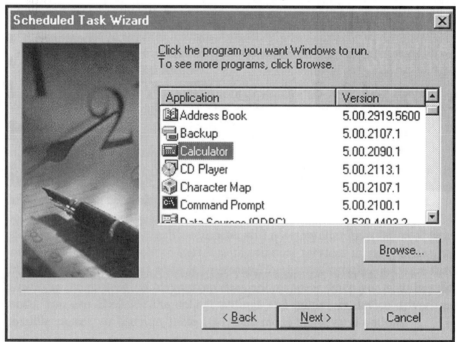

7. Click on the program name (for example, Calculator, as shown in Figure 11-7).

8. Click **Next.**

   ■ The next screen prompts for a name for the scheduled task and for an interval.

9. Enter the name of the scheduled task (for example, the default name of Calculator, as shown in Figure 11-7).

10. Indicate the interval at which the task will occur (for example, you might schedule the task to occur one time only).

11. Click **Next.**

   ■ The next screen prompts for the time and date the scheduled task will occur.

12. Enter the time and date the scheduled task will occur.

13. Click **Next.**

   ■ The next screen prompts for a user and password.

   ■ The program will launch as if that user were performing the action.

14. Enter the name of the user and the user's password. Confirm the password.

15. Click **Next.**

   ■ The next screen confirms your entered settings.

16. Click **Finish.**

   ■ An icon for the Scheduled Task appears in the **Scheduled Tasks** folder.

Lesson 11.4 Explore Control Panel

Control Panel is a collection of programs that are used to customize the hardware and software configurations for a computer. The Control Panel window can be opened from two different locations:

■ Start button, Settings, Control Panel

■ My Computer, Control Panel

To use most of the programs in Control Panel, you will need to be logged on as the administrator or be a member of the administrators group for the computer. Table 11-2 lists the Control Panel programs you would find on a commonly configured domain controller and describes their purpose.

The contents of the Control Panel window may vary depending on the configuration of the computer. Some third-party vendors' products install an icon in

TABLE 11-2 CONTROL PANEL PROGRAMS

CONTROL PANEL

DESCRIPTION

Accessibility Options

The accessibility tools that ship with Windows 2000 are intended to provide a minimum level of functionality for users with special needs. For example, the tools included with Windows 2000 assist users who are hearing impaired by making sounds visual. Most users with disabilities will need utility programs with higher functionality for daily use. Microsoft's Web site offers more utilities.

Add/Remove Hardware

Hardware includes any physical device that is connected to your computer and is controlled by your computer's microprocessor. This Control Panel assists in the proper configuration when adding hardware and also performs the clean-up duties when hardware is removed.

Add/Remove Programs

Add/Remove Programs helps you manage programs on your computer. It prompts you through the steps necessary to add a new program or to change or remove an existing program.

You can use Add/Remove Programs to add Windows 2000 components you chose not to include in the original installation (such as networking options or Indexing Service files), programs (such as Microsoft Excel or Word), Windows updates, or new features from the Internet.

Administrative Tools

This tool provides another way (other than the Start menu) to access the **Administrative Tools** folder.

Date/Time

This tool sets the date, time, and time zone for the computer.

Display

Display customizes the desktop display. Settings include colors, wallpaper, screen saver, refresh rate, video driver, and resolution. Another way to access this Control Panel is to right-click on an open area of the desktop and select Properties from the Context menu.

Fax

Using Fax, you can fax a text document or graphic image as easily as clicking **Print** from an open document in a Windows-based program. Fax supports scanned graphic images and will automatically convert graphics to a .tif file format before you fax them. Also, you can use mail programs to send e-mail and fax messages simultaneously.

Folder Options

Folder Options enables you to change the appearance of your desktop and folder content and to specify how folders open. For example, you can select whether you want a single window to open (instead of cascading windows) when you open folders that are within the selected folder. You can designate if you want network documents to be available off-line. Additionally, you can designate whether folders open with a single-click or double-click.

Fonts

Fonts are used to display text on the screen and to print text. In Windows 2000, a font is the name of a typeface. Fonts have font styles such as italic, bold, and bold italic. Use this Control Panel to add or remove fonts from the computer.

TABLE 11-2 CONTROL PANEL PROGRAMS *CONTINUED*

CONTROL PANEL

Game
Controllers

Internet
Options

Keyboard

Licensing

Mail

Mouse

Network and
Dial-up Co...

Phone and
Modem ...

Power Options

DESCRIPTION

Game adds, removes, or configures game controller hardware such as joysticks and gamepads.

Internet Options configures your Internet display and connections options.

This tool customizes keyboard settings such as how quickly a depressed key repeats, the use of different keyboard layouts, and how fast the cursor blinks.

Licensing is used to change licensing options.

Mail provides Microsoft Outlook profiles.

This tool adjusts how the mouse functions. Settings include adjusting the double-click speed, reversing the mouse buttons, and adjusting the speed of the mouse pointer.

Network and Dial-up Connections provides connectivity between your computer and the Internet, a network, or another computer. With Network and Dial-up Connections, you can gain access to network resources and functionality, whether you are physically located at the network location or in a remote location. Connections are created, configured, stored, and monitored from within the **Network and Dial-up Connections** folder.

This tool configures the telephone dialing rules and modem settings.

Power Options allows you to reduce the power consumption of any number of your computer devices or of your entire system. You do this by choosing a power scheme, which is a collection of settings that manages the power usage by your computer. You can create your own power schemes or use the ones provided with Windows 2000. Power schemes can include options such as turning off your monitor and hard disks automatically to save power and putting the computer on standby when it is idle. Many of these features used to be available only for laptops. This Control Panel makes them available for desktop computers, as long as the computer is set up by the manufacturer to support these features.

Continued

TABLE 11-2 CONTROL PANEL PROGRAMS *CONTINUED*

CONTROL PANEL	DESCRIPTION
Printers	Printers adds, removes, and configures local or network printers. This folder can also be accessed through My Computer by choosing Settings from the Start menu.
QuickTime	QuickTime is Apple's multi-platform, industry standard, multimedia software architecture. Software developers, hardware manufacturers, and content creators use QuickTime to author and publish synchronized graphics, sound, video, text, music, virtual reality, and 3D media.
Regional Options	Regional Options customizes settings for display of time, currency amounts, languages, large numbers and numbers with decimal fractions, and dates. You also can choose the metric or U.S. system of measurement.
Scanners and Cameras	Scanners and Cameras appears in the Control Panel when you install your first scanner or digital camera. Use this feature to install other scanners, digital still cameras, digital video cameras, and image-capturing devices. After a device is installed, Scanners and Cameras can link it to a program on your computer.
Scheduled Tasks	By using Task Scheduler, you can schedule any script, program, or document to run at a time that is most convenient for you. Task Scheduler starts each time you start Windows 2000 and runs in the background. (See Lesson 11.4 for details.)
Sounds and Multimedia	Using Sounds and Multimedia in Control Panel, you can assign sounds to some system events. A system event can occur in a number of ways, including when a computer program performs a task or has a problem performing a task, when you minimize or maximize a program window, or if you try to copy a file to a floppy disk but you do not have a disk inserted into your floppy disk drive.
System	Use System in Control Panel to do the following: view and change settings that control how your computer uses memory and finds certain information, find information about hardware and device properties as well as configure hardware profiles, and view information about your network connection and logon profile.

the Control Panel. In Table 11-2, for example, the icon for the third-party utility called QuickTime was created in the Control Panel by the installation program. Some Control Panel utilities will not be displayed until either hardware or software is installed. For example, the Scanners and Cameras icon did not appear until either a scanner or digital camera was installed.

You should familiarize yourself with each of the Control Panel utilities, but use caution during your learning curve, for you could easily disable your system. The best way to explore is to launch the utility and then click the Cancel button when you are done. This will ensure that any changes you made were not saved. Exercise 11.8 will explore three Control Panel utilities that are commonly used.

EXERCISE

11.8 Exploring Control Panel Utilities

To perform this exercise, you will need:

■ Access to a domain controller

1. Click the Start button.

2. Point to **Settings.**

3. Select **Control Panel.**

4. Double-click on **Add/Remove Programs.**

   ■ The Add/Remove Programs dialog box appears.

   ■ The list indicates the software programs that are currently installed on the computer.

   ■ You can use this utility to uninstall any of the programs.

5. Click on one of the programs.

   ■ The entry is expanded to display more information.

   ■ A Change/Remove button is made available.

6. Click the **Close** button.

7. Double-click on **System.**

   ■ The System Properties dialog box appears.

8. Click on each of the tabs.

   ■ You will use many of these options in the upcoming chapters.

9. Click the **Cancel** button.

10. Double-click on **Folder Options.**

    ■ The Folder Options dialog box appears.

11. Click on the **View** tab (see Figure 11-8).

    ■ The settings on this tab can explain why certain files in Windows Explorer do not appear, even though they exist. For example, if a file is hidden and the option for not displaying hidden files is selected, that file will not appear in the file list.

    ■ Administrators should be able to see all of the files and their extensions.

12. Click the **Cancel** button.

FIGURE 11-8
The View Tab on the Folder Options Dialog Box

Summary

Windows 2000 provides many tools to assist the administrator in maintaining a network. The single-interface approach to system management through the MMC is a new feature with Windows 2000. With the MMC, administrators can create custom consoles for combining similar administrative tasks into one location. Consoles can also be created for the purpose of delegating administrative tasks. When a console is added, its name appears in the Administrative Tools menu. One of the tools administrators can use to save time and effort is the Task Scheduler. Task Scheduler automates the launch of programs and documents at regular intervals or for one time only. This utility can be launched from within the Control Panel. Control Panel utilities are used to configure the hardware and software settings for a local computer. The contents of the Control Panel folder may vary depending on a computer's configuration or installed hardware or software. You must have the appropriate permissions in order to use the Control Panel utilities. Familiarizing yourself with all of the Windows 2000 administrative tools will help make you a more effective administrator.

REVIEW EXERCISE

These questions will help you determine if you have learned enough to move on to the next chapter. If the graphic next to the option is a square (❑), there can be more than one answer for that question. If the graphic is a circle (○), there is only one correct answer. Color in the shape(s) to indicate your answer(s).

1. The MMC is comprised of several elements. Which of the following statements accurately describes the relationships between the elements?

   a. ❑ MMC consoles can contain one or more snap-ins.

   b. ❑ An extension is a snap-in that provides additional functionality to another snap-in.

   c. ❑ Custom consoles are contained within a snap-in.

   d. ❑ Snap-ins can have one or more extensions.

2. Linda is an administrator who only needs to access one snap-in. You do not want her to add any additional snap-ins, but she does need to navigate between all of the snap-ins. What console mode would you use to configure a custom MMC console for her?

   a. ○ Author mode

   b. ○ User mode, Full Access

   c. ○ User mode, Delegated Access, Multiple Windows

   d. ○ User mode, Delegated Access, Single Window

3. What is the extension of an MMC console?

   a. ○ msc

   b. ○ mmc

   c. ○ con

   d. ○ scm

4. Mike is supposed to meet Dawn every Thursday for lunch. Some days he gets so wrapped up in his work that he forgets. What Control Panel utility could Mike use to launch a document at a certain time on Thursdays that reminds him to stop working and go to lunch?

   a. ○ Add/Remove Programs

   b. ○ Time/Date

   c. ○ Task Scheduler

   d. ○ Game Controllers

5. After 14 hours of using a project management program, Kort needs to change the resolution on his monitor so that the image is larger. Which Control Panel utility will he have to use?

   a. ○ System

   b. ○ Regional Options

   c. ○ Monitor Settings

   d. ○ Display

PERFORMANCE CHALLENGES

- Use Task Scheduler to launch three different applications at three different intervals. Print the Task Scheduler screen and the screen that proves the application launched.

- Create a custom MMC console that has two snap-ins. Remove an extension from one of the snap-ins. Print the screen to prove that you made the appropriate changes.

- List the Control Panel utilities that either list or alter a time setting.

MANAGE ACCOUNTS AND GROUPS

OBJECTIVES

After completing this chapter, you should be able to:

- Modify the properties of a user account

- Describe the purpose and function of a user profile

- Create a roaming user profile

- Perform management tasks for user accounts

- Add user accounts to groups

- Move, rename, and delete groups

- Change the scope of a group

- Use Find to locate user accounts and groups

OUTLINE

Lesson 12.1 Modify User Account Properties

    Exercise 12.1—Open the User Account Properties Dialog Box
    Exercise 12.2—Edit the General Tab of the User Account Properties
    Exercise 12.3—Edit the Account Tab of the User Account Properties
    Exercise 12.4—Setting Logon Hours
    Exercise 12.5—Edit the Member Of Tab of the User Account
       Properties

Lesson 12.2 Configure a User Profile

    Exercise 12.6—View Local User Profiles
    Exercise 12.7—Create a Roaming User Profile

Lesson 12.3 Manage User Accounts

    Exercise 12.8—Rename a User Account
    Exercise 12.9—Copy a User Account
    Exercise 12.10—Delete a User Account

Introduction

A farmer's life is a hard life, but it is a life with many rewards. The farmer has the daily responsibility of making sure everything associated with the farm is doing what it was designed to do, including ensuring that the cows are producing milk, the chickens are making eggs, and the crops are growing in the field. The farmer diligently oversees the hundreds of other things that must occur in order for the farm to be successful and is often working when he or she should be resting. What does this have to do with system administration? Instead of cows and chickens, administrators have users and groups. If you want your network to function at its peak, you must be as diligent and knowledgeable about your network as a farmer is about his or her farm. This chapter covers how to manage user accounts and groups.

Lesson 12.1 Modify User Account Properties

In Lesson 8.2 you learned how to create user accounts. In this lesson, you will learn how to edit the properties of a user account so that the account is customized for the user. Customization includes contact information, group membership, where personal files are stored, and more. As explained in Exercise 12.1, the first step in modifying a user account is to open the Properties dialog box for one of the user accounts you created.

EXERCISE

12.1 Open the User Account Properties Dialog Box

To perform this exercise, you will need:

■ Access to a domain controller

■ A previously created user account

1. Log on as administrator.

2. Click the Start button.

3. Point to **Administrative Tools**.

4. Click **Active Directory Users And Computers**.

5. In the console tree, double-click the container object (OU or group) within which the user account is contained.

6. Right-click the user account name.

7. Select **Properties** from the Context menu.

■ The User Account Properties dialog box is displayed (see Figure 12-1).

After a user account is created, only the fields shown in Figure 12-1 are filled in. Customization occurs when specific data are entered on each of the tabs. Table 12-1 provides a description of each tab in the Properties dialog box.

This lesson will cover the tabs that customize information about the user. The remaining tabs are covered in later lessons.

TIP

As you click through the tabs, they seem to change positions erratically. Think of the tabs in terms of rows, with the first row starting with the **General** tab, the second row starting with the **Remote Control** tab, and the third row starting with the **Member of** tab. When you click on any tab in a row, the entire row comes to the forefront and the other rows move back. If you practice clicking on them, you will see the logic in their movement and will not spend too much time searching for the tab you need.

FIGURE 12-1
User Account Properties Dialog Box

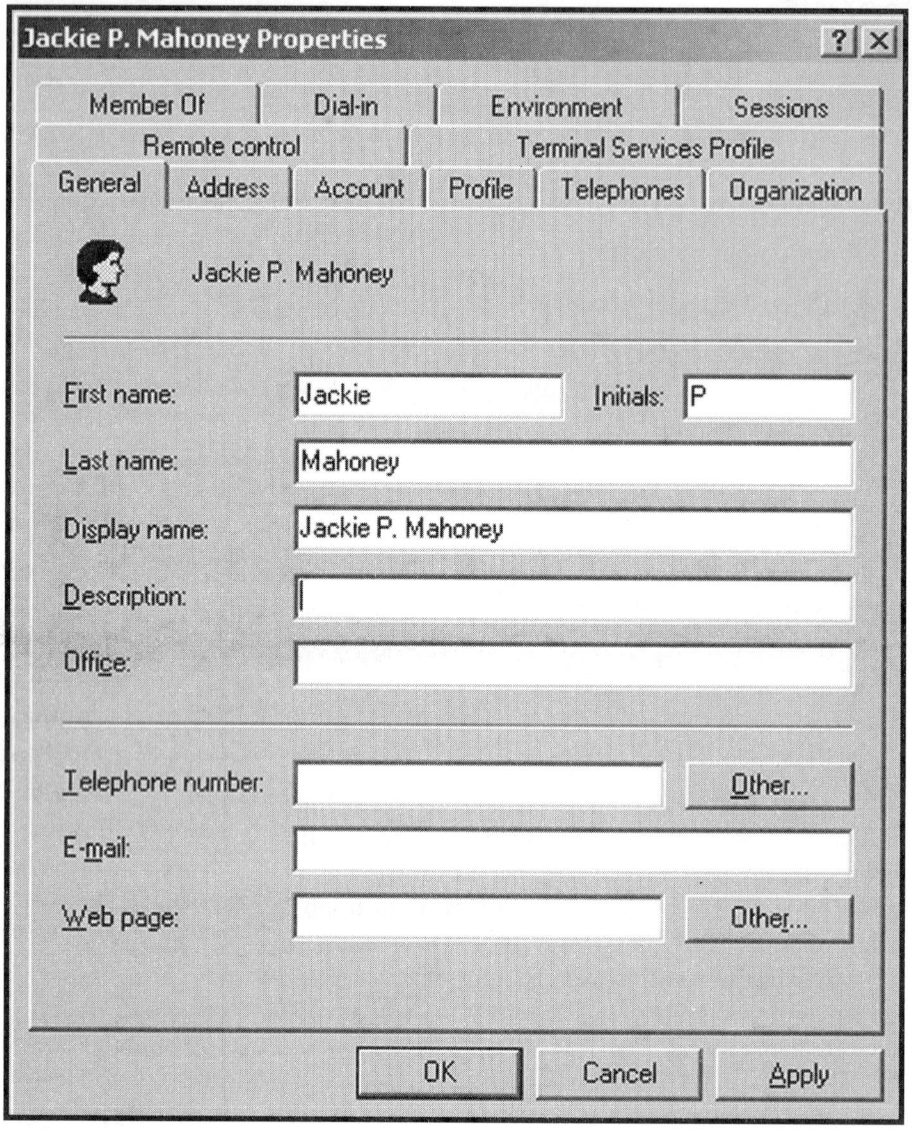

Jackie P. Mahoney Properties   ? ✕

| Member Of | Dial-in | Environment | Sessions |

| Remote control | Terminal Services Profile |

| General | Address | Account | Profile | Telephones | Organization |

Jackie P. Mahoney

First name: Jackie   Initials: P

Last name: Mahoney

Display name: Jackie P. Mahoney

Description: |

Office:

Telephone number: Other...

E-mail:

Web page: Other...

OK   Cancel   Apply

TABLE 12-1 FIELDS ON THE GENERAL TAB OF USER ACCOUNT PROPERTIES

TAB	DESCRIPTION
General	Documents the user's name, including first, middle initial, and last name. Also documents where the user's office is located and the user's office telephone number(s), e-mail address, home page, and additional Web pages.
Address	Documents the user's mailing address.
Account	Documents the user's account options, including user logon name, if and when the user can change his or her password, and if and when the user account expires.
Profile	Sets the profile path, logon script path, home directory, and shared document folder. (Exercise 12.4 will describe these.)
Telephone/Notes	Documents the user's telephone numbers, including home, pager, mobile, fax, and Internet Protocol (IP). There is also room for comments.
Organization	Documents the user's title, department, company, manager, and to whom he or she directly reports.
Member of	Documents the groups to which the user belongs.
Dial-In	Documents the dial-in properties for the user.

EXERCISE

12.2 Edit the General Tab of the User Account Properties

To perform this exercise, you will need:

- Access to a domain controller
- To have performed Exercise 12.1

1. Click on the **General** tab (if it is not in the foreground).

2. In **First name,** type the user's first name.

3. In **Initials,** type the user's middle initial(s).

4. In **Last name,** type the user's last name.

5. Modify **Display name** as desired.
   - This is the name that users will see when they are browsing the network or in user lists.
   - This could be a name such as a nickname or a shortened version of the user's proper name.

6. In **Description,** enter a description of this user.

   - This data will appear in the Description column in the Active Directory Users and Computers window.

7. In **Office,** enter the location or designation of this user's office or cubicle.

8. In **Telephone number,** enter the user's phone number and/or extension.

   - If you want to add more numbers, click the **Other** button.

9. In **E-mail,** enter the user's e-mail address.

10. In **Web page,** enter the address of the user's personal Web page.

11. Click **OK,** or click on the Next tab.

The **Address** tab entries should be self-explanatory. Simply enter the user's mailing address, city, state, and zip code. You can also indicate the region or country in which he or she lives.

EXERCISE

12.3 Edit the Account Tab of the User Account Properties

● ●

To perform this exercise, you will need:

- Access to a domain controller
- To have performed Exercise 12.1

1. Click on the **Account** tab (See Figure 12-2).

2. In **User logon name,** type the name that the user will use to log on.

3. From the drop-down list to the right of the user logon name, click the **UPN suffix** that must be appended to the user logon name (after the @ symbol). (Refer to Lesson 7.3.)

4. If the user will use a different name to log on from computers running Windows NT, Windows 98, or Windows 95, change the user logon name as it appears in **User logon name (pre-Windows 2000)** to the different name.

FIGURE 12-2
The Account Tab in the User Account Properties Dialog Box

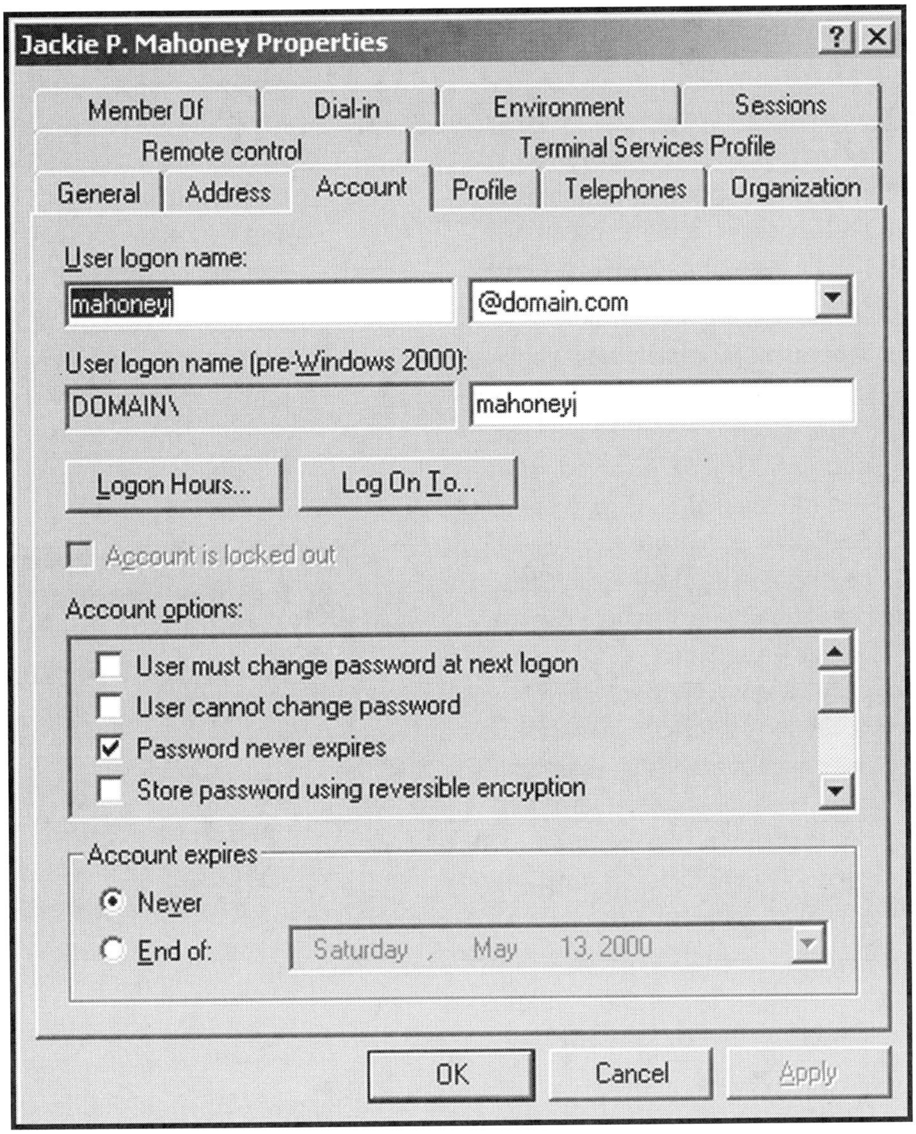

5. In Account options, insert or remove checkmarks according to the appropriate password settings for this user. Notice the scroll bar on the right side of the password settings list, and use it to see the following options:

■ **User must change password at next logon:** If you put a checkmark here, the next time the user logs on, he or she

will be prompted to enter a different password than the one used previously.

■ **User cannot change password:** If the administrator manages passwords, this option would be checked. This is not a recommended option since it places an additional burden on the administrator.

- **Password never expires:** If this checkbox is checked, the password stays in effect until this entry is changed.

- **Store password using reversible encryption:** Encryption adds an additional level of security to the password list. It can also add overhead due to the decryption process.

- **Account is disabled:** When checked, this option will cause the account to be unusable. User accounts can be disabled as a security measure to prevent a particular user from logging on as opposed to deleting the user account, which would erase all of the group memberships and permissions created for this account. By creating disabled user accounts with common group memberships, disabled user accounts can be used as account templates to simplify user account creation.

- **Smart card is required for interactive logon:** To log on to a computer with a **smart card,** users do not need to type CTRL+ALT+DEL. They simply insert the smart card into the **smart card reader** and they are prompted for their **personal identification number (PIN)** instead of their username and password (and, if applicable, domain). This increases security because a hacker must have the user's smart card and PIN. Smart cards lock after several unsuccessful logon attempts. If this checkbox

is marked, the user must have smart card to log on.

- **Account is trusted for delegation:** Select this option to give a user the ability to assign responsibility for management and administration of a portion of the domain namespace to another user, group, or organization.

- **Account is sensitive and cannot be delegated:** This is the opposite of the previous option. This account cannot be assigned for delegation by another account.

- **Use DES encryption types for this account:** Use this option if you need the **Data Encryption Standard (DES).** DES supports multiple levels of encryption.

- **Do not require Kerberos preauthentication:** Select this option if the account uses another implementation of the **Kerberos** protocol. Windows 2000 uses other mechanisms to synchronize time, so using the Kerberos preauthentication option works well.

6. In **Account expires,** select **Never** if the Account will never expire or select **End of** and enter a date if the account has an expiration date.

   - Usually this entry is Never.

   - You could set an account to expire when the user retires, for example.

   - Once the account expires, it is not useable until this entry is altered.

7. Click **OK.**

One of the buttons in the **Account** tab allows you to set when this user account is allowed to log on and/or when the user is restricted from logging on. In Figure 12-3, the colored blocks indicate hours that the user is allowed to log on. White blocks indicate when the user is restricted from logging on. In the example, users are not permitted to work on Sundays and the administrator runs maintenance routines from 2 AM to 3 AM each morning and does not want anyone to log on at that time. Exercise 12.4 demonstrates how to set logon hours.

EXERCISE

12.4   Setting Logon Hours

To perform this exercise, you will need:

■ Access to a domain controller

■ To have performed Exercise 12.1

1. Click on the **Account** tab.

2. Click on the **Logon hours** button.

   ■ The Logon hours dialog box is displayed (see Figure 12-3).

3. To restrict a single hour on a certain day, click on the cell where the day and the time intersect and click the Logon Denied radio button.

   ■ The block will turn white.

4. To restrict a range of hours, click and drag the mouse over the cells and click the Logon Denied radio button.

5. To quickly restrict an entire day, click on the day's name and click the Logon Denied radio button. (Click and drag also works here.)

6. To quickly restrict an hour on every day, click on the number that designates the hour and click the Logon Denied radio button.

7. To permit logon or reverse any of the above changes, perform the mouse action again and click the Logon Permitted radio button.

8. Click **OK** when done.

The **Telephones** tab entries should also be self-explanatory. Simply enter the user's home, pager, mobile, fax, and Internet Protocol (IP) telephone numbers. There is also room for comments such as the best times to call or

FIGURE 12-3
The Logon Hours Dialog Box

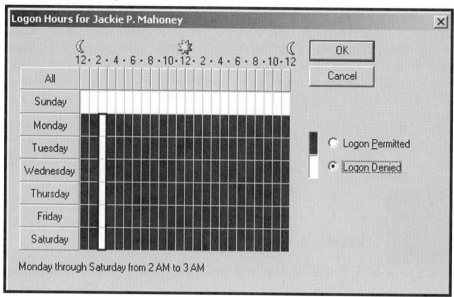

whatever is appropriate. You can click the **Other** button next to each entry to enter additional numbers for that category.

On the **Organization** tab, you enter information about how this user relates to the organization in terms of his or her manager, title, department, and company.

EXERCISE

12.5 Edit the Member Of Tab of the User Account Properties

To perform this exercise, you will need:

■ Access to a domain controller

■ To have performed Exercise 12.1

1. Click on the **Account** tab.

2. Click the **Member of** tab.

   ■ A list of groups the user account belongs to is displayed.

3. To add this user account to another group:

   ■ Click the **Add** button.

   ■ The Select Groups dialog box appears (See Figure 12-4).

   ■ Click on the group name.

   ■ Click on the **Add** button.

FIGURE 12-4
The Member Of Tab in the User Properties Dialog Box

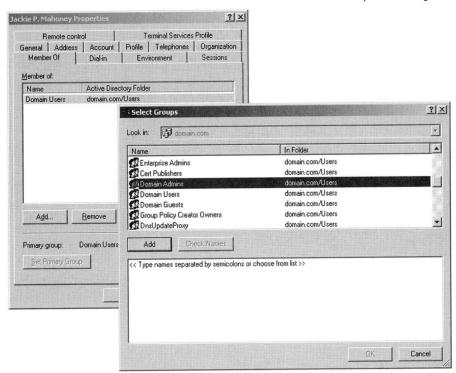

- Click **OK.**

- The group name appears in the list.

4. To remove this user account from a group:

  - Click on the group name.

- Click the **Remove** button.

- The group name is removed from the list.

5. Click **OK,** or click on another tab.

The remaining tabs on the User Account Properties dialog box will be covered in Chapter 13. The **Profiles** tab will be covered in Lesson 12.2.

Lesson 12.2 Configure a User Profile

When you walk into an office, the piece of furniture you usually see first is the person's desk. You can learn a lot about someone from looking at his or her desk, for this is the place where that person gets his or her work done, stores the tools that are most often needed, piles information, and sometimes displays a family picture or two. Almost everything needed for accomplishing tasks is on the top of the desk.

When Microsoft created Windows 95, it introduced the term **desktop** to represent the area of the screen behind where application windows open. Unlike previous versions of Windows, Microsoft made the desktop into a work area where files, folders, and icons could be displayed and easily accessed. Beyond changing the colors of the windows and background, Microsoft also made it possible for users to place a bitmap image under their desktop (like putting photos under glass on top of a desk) and called this bitmap image **wallpaper.** In most organizations, the contents of the desktop and how it appears is left to the discretion of the user. In some situations, however, it is necessary for an administrator to define what those desktop settings are. For example, if two people share a workstation, one person might prefer a bright green color that gives the other user a headache.

To address this issue, Microsoft created **user profiles** that define customized desktop environments. Figure 12-5 demonstrates what constitutes the desktop environment, including all of the entries on the Display Properties dialog box, network and printer connections, icons on the desktop, Start menu options, Toolbar elements, and other specified settings.

Types of User Profiles

The following three types of profiles are available:

- **Local user profile:** The first time the user logs on to a computer, a local user profile is created and stored on a computer's local hard disk. Any changes made to the local user profile are specific to the computer on which the changes were made and do not affect any other computer on the network. When the same user logs on to another computer on the network, he or she would have a different local user profile.

- **Roaming user profile:** A roaming user profile is created by the system administrator and is stored on a server. This profile is available from any

FIGURE 12-5
Desktop Elements

computer on the network. When the user logs on, the roaming profile is downloaded from the server and copied to the local hard drive before the desktop is displayed. In other words, the user profile roams to wherever the user logs on. Any changes the user makes to the desktop settings will be copied to the server when the user logs off.

■ **Mandatory user profile:** A mandatory user profile is a roaming profile that can be used to specify particular settings for individuals or an entire group of users. Only system administrators can make changes to mandatory user profiles. If a user makes changes to the desktop settings during their session, those changes will not be saved.

Viewing User Profiles

User profiles are stored on the local hard drive under the **Documents and Settings** folder. Exercise 12.6 demonstrates how to view the user profiles. Do not make any changes to the folder structure or the entries within the folders at this time.

TIP

Roaming profiles are especially helpful to an administrator. You could configure your desktop so that it contains the utilities you use the most so that wherever you logged on, your utilities would be available to you.

12.6

View Local User Profiles

● ●

To perform this exercise, you will need:

■ Access to a Windows 2000 computer

1. Launch **Windows Explorer.**

2. In the tree pane, double-click **My Computer.**

3. Double-click **Local Disk (C:).**

4. Double-click **Documents and Settings.**

■ Depending on how the computer is configured, you should at least see folders for **Administrator, All Users,** and **Default Users.**

■ You may see other entries depending on who has a user profile established on this computer.

5. Double-click the **Administrator** folder.

■ The folder structure you see under the **Administrator** folder is the Administrator's user profile (see Figure 12-6).

6. Explore the Start menu entries.

7. Double-click the **All Users** folder.

■ The folder structure you see under the **All Users** folder is the common entries all users have in their user profiles.

8. Explore the Start menu entries.

9. Double-click the **Default Users** folder.

■ The folder structure you see under the **Default Users** folder is the user profile that is used when a new user profile is created. It is also used when the user does not have a local cached profile on this computer and he or she does not have access to the user profile from the server (in the case of a roaming profile).

10. Explore the Start menu entries.

11. Exit Windows Explorer without making changes.

Did you notice that some of the folder structures and the Start menu options were different depending on the user profile being explored? User profiles are specific to the user account and are loaded after the user has logged on and has been authenticated.

Table 12-2 lists the folders in the user profile folder structure and what they correlate to on the desktop.

Note that My Documents, My Pictures, Favorites, Start Menu, and Desktop folders are the only folders displayed in Windows Explorer. The NetHood, Print-Hood, Local Settings, Recent, and Templates folders are hidden and do not appear in Windows Explorer. To view these folders and their contents in Windows Explorer, on the **Tools** menu, point to **Folder options,** click the **View** tab, and then click **Show hidden files and folders.**

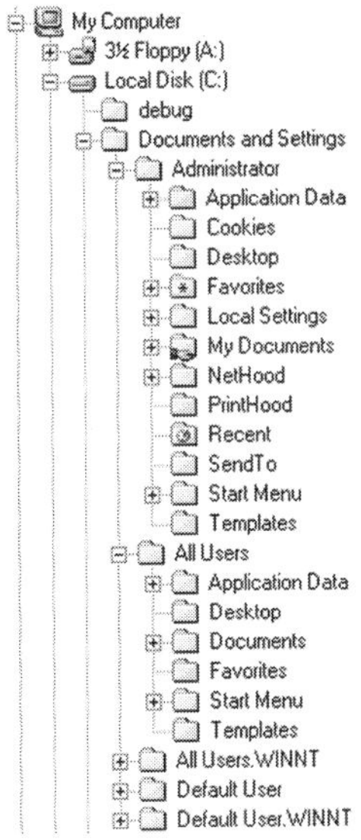

Using Roaming User Profiles

All of the roaming user profiles for all users are stored in a folder on the server. You can assign which folder on the server will hold the user profiles. If you enter a user profile path into a user's domain account, a copy of the user's local user profile is saved on the local hard drive (under **Documents and Settings**) and in the

FIGURE 12-6
User Profiles on a Local Hard Disk

TABLE 12-2 CONTENTS OF THE USER PROFILE FOLDERS

FOLDER NAME	CONTAINS
Application data	Program-specific data—for example, a custom dictionary. Program vendors decide what data to store in the user profile folder.
Cookies	User information and preferences.
Desktop	Desktop items, including files, shortcuts, and folders.
Favorites	Shortcuts to favorite locations on the Internet.
Local Settings	Application data, history, and temporary files. Application data roams with the user by way of roaming user profiles.
My Documents	Documents saved by the user.
My Pictures	Pictures saved by the user.
NetHood	Shortcuts to My Network Places items.
PrintHood	Shortcuts to printer folder items.
Recent	Shortcuts to the most recently used documents and accessed folders.
Send To	Shortcuts to document-handling utilities. The Send To option is provided on the Context-menu of files. You could right-click on the file, point to Send To, and copy the file to a floppy disk, for example.
Start Menu	Shortcuts to program items. This is what the user will see when he or she clicks the Start button.
Templates	User template items.

user profile folder on the server. This copy process occurs when the user logs off. The next time that user logs on, the user profile in the user profile folder on the server is compared to the copy in the local user profile folder, and the most recent copy of the user profile is opened. The local user profile becomes a roaming user profile because its contents come from a centralized location (the server).

If the server is not available, the local cached copy of the roaming user profile is used. If the user has not ever logged on to the computer before, a new local user profile is created. However, if the user profile is not downloaded because of server problems, changes to the user profile during that session are not copied to the server when the user logs off. Before entering roaming profile information in the user account properties, you will need to create a folder on a server and share that folder. The shared folder can be on any server; it does not have to be a domain controller. When the user logs on, Windows checks the user's account to see if there is an entry in the user profile's "Profile path" text box. If there is an entry, the user profile is located by the system and is copied to the local computer. Exercise 12.7 walks you through the steps for creating a roaming profile.

EXERCISE

12.7

Create a Roaming User Profile

To perform this exercise, you will need:

■ Access to a domain controller

1. Log on as administrator.

2. Open the **Active Directory Users and Computers** console.

3. In the details pane, right-click the user account for which the roaming user profile is being created. (You will need to navigate through the appropriate container object to locate the user account.)

4. Select **Properties** from the Context menu.

   ■ The User Account Properties dialog box appears.

5. Click the **Profile** tab.

   ■ The Profile dialog box appears (see Figure 12-7).

6. In **Profile path,** enter the full path that describes the location of the folder on the server where the roaming user profiles are stored as follows:

   ■ *server**share**%username%*

   ■ Where *server* is the name of the server.

FIGURE 12-7

The Profile Path Correlates to the Shared Folder on the Server

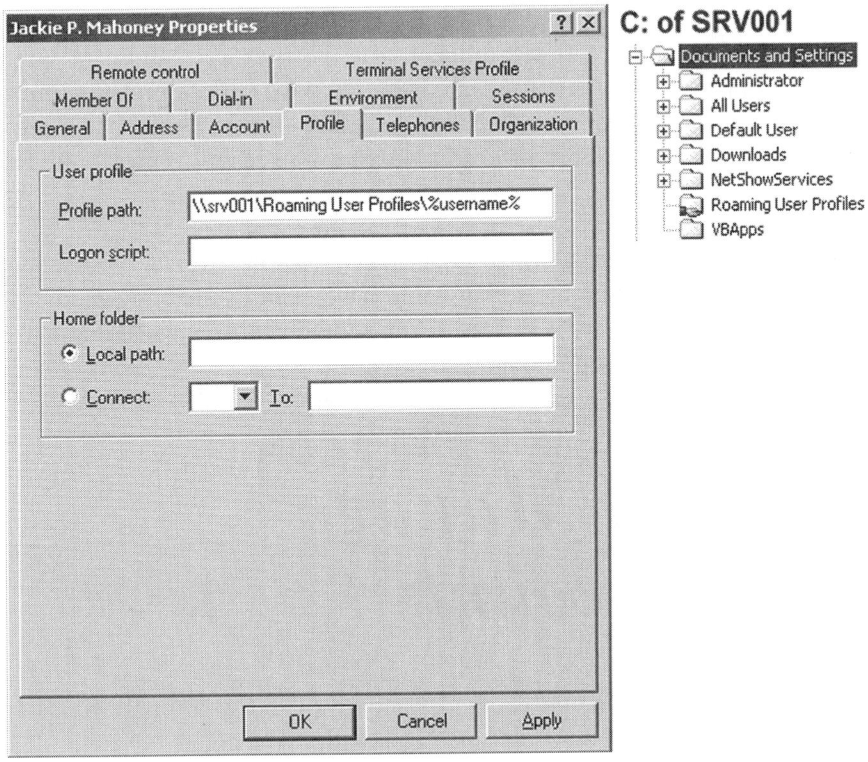

- Where *share* is the shared folder where the roaming profiles are stored.

- Leave *%username%* as is. This is a variable that will pull the username from the logon process. You can put the username there manually, but it is not necessary.

Leaving the variable also saves time when you are copying user profiles because you will not have to alter this entry for each user account.

7. Click **OK.**

Test your roaming profile by logging on to a computer with the user account for whom the roaming profile was created. Make changes to the desktop (colors, for example). Log on to a different computer on the network. You should see the changes made on the first computer's desktop appear on the second computer's desktop.

CAUTION: Because a roaming user profile can be used on various types of client computers, keep in mind that these client computers can have different hardware configurations. For example, the window setup in a user profile created for a computer with a Super VGA monitor might not look correct when loaded on a computer with a regular VGA monitor. When creating a user profile, try to use a computer that has a similar configuration to the computers to which the user will typically be logging on.

Although the folder shown in Figure 12-7 was placed under Documents and Settings, the folder on the server could have been located anywhere. The name of the folder can also be different. You should choose a name that makes sense to you and your team of administrators.

Lesson 12.3 Manage User Accounts

After a user account is created and all of the appropriate fields are filled in, you may not have to do much else with the account for a while. As time goes by, though, you may need to edit the information in the User Account Properties. Change is an inevitable fact of life. A user might be transferred to another department or have a change of address or get married (or all three). A user might even have a change in employment. All of these events require some kind of action on the part of the administrator. This lesson covers the most common tasks an administrator performs when managing user accounts.

Rename a User Account

You would change the name of an account if the user changes his or her name, as in the case of a change in marital status. You might also change the name of a user account if one employee has left the company and another employee will be taking that person's place. By renaming the account, all of the group memberships and permissions are preserved. Exercise 12.8 demonstrates how to rename a user account.

12.8

Rename a User Account

To perform this exercise, you will need:

■ Access to a domain controller

1. Logon as administrator.

2. Open the **Active Directory Users and Computers** console.

3. Click the container object that contains the desired user account.

4. Right-click the user account to be renamed.

5. Select **Rename** from the Context menu.

   ■ An editing box appears with the user account name highlighted.

6. Type the new name, and press Enter.

   ■ The Rename User dialog box appears.

   ■ With the exception of the Full Name, the original information is still intact. You will need to edit the appropriate fields with the change(s).

7. In **First name,** type the user's first name (if necessary).

8. In **Last name,** type the user's last name.

9. In **Display name,** type the name used to identify the user.

   ■ If this rename process is due to a marriage, you might consider temporarily putting the user's maiden name (in parentheses) in this field.

10. In **User logon name,** type the name with which the user will log on.

11. In **User logon name (pre-Windows 2000),** type the name with which the user will log on if he or she is using a non-Windows 2000 computer.

12. Click **OK.**

   ■ The content pane shows the user account with the new name.

Copy a User Account

The larger the organization, the more efficiency in accomplishing administrative tasks becomes important. If you have set up the user account properties, group memberships, and permissions for one user, it would make sense to copy those entries when creating another user account for a user with a similar function within the organization. A less efficient method would be to start from scratch with every user account. Exercise 12.9 demonstrates how to copy a user account.

EXERCISE

12.9   Copy a User Account

To perform this exercise, you will need:
- Access to a domain controller

1. Log on as administrator.

2. Open the **Active Directory Users and Computers** console.

3. Click the container object that contains the desired user account.

4. Right-click the user account to be copied.

5. Select **Copy** from the Context menu.

- The **Copy Object—User** dialog box appears.

6. Enter the appropriate information for the new user account.

- Notice the new user account will be automatically created within the same container object as the original user account.

7. Click the **Next** button.

- The password section of the Copy Object—User dialog box appears.

8. In **Password,** enter the password.

9. In **Confirm Password,** enter the password again.

10. Enter the appropriate checkboxes regarding how the password should be handled.

- On new user accounts, you usually have the user change the password on his or her next logon. The only time you would not do this is if the administrator manages the passwords.

11. Click the **Next** button.

- A summary screen appears detailing the results of the previous steps.

12. Click the **Finish** button.

- The new user account appears in the content pane.

TABLE 12-3 USER ACCOUNT PROPERTIES FIELDS THAT ARE COPIED

TAB	DATA COPIED TO NEW USER ACCOUNT
Address	All except **Street Address**
Account	All except **Logon Name,** which is copied from the **Copy Object—User** dialog box
Profile	All except the **Profile path** and **Home folder** entries, which are modified to reflect the new user's logon name
Organization	All except **Title**
Member of	All

After copying a user account, you will want to edit the User Account Properties of the new user account. Not all of the fields are copied from the original account to the new account. Table 12-3 lists which fields are copied on each of the **Properties** tabs.

Delete a User Account

Occasionally it is necessary to delete a user account. Perhaps an employee has left the company and the position he or she held will no longer be maintained. All group memberships and permissions for the deleted user account are lost and there is no "undelete" function for user accounts.

If you deleted a user account by mistake, you might think you could just create a new user account with the same name as the deleted user account. The new account would not automatically assume the permissions and memberships of the previously deleted account because the security descriptor for each account is unique. To duplicate a deleted user account, all permissions and memberships must be manually recreated, so use delete with caution.

EXERCISE

Delete a User Account

• •

To perform this exercise, you will need:

■ Access to a domain controller

1. Log on as administrator.

2. Open the **Active Directory Users and Computers** console.

3. Click the container object that contains the desired user account.

4. Right-click the user account to be deleted.

5. Select **Delete** from the Context menu.

- An Active Directory warning box appears asking if you are sure you want to delete this object.

6. Click **Yes** to delete the user account, or click **No** to abort the deletion process.

- If you click **Yes,** the user account is removed from the content pane.

Disable a User Account

A safer alternative to deletion is to disable a user account. A disabled user account cannot be used for logon purposes. Consider using disable instead of delete if you think there is any possibility of needing the original user account settings in the future. A user account might be disabled when an employee is either on vacation or on a leave of absence. Another reason might be when an employee has broken some company policy and his or her network privileges are revoked temporarily. You can also use disabled user accounts as templates for creating new user accounts. The disabled account would be copied to another account, and then the **Disable Account** checkbox would be cleared. Exercise 12.11 demonstrates how to disable a user account.

EXERCISE

12.11 Disable a User Account

To perform this exercise, you will need:

- Access to a domain controller

1. Log on as administrator.

2. Open the **Active Directory Users and Computers** console.

3. Click the container object that contains the desired user account.

4. Right-click the user account to be disabled.

5. Select **Disable Account** from the Context menu.

- A message box appears indicating that the object has been disabled (see Figure 12-8).

- A red "X" symbol appears on the user account icon.

FIGURE 12-8
A User Account That Has Been Disabled

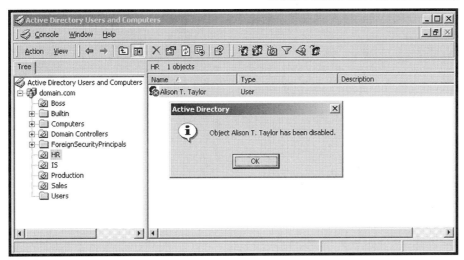

To enable a disabled user account, right-click on the user account and select **Enable Account** from the Context menu.

Move a User Account

You may encounter times when you need to move a user account from one container object to another. One example is when your Active Directory structure reflects the organizational structure and an employee changes departments or divisions. Exercise 12.12 demonstrates how to move a user account.

EXERCISE

12.12 Move a User Account

To perform this exercise, you will need:

■ Access to a domain controller

1. Log on as administrator.

2. Open the **Active Directory Users and Computers** console.

3. Click the container object that contains the desired user account.

4. Right-click the user account to be moved.

5. Select **Move** from the Context menu.

■ The Move dialog box appears (see Figure 12-9).

6. Click the container object to which you want to move the user account.

7. Click **OK.**

■ The user account is moved to the new location.

Find a User Account

In large organizations that have hundreds or thousands of users, locating a particular user within a complicated Active Directory structure would be a challenge. Why not let the computer do the searching for you? Exercise 12.13 demonstrates how to use the Find function to locate a user account.

FIGURE 12-9
The Move Dialog Box

EXERCISE

12.13 Find a User Account

• •

To perform this exercise, you will need:

■ Access to a domain controller

1. Log on as administrator.

2. Open the **Active Directory Users and Computers** console.

3. To search the entire domain, right-click the domain node.

■ If you know which OU the user account is in, right-click the OU.

4. Click **Find.**

■ The Find Users, Contacts, and Groups dialog box appears.

5. In **Name,** type the name of the user you want to find.

■ As an alternative you can type the description of the user.

6. Click **Find Now.**

   ■ If your search is a successful, a results box with the desired name will appear (see Figure 12-10).

   ■ An unsuccessful search will result in a message box indicating that the search was unsuccessful.

7. Double-click on the located user account.

   ■ The User Account Properties dialog box for that user appears.

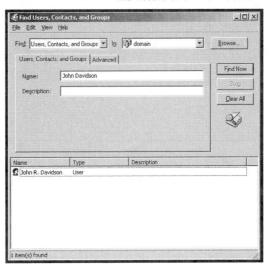

FIGURE 12-10
The Results of a Find Procedure

Reset a Password

The phone rings. It is one of your users, and he says that he cannot remember his password. You verify that he is who he says he is, and then you reset his password. Exercise 12.14 demonstrates how to reset a password.

EXERCISE

Reset a Password

To perform this exercise, you will need:

■ Access to a domain controller

1. Log on as administrator.

2. Open the **Active Directory Users and Computers** console.

3. Click the container object that contains the desired user account.

4. Right-click the user account that needs the password reset.

5. Select **Reset Password** from the Context menu.

   ■ The Reset Password dialog box appears (see Figure 12-11).

FIGURE 12-11
The Reset Password Dialog Box

7. In **Confirm Password,** type the password again.

8. If you want to require the user to change this password at the next logon process, select the **User must change password at next logon** checkbox.

■ This is why you make the password something easy to remember. The password you set in step 7 will not be the permanent password.

9. Click **OK.**

6. In **Password,** type in a password.

■ The password should be something generic and easy to remember (such as happy).

Lesson 12.4 Manage Groups

You learned how to create groups in Chapter 9. This lesson covers how to manage the groups you created.

Explore Group Properties

Every object in Active Directory has properties that can be viewed and altered as necessary, and groups are no exception. When you create a group, entries are made in the group's properties, but not all of the fields are completed. After you create a group, open the Properties dialog box for that group and enter the necessary information. Exercise 12.15 demonstrates how to open the Group Properties dialog box.

EXERCISE

Open the Group Properties Dialog Box

• •

To perform this exercise, you will need:

■ Access to a domain controller

1. Log on as administrator.

2. Open the **Active Directory Users and Computers** console.

3. Click the container object that contains the desired group.

4. Right-click on the group.

5. Select **Properties** from the Context menu.

   ■ The Group Properties dialog box appears (see Figure 12-12).

   ■ Table 12-4 lists the contents of the Group Properties of dialog box tabs.

FIGURE 12-12
The General Tab in the Group Properties Dialog Box

TABLE 12-4 THE TABS OF GROUP PROPERTIES

TAB	DESCRIPTION
General	Documents the group's name, description, and e-mail, indicates the scope and type of group, and has an area for entering comments (see Figure 12-12).
Members	Lists the user accounts that are members of this group. User accounts can be added to the group using the Add button on this page.
Member of	Lists the groups of which this group is a member.
Managed by	Gives the name, address, and contact information for the person who manages this group. The Change button allows the information on the page to be altered.

Adjust Group Membership

The memberships of user accounts in groups can fluctuate as the users move from project to project. Users may even change departments, which would necessitate adjustment of the groups to which they belonged previously and the groups they will need to join.

ADD A MEMBER TO A GROUP

When a new employee is hired, you may want to determine which current employee the new user's tasks will most closely resemble and copy the user account for that employee. When you copy the user account, you also copy the account's group memberships. You also have the option of creating the group memberships manually. Exercise 12.16 demonstrates how to add an object to a group.

12.16 Add a Member to a Group

To perform this exercise, you will need:

- Access to a domain controller

1. Log on as administrator.

2. Open the **Active Directory Users and Computers** console.

3. Click the container object that contains the group to which you are adding a member.

4. Right-click on the group.

5. Select **Properties** from the Context menu.

   - The Group Properties dialog box appears (see Figure 12-12).

6. Click the **Members** tab.

   - The **Members** tab is displayed.

7. Click the **Add** button.

   - The Select Users, Contacts, or Computers dialog box appears.

8. Click the object (usually a user account) to be added to this group.

TIP

In step 8 of Exercise 12.16, you can hold down the Ctrl key while you click multiple objects. Release the Ctrl key and click the Add button. All of the objects will be added at the same time.

9. Click the **Add** button.

10. Repeat steps 8 and 9 for each additional object to be added to the group.

11. Click **OK.**

12. The object(s) on which you clicked appear in the list.

TIP

In addition to users and computers, membership in a particular group can include contacts and other groups.

REMOVE A MEMBER FROM A GROUP

Occasionally you may have to remove a member from a group. For example, a user might change departments or divisions or a project might be completed and the group memberships are no longer needed. Exercise 12.17 demonstrates how to remove a member from a group.

EXERCISE

12.17

Remove a Member from a Group

To perform this exercise, you will need:

■ Access to a domain controller

1. Log on as administrator.

2. Open the **Active Directory Users and Computers** console.

3. Click the container object that contains the group from which you are removing a member.

4. Right-click on the group.

5. Select **Properties** from the Context menu.

■ The Group Properties dialog box appears (see Figure 12-12).

6. Click the **Members** tab.

■ The **Members** tab is displayed.

7. Click on the member you want to remove.

8. Click the **Remove** button.

■ A warning message appears asking if you want to remove the selected member(s) from the group.

9. Click **Yes** to remove the member, or click **No** to retain the member.

Other Management Tasks for Groups

The remaining management tasks for groups are rename, move, delete, and find. Earlier exercises in this chapter demonstrated how to perform these tasks on user accounts. Because the rename, move, delete, and find procedures are the same for all objects, you already know how to perform these actions on a group. If you do not remember the steps, go through the exercises and simply substitute "group" for "user account." Since OUs are also objects, the procedures for rename, move, delete, and find apply to them as well.

CAUTION: Groups can be moved within a domain. However, only groups with universal scope can be moved from one domain to another. The rights and permissions assigned to a group with universal scope are lost when the group is moved to another domain, and new assignments must be made. Domains are security boundaries.

Summary

Windows 2000 Server simplifies user account and group management by placing the most commonly performed tasks for these objects within their respective Properties dialog boxes. Become familiar with the contents of each tab, because these actions are very common in the daily life of a system administrator. Be aware that the changes you make can have far-reaching effects on your network. Deleting a group, for example, affects every user account that is a member of the deleted group. Every permission setting that listed the deleted group would also be affected. It could be the same as the farmer selling the rooster. The hens would have a fit and there would be no one to wake the farmer in the morning, which would seriously upset the cows.

● ● ● ● ● ● ● ● ● ● ● ● ● ●

REVIEW EXERCISE

These questions will help you determine if you have learned enough to move on to the next chapter. If the graphic next to the option is a square (❑), there can be more than one answer for that question. If the graphic is a circle (○), there is only one correct answer. Color in the shape(s) to indicate your answer(s).

1. On which tab in User Account Properties do you set the Logon hours?
   a. ○ General
   b. ○ Address
   c. ○ Account
   d. ○ Profile

2. Esther is working on an important long-term project, but she will be retiring soon. Ken was hired as her replacement and will be working closely with Esther until she retires. Which of the following options could the administrator choose for creating Ken's user account so that he would have the same permissions and group memberships as Esther?

   a. ❑ Delete Esther's account, and then name Ken's account with the same name as the deleted account.

   b. ❑ Copy Esther's account, and customize the new account's Properties for Ken.

   c. ❑ Create Ken's account, and then manually assign all of the permissions and group memberships to match Esther's account.

   d. ❑ Ken cannot have the same permissions and group memberships as Esther. He will have to wait for her to retire.

3. Two users share the same workstation. Dustin uses the computer in the morning for graphic design work, and Denise uses the computer in the afternoon for accounting work. Dustin sets the desktop icons for his job, and then Denise changes them for hers. Every day it is the same. What could the administrator do so that they each can retain their own customized desktop settings?

   a. ⭘ Configure a local user profile for each person.

   b. ⭘ Configure a roaming user profile for each person.

   c. ⭘ Configure a group membership for each person.

   d. ⭘ Connect two monitors to the one computer.

4. Debbie and Sarah work together in the same office. Debbie has forgotten her password, so she asks Sarah for hers. If Sarah obliges, there will be a security breach. After discovering this situation, what options does the administrator have that would allow both users to keep working without compromising security?

   a. ❑ Disable Sarah's account.

   b. ❑ Change both users' account properties to make them change their password the next time they logon.

   c. ❑ Tell Debbie what her original password was.

   d. ❑ Reset the passwords on both user accounts.

5. On which Group Properties tab can you see a list of user accounts that are members of the group?

   a. ⭘ General

   b. ⭘ Members

   c. ⭘ Member of

   d. ⭘ Managed by

PERFORMANCE CHALLENGES

- Complete the User Account Properties information for every user account that you created. Document the list.

- Complete the Group Properties information for every group you created. Document the list.

- Add the appropriate user accounts to the groups to which they belong. Print the screen showing the **Members** tab in the group's Properties dialog box.

- Create a roaming user profile for two users. Log on as one of the users. Print the screen to show the current desktop settings. Make a change to the desktop. Log off and then log on at another workstation. Print the screen to show that the change was copied to the second workstation.

MANAGE RESOURCES

OBJECTIVES

After completing this chapter, you should be able to:

- ■ Configure various addressing methods for TCP/IP

- ■ Install printer drivers and configure a print server

- ■ Map a network drive for access to a shared resource

- ■ Configure home folders for users

- ■ Set up and use the Distributed File System

- ■ Use the Disk Management interface to perform actions on volumes

- ■ Compress files on NTFS drives

- ■ Limit the amount of disk space a user can use for file storage

- ■ Describe the purpose and function of Terminal Services

- ■ Use Device Manager to update a device driver

- ■ Define interoperability

- ■ Compare and contrast RAS and a VPN

- ■ Control access to a Web site

OUTLINE

Lesson 13.1 Configure the Network

Exercise 13.1—Configure TCP/IP for Automatic Addressing
Exercise 13.2—Configure TCP/IP for Dynamic Addressing
Exercise 13.3—Configure TCP/IP for Static Addressing
Exercise 13.4—Configure NWLink
Exercise 13.5—Install a Network Service

Lesson 13.2 Configure Network Printers

Exercise 13.6—Install New or Updated Printer Drivers
Exercise 13.7—Configure the Properties of a Print Server

Introduction

Providing users with access to the resources they need involves a thorough understanding of how a network functions and how to manage resources using the tools available in Windows 2000 Server. If necessity is the mother of invention, as the old saying goes, then technology is the father. As the influence of users expands across town, across the country, or even across the world, the use of technology in conjunction with necessity produces inventions for secure, flexible, and far-reaching access to resources. The **Virtual Private Network (VPN)** is just one example of emerging access technologies. This chapter demonstrates various techniques and technologies for managing access to resources.

Lesson 13.1 Configure the Network

The network itself could possibly be the most important resource in a network environment. Since other resources are not accessible without the network, a solid understanding of how networks function is important. Table 13-1

TABLE 13-1 NETWORK PROTOCOLS

NETWORK PROTOCOLS	DESCRIPTION
Transmission Control Protocol/Internet Protocol (TCP/IP)	TCP/IP is the most popular protocol, and the basis for the Internet. Its routing capabilities provide maximum flexibility in an enterprise-wide network.
Internet Packet Exchange (IPX)	IPX is the native NetWare protocol used on many earlier Novell networks. Lesson 13.10 explains how to integrate Windows 2000 Network and Dial-up Connections clients into a NetWare IPX network.
NetBIOS Extended User Interface (NetBEUI)	NetBEUI is suited for use in small workgroups or LANs. A NetBIOS gateway and the NetBEUI client protocol can be installed on all remote access servers running Windows 2000 and most Windows networking client configuration required for the protocol is a computer name.
AppleTalk	Networking on an Apple Macintosh computer is implemented through the AppleTalk protocol. Applications and processes can communicate across a single AppleTalk network or an AppleTalk internet, which is a number of interconnected AppleTalk networks.

TABLE 13-2 SERVER PROTOCOLS

SERVER PROTOCOLS	DESCRIPTION
Point-to-Point Protocol (PPP)	The PPP is a set of standard protocols that allow remote access software from different vendors to interoperate. A PPP-enabled connection can dial into remote networks through any industry-standard PPP server.
Serial Line Internet Protocol (SLIP)	SLIP is an older remote access standard typically used by UNIX remote access servers.
Point-to-Point Tunneling Protocol (PPTP)	A private network can be accessed through the Internet or other public network by using a virtual private network (VPN) connection with the PPTP.
Layer Two Tunneling Protocol (L2TP)	A private network can be accessed through the Internet or other public network by using a VPN connection with the L2TP. L2TP is an industry-standard Internet tunneling protocol with roughly the same functionality as the PPTP. The Windows 2000 implementation of L2TP is designed to run natively over IP networks.
AppleTalk Control Protocol (ATCP)	With ATCP, Macintosh clients can run the AppleTalk network protocol over the PPP. With ATCP support, a remote user can access a Web server over TCP/IP, print a document to an AppleTalk printer, and connect to a Macintosh file server (over TCP/IP or AppleTalk), all with the same dial-up connection over PPP.

TABLE 13-3 ACCESS METHODS

NETWORK PROTOCOLS	ACCESS METHODS	SERVER PROTOCOLS
TCP/IP	Phone lines and modems	PPP
IPX	ISDN access	SLIP
NetBEUI	Using X.25	PPTP
AppleTalk	Serial (RS-232) access	L2TP
	DirectParallel access	ATCP

and Table 13-2 describe network protocols and server protocols, two elements that provide a communications link between a computer and the network.

Table 13-3 demonstrates how the network protocols and server protocols can be related. It also adds possible access methods.

Configure Network Protocols

After a connection is made, communication cannot occur without matching protocols. For example, if a person who only spoke Portuguese tried to talk on the phone to a person who only spoke English, communication would not occur even though the connection was made. They need a common language in order to communicate with understanding. Knowing how to configure the chosen protocol is important. The first step in network protocol configuration in a Windows 2000 environment is to use the Network and Dial-up Connections utility.

EXPLORE NETWORK AND DIAL-UP CONNECTIONS

The Network and Dial-up Connections utility in Control Panel is used to configure the connection between a computer and the Internet, a network, or another computer. The utility is used to create, configure, store, and monitor connections to network resources both locally and remotely.

Initially, the Network and Dial-up Connections folder has only one icon: Make New Connection. As you create outgoing connections that contact a remote access server by using a configured access method (LAN, modem, ISDN, and so on) to establish a connection with the network. Or, you can create an incoming connection that enables a computer running Windows 2000 Professional or a stand-alone computer running Windows 2000 Server to be contacted by other computers. This means makes the computer operate as a remote access server.

No other management tools beyond Network and Dial-up Connections are necessary, because all services and communication methods are configured within the connection. For example, the settings for a dial-up connection include features to be used before, during, and after connecting. Even the connection status, which includes the duration and speed of a connection, is viewed from the connection itself.

The Network and Dial-up Connections utility can be launched in two ways:

1. Right-click My Network Places, then select Properties.

2. Open Control Panel, then double-click Network and Dial-up Connections.

TCP/IP OVERVIEW

Transmission Control Protocol/Internet Protocol (TCP/IP) is the most popular network protocol and is the basis for the Internet. It is the protocol used by most servers, although additional and/or different network adapters and their associated protocols can also be used. **Setup** and the **Configure Your Server** program are designed to assist in configuring TCP/IP and the services that support it.

To use TCP/IP, each server must be provided with an IP address. The IP address can be either a dynamic or automatic address provided through software, or it can be a static address that you obtain and set. Because these addresses are numbers and, therefore, are hard to remember, you will also have to provide users with names that are easier to use. Mapping this type of name to an IP address is called *name resolution* and can be accomplished by various methods, including the **Domain Name System (DNS)** and **Windows Internet Name Service (WINS).**

CONFIGURE TCP/IP

TCP/IP is configured in Windows 2000 Server by using one of three configuration methods: automatic, dynamic, and manual.

Automatic Configuration. By using the new Automatic Private IP Addressing (APIPA) feature, Windows 2000 provides default automatic configuration of the IP address in the reserved range from 169.254.0.1 through 169.254.255.254 and a subnet mask of 255.255.0.0. There is no automatic configuration of a default gateway, DNS server, or WINS server. Since APIPA is designed for networks that consist of a single network segment that is not connected to the Internet, you do not need to configure the default gateway, DNS server, and WINS server.

EXERCISE

13.1 Configure TCP/IP for Automatic Addressing

To perform this exercise, you will need:

■ Access to a domain controller

1. Log on as an administrator.

2. Click the Start button.

3. Point to **Settings.**

4. Select **Network and Dial-up Connections.**

   ■ The Network and Dial-up Connections window opens.

5. Right-click the network connection to be configured.

6. Select **Properties** from the Context-menu.

7. Click the **General** tab (for a local connection) or the **Networking** tab (for all other connections).

8. Click on **Internet Protocol (TCP/IP).**

9. Click the **Properties** button.

10. Click **Obtain an IP address automatically** (see Figure 13-1).

11. Click **OK.**

FIGURE 13-1
TCP/IP Properties Dialog Box

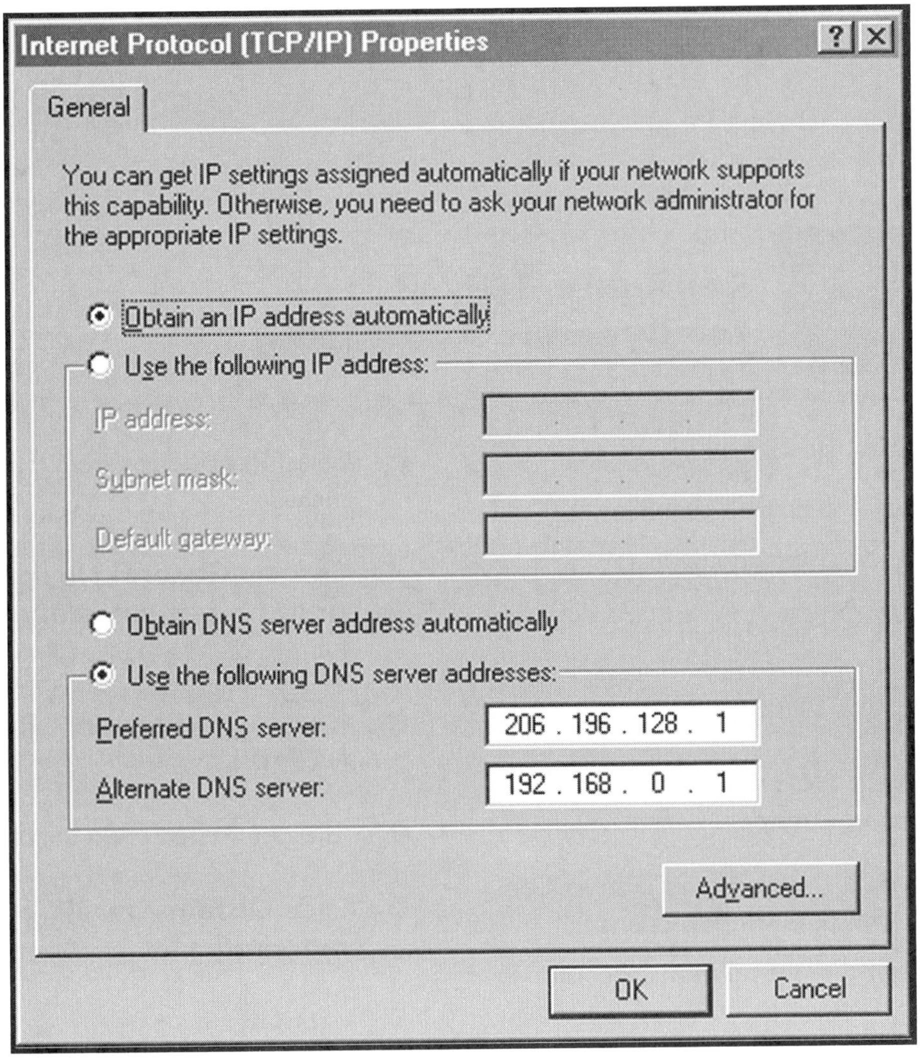

Internet Protocol (TCP/IP) Properties

General

You can get IP settings assigned automatically if your network supports this capability. Otherwise, you need to ask your network administrator for the appropriate IP settings.

◉ Obtain an IP address automatically
◯ Use the following IP address:

IP address:
Subnet mask:
Default gateway:

◯ Obtain DNS server address automatically
◉ Use the following DNS server addresses:

Preferred DNS server: 206 . 196 . 128 . 1
Alternate DNS server: 192 . 168 . 0 . 1

Advanced...

OK   Cancel

Dynamic Configuration.   By using Dynamic Host Configuration Protocol (DHCP), TCP/IP configuration is done dynamically and automatically when the computer is started. Dynamic configuration requires the configuration of a DHCP server, and computers running Windows 2000 are DHCP clients by default. When the DHCP server is properly configured, TCP/IP hosts can obtain IP address, subnet mask, default gateway, DNS server, NetBIOS node type, and WINS server configuration information. Dynamic configuration (using DHCP) is recommended for medium to large TCP/IP networks.

The steps listed in Exercise 13.2 are only required if a static TCP/IP configuration was previously used. By default, Windows 2000 attempts to obtain the TCP/IP configuration from a DHCP server on the network.

13.2 Configure TCP/IP for Dynamic Addressing

To perform this exercise, you will need:

■ Access to a domain controller

1. Log on as an administrator.

2. Click the Start button.

3. Point to **Settings.**

4. Select **Network and Dial-up Connections.**

   ■ The Network and Dial-up Connections window opens.

5. Right-click the network connection to be configured.

6. Select **Properties** from the Context menu.

7. Click the **General** tab (for a local connection) or the **Networking** tab (for all other connections).

8. Click on **Internet Protocol (TCP/IP).**

9. Click the **Properties** button.

10. Click **Obtain an IP address automatically.**

11. Click **OK.**

Manual Configuration. By manually configuring the properties of the TCP/IP protocol through the properties of a network connection, you can assign an IP address, subnet mask, default gateway, DNS server, and WINS server. Manual configuration is required in a network with multiple network segments when no DHCP server is present. Exercise 13.3 demonstrates how to configure TCP/IP so that the IP address does not change from session to session.

MICROSOFT EXAM OBJECTIVE

Configure the properties of a connection.

EXERCISE

13.3 Configure TCP/IP for Static Addressing

To perform this exercise, you will need:

■ Access to a domain controller

1. Log on as an administrator.

2. Click the Start button.

3. Point to **Settings.**

4. Select **Network and Dial-up Connections.**

   ■ The Network and Dial-up Connections window opens.

5. Right-click the network connection to be configured.

6. Select **Properties** from the Context menu.

7. Click the **General** tab (for a local connection) or the **Networking** tab (for all other connections).

8. Click on **Internet Protocol (TCP/IP).**

9. Click the **Properties** button.

10. Click **Use the following IP address,** and do one of the following:

    ■ For a local area connection, in **IP address, Subnet mask,** and **Default gateway,** type the IP address, subnet mask, and default gateway addresses.

    ■ For all other connections, in **IP address,** type the IP address.

11. Click **Use the following DNS server addresses.**

12. In **Preferred DNS server** and **Alternate DNS server,** type the primary and secondary DNS server addresses.

13. To configure advanced settings, click **Advanced,** and do one or more of the following:

    ■ To configure additional IP addresses:

       1. On the **IP Settings** tab, in **IP addresses,** click **Add.**

       2. In **IP Address** and **Subnet mask,** type an IP address and subnet mask, and then click **Add.**

       3. Repeat step 1 for each IP address you want to add, and then click **OK.**

    ■ To configure additional default gateways:

       1. On the **IP Settings** tab, in **Default gateways,** click **Add.**

       2. In **Gateway** and **Metric,** type the IP address of the default gateway

and the metric, and then click **Add.**

3. Repeat step 1 for each default gateway you want to add, and then click **OK.**

■ To configure a custom metric for this connection, type a metric value in **Interface metric.**

14. Click **OK** to close the Advanced dialog box.

15. Click **OK** to apply the changes and to exit the Properties dialog box.

IPX

Internet Packet Exchange (IPX) is the NetWare protocol used on many earlier Novell networks. In order for a computer to see a Novell NetWare network, the computer must run a NetWare redirector. In computers running Windows 2000 Professional, this redirector is called **Client Service for NetWare.** In computers running Windows 2000 Server, this redirector is called **Gateway Service for NetWare.** These two redirectors are covered in Lesson 13.7.

Included with both Windows 2000 Server and Windows 2000 Professional, **NWLink** is the Windows 2000 implementation of the IPX/SPX protocol. NWLink supports connectivity between computers running Windows 2000 and computers running NetWare and compatible systems. Exercise 13.4 demonstrates how to configure NWLink. To configure NWLink, you must first install the NWLink IPX/SPX/NetBIOS Compatible Transport Protocol and be a member of the Administrators group. You can perform this exercise without having a Novell system to connect to, but you will not be able to test the configuration.

EXERCISE

13.4 Configure NWLink

● ●

To perform this exercise you will need:

■ Access to a Windows 2000 computer

1. Open **Network and Dial-up Connections.**

2. Right-click a local area connection, and then click **Properties.**

3. On the **General** tab, click **NWLink IPX/SPX/NetBIOS Compatible Transport Protocol.**

4. Click the **Properties** button.

5. On the **General** tab, type a value for **Internal Network Number,**

or leave this setting at the default value of **00000000.**

6. Do one of the following:

- Click **Auto frame type detection,** and then click **OK.**

- Click **Manual frame type detection,** and do the following:

    - Click **Add.**

    - In the **Manual Frame Detection** dialog box, in **Frame type,** click a frame type. By default, NWLink automatically detects the frame type used by the network adapter to which it is bound. If NWLink detects no network traffic or if multiple frame types are detected in addition to the 802.2 frame type, NWLink sets the frame type to 802.2.

- In **Network number,** type a network number, and then click **Add.**

- Repeat these steps for each frame type you want to include, and then click **OK.**

APPLETALK

Networking on an Apple Macintosh computer is implemented through the AppleTalk protocol. By using AppleTalk, applications and processes can transfer and exchange data and share resources, such as printers and file servers. The ATCP supports remote access for AppleTalk.

With ATCP, Macintosh clients can run the AppleTalk network protocol over PPP. With ATCP support, a remote user can access a Web server over TCP/IP, print a document to an AppleTalk printer, and connect to a Macintosh file server, all with the same dial-up connection over PPP.

NETBEUI

NetBIOS Extended User Interface (NetBEUI) is suited for use in small workgroups or LANs. NetBEUI is not routable, and the only configuration required for the protocol is a computer name. A NetBIOS gateway and the NetBEUI client protocol can be installed on all remote access servers running Windows 2000 and most Windows networking clients. Previous Windows NT remote access clients, LAN Manager remote access clients, MS-DOS remote access clients, and Windows for Workgroups remote access clients may use NetBEUI.

NOTE: For information on troubleshooting network protocols and connectivity, see Lesson 17.6.

Install Network Services

File and printer sharing are examples of features network services provide. Exercise 13.5 demonstrates how to install a network service.

> **MICROSOFT EXAM OBJECTIVE**
>
> Install and configure network services

13.5

Install a Network Service

• •

To perform this exercise, you will need:

■ Access to a domain controller

1. Log on as an administrator.

2. Click the Start button.

3. Point to **Settings.**

4. Select **Network and Dial-up Connections.**

■ The Network and Dial-up Connections window opens.

5. Right-click the network connection to be configured.

6. Select **Properties** from the Context menu.

7. Click the **Install** button.

■ The Select Network Component Type dialog box appears.

8. Click **Service.**

9. Click **Add.**

■ The Select Network Service dialog box appears.

10. Click the service you want to install.

11. Click **OK.**

To configure a network service, click on the service in the Properties dialog box of the Network and Dial-up Connections control panel. Click the **Properties** button, and alter the configuration as needed.

Lesson 13.2 Configure Network Printers

Understand Network Printers

A printer is a device that places text and graphics on media. Many types of media exist, including paper, transparencies, labels, and film. Printers come in several forms, and each form has a specific application, including dot-matrix, laser,

MICROSOFT EXAM OBJECTIVE

Monitor, configure, troubleshoot, and control access to printers.

and color. Every printer must have a device driver installed in order to translate the information coming from a computer into printed material. Printers can be local, which means that the printing device is connected to the local computer, or printers can be network, which means that the printing device is connected either to a network computer or directly to the network itself. Windows 2000 offers a wizard to assist administrators and/or users with connecting to a printer (see Lesson 13.3).

Before a printer can be made available to users, it must be installed by copying the device driver to the hard drive and giving the printer a name. Although Windows 2000 will automatically install most printers, you may need the device driver if the printer is an older model. The Hardware Compatibility List should also be consulted before attempting to connect a printer to the network.

Configure a Network Printer

During the boot process, Windows 2000 runs a system check to detect if any new hardware has been added to the system. If possible, the operating system will install the printer at that time. You can also initiate a scan by using the Add/Remove Hardware tool in Control Panel. Occasionally printer manufacturers will develop a printer driver that is better than the driver they supplied to Microsoft or the driver they included on a disk in the printer box. When this happens, you should install the printer driver as soon as possible, for updated drivers for printers often enhance the printer's speed, and might also add other functionality. Exercise 13.5 demonstrates how to install new or updated printer drivers.

EXERCISE

13.6 Install New or Updated Printer Drivers

To perform this exercise, you will need:

- Access to a Windows 2000 computer

- A printer that is connected to the network according to the printer manufacturer's instructions

- The device driver for the printer (Windows 2000 will automatically install most printers, but you may need the device driver if the printer is an older model).

1. Click the Start button.

2. Point to **Settings.**

3. Select **Printers.**

   - The **Printers** folder opens.

4. Right-click on the printer for which the driver will be changed.

5. Select **Properties** from the Context menu.

- The Printer Properties dialog box appears.

6. Click the **Advanced** tab.

7. Click the **New Driver** button.

- The **Add Printer Driver** wizard launches.

8. Click **Next.**

- The wizard loads the list of printer drivers available as part of Windows 2000.

9. Select the appropriate manufacturer and model number for your printer.

- If the printer is not on the list or if you have a newer driver (usually sent by the manufacturer or downloaded from the manufacturer's Web site), click the **Have Disk** button.

- The wizard will prompt you to insert the disk and to identify the driver file.

- A closing screen appears indicating your successful installation of the driver file.

10. Click **Finish.**

Print Servers

A print server is a computer that is dedicated to managing the printers on a network. Any computer on the network can be a print server. Exercise 13.6 demonstrates how to configure the settings for a print server. The changes made to this dialog box affect all of the printers on the print server.

EXERCISE

13.7 Configure the Properties of a Print Server

● ●

To perform this exercise, you will need:

- Access to the Windows 2000 server that is the print server

1. Click the Start button.

2. Point to **Settings.**

3. Select **Printers.**

4. From the File menu, select **Server Properties.**

- The Print Server Properties dialog box appears.

5. Change settings according to your network needs on the following tabs:

- **Forms:** This tab allows you to specify the physical characteris-

FIGURE 13-2
The Drivers Tab of the Print Server Properties Dialog Box

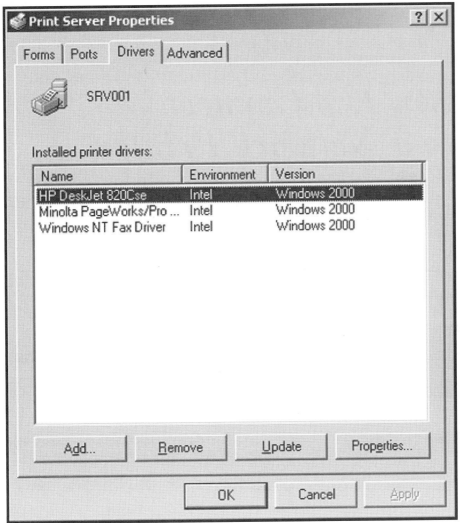

tics of the documents (such as paper size and margin settings) that will be generated on the print server. You can create multiple forms or use the default forms.

- **Ports:** A port is a connection point for communication between the computer and a peripheral device. One example of a port is a parallel port (LPT1) where a printer can be connected to a

computer. This tab allows you to add ports, delete ports, and configure ports.

- **Drivers:** This tab displays the printer drivers that are currently installed on the computer and allows for additional printer drivers to be added (see Figure 13-2).

■ **Advanced:** This tab lists the error-logging options for the print server. You can also see where on the hard drive documents waiting to be printed are spooled.

6. Click **OK.**

Lesson 13.3 Connect to a Network Printer

Once a printer is shared, users can connect to the printer and then send print jobs to the printer. Exercise 13.8 demonstrates how to connect to a network printer.

EXERCISE

13.8

Use the Add Printer Wizard to Connect to a Network Printer

To perform this exercise, you will need:

■ Access to a Windows 2000 computer

■ A printer that is connected to the network according to the printer manufacturer's instructions

■ The device driver for the printer (Windows 2000 will automatically install most printers, but you may need the device driver if the printer is an older model).

1. Click the Start button.

2. Point to **Settings.**

3. Select **Printers.**

   ■ The **Printers** folder opens.

4. Double-click the **Add a Printer** icon.

   ■ The Add Printer wizard appears.

5. Click **Next.**

   ■ The Local or Network Printer page appears.

6. Click the **Network** button.

7. Click **Next.**

   ■ The Locate Your Printer page appears.

8. Enter the name of the printer.

   ■ If you know the name of the printer, you can type the name in the **Printer Name** box.

FIGURE 13-3
The Browse For Printer Window in the Add a Printer Wizard

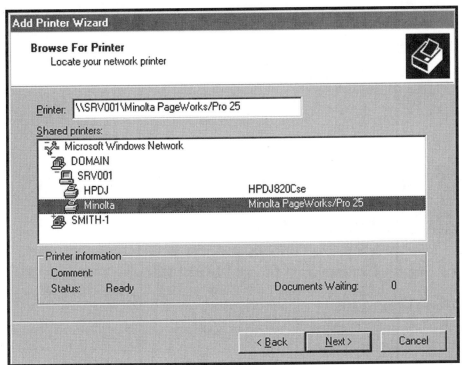

- If you do not know the name of the printer, leave the text box blank (clicking **Next** will initiate a browse procedure).

- It is suggested that you browse to the printer, even if you know the name. If you make a typo while manually entering the name, the printer will not be accessible.

9. Click **Next.**

   - The Browse For Printer page appears (see Figure 13-3).

10. Navigate through the network to locate the desired printer.

11. Click on the printer name.

    - Ensure that the name of the printer is accurately entered in the **Printer** text box.

12. Click **Next.**

    - The Default Printer page appears.

13. Indicate if you want this printer to be the default printer for this computer.

    - When the user selects Print from an application's File menu, the default printer will be selected. The user would have to use a pull-down list to select an alternate printer.

14. Click **Next.**

- A closing screen appears indicating your success.

15. Click **Finish.**

- The icon for the printer appears in the **Printers** folder.

- The black checkmark on one printer's icon indicates that printer is the default printer.

Lesson 13.4 Configure Access to Files, Folders, and Shared Folders

Permissions

Lesson 10.3 introduced you to permissions. NTFS permissions control access to files and folders, while share permissions control access to network resources. The most common problem with permissions is when permissions conflict and when a user cannot have access to a certain file. When permissions conflict, remember the rules that govern multiple permissions.

If a user belongs to two groups each with a different NTFS permission setting, the permissions are *cumulative.* This gives the user the permission that is the least restrictive. The only exception is in the case of **deny,** which overrides all other permissions and denies access. When a shared permission on a resource such as a folder conflicts with the NTFS permission on the resource, the *most restrictive* permission is applied.

> **MICROSOFT EXAM OBJECTIVE**
>
> Monitor, configure, troubleshoot, and control access to files, folders, and shared folders.

If a user requests access to a file that he or she does not have permission to access, you may have to talk with the user's supervisor or with the owner of the resource before granting access. Some users can be very persuasive, but you must keep in mind that there is a reason for the supervisor or owner requesting those permissions from you in the first place. The resource really belongs to the supervisor or owner, so the decision is that person's to make.

Map a Network Drive

Once a resource is shared on the network, other users can have access to the resource. One way for them to access the resource is to map a drive letter to a network computer or folder. Typically this process is called *mapping a network*

FIGURE 13-4
The Map Network Drive Dialog Box

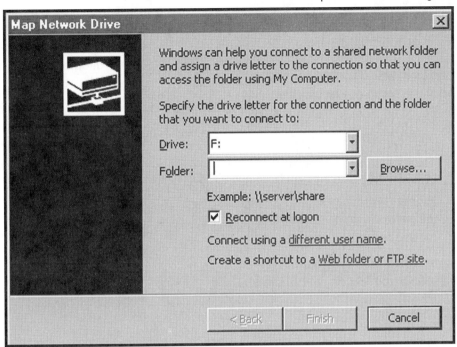

drive. After mapping a network drive, the connection to the resource over the network will appear as a drive letter on the local computer. To access the resource, the user simply double-clicks the drive letter and the contents of the shared folder are displayed. Exercise 13.9 demonstrates how to map a network drive.

EXERCISE

13.9 Map a Network Drive

To perform this exercise, you will need:

■ Access to a Windows 2000 computer

■ Access to a shared folder (Exercise 10.5)

1. Open **Windows Explorer.**

2. Click on the Tools menu.

3. Select **Map Network Drive.**

   ■ The Map Network Drive dialog box appears (see Figure 13-4).

4. Use the pull-down list box next to **Drive:** to select the drive letter that will represent the shared resource on the local computer.

5. In the **Folder** text box, type the server and share name of the resource.

   ■ Use the following form: *servername**sharename*

   ■ You also can click the **Browse** button and double-click the shared resource after navigating the network structure and locating the resource.

6. To reconnect to the mapped drive every time you log on, put a check-mark in the **Reconnect at logon** checkbox.

   ■ Mapped drives are available only when the host computer is also available.

      ■ You can assign a mapped drive to a different drive letter by disconnecting from the drive and then remapping it to a new drive letter.

7. Click the **Finish** button.

   ■ The designated drive letter appears in the tree pane of Windows Explorer.

Home Folder

Many of the files generated by a user are for his or her own information and are not necessarily created for the use of others. Windows 2000 Server allows for the creation of a folder called the **home folder,** which is designated for file storage by a particular user. The security is typically set for only that user to have access. Some applications will automatically point to the home folder when performing Open and Save procedures, and other applications will point to My Documents.

Configuring home folders involves the following three procedures:

■ **Create the folder:** Choose a location on a server with disk space sufficient to store the contents of the home folder for the users. While you could use multiple servers or even create the folder on the local hard drive, keeping the home folders in one location, makes backups and restores easier and simplified administration. Often administrators will create one folder with a name such as **Home folders** and then will create a subfolder for each user who will have a home folder. The name of the subfolder could be the same as the username.

> **MICROSOFT EXAM OBJECTIVE**
>
> Install, configure, and troubleshoot shared access.

- **Share the folder:** If the folder is not created on the local computer, you will need to share the folder on the network drive. Assign the permissions for access by the user at this time.

- **Configure the User Profile:** Enter the name of the shared folder, and assign a drive letter in the user's User Profile.

Exercise 13.10 demonstrates how to configure a home folder for a user.

EXERCISE

13.10   Configure a Home Folder

● ●

To perform this exercise, you will need:

- Access to a domain controller

- A location for creation of the folder that will be the home folder

- A user account that will use the home folder

1. Log on as administrator.

2. Open **Windows Explorer.**

3. Create the folder that will be the user's home folder.

4. Share the folder.

5. Open **Active Directory Computers and Users.**

6. Navigate through the console tree, and double-click on the container object that holds the user account.

7. Right-click on the **user account.**

8. Select **Properties** from the Context menu.

- The Properties dialog box for the user account appears.

9. Click on the **Profile** tab.

- The Profile page appears.

10. Enter the appropriate information in the **Home folder** section.

- **Local Path:** Enter the path for the folder if the folder is stored on the local hard drive.

- **Connect:** Use the pull-down list button to select a drive letter. Often administrators use **H:** for Home.

- **To:** Enter the server and share name of the resource (*servername**sharename*). Unfortunately, there is no **Browse** button, so you must enter this information manually and *precisely*. If you make even one simple typo, the home folder will not work.

11. Click **OK.**

- When the user logs on and then accesses his or her directory structure, the home folder drive letter will appear.

TIP

Encourage users to save their files in their home folders and to save files they share with other users in folders configured for access by multiple users.

Logon Scripts

On the **Profile** tab for a user account, you might have noticed the Logon script text box that we have not discussed yet. A **logon script** is a series of commands contained within a file that execute after the user logs on. Administrators use logon scripts to automate administrative tasks to be performed on behalf of one user, a group of users, or even all users. The administrative tasks might be as simple as synchronizing the time of the workstation to a particular server or as complicated as patching software problems.

To enable a logon script, you would enter the path and executable filename for the logon script file in the **User Account Properties Profile** tab. Although logon scripts can be written as command lines in a batch file, programs exist that make script writing more intuitive and flexible. Windows 2000 includes **Windows Scripting host,** a language-independent scripting host for 32-bit Windows platforms that includes both Visual Basic Scripting Editions (VBScript) and Jscript scripting engines. Full coverage of this topic is beyond the scope of this book. For more information, see Windows 2000 Server Help.

Understand Distributed File System

A user can spend a lot of time searching for and retrieving the information he or she needs, especially if the information is stored in several different locations on the network. With the **Distributed file system (Dfs),** files that are distributed across multiple servers appear to users as if they reside in one place on the network. Users no longer need to know and specify the actual physical location of files in order to access them. Consider implementing Dfs if

- Users who access shared folders are distributed across a site or sites.

- Most users require access to multiple shared folders.

- Server load balancing could be improved by redistributing shared folders.

- Users require uninterrupted access to shared folders.

- The organization has Web sites for either internal or external use.

DFS TOPOLOGY

A Dfs topology consists of the following:

- **Dfs root:** A container for files and Dfs links.

- **Dfs link(s):** A link from a Dfs root to one or more shared files or another Dfs root or to a domain-based volume.

- **Dfs shared folder(s), or replica(s):** A folder in a replica set to which each Dfs link points. A replica is a folder that participates in replication.

The domain server on which a Dfs root resides is known as a *host server*. You can replicate a Dfs root by creating *root shares* on other servers in the domain. This provides file availability when the host server becomes unavailable.

To users, a Dfs topology provides unified and transparent access to the network resources they need. To system administrators, a Dfs topology is a single DNS name space. With domain-based Dfs, the DNS names for the Dfs root shares resolve to the host servers for the Dfs root.

Because the host server for a domain-based Dfs is a member server within a domain, the Dfs topology is automatically published to Active Directory by default, which provides synchronization of Dfs topologies across host servers. This, in turn, provides fault tolerance for the Dfs root and supports optional replication of Dfs shared folders.

You can expand a Dfs topology by adding a Dfs link to the Dfs root. The only constraint on the number of hierarchical levels in a Dfs topology is imposed by the Windows 2000 limit of 260 characters for any file path. A new Dfs link can refer to a shared folder with or without subfolders or to an entire Windows 2000 volume. If you have adequate permissions, you can also access any local subfolders that exist in or are added to a Dfs shared folder.

STAND-ALONE VS. DOMAIN-BASED

Two types of Dfs root configurations exist: **stand-alone** and **domain-based.** In a domain-based implementation of Dfs, the Dfs structure is stored in Active Directory. In a stand-alone implementation, the Dfs structure does not use Active Directory. A stand-alone configuration can have only a single level of Dfs links, whereas a domain-based configuration is only limited to the Windows 2000 path length limit of 260 characters. A domain-based configuration can also have folders at the root level that are shared, but a stand-alone configuration cannot.

CREATE A DFS ROOT

Using the Dfs console, a shared folder is designated as the Dfs root. In addition to accessing this shared folder, users can access any subfolders of this shared folder.

MICROSOFT EXAM OBJECTIVE

Configure, manage, and troubleshoot a stand-alone Distributed file system (Dfs). Configure, manage, and troubleshoot a domain-based Distributed file system (Dfs).

13.11

Create a Dfs Root

To perform this exercise, you will need:

■ Access to the domain controller that will be the host for the Dfs root. (Any member server or domain controller can host a Dfs root. Currently a host server is limited to one Dfs root. Although the Dfs root may be located in a FAT partition, NTFS offers security advantages.)

1. Log on as administrator.

2. Click the Start button.

3. Point to **Administrative Tools.**

4. Select **Distributed File System.**

■ The Dfs console appears.

5. From the Action menu, select **New Dfs Root.**

■ The welcome page of the New Dfs Root wizard appears.

6. Click **Next.**

■ The Select the Dfs Root Type page appears.

7. Select the type of Dfs root to create (either *domain-based* or *stand-alone*).

8. Click **Next.**

■ The Select the Host Domain for the Dfs Root page appears.

9. Enter the domain that will host the Dfs root, or click a name from the list of available domains.

10. Click **Next.**

■ The Select the Host Server for the Dfs Root page appears.

11. Enter the name of the host computer for the Dfs root, or click a name from the list of available servers.

12. Click **Next.**

■ The Specify the Dfs Root Share page appears.

13. Click an existing shared folder, or specify the path and name of a new shared folder to create.

14. Click **Next.**

■ The Name the Dfs Root page appears.

15. Accept the default name for the Dfs root, or specify a new name.

16. Click **Next.**

■ The Summary page appears.

17. Click **Finish.**

■ The new Dfs Root appears in the tree pane of the Dfs console.

ADD A DFS LINK

You can add a Dfs link at the root of the Dfs topology. Currently the maximum number of Dfs links that can be assigned to a Dfs root is 1,000.

EXERCISE

13.12   Create a Dfs Link

To perform this exercise, you will need:

■ Access to the domain controller that will be the host for the Dfs root

■ To have completed Exercise 13.11

1. Log on as administrator.

2. Click the Start button.

3. Point to **Administrative Tools.**

4. Select **Distributed File System.**

   ■ The Dfs console appears.

5. Right-click the Dfs Root you created in Exercise 13.11.

6. Select **New Dfs Link** from the Context menu.

   ■ The Create a New Dfs Link dialog box appears (see Figure 13-5).

FIGURE 13-5
The New Dfs Link Dialog Box

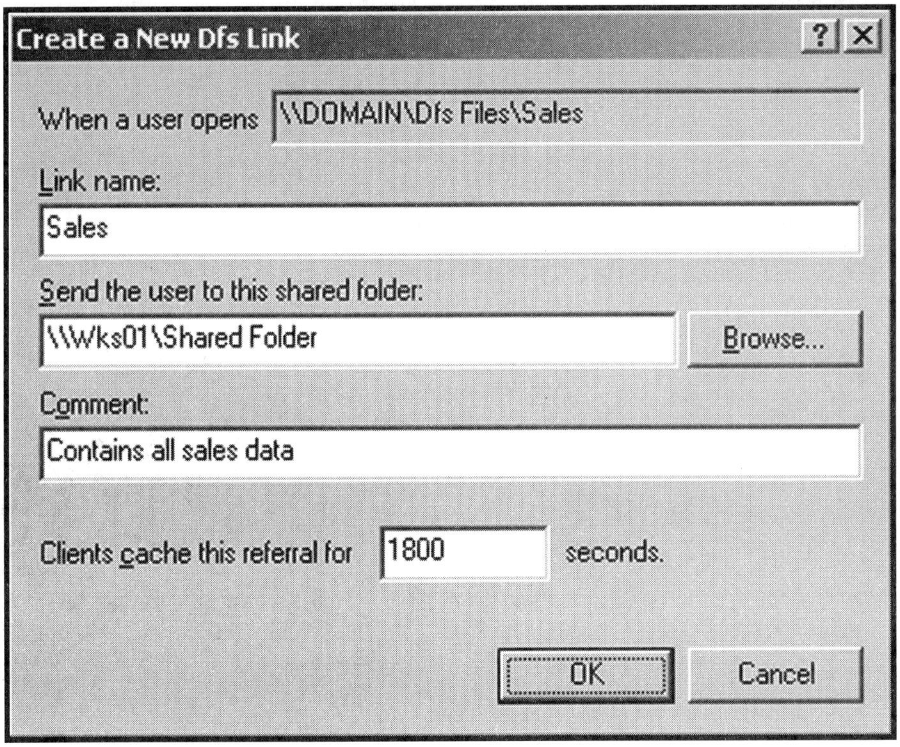

7. Type a name and path for the new Dfs link, or click **Browse** to select from the list of available shared folders.

- If desired, enter a comment to further identify or describe the Dfs link.

- Often the name of the link is not enough information for a user to determine if that is the area he or she is seeking.

8. Click **OK.**

- The new link appears in the Dfs console.

DFS SHARED FOLDERS, OR REPLICAS

For each Dfs link you can create a set of Dfs shared folders (also called replicas) to which the Dfs link points. Within a set of Dfs shared folders, the first folder is added to the set when you create the Dfs link. Subsequent Dfs folders are added by right-clicking the link and selecting **New Replica** from the Context menu. The maximum number of shared folders allowed in a set of shared folders is 32. Figure 13-6 shows two replicas for one link.

When users access the link via their browser, they will see the two folders shown in Figure 13-6 as being directly beneath the sales folder, even though the actual folders are on two different computers and nested in separate folder structures. The power of Dfs is seen in increased efficiency for the users.

FIGURE 13-6
Two Replicas for One Link

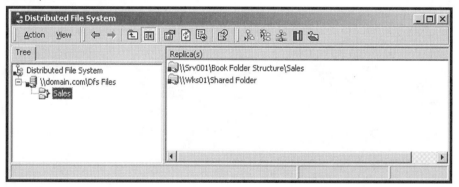

Lesson 13.5 Manage Disks and Volumes

Disk Terminology

Storage space on hard drives is an important part of any network. The files that must be accessible to the users are stored on hard drives that are installed in computers. Before learning how to manage the hard drives, the Windows 2000 terminology provided in Table 13-4 must be understood. You will more fully understand the contents of this table as you study the remainder of this lesson.

Use Disk Management

Disk Management is a utility for managing hard disks and the volumes, or partitions, they contain. Some of the tasks you can perform using Disk Management include creating volumes, formatting volumes with file systems, initializing disks, and creating fault-tolerant disk systems. Disk Management replaces the Disk Administrator utility used in Windows NT 4.0. The utility offers many new features, including the following:

> **MICROSOFT EXAM OBJECTIVE**
>
> Monitor, configure, and troubleshoot disks and volumes.

- **Dynamic disks:** Dynamic disks allow you to accomplish administrative tasks without shutting down the system or interrupting users. For example, you can create, extend, or mirror a volume without restarting the system. You can also add a new disk without restarting the computer.

- **Local and network drive management:** From any Windows 2000 computer on your network, you can manage any other network computer that runs either Windows 2000 or Windows NT 4.0 and on which you are an administrator.

- **Simplified tasks and intuitive user interface:** Because it has the same graphical interface as other Windows 2000 programs, Disk Management is easy to use. Many wizards assist you with both common and complex tasks.

- **Mounted drives:** You can use Disk Management to connect, or mount, a local drive at any empty folder on a local NTFS-formatted volume. Mounted drives make data more accessible and provide the flexibility to manage data storage based on the work environment and system usage.

TABLE 13-4 HARD DRIVE TERMINOLOGY

TERM	DESCRIPTION
Basic disk configuration	Basic disks have the same partition-oriented scheme of disk configuration as Windows NT Server 4.0.
Dynamic disk configuration	Dynamic disks are new with Windows 2000. They allow you to accomplish administrative tasks without shutting down the system or interrupting users. Both basic and dynamic disk configurations are supported by Windows 2000, but dynamic provides more features and flexibility.
Volume	A volume is a portion of a physical disk that functions as though it were a physically separate disk.
Partition	As with a volume, a partition is a portion of a physical disk that functions as though it were a physically separate disk. Partitions can only be created on basic disks. Types of partitions include primary, extended, boot, system, and active.
System and boot partitions System and boot volumes	System and boot partitions contain the hardware-specific files needed to load Windows 2000. The system partition can be but does not have to be the same as the boot partition. On a dynamic disk, system and boot partitions become system and boot volumes.
Active partition and active volume	The partition or volume from which the computer starts up. The active partition must be the primary partition on a basic disk. With Windows 2000, the active volume must be a simple volume on a dynamic disk.
Extended partition	A portion of a basic disk that can contain logical drives. Only one of the allowed four partitions can be the extended partition. Extended partitions can only be created on basic disks. On a dynamic disk, extended partitions become volumes and unallocated space.
Logical drive	A logical drive is a volume you create on an extended partition on a basic disk. It cannot span multiple disks. On a dynamic disk, a logical drive would be converted to a simple volume.
Simple volume	A simple volume is made up of disk space from a single disk. If the volume is expanded to multiple disks, it becomes a spanned volume.
Volume set	A volume set is a partition consisting of disk space on one or more physical disks that was created with Windows NT 4.0 or earlier. Only Windows 2000 can delete a volume set. Dynamic disks convert volume sets to a spanned volume.
Spanned volume	A spanned volume consists of disk space on multiple physical disks. Only dynamic disks have spanned volumes. Spanned disks cannot be mirrored.
Stripe set	A stripe set is a partition created with windows NT 4.0 or earlier that stores data in stripes on two or more physical disks. Stripe sets on basic disks are converted to a striped volume on dynamic disks.

Continued

TABLE 13-4 HARD DRIVE TERMINOLOGY *CONTINUED*

TERM	DESCRIPTION
Striped volume	A striped volume on a dynamic disk configuration stores data in stripes on two or more physical disks. Striped volumes offer the best performance of all volumes available under Windows 2000. Striped volumes cannot be mirrored or extended and are not fault tolerant. (If one of the stripes is lost, all of the data is lost.) Use RAID-5 to provide stripes with fault tolerance.
Mirrored volume	A fault-tolerant volume that duplicates the data on two physical disks. If one mirror becomes unavailable (hard drive failure, for example), the system can use the data stored on the other mirror. A mirrored volume is slower than a RAID-5 volume in read operations but is faster in write operations. Mirrored volumes can only be created on dynamic disks. Basic disks call this configuration a **mirror set.**
RAID-5	RAID stands for **redundant array of independent disks.** It is a fault-tolerant volume with data and parity striped intermittently across three or more physical disks. If one of the disks fails, the data that were on the failed disk can be reconstructed from data on the remaining disks. RAID-5 volumes can only be used on dynamic disks and cannot be mirrored or extended. In Windows NT 4.0, a RAID-5 volume was referred to as a **striped set with parity.**

EXERCISE

13.13 Launch Disk Management

To perform this exercise, you will need:

■ Access to a domain controller

1. Log on as administrator.

2. Click the Start button.

3. Point to **Administrative Tools.**

4. Click **Computer Management.**

   ■ The Computer Management window opens.

5. In the left pane, double-click the folder under Storage named **Disk Management.**

   ■ The right pane displays the Disk Management utility's opening window (see Figure 13-7).

FIGURE 13-7
The Opening Window of Disk Management

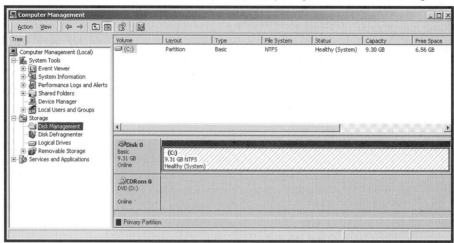

BASIC AND DYNAMIC DISKS

Disk Management supports two types of disk configurations: **basic** and **dynamic. Basic disks** have the same partition-oriented scheme of Windows NT Server 4.0. For upgrades, partitioned disks are automatically initialized as basic disks, so you can maintain partitions and volumes created with Windows NT Server 4.0. A **dynamic disk** is a physical disk that contains dynamic volumes. Dynamic disks cannot contain partitions or logical drives, and they cannot be accessed using MS-DOS. New or empty disks can be initialized as either basic or dynamic after installation. Table 13-5 identifies the actions you can perform on each kind of disk.

Storage on a dynamic disk is divided into volumes instead of partitions. Basic storage can be upgraded to dynamic storage at any time. When upgrading to dynamic storage, existing partitions are converted into volumes as shown in Table 13-6.

TIP

When you see the word *dynamic,* it usually means that the associated action will occur while the computer is running. For example, with Windows NT 4.0 and with Windows 2000 Basic disks, when a new disk is added to the system, you must reboot the computer. A disk configured as dynamic would be accessible without the computer having to be rebooted; the computer continues to run during the entire process.

TABLE 13-5 ACTIONS THAT CAN BE PERFORMED ON BASIC AND DYNAMIC DISKS

BASIC

Create and delete primary and extended partitions.

Create and delete logical drives within an extended partition.

Format a partition and mark it as active.

Delete volume sets, stripe sets, mirror sets, and stripe sets with parity.

Break a mirror from a mirror set and repair a mirror set or a stripe set with parity.

DYNAMIC

Create and delete simple, spanned, striped, mirrored, and RAID-5 volumes.

Extend a simple or spanned volume.

Remove a mirror from a mirrored volume or split the volume into two volumes.

Repair mirrored or RAID-5 volumes.

Reactivate a missing or offline disk.

BOTH

Check disk properties such as capacity, available free space, and current status.

View volume and partition properties such as size, drive-letter assignment, label, type, and file system.

Establish drive-letter assignments for disk volumes or partitions and for CD-ROM devices.

Establish disk sharing and security arrangements for a volume or partition.

Upgrade a basic disk to dynamic or revert a dynamic disk to basic.

TABLE 13-6 CONVERSION OF ELEMENTS FROM A BASIC DISK TO A DYNAMIC DISK

BASIC DISK ORGANIZATION	DYNAMIC DISK ORGANIZATION
Partition	Volume
System and boot partitions	System and boot volumes
Active partition	Active volume
Extended partition	Volumes and unallocated space
Logical drive	Simple volume
Volume set	Spanned volume
Stripe set	Striped volume
Mirror set	Mirrored volume

13.14 Upgrade from Basic to Dynamic Disk Configuration

To perform this exercise, you will need:

■ Access to a domain controller

■ To have performed Exercise 13.13— Launch Disk Management

1. In the lower right pane, right-click on the disk description for the basic disk that will become a dynamic disk (see Figure 13-8).

2. Select **Upgrade to Dynamic Disk** from the Context menu.

  ■ The Upgrade to Dynamic Disk dialog box appears and lists the available drives on the computer.

3. Place a checkmark beside each disk to be upgraded.

4. Click **OK.**

  ■ The Disks to Upgrade dialog box appears and lists the drives that will be upgraded.

5. Click the **Upgrade** button.

  ■ Disk Management displays a warning message indicating that once the upgrade is complete, you will not be able to boot any other operating systems from this drive except for Windows 2000.

6. Click **Yes** to continue the upgrade, or click **No** to abort the procedure.

  ■ Another warning message appears indicating that any mounted drives on the disk(s) to be upgraded will be force dismounted.

■ A **mounted drive** is a drive attached to an empty folder under NTFS. Mounted drives are referred to by labels instead of by drive letters. This is a useful function when all of the 26 available letters for drives have been assigned.

■ If you had set up some mounted drives, this upgrade process would dismount (disconnect) the mounted drive configurations.

7. Click **Yes** to continue the upgrade, or click **No** to abort the procedure.

  ■ A message appears indicating that the computer will have to be rebooted.

8. Click **OK.**

  ■ Windows 2000 Server performs a controlled shut down and restart of the computer.

FIGURE 13-8
Context Menu for Upgrading from Basic to Dynamic Disk

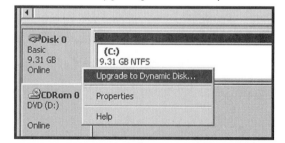

CREATING AND EXTENDING SIMPLE VOLUMES

Simple volumes can only be created on dynamic disks. They cannot contain partitions or logical drives, and they cannot be accessed by MS-DOS or by Windows operating systems other than Windows 2000.

If you want to increase the capacity of a simple volume after it has been created, you can extend it by the amount of unallocated space left on the disk. To extend a simple volume, the volume must be formatted with the version of NTFS used in Windows 2000. You cannot extend simple volumes that were formerly partitions on basic disks, but you can extend a simple volume to regions on other disks on the same computer. Exercise 13.15 demonstrates how to create a simple volume.

EXERCISE

13.15 Create a Simple Volume

To perform this exercise, you will need:

- Access to a domain controller

- To have performed Exercise 13.13—Launch Disk Management

1. In the lower right pane, right-click the unallocated space on the dynamic disk where you want to create the simple volume.

2. Select **Create Volume** from the Context menu.

- The opening screen of the Create Volume wizard appears.

3. Click **Next.**

- The Select Volume Type screen appears.

4. If an option is gray, you are unable to create a volume of that type at this time.

5. Click **Simple volume.**

6. Click **Next.**

- The Select Disks screen appears.

7. Click on the dynamic disk on which the simple volume will exist.

8. Set the size of the volume if it is different than the entire amount of unallocated space.

9. Click **Next.**

- The Assign Drive Letter or Path screen appears.

10. Accept the default drive letter, or change the entries on the screen according to your situation.

11. Click **Next.**

- The Format Volume screen appears.

12. From the pull-down lists, indicate the following settings:

- **File System:** Select the appropriate file system with which you want to have the drive formatted (NTFS is usually the best).

- **Allocation unit size:** Leave this setting as the default.

- **Volume label:** Enter a name that describes the purpose of the volume.

- **Quick Format:** Put a checkmark here if the volume has been previously formatted. The new format procedure will be faster because the operating system does not have to do a surface check of the hard drive on a quick format.

- **Enable File and Folder Compression:** Put a checkmark here if you want the option of using compression. You can enable this feature later as well.

13. Click **Next.**

- The wizard's summary screen appears.

14. Click **Finish.**

- Disk Management creates the volume, formats the drive, and puts the volume label on the display where the word "unallocated" was previously.

- The volume is now ready to store files.

ASSIGNING DRIVE LETTERS

You can create more than 26 volumes with Windows, but you cannot assign more than 26 drive letters for accessing these volumes. Drive letters A and B are reserved for floppy disk drives. However, if you do not have a floppy disk drive B, you can use the letter B for a network drive.

Windows 2000 allows the assignment of **static drive letters,** which means that a drive letter can be permanently assigned to a specific hard disk and volume. When a new hard disk is added to an existing computer system, it does not affect statically assigned drive letters. Some administrators will use drive letters that remind them of the volume's purpose. For example, they might use H: for Home Directories, D: for Data, or P: for Public.

CAUTION: Be careful when making drive-letter assignments because many programs for MS-DOS and Windows make references to a specific drive letter. For example, a program may only be able to find data files if the files are stored on the D: drive. During installation, most of these types of programs will put an entry in the **Autoexec.bat** file on the PATH line. If you are using legacy software, check the path before assigning drive letters.

Configure Data Compression

When you look at the details for a list of files in Windows Explorer, you will see that files take up space on a hard drive. Some files, such as graphics files, take a significant amount of disk space. Since the operating system needs a certain amount of open disk space in order to function efficiently, performance drops when disk space becomes low. Several options exist for increasing the amount of disk space in a system, including purchasing additional hard drives. A less expensive option is to compress the data within the files so that it takes up less space, and Windows 2000 Server supports data compression as a part of NTFS. Exercise 13.16 demonstrates how to compress an entire drive, and Exercise 13.17 demonstrates how to compress a single file.

> **MICROSOFT EXAM OBJECTIVE**
>
> Configure data compression.

EXERCISE

13.16

Compress an NTFS Drive

To perform this exercise, you will need:

- Access to a Windows 2000 computer
- A volume formatted as NTFS

1. Open **My Computer** or **Windows Explorer.**

2. Right-click the NTFS drive you want to compress.

3. Select **Properties** from the Context menu.

- The Properties dialog box for the disk appears.

4. Place a checkmark in the checkbox at the bottom of the screen next to **Compress drive to save disk space.**

5. Click **OK.**

- The Confirm Attribute Changes dialog box appears.

6. Indicate if you want the compression to affect only the root (C:\, for example) of the hard drive or the root and all of the drive's subfolders.

7. Click **OK.**

- The compression takes effect.

13.17

Compress a File on an NTFS Drive

● ●

To perform this exercise, you will need:

- Access to a Windows 2000 computer

- A volume formatted as NTFS

1. Open **My Computer** or **Windows Explorer.**

2. Right-click the file you want to compress.

- You can also compress a folder and all of its files and subfolders.

3. Select **Properties** from the Context menu.

- The Properties dialog box for the file appears.

4. Click the **Advanced** button.

- The Advanced Attributes dialog box appears (see Figure 13-9).

5. Place a checkmark next to **Compress contents to save disk space.**

FIGURE 13-9

The Advanced Attributes for a File with the Compression Attribute Set

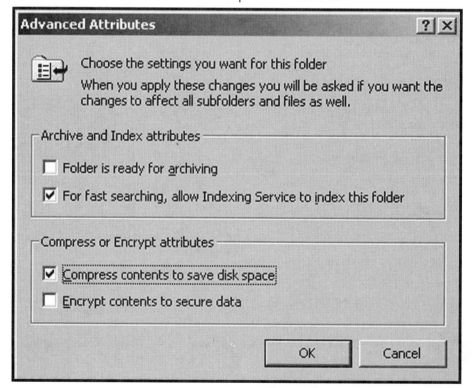

6. Click **OK** to exit the Advance Attributes dialog box.

7. Click **OK** to exit the file's Properties dialog box and to save the changes.

- The compression of the file takes effect.

MOVING OR COPYING FILES TO A COMPRESSED FOLDER

If a file is added or copied into a compressed folder, it is compressed automatically. If a file is moved from a *different* NTFS drive into a compressed folder, it is also compressed. However, if a file is moved from the *same* NTFS drive into a compressed folder, the file retains its original state, either compressed or uncompressed. Compressed files and folders cannot be encrypted.

EXERCISE

13.18 View Compressed Files in a Different Color

To perform this exercise, you will need:

- Access to a Windows 2000 computer
- To have performed at least one compression as in Exercise 13.17

1. Open **Control Panel.**

2. Double-click **Folder Options.**

- The Folder Options dialog box appears.

3. Click the **View** tab.

- The View page is displayed.

4. Place a checkmark beside **Display compressed files and folders in an alternate color.**

5. Click **OK.**

6. Launch Windows Explorer to see the results.

OTHER COMPRESSION SITUATIONS

Drives and files are not the only types of information that can be compressed. For example, HTTP compression conserves bandwidth and provides faster transmission of pages between the Web server and compression-enabled clients. In modem communications, data compression enables information to be transmitted beyond the actual connection speed. Data, particularly text and graphics, usually contain repeated sequences of identical information. Data compression works by replacing many characters of repeated information with a few characters and transmitting only one copy of repeated sequences of data.

Configure Disk Quotas

To understand the significance of disk quotas, consider the following example. Jane works in the accounting department. When there are no numbers to crunch, she likes to surf the Internet and download pictures she can use for wallpaper. One day, the administrator is searching frantically for available disk space when she discovers that Jane has saved over 3 gigabytes of graphic files. Although Windows NT Server 4.0 offered no way to limit the amount of disk space a user could use, Windows 2000 Server offers **disk quotas** to track and control disk space usage for volumes.

Two values are available for setting disk quotas: the **disk quota limit** and the **disk quota warning level.** The disk quota limit specifies the amount of disk space a user is allowed to use, and the disk quota warning level specifies the point at which a user is nearing his or her quota limit. For example, a user's disk quota limit could be set to 100 megabytes (MB), and the disk quota warning level could be set to 95 MB. In this case, the user can store no more than 100 MB of files on the volume. If the user stores more than 95 MB of files on the volume, the disk quota system can log a system event.

You can allow users to exceed their quota limit. Enabling quotas and not limiting use of disk space are useful when you do not want to deny users access to a volume but want to track disk space use on a per-user basis.

You can enable quotas on both local volumes and network volumes but only on those volumes that are shared from the volume's root directory and are formatted with the NTFS file system. Some additional rules that apply to quotas are as follows:

- A disk volume must be formatted with the version of NTFS used in Windows 2000.

- To administer quotas, you must be a member of the Administrators group on the computer where the drive resides.

- If the volume is not formatted as NTFS or if you are not a member of the Administrators group on the local computer, the **Quota** tab is not displayed on the volume's Properties page.

- File compression does not affect quota statistics. For example, if a user is limited to 3 MB of disk space, he or she can store only 3 MB worth of files even if the files are compressed.

EXERCISE

13.19 Enable Disk Quotas

To perform this exercise you will need:

- Access to a domain controller

- A volume where user files are stored

1. Open **My Computer.**

2. Right-click on the disk volume for which disk quotas will be enabled.

3. Select **Properties** from the Context menu.

   - The Properties dialog box for the volume appears.

4. Click the **Quota** tab.

   - The Quota page is displayed (see Figure 13-10).

5. Click the **Enable quota management** checkbox.

6. Fill in the remaining sections of the dialog box according to your organization's needs.

7. Click **OK.**

   - A message appears indicating that you should only enable disk quotas if you intend to use them since updating the volume could take several minutes.

8. Click **OK.**

FIGURE 13-10
Disk Quota Settings

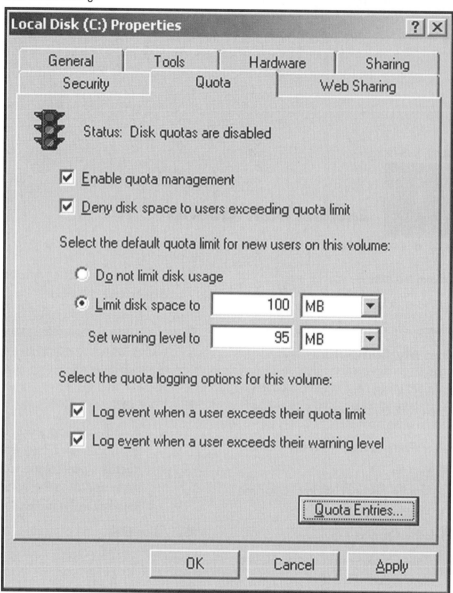

EXERCISE

13.20 Set a Disk Quota for a User

To perform this exercise, you will need:

- Access to a domain controller

- To have performed Exercise 13.19

1. Open **My Computer.**

2. Right-click on the disk volume for which disk quotas have been enabled and on which the user's files are stored.

3. Select **Properties** from the Context menu.

4. Click the **Quota** tab.

5. Click the **Quota Entries** button.

   ■ The Quota Entries window opens (see Figure 13-11).

6. From the Quota menu, select **New Quota Entry.**

   ■ The Select Users dialog box appears.

7. Use the Look in list box to select the domain or workgroup for the user.

8. Click the **Add** button.

9. Click **OK.**

   ■ The Add New Quota Entry dialog box appears.

10. Enter specific settings for the user, including the user's quota limit.

11. Click **OK.**

   ■ The new quota entry is listed in the Quota Entries window.

FIGURE 13-11
The Quota Entries Window

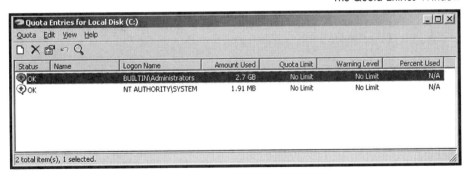

Lesson 13.6 Working with Device Drivers

Configuring Hardware Devices

Many of the resources available on a network are hardware resources. In order for hardware to function, it must have a driver and it must be configured to work properly with other devices installed in the computer. Windows 2000 supports plug and play, which enables the operating system to automatically configure a plug-and-play compatible device. As part of that configuration process, Windows 2000 assigns a unique set of system resources to the device. These resources can include IRQ line numbers, DMA channels, I/O port addresses, and Memory address ranges.

MICROSOFT EXAM OBJECTIVE

Configure hardware devices.

Each resource that is assigned to the device must be unique or the device will not function properly. Occasionally two devices require the same resources, resulting in a device conflict. If this occurs, the resource settings can be manually changed so that each setting is unique.

Resource settings for a non–plug-and-play device are not automatically configured. Depending on the type of device being installed, you might have to manually configure these settings, which should be supplied in the instruction manual that came with the device. Devices can be configured using the Add/Remove Hardware wizard or the **Device Manager.**

Update Device Drivers

LOCATING THE DEVICE DRIVER

Most device drivers are included in the packaging for the hardware device, typically as a file on a floppy disk or CD-ROM. In the Add/Remove Hardware utility, the **Have Disk** button is used to point to the driver file for installation. Having the most current driver can increase functionality and compatibility, and occasionally the driver that is included with the hardware is not the most current driver. Sources for updated drivers include the manufacturer (and/or the manufacturer's Web site), Web sites dedicated to providing hardware drivers, and the Windows 2000 CD-ROM.

MICROSOFT EXAM OBJECTIVE

Update device drivers.

USE DEVICE MANAGER

Before Windows 95, the process for installing, updating, and configuring devices was as varied as the devices themselves. Device Manager was introduced by Microsoft to provide one location for managing all devices. The utility displays all of the installed hardware in a hierarchical and graphical format. Using Device Manager, you can do the following:

- Determine whether the hardware on the computer is working properly.

- Change hardware configuration settings.

- Identify the device drivers that are loaded for each device and obtain information about each device driver.

- Change advanced settings and properties for devices.

- Install updated device drivers.

- Disable, enable, and uninstall devices.

- Identify device conflicts and manually configure resource settings.

- Print a summary of the devices that are installed on your computer.

> **MICROSOFT EXAM OBJECTIVE**
>
> Install, configure, and troubleshoot network adapters and drivers.

Device Manager is a good tool for checking the status of the hardware and for identifying the applied driver. You should not need to use Device Manager to change resource settings because resources are allocated during the hardware setup process. Although Device Manager can only be used to change settings on the local computer, remote computers can access Device Manager information in read-only mode. Exercise 13.21 demonstrates how to launch and explore Device Manager and how to configure network adapter drivers. Review the information provided in each window, but do not make any changes.

CAUTION: Changing resource settings improperly can disable the hardware and cause the computer to malfunction or stop working altogether. Only users who have expert knowledge of computer hardware and hardware configurations should change resource settings.

EXERCISE

Configure Network Adapter Drivers

To perform this exercise, you will need:

- Access to a Windows 2000 computer with an installed network adapter

1. Log on as an administrator.

2. Open **Control Panel.**

3. Double-click on **System.**

4. Click the **Hardware** tab.

5. Click the **Device Manager** button.

■ The Device Manager window opens.

6. Expand the Network adapters branch (see Figure 13-12).

7. Double-click on the listed network adapter.

FIGURE 13-12
The Device Manager Interface

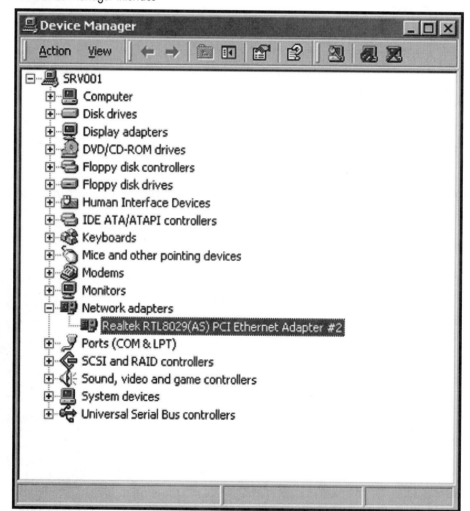

- The Properties dialog box appears and offers the following tabs:

    - **General:** Lists the type of device, the manufacturer, and where it is installed in the computer. The page also indicates the status of the device (whether or not it is functioning properly) and offers a **Troubleshooter** button for troubleshooting a malfunctioning device.

    - **Driver:** Displays information about the driver, including who provided the driver, the date and version of the driver, and the digital signer (covered in the next section). To see more about the driver, such as the folder where the driver is installed, click the **Driver**

Details button. To uninstall the device, click the **Uninstall** button. To launch the Update Device Driver wizard, click the **Update Driver** button. The wizard will prompt you for the source of the new driver file and will then install the driver in the appropriate location.

- **Resources:** Lists the allocated settings for the resource and indicates if any resource conflicts exist.

8. After exploring the tabs, click **OK** to close the Properties dialog box.

9. Exit the Device Manager window.

10. Click **OK** to exit the System dialog box.

11. Exit Control Panel.

Configure Driver Signing Options

Consider the following scenario. While browsing the Internet, you discover a third-party driver for your video card that has a more recent date than the driver you are currently using. You download the file and use Device Manager to update the driver on the computer. Upon rebooting, the computer is functional but the monitor is black. All is not lost, since you know that Safe Mode is available. If only you had known that the new driver was not going to work, you could have saved yourself some time and effort.

To help you avoid situations like this, Windows 2000 drivers and operating system files have been digitally signed by Microsoft to ensure their quality. A digital signature from Microsoft ensures

MICROSOFT EXAM OBJECTIVE

Configure driver signing options.

that the file has been tested and that it has not been altered or overwritten by another program's installation process.

Digital signatures offer an additional level of system integrity protection. An administrator can configure Windows 2000 to either ignore device drivers that are not digitally signed, to display a warning when it detects device drivers that are not digitally signed (the default), or to prevent the installation of device drivers without digital signatures. Exercise 13.22 demonstrates how to configure driver signing options.

EXERCISE

13.22 Configure Driver Signing Options

● ●

To perform this exercise, you will need:

■ Access to a Windows 2000 computer

1. Log on as an administrator.

2. Open **Control Panel.**

3. Double-click on **System.**

4. Click the **Hardware** tab.

5. Click the **Driver Signing** button.

   ■ The Driver Signing Options dialog box opens and offers the following options:

      ■ **Ignore:** Allows all device drivers to be installed on this computer, regardless of whether they have a digital signature.

      ■ **Warn:** Displays a warning message whenever an

installation program attempts to install a device driver without a digital signature.

      ■ **Block:** Prevents an installation program from installing device drivers without a digital signature.

      ■ **Apply setting as system default:** Applies the selected setting as the default for all users who log on to this computer.

6. Click **OK** to close the Driver Signing Options dialog box.

7. Click **OK** to close System.

8. Exit Control Panel.

Lesson 13.7 Configure Network Services for Interoperability

Understand the Need for Interoperability

Windows 2000 is not the only operating system available on the market today, and one of Microsoft's largest competitors in this area is Novell's NetWare. Most companies will run one operating system on all of their computers, but there are some situations where a combination of operating systems must coexist. In order for the network to be fully functional, the two operating systems must be able to communicate and exchange information. This interaction is referred to as **interoperability,** or the ability to interoperate.

Windows 2000 Server and Windows 2000 Professional provide several services that enable computers running Windows 2000 to coexist and interoperate with Novell NetWare networks and servers. Table 13-7 lists the most commonly used interoperability services.

MICROSOFT EXAM OBJECTIVE

Install and configure network services for interoperability.

TABLE 13-7 WINDOWS 2000 INTEROPERABILITY SERVICES

SERVICE	DESCRIPTION
NWLink (IPX/SPX/NetBIOS Compatible Transport Protocol)	Included with both Windows 2000 Server and Windows 2000 Professional, NWLink is the Windows 2000 implementation of the IPX/SPX protocol. NWLink supports connectivity between computers running Windows 2000 and computers running NetWare and compatible systems.
Gateway Service for NetWare	Included with Windows 2000 Server, this tool enables a Windows 2000 Server to connect to computers running NetWare 3.*x* or 4.*x* server software. In addition, Gateway Service for NetWare can be used to enable computers running only Microsoft client software to access NetWare resources through a gateway.
Client Service for NetWare	Included with Windows 2000 Professional, this tool enables workstations to make direct connections to file and printer resources on NetWare servers running NetWare 2.*x*, 3.*x*, or 4.*x* software.
Directory Service Migration Tool	Included with Windows 2000 Server, this tool enables the migration of user accounts, groups, files, and permissions from a NetWare server to Windows 2000 Active Directory.
File and Print Services for NetWare	This tool is a separate product that enables a Windows 2000 Server to provide file and print services directly to NetWare and compatible client computers. No changes or additions to the NetWare client software are necessary.

The Gateway Service for NetWare

INSTALLATION

You can install the Gateway Service for NetWare during the installation of Windows 2000 Server, or you can install it later using Network and Dial-up Connections. NWLink and Client Service for NetWare are also installed during the Gateway Service for NetWare installation process. Exercise 13.23 demonstrates how to install these services. (Your instructor might not require you to perform this exercise, depending on the configuration of your network.)

EXERCISE

13.23 Install the Gateway Service for NetWare

To perform this exercise you will need:

■ Access to a Windows 2000 workstation

1. Log on as an administrator.

2. Click the Start button.

3. Point to **Settings.**

4. Select **Network and Dial-up Connections.**

5. Right-click a local area connection.

6. Select **Properties** from the Context menu.

7. Click the **Install** button.

   ■ The Select Network Component Type dialog box appears.

8. Click on **Client.**

9. Click the **Add** button.

   ■ The Select Network Client dialog box appears.

10. Click **Client Services for NetWare.**

11. Click **OK.**

   ■ After the service is activated, a message box appears indicating that the computer will have to be rebooted for the changes to take effect. You are prompted to click Yes to reboot the computer now or No to reboot later.

   ■ If you do nothing and wait a moment, the Select Network Logon dialog box will appear and offers the following options:

      ■ **Preferred server:** If your network does not

support NDS (see Terminology box), indicate the server to which you want to automatically log on upon booting.

- **Default Tree and Context:** If your network supports NDS, enter the tree name and user context.

- **Run Logon Script:** Runs a NetWare logon script after logon.

12. Enter the appropriate information.

13. Click **OK.**

14. Click **Yes** to reboot the computer.

ACTIVATION

Now that you have installed the Gateway Service for NetWare on the client computer, you must enable gateways on the server before you can activate the gateway. You can create gateways only to NetWare servers that recognize the user account specified in **Gateway Account** and that have an NTGATEWAY group containing the gateway account. To create a gateway to an NDS volume, the volume must be in the same container as the NTGATEWAY group and the gateway account must be a member of the NTGATEWAY group in that container. To be fully understood these NetWare configurations require a more in-depth understanding of how NetWare works. Your instructor will determine how much more you need to know about this topic and if you can perform the following exercise. Exercise 13.24 demonstrates how to create a gateway to a file that is a resource on a NetWare server.

EXERCISE

13.24 Activate a Gateway to a NetWare File Resource

To perform this exercise, you will need:

- Access to a Windows 2000 workstation

- To have installed the Gateway Service for NetWare on the client and activated gateways on the server

1. Log on as an administrator.

2. Open **Control Panel.**

3. Double-click **GSNW.**

4. Click **Gateway.**

5. Select the **Enable Gateway** checkbox.

6. Click the **Add** button.

7. In **Share Name,** type a share name that Microsoft clients will use to access the NetWare resource.

8. In **Network Path,** type the network path of the NetWare volume or directory you want to share.

9. In **Use Drive,** enter the default drive you want to use, if necessary.

10. Click **Unlimited** to indicate no limitations on the numbers of concurrent users, or click **Allow** and enter the maximum number of concurrent users.

11. Click **OK.**

The configuration of interoperability components can be complicated and requires adequate knowledge of the Microsoft Windows 2000 operating system, the Novell NetWare operating system, and how they are each implemented within a network. Consider this to be an area for further study after you complete this course. After studying the topic, you will most likely understand why most companies choose to perform a *total* migration from one operating system to another.

Lesson 13.8 Configure Terminal Services

Understand Terminal Services

Terminal Services provides remote access to a server desktop through "thin client" software, serving as a terminal emulator. **Thin client** means that the server computer does the majority of the processing tasks, allowing the client to be less powerful in its hardware configuration. Terminal Services transmits only the user interface of the program to the client. The keyboard and mouse clicks from the client are then returned back to the server for processing.

MICROSOFT EXAM OBJECTIVE

Install, configure, monitor, and troubleshoot Terminal Services. Remotely administer servers by using Terminal Services. Configure Terminal Services for application sharing. Configure applications for use with Terminal Services.

Terminal Services can be deployed in either application server or remote administration mode. As an application server, Terminal Services can be used to distribute Windows-based programs using a network server. In application server mode, Terminal Services delivers the Windows 2000 desktop and applications to computers that might not normally be able to run Windows. When used for remote administration, Terminal Services provides remote access for administering the server from virtually anywhere on the network.

During the Terminal Services setup, a connection is configured for TCP/IP. The connection provides the link that clients use to log on to a session on the server. After installation, the **Terminal Services Configuration** tool is used to change the properties of this connection or to add new connections. The tool can also be used to:

■ Name a connection.

■ Specify a connection type.

■ Specify a connection transport and transport properties.

■ Set the maximum number of sessions allowed.

■ Enable or disable logons through the connection.

■ Set connection time-outs.

■ Set the level of encryption.

■ Set whether to disconnect broken connections.

■ Enable or disable session remote control.

■ Enable or disable automatic logons.

■ Specify a program to run automatically when a user logs on.

■ Override user profile settings for wallpaper.

■ Set permissions on the connection.

■ Set client device mapping and connection parameters.

Enable Terminal Services in Application Server Mode

Microsoft recommends that Terminal Services be deployed in application server mode on a stand-alone server, and not on a domain controller because of the extra processing domain controllers perform as a part of a normal network. Terminal Services should be installed on a server installed on an NTFS file system partition because NTFS provides greater security for users in a multi-session environment. Lastly, Microsoft recommends that programs designated for use with Terminal Services be installed *after* Terminal Services is enabled. This allows Terminal Services to register the programs for multi-session access, making the programs easier to manage. After considering these recommendations and taking appropriate action, you are ready to enable Terminal Services. Exercise 13.25 demonstrates how to enable Terminal Services.

13.25 Enable Terminal Services in Application Server Mode

● ●

To perform this exercise you will need:

■ Access to a Windows 2000 Server

1. Log on as an administrator.

2. Open **Control Panel.**

3. Double-click **Add/Remove Programs.**

4. Click **Add/Remove Windows Components.**

   ■ The Windows Components wizard launches.

5. Place a check mark next to **Terminal Services.**

6. Click **Next.**

   ■ The Terminal Services Setup page appears and describes the two terminal modes.

7. Click **Application server mode.**

8. Click **Next.**

   ■ Another Terminal Services Setup page lists programs that may not work properly when Terminal Services is enabled.

   ■ You may need to reinstall those programs for multi-session access.

9. Click **Next.**

10. You will be prompted to insert the Windows 2000 Server CD-ROM, so do it.

11. Click **OK.**

   ■ The Terminal Services Licensing Setup page appears.

12. Specify whether you want the license server to serve the entire enterprise or the domain/workgroup

13. Provide the directory location for the database.

14. Click **Next.**

15. Click **Finish.**

   ■ The required files are copied to your hard disk, and server software can be used after restarting the system.

Understand Terminal Services Licensing

Terminal Services has its own method for licensing clients that log on to Terminal servers. This licensing is different than the licensing method for Windows 2000 Server clients. Terminal Services clients must receive a valid license issued by a **license server** before they are allowed to log on to a Terminal server in application server mode.

The license server must be activated through Microsoft. Before licenses can be issued to clients, a license server must be installed on the network. The license server is activated using the **Microsoft Clearinghouse**. Lastly, you must install client license key packs on the license server.

MICROSOFT CLEARINGHOUSE

The Microsoft Clearinghouse is the database Microsoft maintains to activate license servers and install client license key packs on license servers that request them. The Microsoft Clearinghouse is accessed from Terminal Services Licensing.

LICENSE SERVER

A license server stores all client licenses that have been installed for a Terminal server and tracks the licenses that have been issued to client computers or terminals. A Terminal server must be able to connect to an activated license server before clients can be issued licenses.

For Windows 2000 domains, a license server must be installed on a domain controller. Two types of license servers are available: a **domain license server** or an **enterprise license server.** By default, a license server is installed as a domain license server. This type is appropriate if a separate license server will be maintained for each domain. Terminal servers can only access domain license servers if they are in the same domain as the license server. The enterprise license server is appropriate if the network has many domains. An enterprise license server can serve Terminal servers on any Windows 2000 domain.

EXERCISE

13.26 Enable Terminal Services Licensing

To perform this exercise you will need:

- Access to the Windows 2000 Server for Terminal Services

1. Log on as an administrator.

2. Open **Control Panel.**

3. Double-click **Add/Remove Programs.**

4. Click **Add/Remove Windows Components.**

- The Windows Components wizard launches.

5. Place a check mark next to **Terminal Services Licensing.**

6. Click **Next.**

7. The Terminal Services Licensing page appears and offers the following options:

8. If your network includes several domains, click **Your entire enterprise,** and then provide the database location. An enterprise license server can serve Terminal servers on any domain, but the domain must be a Windows 2000 domain.

9. If you want to maintain a separate license server for each domain, or if your network includes workgroups or Windows NT 4.0 domains, click **Your domain or workgroup,** and then provide the database location.

10. Click **Next.**

11. Click **Finish.**

Enable Terminal Services in Remote Administration Mode

In Remote Administration mode, Terminal Services will enable an administrator to perform administrative tasks on a server without having to physically sit at the server. Anytime you can do your work without having to move yourself around the building, you are being more efficient.

Terminal Services Licensing does not need to be enabled when enabling Terminal Services in remote administration mode. A maximum of two concurrent connections are automatically allowed on a Terminal server in remote administration mode.

EXERCISE

13.27 Enable Terminal Services in Remote Administration Mode

• •

To perform this exercise you will need:

■ Access to the Windows 2000 Server for Terminal Services

1. Log on as an administrator.

2. Open **Control Panel.**

3. Double-click **Add/Remove Programs.**

4. Click **Add/Remove Windows Components.**

   ■ The Windows Components wizard launches.

5. Place a check mark next to **Terminal Services.**

6. Click **Next.**

   ■ The Terminal Services Setup page appears and describes the two terminal modes.

7. Click **Remote administration mode.**

8. Click **Next.**

   ■ The necessary files are copied to the hard drive.

   ■ You will be prompted to restart the computer in order for the changes to take affect.

Configure Applications to Use Terminal Services

Many commonly used programs have been tested for compatibility with Terminal Services, but some programs may need tuning in order to work correctly for a multisession environment. If a program requires minor changes to the installation, a script must be run after the program installation is complete. Before installing a program, check the **Application compatibility scripts** for a list of programs that require scripts and information about how to use them. Scripts are located in the %systemroot%\Application Compatibility Scripts\Install folder.

Two options exist for installing programs for multisession application server access: **Add/Remove Programs** in Control Panel, and the **change user** command at the command prompt before and after installing the program.

CHANGE USER COMMAND

In order to make programs available for multisession access, program files must be installed to the %systemroot% folder rather than the windows folder of the user's home folder (%homepath%\windows). The change user command ensures that this is the case.

Before the program is installed, **change user /install** places the system in install mode and

---

TERMINOLOGY

%systemroot% refers to the directory in which you installed Windows 2000 Server. Usually, the systemroot directory is C:\WINNT. Whenever you see those characters, substitute the path that corresponds to your installation directory.

TERMINOLOGY

An **Application Program Interface (API)** is a subset of programming code usually provided by Microsoft that performs a specific function. The Open dialog box is an example of an API. Programmers can insert the API into their program with a single line of code instead of re-writing the many lines of code required to perform the actual procedure.

turns off .ini file mapping. The system then records how the setup APIs initially install the program.

After the program is installed, **change user /execute** returns the system to execute mode, restores .ini file mapping, and redirects user-specific data to the user's home directory. When the user opens the program, user-specific registry setting files (.ini, .dll, .ocx, and so on) are automatically propagated as needed to the user's home directory.

ADD/REMOVE PROGRAMS

Add/Remove Programs is located in Control Panel and provides a wizard to assist in adding, changing, or removing programs from the system. When using Add/Remove Programs, only programs that were written for Windows operating systems can be installed.

Add/Remove Programs, which automatically runs the **change user** command, is the preferred method of installing applications for use with Terminal services. Enter **change user** at the command prompt only when you install a program by another method and want to ensure multisession access. For example, when Internet Explorer 5 prompts you to install an add-on program, use **change user** at the command prompt to ensure that the program is installed for multisession access.

EXERCISE

13.28 Install a Program for Use with Terminal Services

To perform this exercise you will need:

- Access to the Windows 2000 Server for Terminal Services

- To have enabled Terminal Services (Exercise 13.27)

1. Log on as an administrator.

2. Open **Control Panel.**

3. Open **Add/Remove Programs.**

- The Add/Remove Programs screen appears.

4. Insert the program's CD or Floppy in the drive.

5. Click the **Add New Programs** icon on the left of the screen.

6. Indicate the source of the program files (usually **CD or Floppy**).

- An installation wizard appears.

7. Indicate the source drive (usually displayed by default).

8. Click **Finish.**

   ■ The program's installation procedure will launch.

9. Follow the instructions on the screen.

10. If the program requires a script to be run, locate the appropriate script and double-click it.

Managing Users with Terminal Services

Consider the following suggestions when managing users with Terminal Services.

■ **Use Terminal Services specific groups:** Create groups that are specifically for Terminal Services users. Maintaining users through groups is much easier and less time consuming than managing users individually.

■ **Use Terminal Services specific profiles:** Assign a separate profile for logging onto Terminal Services. Many of the common options that are stored in profiles, such as screen savers and animated menu affects, are not desirable when using Terminal Services because of their overhead. Assigning a specific profile allows users to get the most out of the system they are working with without expending additional server resources.

■ **Use mandatory profiles:** Use a mandatory Terminal Services profile that will meet the needs of different types of clients and that provides the best server performance.

■ **Set time limits:** Setting limits on the duration of client connections can improve server performance. You can set the limits on how long a session lasts, how long a disconnected session is allowed to remain active on the server, and the time allowed for a session to remain connected, yet idle.

■ **Create pre-configured connections for users or groups of users:** To make connecting to Terminal Services easier, you can supply users with pre-configured connections. Collections of connections can also be made either for different departments within your organization or for different job titles. Pre-configured connections are created using Client Connection Manager.

Troubleshooting Terminal Services

Once you have enabled Terminal Services and installed applications, do not switch Terminal Services on and off. Programs that were installed while Terminal Services was installed might not work correctly when Terminal Services is turned off because Terminal Services installs programs for use in a multisession environment. If Terminal Services must be removed, you should reinstall all programs previously installed for Terminal Services.

Do not copy program files from one directory to another or manually edit the registry during installation.

To improve program performance, install programs on the Terminal server local drive rather than on a file server.

Install programs on NTFS file system formatted drives rather than on FAT formatted drives. You can only set file permissions on NTFS drives.

When shutting down a Terminal server, use the **tsshutdn** command instead of the **Shut Down** option on the **Start** menu. This will shut down the server in a controlled manner. The **Shut Down** option on the **Start** menu does not notify users before ending user sessions and is not recommended. Ending a user's session without warning can result in loss of data at the client.

Be aware that 16-bit computers and Windows-based Terminals might not support some screen resolutions.

Lesson 13.9 Configure Remote Access

Understand Remote Access

Remote Access Service is a standard term in the Information Technology industry. RAS describes a method for users to connect to the company LAN or WAN from public networks. The RAS server works as a router for the remote clients. The RAS server normally transfers whatever is sent to the RAS server from the remote clients to the company network. Windows 2000 supports two RAS technologies: **Dial-up Remote Access** and **Virtual Private Networking.** Dial-up Remote Access is covered in this section, and Virtual Private Networking is covered in Lesson 13.10.

Dial-up Remote Access allows a remote client to dial in directly to the RAS server. The connection normally is made through the public telephone system, and a user must be authorized to use RAS in the Active Directory. The RAS server might simply allow the user to connect, or (if it is a long-distance call for the user) it might allow the user to specify a number to call back. If tighter security is required, the RAS server may be configured to always call users back at a specified number. A required callback prevents someone from using a stolen username and password if that person is not in that user's home.

Configure Remote Access

When users want to connect to the network with dial-up remote access, they create a physical connection to a port on the RAS server using a public telephone system. This is typically done using a modem or ISDN adapter to dial in to the RAS server. Dial-up remote access is good for small companies who have a small number of dial-in users that are connecting within the local calling area (not long distance).

MICROSOFT EXAM OBJECTIVE

Configure, monitor, and troubleshoot remote access. Configure inbound connections. Create a remote access policy. Configure a remote access profile.

CONFIGURE THE HARDWARE

To configure support for remote access, the telephone company needs to install a phone line for each analog modem that accepts incoming calls. When the remote access clients dial in, they will use the numbers designated for the installed phone lines. Each modem in the RAS server requires a serial port.

CONFIGURE THE SOFTWARE

Windows 2000 Server provides a wizard for configuring remote access. Once you complete the wizard steps correctly, the wizard will configure all of the modems and ISDN adapters to be available for remote users.

EXERCISE

13.29 Configure Remote Access Service

To perform this exercise you will need:

■ Access to a domain controller

1. Log on as an administrator.

2. Click the Start button.

3. Point to **Programs.**

4. Point to **Administrative Tools.**

5. Select **Routing and Remote Access.**

   ■ The Routing and Remote Access console appears.

   ■ When the tool is opened for the first time, the server name is listed on the left side with the instructional text in the right pane.

6. Right-click the server that will be the remote access server.

   ■ Only the server you are logged on to will appear in the list,

unless you add other servers by right-clicking on **Routing and Remote Access** (at the top of the tree pane) and selecting **Add Server.** Browse to the appropriate server.

7. Select **Configure and Enabling Routing and Remote Access** from the Context menu.

   ■ The Routing and Remote Access Server Setup wizard welcome screen appears.

8. Click **Next.**

9. The **Common Configurations** page appears.

10. Select **Remote access server.**

11. Click **Next.**

12. The **Remote Client Protocols** page appears.

- This screen shows the protocols installed on the server so that you can indicate which networking protocol you want to use for remote clients.

- You will use TCP/IP for this exercise.

13. TCP/IP appears on the list, so select **Yes, all of the required protocols are on this list.**

14. Click **Next.**

- The IP Address Assignment page appears.

15. Select **Automatically** because the server will use the existing DHCP to assign IP addresses to the remote access clients when they connect.

16. Click **Next.**

- The Managing Multiple Remote Access Servers page appears.

- RADIUS servers can be used to manage authentication and remote access group policy.

- For this exercise, Active Directory is used to authenticate remote clients.

17. Choose the default of **No, I don't want to set up this server to use RADIUS now.**

18. Click **Next.**

- The Summary page appears.

19. Click **Finish.**

Configure Inbound Connections

In order for remote users to connect to the network using dial-up networking, access permissions must be set. Exercise 13.30 demonstrates how to set remote access permissions.

13.30 Set Remote Access Permissions

To perform this exercise you will need:

- Access to a domain controller

1. Log on as an administrator.

2. Click the Start button.

3. Point to **Programs.**

4. Point to **Administrative Tools.**

5. Select **Active Directory Users and Computers.**

6. Navigate to the **Users** folder under the appropriate domain name.

7. Right-click on the user who will be given remote access permissions.

8. Select **Properties** from the Context menu.

   ■ The User Account Properties page appears.

9. Click on the **Dial-in** tab.

10. In the Remote Access Permission (Dial-in or VPN) section, select **Allow access.**

11. In the Callback Option section, indicate if or how callback will occur.

   ■ **No Callback:** The caller is able to connect without being called back.

   ■ **Set by Caller:** The caller can indicate to which phone number they would like the RAS server to call back. This is helpful when the user changes locations and wants to save long-distance call costs.

   ■ **Always Callback to:** This is a security measure that designates a specific number the RAS server will call.

12. Click **OK.**

You can specify if a port can be used for an inbound connection or not. Exercise 13.31 demonstrates how to configure a port to be used for an inbound connection.

EXERCISE

13.31 Configure an Inbound Connection

• •

To perform this exercise, you will need:

■ Access to a domain controller with a modem

1. Log on as an administrator.

2. Click the Start button.

3. Point to **Programs.**

4. Point to **Administrative Tools.**

5. Select **Routing and Remote Access.**

   ■ The Routing and Remote Access console appears.

6. Expand the tree of the server to be configured.

7. Right-click on **Ports.**

8. Select **Properties** from the Context menu.

   ■ The Ports Properties dialog box appears.

9. Select a device such as a modem.

10. Click the **Configure** button.

    ■ The Configure Device—Device Name dialog box appears and gives the following options:

■ **Remote access connections (inbound only):** Enables this device to accept inbound connections

■ **Demand-dial routing connections (inbound and outbound):** Enables this device to accept inbound connections and become a router for outbound connections

11. For this exercise, select **Remote access connections (inbound only).**

12. Click **OK.**

Create a Remote Access Policy

You can override the client settings by creating a Remote Access Policy. This simplifies administration by enabling remote access availability by default instead of making changes to each client individually. In the Routing and Remote Access console, you can create a new Remote Access Policy by expanding the server's branch, right-clicking Remote Access Policy, and selecting New Remote Access Policy from the Context menu. A wizard will launch to walk you through the steps. Another option is to edit the default Remote Access Policy that has the many settings preconfigured. Double-click the default Remote Access Policy in the left pane. The policy settings include the following options:

■ **Edit** button: Edits the permitted connect hours.

■ **Edit Profile** button: This button will be explained in the following paragraphs.

■ **Add** button: Allows you to set attributes for the policy.

Configure a Remote Access Profile

When you click the **Edit Profile** button when creating a new policy or when editing the default policy, the Edit Profile dialog box appears, as shown in Figure 13-13. The dialog box offers the following tabs:

FIGURE 13-13
The RAS Profile Dialog Box

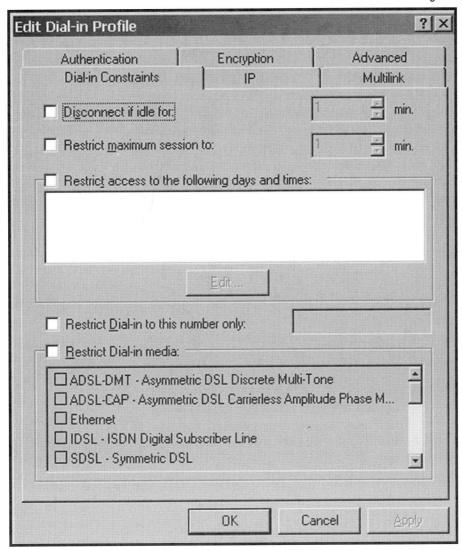

- **Dial-in Constraints:** Allows you to restrict which media is valid for remote users and for how long sessions can last or be idle.

- **IP:** Determines whether a server supplies the IP address, the client requests the IP address, or the server refers to the default server policy.

- **Multilink:** Determines whether multilink (allows a user to employ multiple modems simultaneously to increase bandwidth) is enabled.

- **Authentication:** Determines what authentication protocol is used.

- **Encryption:** Determines what level of encryption is used.

- **Advanced:** Offers additional connection attributes.

Lesson 13.10 Configure a Virtual Private Network

Understand Virtual Private Networks

Virtual Private Networking (VPN) is an enhancement to RAS in Windows 2000. One unfortunate aspect of maintaining a RAS server is upgrading the infrastructure each time telecommunications technology improves. Companies that have used RAS since the original use of Windows NT probably started with 9600 bps modems and then upgraded several times. In a quest for speed, companies may have upgraded in steps to 19.2 Kbps, 28.8 Kbps, 33.6 Kbps, and 56 Kbps. Some companies may have even tried to support ISDN or DSL technology.

This can become very expensive when you consider that a company is probably trying to support multiple simultaneous connections and may need to purchase 10 or 20 devices each time the technology changes. RAS may also become expensive if your remote users need to make long-distance phone calls; if you are using a callback strategy, the company pays the long-distance charges.

VPN tries to address deficiencies in RAS. The users do not make a phone call to the RAS server. The RAS server is connected to the Internet. The users connect to an Internet Service Provider and then connect to the RAS server through the Internet. Figure 13-14 shows how the components work together to form the VPN. It is a virtual private network because users access a public network (the Internet) as part of the connection, but it is private because the data that are sent between the clients and the RAS server are encrypted.

Windows 2000 supports two types of remote access VPN technology: **Point-to-Point Tunneling**

FIGURE 13-14
How a VPN Works

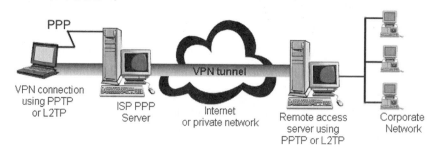

PPP

VPN connection using PPTP or L2TP

ISP PPP Server

VPN tunnel

Internet or private network

Remote access server using PPTP or L2TP

Corporate Network

Protocol (PPTP) and **Layer 2 Tunneling Protocol over IP Security (L2TP/IPSec).** Although PPTP is the current standard, L2TP is an evolving standard that uses Internet protocol security for encryption and authentication services. See the Windows 2000 Help and Windows 2000 Resource Kit for more information on these protocols.

Configure a VPN

CONFIGURE THE HARDWARE

To allow VPN clients access to the network, a VPN server will need to be attached to the internal network as well as to the Internet. Typically one NIC in the VPN server is connected to the local network, and there is also a connection to the Internet by a dedicated line to either the VPN server or to the LAN. Dedicated line technologies include a cable modem, DSL, a dial-up connection, or an ISDN link.

CONFIGURE THE SOFTWARE

In Exercise 13.29, when you selected **Remote access server** from the Common Configurations screen in the Routing and Remote Access Server Setup wizard, the server was configured to act as a RAS server and as a VPN server. The wizard also configured the server for five PPTP and five L2TP/IPSec connections. Open the server's **Ports** option in the **Routing and Remote Access console** to view the connections.

EXERCISE

13.32   Create a VPN Connection

To perform this exercise you will need:

■ Access to the computer that will be used to make the connection to the Internet

1. Log on as an administrator.

2. Right-click **My Network Places.**

3. Select **Properties.**

4. Double-click the **Make New Connection** icon.

   ■ The welcome screen for the Network Connection wizard is displayed.

5. Click **Next.**

   ■ The Network Connection Type page appears.

6. Select **Connect to a private network through the Internet.**

7. Click **Next.**
   - The Public Network page appears and displays two choices:
     - Do not dial the initial connection.
     - Automatically dial this initial connection.

8. Select **Do not dial the initial connection.**

9. Click **Next.**
   - The Destination Address page appears.

10. Enter the host name or IP address of the computer or network to which you are connecting.

11. Click **Next.**
    - The Connection Availability page appears and displays two choices for how the connection will be used:
      - For all users.
      - Only for myself.

12. Click **For all users.**

13. Click **Next.**
    - The final page of the wizard appears.

14. Enter a name for the connection.

15. Click **Finish** to save the connection in the Network and Dial-up Connections folder.
    - The Connect Virtual Private Connection dialog box appears.

16. Enter the username and password that will be used for authentication during connection procedures.

17. Click the **Connect** button to make the VPN connection or **Cancel** to exit the dialog box.

Lesson 13.11 Configure Internet Information Services

Understand Internet Information Services

Internet Information Services (IIS) is installed by default during the Windows 2000 Server installation. IIS is the Windows component that makes it easy to publish information and bring business applications to the Web, and it enables a Windows 2000 server to become an **Internet** or **Intranet server.** Internet/Intranet servers host Web sites and FTP (file transfer protocol) sites. Internet servers (as the name implies) are connected to the Internet. Intranet servers use Internet technologies but are limited to users within one organization. Windows 2000 offers a full range of security, configuration, and monitoring options for IIS.

EXERCISE

13.33 Start Internet Information Services

To perform this exercise, you will need:

- Access to a domain controller

1. Log on as an administrator.

2. Click the Start button.

3. Point to **Programs.**

4. Point to **Administrative Tools.**

5. Select **Computer Management.**

6. Expand the **Server Applications and Services** node in the console tree.

7. Select **Internet Information Services.**

Software Requirements

Internet Information Services requires that the Windows TCP/IP Protocol and Connectivity Utilities be installed on the computer prior to installation. If you are publishing on the Internet, your ISP must provide your server's IP address, subnet mask, and the default gateway's IP address. (The default gateway is the ISP computer through which your computer routes all Internet traffic.)

The following optional components are recommended:

> **MICROSOFT EXAM OBJECTIVE**
>
> Monitor, configure, troubleshoot, and control access to Web sites.

- **The Domain Name System (DNS) service** installed on a computer in your intranet. This step is optional, but it does allow users to have user-friendly text names instead of IP addresses. On the Internet, Web sites usually use the Domain Name System. If you register a domain name for your site, users can type your site's domain name in a browser to contact your site.

- For security purposes, Microsoft recommends that all drives used with IIS be formatted with NTFS.

- **Microsoft FrontPage** or other Web authoring software to create and edit HTML pages for the Web site. FrontPage is a WYSIWYG editor that provides a friendly, graphical interface for tasks such as inserting tables, graphics, and scripts.

- **Microsoft Visual InterDev** to create and develop interactive Web applications.

Configure Access to a Web Site

In addition to normal Windows 2000 security (which allows users to access only what their account permits), IIS can also be configured to allow *Anonymous* access.

Since there is no anonymous access in Windows 2000, IIS uses an account it creates for the anonymous users. By default the special account used by anonymous users is called *Iusr_<servername>*. IIS can be monitored using, for example, the FTP Service and Web Service objects in the Performance Monitor console.

EXERCISE

13.34   Control Access to a Web Site

• •

To perform this exercise, you will need:

- Access to a domain controller
- To have performed Exercise 13.33— Start Internet Information Services

1. Expand **Internet Information Services** in the tree console:

2. Right-click **Default Website.**

3. Select **Properties** from the Context menu.

    - The Default Website Properties dialog box appears (see Figure 13-15).

4. Click the **Directory Security** tab.

    - The following options are offered:

        - **Anonymous access and authentication control:** Allows any user to have access to the resource even if the user does not have a username or password. Various methods of authentication are offered with the default being Windows authentication.

        - **IP address and domain name restrictions:** Allows access by any computer, no matter what the IP address is. You can also deny access to all computers except those with IP addresses you specify.

        - **Secure communications:** Requires secure communications between the server and client. The issuance of certificates is managed through this section.

5. After making the appropriate entries, click **OK** to save the changes.

FIGURE 13-15
The Default Web Site Properties Dialog Box

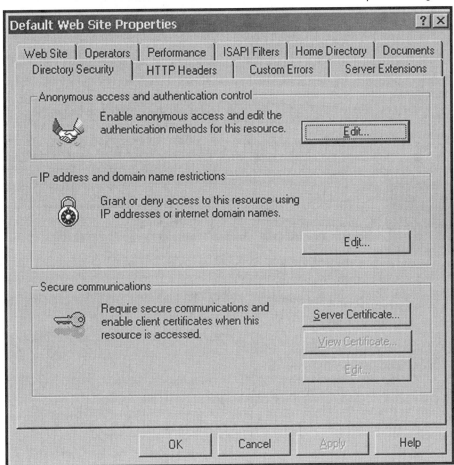

After using Web authoring software to create your Web site, you can test your installation by using Internet Explorer to view the files in your home directory.

EXERCISE

13.35 Test a Web Site Connected to the Internet

To perform this exercise, you will need:

■ A Web server

■ HTML files in the **wwwroot** folder

■ A Web browser

■ An active connection to the Internet

1. Launch the Web browser.

2. In the Address field, type in the URL for the home directory of your new Web site.

3. Press Enter.

EXERCISE

13.36

Test a Web Site on an Intranet

To perform this exercise, you will need:

■ An active network connection

■ The WINS server service (or other name resolution method) to be functional

■ HTML files in the **wwwroot** folder

■ A Web browser

1. Launch the Web browser.

2. Type in the URL for the home directory of your new server.

3. Press Enter.

Summary

From drivers to hard disks to networks, managing resources is a challenge. Fortunately most networks start small and are not in need of many resource management tools. Growth over time allows the administrator to ease into new technologies and gradually increase network functionality. Some of the topics in this chapter would not apply to every network. For example, not every network will have a Windows 2000 server that needs to coexist with a NetWare server. Nonetheless, Microsoft still requires that you understand these concepts in order to gain MCSE certifications. Knowledge and experience will be your best friends when it comes to effectively and efficiently managing resources.

REVIEW EXERCISE

These questions will help you determine if you have learned enough to move on to the next chapter. If the graphic next to the option is a square (❑), there can be more than one answer for that question. If the graphic is a circle (○), there is only one correct answer. Color in the shape(s) to indicate your answer(s).

1. Which TCP/IP configuration methods will automatically assign an IP address when the computer is started?

   a. ❑ Automatic

   b. ❑ Dynamic

   c. ❑ Manual

   d. ❑ Overdrive

2. Which two of the following settings are configured from within the same dialog box?

   a. ❑ Logon scripts

   b. ❑ Disk Management

   c. ❑ Dfs

   d. ❑ Home folders

3. With which type of disk configuration can you check disk properties such as capacity, available free space, and current status?

   a. ○ Only Basic

   b. ○ Only Dynamic

   c. ○ Both Basic and Dynamic

   d. ○ Neither Basic nor Dynamic

4. Bill suspects that either his hard drive or its controller is malfunctioning. Which utility does he launch to check whether the hardware on the computer is working properly?

   a. ○ Disk Managment

   b. ○ Device Manager

   c. ○ Properties dialog box of My Computer

   d. ○ Terminal Services

5. The company that Carl works for has just purchased a new server that has a fast CPU and multiple hard drives. Unfortunately they were unable to purchase new workstations. Which of the following programs would compensate for the lower powered workstations and take advantage of the new server's capabilities?

a. ❏ Dfs

b. ❏ Terminal Services—Application server mode

c. ❏ RAID-5

d. ❏ Terminal Services—Remote server mode

6. Which of the following steps must be completed in order for an application to function with Terminal Services?

a. ❏ The application must be installed before Terminal Services is installed.

b. ❏ The application must be installed after Terminal Services is installed.

c. ❏ Before installing an application, check the **Application compatibility scripts** to see if the application is listed.

d. ❏ If the application needs a script, run the script after installing the application.

7. What two types of remote access VPN technology does Windows 2000 support?

a. ❏ RAS/VPN

b. ❏ PPTP

c. ❏ L2TP/IPSec

d. ❏ IPX/SPX

▼PERFORMANCE CHALLENGES

■ Invent a user who has the worst network-usage habits a user could have. List at least four bad habits and then describe how you could counteract the negative impact.

■ Contrast and compare at least five features of Windows 2000 and Novell NetWare. Print your results.

TUNE THE PERFORMANCE

OBJECTIVES

After completing this chapter, you should be able to:

- Define bottlenecks and describe what causes them

- Use Performance Monitor to analyze a computer system

- Capture and evaluate network data using Network Monitor

- Defragment files on a hard disk

- Remove unnecessary files to free disk space

- Stop or start a Windows 2000 service

- Make a computer's performance more efficient

- Change the status of the paging file for virtual memory

OUTLINE

Introduction

Imagine seven lanes of traffic that funnel into two lanes within a distance of 300 feet. Cars are lurching forward, stopping suddenly, and angling for position. The drivers are caught in a traffic bottleneck. The same bottlenecks can occur on a computer or even on a network, and they cause system response to slow. Because users are unhappy when either their computers or the network is slow, you must identify what is causing the bottleneck. This chapter provides ideas, solutions, and tools for identifying and solving problems with performance. Before you begin to explore these concepts, however, review Table 14-1 for terms that are helpful to know when tuning performance.

TABLE 14-1 PERFORMANCE TUNING TERMINOLOGY

TERM	DESCRIPTION
Resources	Hardware components that provide some quantifiable work capacity
Bottlenecks	Resources with performance limitations that affect responsiveness
Load	Amount of work that a resource has to perform
Optimizations	Measures taken to reduce the impact of a bottleneck on performance
Throughput	Measure of information flow through a resource
Processes	Software services running concurrently that perform a certain function
Threads	Software chains of execution that run concurrently to perform functionality and basic units of division among processors in a multiprocessing environment

Lesson 14.1 Identify Bottlenecks

Anything that limits the performance in a computer or network is a bottleneck. In a computer, the bottleneck might be a slow CPU, insufficient RAM, or an old hard drive. There will always be a bottleneck in system performance—something that is slower than everything else. Ideally, the bottleneck will be you.

Demand may become extreme enough to cause resource bottlenecks for the following reasons:

- Resources are insufficient and additional or upgraded components are required.

- Resources are not sharing workloads evenly and need to be balanced.

- A resource is malfunctioning and needs to be replaced.

- A program is monopolizing a particular resource; this may require substituting another program, having a developer rewrite the program, adding or upgrading resources, or running the program during periods of low demand.

- A resource is incorrectly configured and configuration settings should be changed.

In order to find a bottleneck, you need to have knowledge of how computers work and access to the necessary monitoring tools. You must also be able to measure the speed of the resources in order to find the one resource that is performing at its peak (doing all it can do) and is, therefore, causing the bottleneck. You also need to know what the measurements are for various resources. Disk throughput, for example, is measured in *megabytes* per second, while interrupt activity is measured in *interrupts* per second.

Steps in Locating Bottlenecks

To locate a bottleneck, complete the following steps:

1. Run performance monitoring software (covered in Lesson 14.2).

2. Create a load that causes the system to run slower than desired.

3. Using the performance monitoring software, examine general areas that will indicate the problem areas to probe more deeply.

Eliminating Bottlenecks

To eliminate a bottleneck means to make the resource fast enough that something else is the primary bottleneck. Because so many types of resources exist and each resource may have its own peculiarities, no text could adequately describe how to eliminate every bottleneck. You must determine how to relieve the load placed on the resource. Sometimes relieving the load is as simple as adjusting a setting in Control Panel, and sometimes you may have to replace a slow hard drive or upgrade a network device. In general, your options are as follows:

1. Adjust software and/or hardware configurations.

2. Redirect the load from the slow device to another device.

3. Replace the component with a better component.

The Cycle Never Ends

Most hardware in a modern network has a life span—a certain amount of time in which the component can handle the task it was designed to perform. Technology advances and eventually all of the hardware (as resources are gradually replaced) will have to be upgraded. You will achieve maximum performance from the hardware through a continuous cycle of improvement. Once the primary bottleneck is eliminated, start working on the next resource, then the next one, and so on. About the time you finish, you will probably be back to the original resource!

Lesson 14.2 Use Performance Monitor

Performance tuning is the systematic process of finding a resource experiencing the most load and then relieving that load. Windows 2000 Server includes a utility called Performance Monitor that allows you to monitor the performance of resources.

In Windows 2000, Performance Monitor has been renamed **System Monitor.** System Monitor is part of the **Performance** tool, which is located in **Administrative Tools.** The Performance tool has the following two parts:

> **MICROSOFT EXAM OBJECTIVE**
>
> Monitor and optimize usage of system resources.

- **System Monitor** is used to collect and view real-time (while it is happening) data about memory, disk, processor, network, and other activities. The data can be represented in a graph, histogram, or report.

- **Performance Logs and Alerts** are used to configure logs to record performance data and to set system alerts to notify you when a value is above or below your specifications.

Objects and Counters

Whenever a system component is functioning, it is generating performance data called **performance objects.** Performance objects are usually named after the component that is generating the data. For example, the Processor object is a collection of performance data about processors in the computer.

Windows 2000 Server has many built-in performance objects for the major hardware components such as memory and processors. Other services such as WINS or server programs such as Microsoft Exchange may install their own performance objects.

Each performance object provides **counters,** which are values that represent data on specific aspects of a system or service. For example, the Pages/sec counter provided by the Memory object tracks the rate of memory paging. Even though many objects are available on a typical system, the following objects are used most frequently to monitor system components:

- Cache
- Memory
- Objects
- Paging File
- PhysicalDisk
- Process
- Processor
- Server
- System
- Thread

EXERCISE

14.1 Launch Performance Monitor

• •

To perform this exercise, you will need:

- Access to a domain controller

1. Log on as administrator.

2. Click the Start button.

3. Point to **Program Files.**

4. Point to **Administrative Tools.**

5. Click **Performance.**

   - The Performance window opens (see Figure 14-1).

FIGURE 14-1
The Performance Window

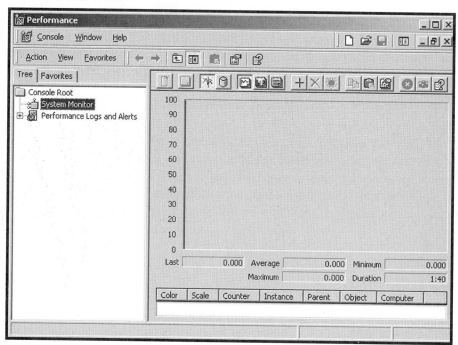

EXERCISE

14.2   Add a Counter

To perform this exercise, you will need:

- Access to a domain controller
- To have performed Exercise 14.1—Launch Performance Monitor

1. Right click the System Monitor details pane.

2. Click **Add Counters.**

   - The Add Counters dialog box appears (see Figure 14-2).

3. Use the pull-down list button for **Performance object** and select an object.

   - For example, you might select Processor, as shown in Figure 14-2.

4. In **Select counters from list,** click the counter for which you want information.

   - For example, you might select % Processor Time, as shown in Figure 14-2.

FIGURE 14-2
The Add Counters Dialog Box

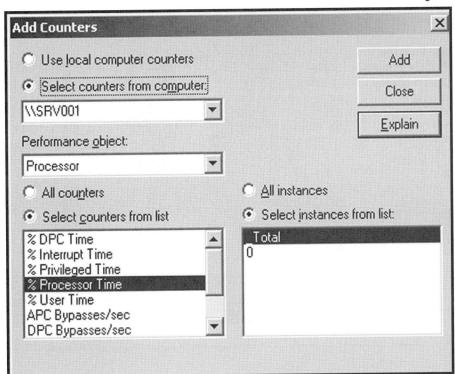

5. Click the **Add** button.

  ■ Repeat steps 4 and 5 for each additional counter you want to add to this session.

6. Click the **Close** button.

  ■ The System Monitor details pane immediately begins to graph the counters you selected (see Figure 14-3).

TIP

The **Explain** button in the Add Counters dialog box will open a small window that gives a description of the highlighted counter. Read through each of the descriptions.

FIGURE 14-3
The System Monitor Detail Pane After Adding Two Counters

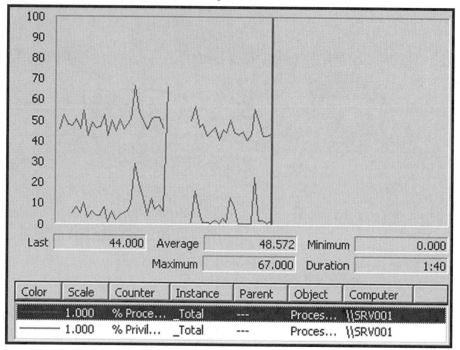

Color	Scale	Counter	Instance	Parent	Object	Computer	
	1.000	% Proce...	Total	---	Proces...	\\SRV001	
	1.000	% Privil...	_Total	---	Proces...	\\SRV001	

Last 44.000 Average 48.572 Minimum 0.000
Maximum 67.000 Duration 1:40

Performance Logs and Alerts

With **Performance Logs and Alerts,** performance data can be collected automatically from local or remote computers. Logged counter data can be viewed using System Monitor, or data can be exported to spreadsheet programs or databases for analysis and report generation. Performance Logs and Alerts offers the following capabilities:

■ Data are collected in a comma-separated or tab-separated format for easy export to spreadsheet programs.

■ Collected counter data can be viewed during collection as well as after collection has stopped.

■ Because logging runs as a service, data collection occurs regardless of whether any user is logged on to the computer being monitored.

■ Start and stop times, filenames, file sizes, and other parameters can be designated for automatic log generation.

■ Multiple logging sessions can be managed from a single console window.

■ An alert can be set on a counter that causes a message to be sent, a program to be run, or a log to be started when the selected counter's value exceeds or falls below a specified setting.

EXERCISE

14.3

Create a Counter Log

To perform this exercise, you will need:

■ Access to a domain controller

■ To have performed Exercise 14.1—Launch Performance Monitor

■ To have defined at least one counter (see Exercise 14.2—Add a Counter)

1. Double-click **Performance Logs and Alerts.**

2. Click **Counter Logs.**

   ■ Any existing logs will be listed in the details pane.

   ■ A green icon indicates that a log is running.

   ■ A red icon indicates that a log has been stopped.

3. Right-click a blank area of the details pane.

4. Select **New Log Settings** from the Context menu.

   ■ The New Log Settings dialog box appears.

5. In **Name,** type the name of the log (for example, *Processor*).

6. Click **OK.**

   ■ A dialog box labeled with the name of the log appears (see Figure 14-4).

7. On the **General** tab, click **Add.**

   ■ The Add Counters dialog box appears (see Figure 14-2).

8. Select the counters you want to log.

9. Click **Close** to close the Add Counters dialog box.

10. If you want to change the default file and schedule information, make the changes on the **Log Files** tab and the **Schedule** tab.

11. Click **OK** to close the log properties dialog box.

12. If the log folder does not exist, you will be asked if you want the file to be created. Click **Yes** to create the file.

    ■ The name of the new log file appears in the details pane.

FIGURE 14-4
The Counter Log Properties Dialog Box

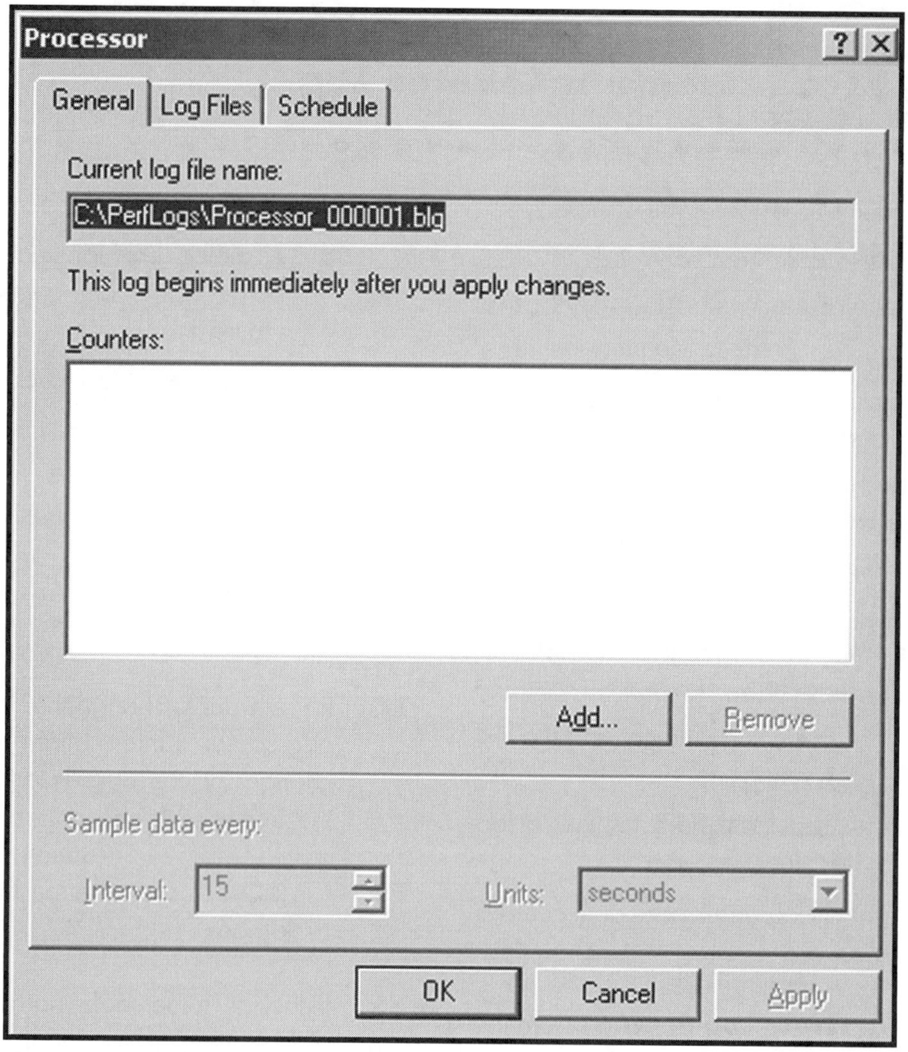

Choosing How Often to Monitor

A report is only good if you have time to evaluate the results. If you collect too much information, you will not be able to look through all of it in a reasonable amount of time. You must decide how often you are going to take a reading and how long the log file will be in effect.

For routine monitoring, start by logging activity over 15-minute intervals. If you are monitoring activity of a specific process at a specific time, set a frequent update interval. If you are monitoring a problem that manifests itself slowly such as a memory leak, use a longer interval.

Also consider the overall length of time you want to monitor when choosing this interval. Updating every 15 seconds is reasonable if you will be monitoring for no more than four hours. When monitoring a system for eight hours or more, do not set an interval shorter than 300 seconds (five minutes). Setting the update interval to a frequent rate (low value) can cause the system to generate a large amount of data, which can be difficult to work with and can increase the overhead of running Performance Logs and Alerts.

Monitoring a large number of objects and counters can also generate large amounts of data and consume disk space. Try to strike a balance between the number of objects you monitor and the sampling frequency to keep log file size within manageable limits.

Evaluating the Data

Analyzing the data you have collected involves examining counter values that are reported while the system is performing various operations. During this process you should determine which processes are most active and which programs or threads, if any, are monopolizing a resource. Using this type of analysis you should be able to understand how the system is responding to workload demands.

As a result of this analysis, you may find that your system performs satisfactorily at some times and unsatisfactorily at others. Depending on the causes of these variations and the degree of difference, you may choose to take corrective action or to accept these variations and delay tuning or upgrading resources to a later time.

The level of system performance that you consider acceptable when the system is handling a typical workload and running all required services is its **baseline.** The baseline performance is a subjective standard that the administrator determines based on the work environment. It may correspond to a range of counter values, including some that are temporarily unacceptable, that generally indicate the best possible performance under the administrator's specific conditions. The baseline can be the measure used for setting performance expectations of the users.

DETERMINE ACCEPTABLE VALUES FOR COUNTERS

In general, deciding whether or not the system's performance is acceptable is a subjective judgment on your part. Table 14-2 contains threshold values for specific counters that can help you determine whether values reported by the computer indicate a problem. If System Monitor consistently reports these values, it is likely that bottlenecks exist on the system and you should take action to tune or upgrade the affected resource.

UNDERSTAND VARIATIONS IN PERFORMANCE DATA

Keep in mind that resource usage can vary dramatically based on what the users are doing with the system during the day. Peak usage times will give different results than low usage times (during lunch, for example).

Also, it is better to evaluate performance based on intervals rather than averages of instantaneous counter values. Averages can include data for service startup and other events that make the numbers go far out of the normal range for a brief period. This makes the resulting data inaccurate.

TABLE 14-2 THRESHOLD VALUES TO CONSIDER

RESOURCE	OBJECT/COUNTER	SUGGESTED THRESHOLD	COMMENTS
Disk	PhysicalDisk\ % Disk Time	90%	
Disk	PhysicalDisk\ Disk Reads/sec, PhysicalDisk\ Disk Writes/sec	Depends on manufacturer's specifications	Check the specified transfer rate for your disks to verify that this rate does not exceed the specifications. In general, Ultra Wide SCSI disks can handle 50 I/O operations per second.
Disk	PhysicalDisk\ Current Disk Queue Length	Number of spindles plus 2	This is an instantaneous counter; observe its value over several intervals. For an average over time, use PhysicalDisk\ Avg. Disk Queue Length.
Memory	Memory\ Available Bytes	Less than 4 MB	Research memory usage and add memory if needed.
Memory	Memory\ Pages/sec	20	Research paging activity.
Network	Network Segment\ % Net Utilization	Depends on type of network	You must determine the threshold based on the type of network you are running. For Ethernet networks, for example, 30% is the recommended threshold.
Paging File	Paging File\ % Usage	99%	Review this value in conjunction with Available Bytes and Pages/sec to understand paging activity on your computer.
Processor	Processor\ % Processor Time	85%	Find the process that is using a high percentage of processor time. Upgrade to a faster processor or install an additional processor.
Processor	Processor\ Interrupts/sec	Depends on processor.	A dramatic increase in this counter value without a corresponding increase in system activity indicates a hardware problem. Identify the network adapter causing the interrupts.

TABLE 14-2 THRESHOLD VALUES TO CONSIDER *CONTINUED*

RESOURCE	OBJECT/COUNTER	SUGGESTED THRESHOLD	COMMENTS
Server	Server\ Bytes Total/sec		If the sum of Bytes Total/sec for all servers is roughly equal to the maximum transfer rates of your network, you may need to segment the network.
Server	Server\ Pool Paged Peak	Amount of physical RAM	This value is an indicator of the maximum paging file size and the amount of physical memory.
Server	Server Work Queues\ Queue Length	4	If the value reaches this threshold, there may be a processor bottleneck. This is an instantaneous counter; observe its value over several intervals.
Multiple Processors	System\ Processor Queue Length	2	This is an instantaneous counter; observe its value over several intervals.

Lesson 14.3 Use Network Monitor

Monitoring a network usually consists of watching server resource utilization and measuring overall network traffic. Although you can do both of these with System Monitor, for in-depth traffic analysis you should use **Network Monitor.**

Network Monitor is used to capture and display the frames (also called packets) that a computer running Windows 2000 Server receives from a local area network (LAN). Administrators can use Network Monitor to detect and troubleshoot networking problems that the local computer might experience. Frames captured by Network Monitor can even be saved to a file and then sent to professional network analysts or support organizations. Network Monitor is only available in Windows 2000 Server.

The **Network Monitor driver** must be installed before Network Monitor can be used. The Network Monitor driver enables Network Monitor to receive packets from a network adapter.

14.4   Install the Network Monitor Driver

To perform this exercise, you will need:

■ Access to a domain controller

1. Log on as an administrator.

2. Open **Network and Dial-up Connections** from Control Panel.

   ■ The Network and Dial-up Connection window opens.

3. Right-click **Local Area Connection.**

   ■ The Local Area Connection Properties dialog box appears (see Figure 14-5).

4. Click the **Install** button.

   ■ The Select Network Component Type dialog box appears.

5. Click on **Protocol.**

6. Click the **Add** button.

   ■ The Select Network Protocol dialog box appears.

7. Click **Network Monitor Driver.**

   ■ If you have already installed Network Monitor, **Network Monitor Driver** does not appear in the **Select Network Protocol** dialog box, because the driver is installed automatically with Network Monitor. If this is the case, abort this exercise.

8. Click **OK.**

   ■ If you are prompted for additional files, insert your Windows 2000 CD or type a path to the location of the files on the network.

FIGURE 14-5
The Local Area Connection Dialog Box

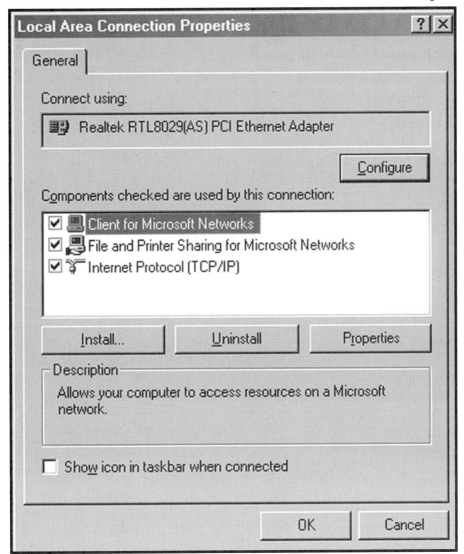

FIGURE 14-5
The Local Area Connection Dialog Box

EXERCISE

14.5 Install Network Monitor

• •

To perform this exercise, you will need:

■ Access to a domain controller

1. Log on as an administrator.

2. Open **Control Panel.**

3. Double-click **Add/Remove Programs.**

4. Click **Add/Remove Windows Components** from the left pane.

   ■ The Windows Components wizard appears.

5. Click **Next.**

6. Select **Management and Monitoring Tools** (see Figure 14-6).

7. Click the **Details** button.

   ■ The Management and Monitoring Tools window appears.

8. Put a checkmark in the **Network Monitor** box.

9. Click **Next.**

   ■ The installation occurs.

10. Click **Finish.**

Capturing Network Data

Network Monitor monitors the **network data stream,** which consists of all information transferred over a network at any given time. The process by which Network Monitor copies frames is referred to as **capturing.** All network traffic to and from the local network card can be captured. You can also set a

FIGURE 14-6
Adding Management and Monitoring Tools Using the Windows Components Wizard

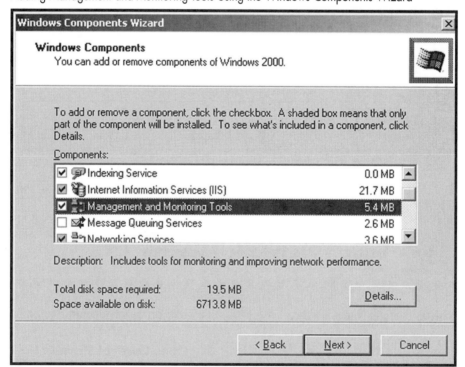

capture filter and capture a subset of frames. After the data are captured, you can view the data. Network Monitor does much of the data analysis by translating the raw capture data into its logical frame structure.

EXERCISE

14.6 Capture Network Data

To perform this exercise, you will need:

- Access to a domain controller

- To have completed Exercise 14.5—Install Network Monitor

1. Log on as an administrator.

2. Open **Administrative Tools.**

3. Double-click **Network Monitor.**

- The Network Monitor window opens (see Figure 14-7).

FIGURE 14-7
The Network Monitor Interface

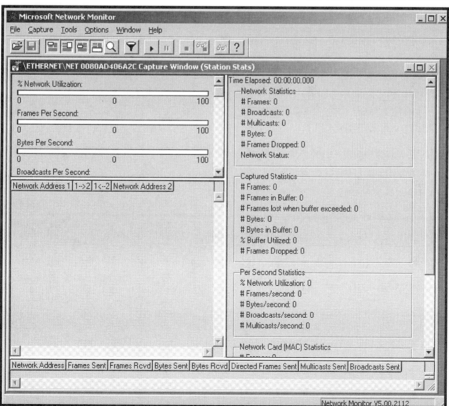

FIGURE 14-8
The Select a Network Dialog Box

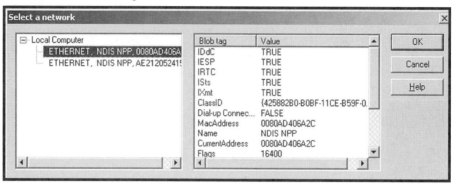

FIGURE 14-9
The Network Monitor Interface During a Capture Procedure

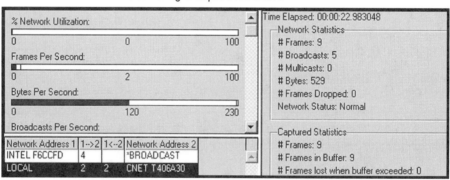

- The first time this program launches, you may be prompted for a valid network.

- If this happens, the Select Network dialog box appears (see Figure 14-8).

- Click **Local Computer.**

- Click on the appropriate network name.

- Click **OK.**

4. Click the Capture menu.

5. Select **Start.**

- Data collection begins immediately (see Figure 14-9).

- Notice the right pane has a timer showing elapsed time.

6. After the amount of time has elapsed that you wanted to monitor, click the Capture menu.

7. Select **Stop and View.**

- Data collection ceases, and a capture summary window is displayed (see Figure 14-10).

FIGURE 14-10
The Results of a Network Monitor Capture

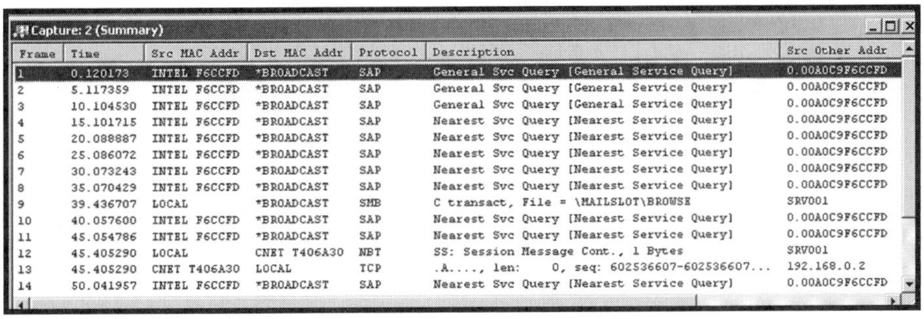
Capture: 2 (Summary)

Frame	Time	Src MAC Addr	Dst MAC Addr	Protocol	Description	Src Other Addr
1	0.120173	INTEL F6CCFD	*BROADCAST	SAP	General Svc Query [General Service Query]	0.00A0C9F6CCFD
2	5.117359	INTEL F6CCFD	*BROADCAST	SAP	General Svc Query [General Service Query]	0.00A0C9F6CCFD
3	10.104530	INTEL F6CCFD	*BROADCAST	SAP	General Svc Query [General Service Query]	0.00A0C9F6CCFD
4	15.101715	INTEL F6CCFD	*BROADCAST	SAP	Nearest Svc Query [Nearest Service Query]	0.00A0C9F6CCFD
5	20.088887	INTEL F6CCFD	*BROADCAST	SAP	Nearest Svc Query [Nearest Service Query]	0.00A0C9F6CCFD
6	25.086072	INTEL F6CCFD	*BROADCAST	SAP	Nearest Svc Query [Nearest Service Query]	0.00A0C9F6CCFD
7	30.073243	INTEL F6CCFD	*BROADCAST	SAP	Nearest Svc Query [Nearest Service Query]	0.00A0C9F6CCFD
8	35.070429	INTEL F6CCFD	*BROADCAST	SAP	Nearest Svc Query [Nearest Service Query]	0.00A0C9F6CCFD
9	39.436707	LOCAL	*BROADCAST	SMB	C transact, File = \MAILSLOT\BROWSE	SRV001
10	40.057600	INTEL F6CCFD	*BROADCAST	SAP	Nearest Svc Query [Nearest Service Query]	0.00A0C9F6CCFD
11	45.054786	INTEL F6CCFD	*BROADCAST	SAP	Nearest Svc Query [Nearest Service Query]	0.00A0C9F6CCFD
12	45.405290	LOCAL	CNET T406A30	NBT	SS: Session Message Cont., 1 Bytes	SRV001
13	45.405290	CNET T406A30	LOCAL	TCP	.A...., len: 0, seq: 602536607-602536607...	192.168.0.2
14	50.041957	INTEL F6CCFD	*BROADCAST	SAP	Nearest Svc Query [Nearest Service Query]	0.00A0C9F6CCFD

Interpreting Captured Data

The more knowledge you have about networking, the more sense the captured data from Network Monitor will make. To serve as an example, Exercise 14.7 demonstrates how to identify the largest broadcaster on the network.

EXERCISE

14.7 Identify the Largest Broadcaster on the Network

To perform this exercise, you will need:

- Access to a domain controller
- To capture some network data (Exercise 14.6)

1. In the Station Statistics pane (the lowest pane on the Network Monitor interface), double-click the **Broadcasts Sent** column header.
   - You can also right-click in the **Broadcasts Sent** column and select **Sort Column** from the Context menu.
   - If the Graph pane indicates a high percentage of network use and if network operations are unusually slow, an abrupt increase in broadcasts may be the source of the problem.
   - The row containing the highest number of broadcasts that were sent appears at the top of the list. The network address in this row represents the highest broadcaster on the network.

Lesson 14.4 Optimize Disk Performance

If while monitoring disk performance you discover that one or more hard drives are the bottleneck, you have the following options for optimizing disk performance:

- You can upgrade to a higher speed disk or add disks. You will also want to upgrade the disk controller and the bus.

- On servers, you can use **Disk Management** to create striped volumes on multiple physicaldisks. This solution increases throughput because I/O commands can be issued concurrently to multiple drives.

> **MICROSOFT EXAM OBJECTIVE**
>
> Manage and optimize availability of system state data and user data.

- You can distribute programs among servers. **Distributed file system (Dfs)** can be used to balance workload. (See the following section for more on workload balancing.)

- You can isolate tasks that heavily utilize disk I/O on separate physical-disks or disk controllers.

- You can use **Disk Defragmenter** to optimize disk space.

- To improve the efficiency of disk access, consider installing the latest driver software for the host adapters. Contact your adapter manufacturer for information.

> **MICROSOFT EXAM OBJECTIVE**
>
> Optimize disk performance.

Balancing the Workload among Servers

Imagine a crew of workers whose task is to make a road. Which method would get the job done more efficiently: one man on the crew does most of the work while the other guys stand around, or all of the workers do their share of the total workload. Of course, the more workers you have working, the less the load is on a single person. The same concept applies to servers. When one server is getting more read and write requests than any other server, network performance can slow.

To balance loads on network servers, you need to know how busy the server disk drives are. Use the PhysicalDisk\ % Disk Time counter, which indicates the percentage of time a drive is active. If % Disk Time is over 90 percent, check the PhysicalDisk\ Current Disk Queue Length counter to see how many system requests are waiting for disk access. The number of waiting I/O requests should be sustained at no more than 1.5 to 2 times the number of spindles making up the physicaldisk.

Most disks have one spindle, although **Redundant Array of Independent Disks (RAID)** devices usually have more. A hardware RAID device appears as one physicaldisk in System Monitor; RAID devices created through software appear as multiple drives (instances). You can either monitor the PhysicalDisk counters for each physical drive (other than RAID), or you can use the _Total instance to monitor data for all of the computer's drives.

Use the values of the Current Disk Queue Length and % Disk Time counters to detect bottlenecks with the disk subsystem. If Current Disk Queue Length and % Disk Time values are consistently high, consider upgrading the hard drive or moving some files to an additional disk.

Use Disk Defragmenter

When a file is saved to a hard disk, Windows 2000 will attempt to place the file in one contiguous block (a block that is unbroken). As a hard drive fills up and reaches approximately 75 percent of capacity, the entire contents of a single file may not be able to be saved in one location; part of the file will be in one location on the hard drive and the remainder of the file will be saved in one or more additional locations. When this occurs, the file is *fragmented*. When a disk is fragmented, file access is slowed because the hard drive head must travel to multiple locations in order to load a single file into memory. The Disk Defragmenter utility in Windows 2000 can restructure the file storage and put fragmented files back together into contiguous blocks.

EXERCISE

14.8 **Use Disk Defragmenter**

● ●

To perform this exercise, you will need:

■ Access to a Windows 2000 computer

1. Open **My Computer.**

2. Right-click on the drive to be defragmented.

3. Select **Properties** from the Context menu.

   ■ The Disk Properties dialog box appears.

4. Click the **Tools** tab.

5. Click the **Defragment Now** button.

   ■ The Defragment disk dialog box appears (see Figure 14-11).

FIGURE 14-11
The Disk Defragmenter Dialog Box

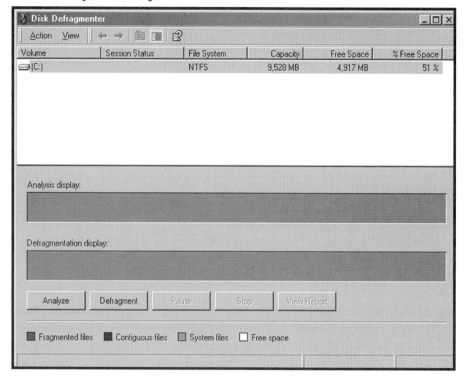

6. Click the **Analyze** button.

   ■ When the analysis is complete, the utility will either suggest that you defragment the drive or it will state that the drive is not fragmented enough to warrant a defragment process.

7. Click **View Report** to see a textual analysis of the drive.

8. Click the **Defragment Drive** button.

   ■ The utility performs the defragmentation process.

   ■ The color coded graphical display indicates the progress of the process.

Use Disk Cleanup Wizard

Windows 2000 includes a utility for cleaning up extraneous files that accumulate on a computer system over a period of time. The utility is called the Disk Cleanup wizard, and it can perform the following tasks in order to clear space on a hard disk:

- Remove temporary Internet files
- Remove any downloaded program files (ActiveX controls and Java applets downloaded from the Internet)
- Empty the Recycle Bin
- Remove Windows 2000 temporary files
- Remove Windows 2000 components not in use
- Remove installed programs that are no longer used

EXERCISE

14.9 Use the Disk Cleanup Wizard

To perform this exercise, you will need:

- Access to a domain controller

1. Click the Start button.

2. Select **Run.**

3. Type **cleanmgr.**

4. Press **Enter,** or click **OK.**

   - The Select Drive dialog box appears.
   - Use the pull-down list to select the drive that you want to clean up.

5. Click **OK.**

   - The Disk Cleanup wizard scans the drive for files that can be deleted.
   - When the scan is complete, the Disk Cleanup dialog box appears.

6. Use the checkboxes to select or de-select the types of files you want the utility to delete (see Figure 14-12).

7. Click **OK.**

   - The files are deleted, and the indicated disk space is now available.

FIGURE 14-12
The Disk Cleanup Wizard Dialog Box

Lesson 14.5 Manage Services and Processes

The collection of programs that comprise Windows 2000 Server have many components that enable the operating system to function. Some of those supportive components are called services. A service is a program, routine, or process that performs a specific function to support other programs. Some examples of Windows 2000 services include Security Accounts Manager service and the File Replication service. Services are installed when the program is installed; they may or may not be active and can be started and stopped according to configuration needs. For example, one service controls the print spooler, which is the service that controls the storage of print jobs that are waiting to be printed. Occasionally, because of a paper jam or a network problem, print jobs are unable to print due to a failed print attempt. Stopping and restarting the print spooler service will clear the error and allow the waiting print jobs to print. Exercise 14.10 demonstrates how to stop and restart the print spooler service.

CAUTION: Do not start or stop services without an understanding of the results of your actions.

EXERCISE

14.10 Start and Stop the Print Spooler Service

To perform this exercise, you will need:

- Access to a domain controller

1. Open the **Computer Management console.**

2. Expand **Services and Applications.**

3. Click on **Services.**

   - The available services appear in the right pane.

4. Double-click the **Print Spooler** service.

   - The Print Spooler dialog box appears (see Figure 14-13).

5. Click the **Stop** button.

   - The Service Status: indicator displays "Stopped."

6. Click the **Start** button.

   - The Service Status: indicator displays "Started."

FIGURE 14-13

The Services Section of the Computer Management Console

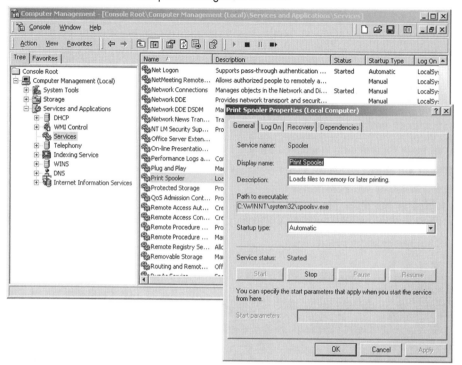

Managing Processes

When a service is running, it will initiate one or more **processes.** When you stop a service, you stop all the processes associated with that service. Individual processes can be started and stopped. The Processes tab of the Task Manager utility is used to view and manage running processes. The Task Manager allows you to end processes, view process details, and set the priority of processes to enhance system performance. Exercise 14.11 demonstrates some of these activities.

> **MICROSOFT EXAM OBJECTIVE**
>
> Manage processes. Set priorities and start and stop processes.

EXERCISE

Manage Processes with Task Manager

To perform this exercise you will need:

■ Access to a Windows 2000 computer

1. Log on as administrator.

2. Right-click an empty portion of the Taskbar.

3. Select **Task Manager** from the context-menu.

   ■ Task Manager can also be selected from a button after pressing Ctrl+Alt+Del or by entering taskmgr.exe in the Run dialog box.

4. Click the **Applications** tab.

5. Click the **New Task** button.

   ■ The Create New Task dialog box appears.

6. Type **notepad.exe** and click **OK.**

   ■ Notepad launches.

7. Click on the **Processes** tab.

   ■ The list of active processes is displayed.

   ■ Process headings include:

      ■ **Image Name** is the name of the process or executable filename.

      ■ **PID** is the Process Identification, a number that is assigned to the process.

      ■ **CPU** indicates the percentage of the CPU being used by the process.

      ■ **CPU time** displays the total amount of time the process has used or is using the processor.

      ■ **Memory Usage** indicates the amount of RAM the process is using.

8. Click any of the heading to sort the information according to the heading.

9. Click the heading again to switch between sorting in ascending and descending order.

10. Right-click on notepad.exe in the Image Name column.

11. In the context-menu, point to **Set Priority.**

   ■ The list of available process priorities is displayed from the highest to the lowest.

   ■ Setting a process to a higher priority will increase the availability of system resources to the process.

12. Select one of the priority levels.

   ■ If a warning message appears, click **No** to abort the procedure.

13. Click on notepad.exe.

14. Click the **End Process** button.

15. When the warning message appears, click **Yes** to end the process.

   ■ Notepad.exe is no longer running.

16. Exit the Task Manager utility.

Using the Start Utility

Another way to start processes is by using a command named Start. Using a command-line utility has several advantages:

- Through the use of switches, you can launch a program with the priorities, window settings (new window, minimized, maximized, and so on), and other configurations in place. Without this ability, you would have to configure the settings after the program is launched.

- Command lines can be used in scripts that are scheduled to run at particular times.

- The command has additional functionality that Task Manager does not offer.

Exercise 14.12 demonstrates how to view Start command options and also how to start a program using the Start utility.

EXERCISE

Using the Start Command

To perform this exercise you will need:

- Access to a Windows 2000 computer

1. Log on as administrator.

2. Click the **Start** button.

3. Point to **Programs.**

4. Point to **Accessories.**

5. Click on **Command Prompt.**

6. Type **Start /?.**

   - The syntax and switches for the Start command are displayed.

7. Press the **spacebar** to display each paused page until the command prompt is available again.

8. Type **Start /MIN notepad.exe.**

   - Notepad will be launched and the window will be minimized.

9. Type **Start /MAX notepad.exe.**

   - Notepad will be launched and window will be maximized.

10. Close both notepads.

11. Click on the command prompt window.

12. At the prompt, type **Exit** to exit the command prompt window.

Lesson 14.6 Enhance System Performance

The System utility in Control Panel offers another way to optimize a computer's performance. Exercise 14.13 opens the Performance Options dialog box.

EXERCISE

14.13 Launch Performance Options

To perform this exercise, you will need:

■ Access to a domain controller

1. Log on as administrator.

2. Open **Control Panel.**

3. Double-click the **System** icon.

   ■ The System Properties dialog box appears.

4. Click the **Advanced** tab.

5. Click the **Performance Options** button.

   ■ The Performance Options dialog box appears.

Application Response

Application Response is defined as the priority of foreground applications versus background applications and Virtual Memory. A foreground application is the application with an active window, which is usually indicated by a colored title bar in Windows 2000. Any program that is not the foreground application is a background application (see Figure 14-14).

FIGURE 14-14
Background Applications and the Foreground Application

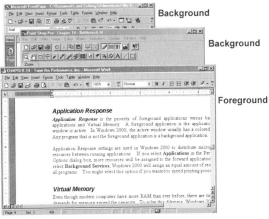

Application Response settings are used in Windows 2000 to distribute microprocessor resources between running applications. If you select **Applications** in the Performance Options dialog box, more resources will be assigned to the forward application. If you select **Background Services,** Windows 2000 will assign an equal amount of resources to all programs. For example, you might select this option if you wanted to speed printing processes.

Virtual Memory

Even though modern computers have more RAM than ever before, there are times when demands for memory exceed the capacity. To solve this dilemma, Windows 2000 uses a **virtual-memory paging file.** When more memory is needed for the active application, the operating system will copy information from memory into the page file that is stored on the hard drive. When the information that was stored on the hard drive is needed, the operating system will copy the information from the hard drive back into memory. This process is called **demand paging.**

The minimum page file size is 2 MB. The default paging size is equal to the lesser of the total amount of RAM plus 12 MB or the amount of available disk space. Normally the default paging file size is sufficient and does not need adjustment, and paging files never decrease below the initial size that was set during installation.

When the computer boots, the paging files are set to their initial size. As needed, a paging file grows from its initial to the maximum configured size. System performance degrades when the maximum size is reached. Thus, there may be times when a larger paging file is required to improve system performance (for example, when you are running many applications at the same time). You can increase the size of the paging file or even have the paging file spread across multiple disks. By configuring a paging file on each disk, the file takes up less room on each disk and increases access times because of multiple hard drive heads transferring information concurrently.

During particularly heavy usage, a user may receive a message indicating that virtual memory is limited. He or she can usually resolve the error by closing some applications, but if that is not acceptable, an administrator would change the paging file properties to accommodate the user's extended needs. Exercise 14.14 demonstrates how to change the status of the paging file.

FIGURE 14-15
The Virtual Memory Dialog Box

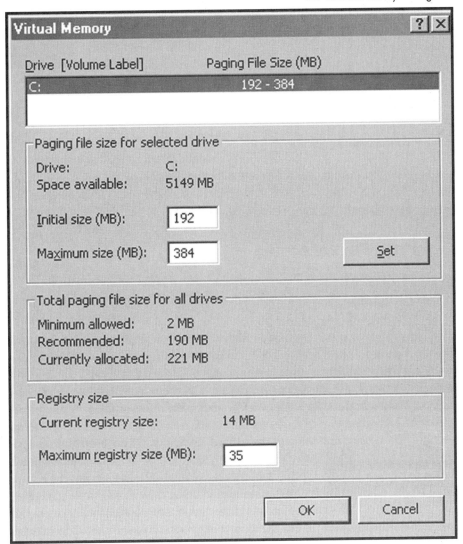

EXERCISE

Configure Virtual Memory

To perform this exercise, you will need:

■ Access to a Windows 2000 computer

■ To have performed Exercise 14.13—
Launch Performance Options

1. Click the **Change** button in the Virtual Memory section.

   ■ The Virtual Memory dialog box appears (see Figure 14-15).

2. From the Drive list, select the drive that will have a paging file.

3. Adjust the **Initial Size** as necessary.

4. Adjust the **Maximum Size** as necessary.

5. Click the **Set** button.

6. Click **OK.**

System performance can also be enhanced by setting the intial size of the paging file to the value displayed in the Maximum Size box. This eliminates the time required to enlarge the file from the initial size to the maximum size.

Summary

To keep a system running efficiently requires vigilance on the part of the administrator. The primary system to monitor and maintain is the server(s). Use Performance Monitor on a regular basis to determine any developing bottlenecks. You will probably hear from your users when either their local computer or the network is slow. Network statistics can be evaluated using Performance Monitor, but a more in-depth analysis can be obtained by using Network Monitor. File management will help hard drives work efficiently, and disk defragmentation should be a regularly scheduled task. It is best to initiate a defragmentation process when the user is not using his or her computer because open files are not defragmented. Cleaning unnecessary files from a hard drive is not as critical as defragmentation, so the procedure could be performed less frequently. Making adjustments to the paging file is not a common occurrence but may be necessary especially when the system frequently alerts the user that virtual memory is low. Consider configuring a paging file on each disk. Some of these tasks are what administrators focus on during their slower times.

● ● ● ● ● ● ● ● ● ● ● ● ●

REVIEW EXERCISE

These questions will help you determine if you have learned enough to move on to the next chapter. If the graphic next to the option is a square (❑), there can be more than one answer for that question. If the graphic is a circle (○), there is only one correct answer. Color in the shape(s) to indicate your answer(s).

1. What program would you launch to collect and view real-time data about memory, disk, processor, network, and other activities?

   a. ○ System Monitor

   b. ○ Performance Options

   c. ○ Disk Defragmenter

   d. ○ Computer Management console

2. Charles is a programmer with heavy usage needs on the local computer. Progressively, his computer has slowed down. He calls Lucas, the system administrator, and explains his frustrations. What should Lucas do first to alleviate the problem?

   a. ○ Stop and restart the print spooler service

   b. ○ Launch Network Monitor and determine the largest broadcaster on the network

   c. ○ Increase the paging file size

   d. ○ Use Performance Monitor while the load exists on the system to determine the bottleneck

3. Marilee just learned about a utility that will automatically delete unnecessary files from Windows 2000 hard drives. What steps would she have to perform to launch the utility?

   a. ○ My Computer, System, Performance Options, Delete Files

   b. ○ Control Panel, Administrative Tools, Clean Disk

   c. ○ Start, Run, cleanmgr, OK

   d. ○ Right-click drive, Properties, Tools, Defragment Now

4. Which program is used to configure logs to record performance data and to set system alerts to notify you when a value is above or below your specifications?

   a. ○ Performance Options

   b. ○ Performance Logs and Alerts

   c. ○ Application Response

   d. ○ Disk Management

5. Megan has seven applications running at the same time. While transferring a graphic from one program to another, her system suddenly slows to a crawl and then a warning dialog box appears that says her virtual memory is low. What could she do to alleviate this problem?

a. ❑ Change Performance Options so that the background services have more processor time than the applications

b. ❑ Close applications until adequate system performance is restored

c. ❑ Call the administrator to ask for an increase in the paging file size on her computer

d. ❑ Let the computer rest, get a pop, and hope performance comes back to 100 percent

▼ PERFORMANCE CHALLENGES

- ■ Initiate three counters for disk performance. Make a screen capture of the counters while they are making the graph.

- ■ Use both System Monitor and Network Monitor to capture network information for 10 minutes. Print the results of each capture. Describe the differences between the two utilities and what they were able to capture.

EDIT THE REGISTRY

OBJECTIVES

After completing this chapter, you should be able to:

- Describe the structure and purpose of the registry

- Launch the Registry Editor

- Navigate through the registry hierarchy

- Edit a value in the registry

- Understand why you should not edit the registry without a good reason

OUTLINE

Introduction

The Windows 2000 **registry** is a database that contains configuration information. The registry contains profiles for each user of the computer and information about system hardware, installed programs, and property settings. As Windows 2000 is running, it is continually referencing this information. Most of the Windows 2000 programs access and/or modify the registry as needed. You can modify the registry directly by using one of two registry editor programs, but one wrong entry could corrupt the entire database. Lesson 15.3 gives more details on why Microsoft strongly recommends that you do not edit registry settings manually.

Lesson 15.1 Understand the Registry

Structure of the Registry

The registry is organized in a hierarchical structure and has an appearance similar to that of Windows Explorer, as shown in Figure 15-1. Instead of files and folders, the registry has **subtrees** and their **keys, subkeys,** and **value entries.** These terms are described in Table 15-1.

REGISTRY SUBTREES

Two registry subtrees exist in Windows 2000: **HKEY_LOCAL_MACHINE** and **HKEY_USERS.** However, to make the information in the registry easier to find, the Registry Editor utilities will display the contents of the two subtrees as five **root trees.** The root trees are listed in Table 15-2.

FIGURE 15-1
The Registry Editor Interface

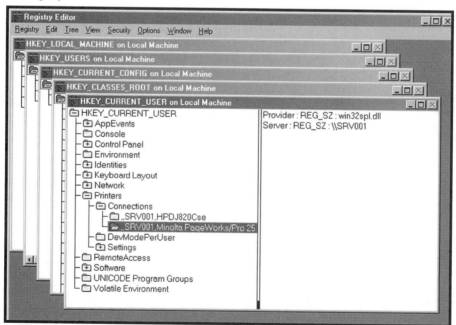

TABLE 15-1 ELEMENTS OF THE REGISTRY

REGISTRY ELEMENT	DESCRIPTION
Subtrees	A subtree is the primary node in the registry hierarchical structure. This would relate in concept to the root-level folders in Windows Explorer.
Keys	In Registry Editor, keys appear in the left pane. A key can contain subkeys and values.
Subkeys	A subkey is a key within a key. Subkeys can be nested within other subkeys and can carry out functions.
Value Entries	A value entry is the string of data that defines the value of the current key. A value entry has three parts: name, data type, and value.

TABLE 15-2 ROOT TREES IN THE WINDOWS 2000 REGISTRY

ROOT TREE	DESCRIPTION
HKEY_LOCAL_MACHINE	Contains configuration information particular to the computer (for any user), including hardware and operating system data such as bus type, system memory, device drivers, and startup control data.
HKEY_CLASSES_ROOT	Contains information used by various OLE technologies and file-class association data (equivalent to the registry in Windows for MS-DOS). This is a subkey of HKEY_LOCAL_MACHINE\Software. The information stored here ensures that the correct program opens when you open a file by using Windows Explorer.
HKEY_CURRENT_USER	Contains the user profile for the user who is currently logged on interactively (as opposed to remotely), including environment variables, desktop settings, network connections, printers, and program preferences. This subtree is an alias of the **HKEY_USERS** subtree and points to **HKEY_USERS**_security ID of current user._
HKEY_USERS	Contains information about actively loaded user profiles and the default profile. This includes information that also appears in **HKEY_CURRENT_USER.** Users who are accessing a server remotely do not have profiles under this key on the server; their profiles are loaded into the registry of their own computers.
HKEY_CURRENT_CONFIG	Contains information about the hardware profile used by the local computer system at startup. This information is used to configure settings such as the device drivers to load and the display resolution to use. This subtree is part of the HKEY_LOCAL_MACHINE subtree.

NOTE: Each root key name begins with **HKEY_** to indicate to software developers that this is a handle that a program can use. A handle is a value used to identify a resource so that a program can access it.

VALUE ENTRIES

Each registry key or subkey can contain data called **value entries.** A value entry has three parts: the name of the value, the data type of the value, and the value itself. The data types describe the format of the data. Some data types are raw binary data (1's and 0's), while others are a data string that humans can read and understand. As you browse through the registry in the next few exercises, you will encounter the various data types and values.

Lesson 15.2 Use the Registry Editor

After looking through Table 15-2, you can probably see why editing the registry is discouraged. However, there are times when editing the registry is necessary. Two programs exist for editing the registry: **regedt32.exe** (called the **Registry Editor**) and **regedit.exe** (called **regedit**). Regedit existed before the Registry Editor and has one major drawback: any changes you make are immediately in effect. With the Registry Editor, changes are not made until you exit the program. Their interfaces are different as well; regedit shows all of the registry elements in one window, whereas Registry Editor displays each key in its own window.

EXERCISE

15.1 Launch the Registry Editor

To perform this exercise, you will need:

■ Access to a domain controller

1. Log on as administrator.

2. Click the Start button.

3. Select **Run.**

4. Type **regedt32.**

5. Press **Enter,** or click **OK.**

   ■ The Registry Editor window is opened (see Figure 15-1).

Registry Editor is an advanced tool for viewing and changing settings in the registry. An advanced user who is prepared to both edit and restore the registry can safely use Registry Editor for such tasks as eliminating duplicate entries or deleting entries for programs that have been uninstalled or deleted.

CAUTION: As you perform the following exercises, be careful to not alter any values without being instructed to do so. You could disable the system.

The contents of the registry will vary from computer to computer depending on that computer's hardware and software configurations. Keep this in mind as you explore the registry in Exercise 15.2.

EXERCISE

15.2 Explore the Registry Editor

To perform this exercise, you will need:

■ Access to a domain controller

■ To have performed Exercise 15.1— Launch the Registry Editor

1. Click on each of the following menu choices:

   ■ **Registry:** Select Computer allows you to view the registry of any computer on the network. This menu also allows you to print portions of the registry (be careful, there can be hundreds of pages in some of the keys).

   ■ **Edit:** Facilitates the entering of a new value or key.

   ■ **Tree:** Assists in navigating through the structure (double-clicks do the same thing).

   ■ **View:** Changes how the interface displays registry informa-

tion. Also contains the search feature within the menu choice called **Find Key.**

■ **Security:** Allows you to set permissions on who has the authority to edit the registry.

■ **Options:** Changes miscellaneous settings like making the registry read-only and save settings on exit. As a safety feature, you can also have the Registry Editor ask for confirmation on deletion procedures.

■ **Window:** Navigates through the windows, bringing the selected window to the foreground. You can also click on any visible part of the window.

■ **Help:** Launches the Help program.

2. Make the **HKEY_LOCAL_MACHINE** key the active window.

3. Double-click the **HARDWARE** key.

4. Double-click the **DESCRIPTION** subkey.

5. Double-click the **System** subkey.
   - Notice the values that appear.
   - You can expand the subkeys under system if you want.

6. Double-click on the **CentralProcessor** subkey.

7. Click on the **0** subkey.
   - Values appear in the right pane.

8. Double-click on the first value.
   - An editing dialog box appears.

   - This is where you would make changes, if you knew the ramifications of the changes you were making.

9. **Cancel** out of the dialog box (make *no* changes).

10. Repeat steps 8–10 for each of the values.
    - Note the various editors open depending on the type of data or value.

11. Explore the remaining subtrees.

12. Exit the Registry Editor (either click the X or pull down the Registry menu and select **Exit**).

Lesson 15.3 Do Not Use the Registry Editor

Hopefully you have seen enough warnings about not changing the registry without knowing how the changes will affect the system. Now you need to know why you should not have to edit the registry and what to do if an edit causes system failure.

How Windows 2000 Uses the Registry

Many of the consoles and control panel programs you use to administer the computer edit the registry. Perhaps you noticed some of the following settings as you explored the registry:

- **Setup:** Both the Windows 2000 Setup program and other setup programs (for programs or hardware) add configuration data to the registry. For example, new information is added when a new SCSI adapter is installed or settings for the display are changed. Setup also reads information from the registry to determine if the prerequisite components are installed.

- **Recognizer:** Each time a computer running Windows 2000 is started, the recognizer places hardware configuration data in the registry. These data include a list of hardware detected in your system.

- **Windows 2000 kernel:** During system startup, the Windows 2000 kernel extracts information from the registry, such as which device drivers to load and their load order.

- **Device drivers:** Device drivers send and receive load parameters and configuration data from the registry. A device driver must report the system resources that it uses, such as hardware interrupts and DMA channels, so that the system can add this information to the registry. Programs and device drivers can access this registry information to provide users with smart installation and configuration programs.

- **Administrative tools:** The options and administrative tools in Windows 2000 (such as those provided in the **Administrative Tools** folder in Control Panel) can be used to modify configuration data indirectly. These programs should be able to make any configuration changes to the registry that are necessary.

TIP

If you must edit the registry, at least take some precautions to protect yourself from disaster. See Lesson 16.3 for a description of how to back up, restore, and recover the registry.

Summary

The registry is the database that holds all of the configuration information for Windows 2000. The structure of the registry is hierarchical in nature with subtrees being at the top level. Keys are subordinate to subtrees, and subkeys can be nested within keys and other subkeys. When a value entry for a subkey appears in the right pane, double-clicking will open an editing dialog box. Because of the many programs, tools, and utilities available, most administrators do not have to edit the registry directly.

● ● ● ● ● ● ● ● ● ● ● ● ● ● ●

REVIEW EXERCISE

These questions will help you determine if you have learned enough to move on to the next chapter. If the graphic next to the option is a square (❏), there can be more than one answer for that question. If the graphic is a circle (○), there is only one correct answer. Color in the shape(s) to indicate your answer(s).

1. What is the filename of the Registry Editor?

   a. ○ regedit.exe

   b. ○ regedt32.exe

   c. ○ regedt32.bat

   d. ○ regedt.exe

2. Regarding subtrees, which of the following statements are true?

   a. ❏ Three registry subtrees exist in Windows 2000.

   b. ❏ The five root trees that Registry Editor displays are actually portions of the two subtrees.

   c. ❏ Subtrees are the primary nodes in the registry hierarchical structure.

   d. ❏ Keys and subkeys are subordinate to subtrees.

3. Shawn is searching for a certain key in the registry. He has searched for a long time and cannot find it by navigating through the structure. He calls Jennifer, and she tells him that the Registry Editor has a search feature. On which menu does she tell him to click?

   a. ○ Registry

   b. ○ Search

   c. ○ View

   d. ○ Window

4. Under which two subtrees would you find information about device drivers?

   a. ❏ HKEY_LOCAL_MACHINE

   b. ❏ HKEY_CLASSES_ROOT

   c. ❏ HKEY_CURRENT_USER

   d. ❏ HKEY_CURRENT_CONFIG

PERFORMANCE CHALLENGES

- Use the search feature to locate the following keys. Print each screen to prove you found the keys.

    - Hardware Profiles

    - .ini

    - SERVICES

    - WindowMetrics

- Launch and explore regedit (without making any changes). Describe the differences between regedit and the Registry Editor. Make two print screens—one using regedit and the other using the Registry Editor—showing the same registry key.

5

DISASTER PROTECTION AND RECOVERY

PROTECT THE NETWORK

OBJECTIVES

After completing this chapter, you should be able to:

- Define a computer disaster

- Restart a computer that will not start

- Know when to use Safe Mode

- Describe the purpose of the Recovery console

- Understand the purpose of the Emergency Repair Disk

- Create an Emergency Repair Disk

- Perform backup and restore procedures

- Encrypt data files and folders

OUTLINE

Introduction

Networks are valuable components of the information age. Some companies would not survive an extended period of time without their network. For example, a manufacturing plant could lose millions of dollars in a matter of hours when the network is down because of not being able to make, test, sell, support, or ship their product. Many events can cause a network or its computers to fail, including (but not limited to) poor maintenance, hardware failure, insufficient planning for expansion, software bugs, power outages or surges, viruses, user mistakes, acts of nature, and unauthorized access. Anything that causes a computer to stop running or to be unable to start running again is classified as a computer disaster. The value of all network components makes implementing disaster recovery procedures vital to the success of the organization.

Lesson 16.1 Recover from Disaster

Disaster recovery is the restoration of a computer so that a user can log on and access system resources after a computer disaster has occurred. Windows 2000 provides the following options to help in the identification of and recovery from computer disasters:

- Safe mode
- Recovery console
- Emergency Repair Disk (ERD)

Safe Mode

If the computer will not start, you may be able to start it in **safe mode.** In safe mode, Windows 2000 uses default settings, including a VGA video driver, Microsoft mouse driver, no network connections, and the minimum device drivers required to start Windows. For example, if a computer will not start after installation of new software, you may be able to start it with minimal services in safe mode and then change the computer settings or remove the newly installed software that is causing the problem. If a symptom does not reappear when you start in safe mode, you can eliminate the default settings and minimum device drivers as possible causes. As listed in Table 16-1, safe mode has several options.

> **MICROSOFT EXAM OBJECTIVE**
>
> Recover systems and user data. Troubleshoot system restoration by using Safe Mode. Recover system and user data by using the Recovery Console.

TABLE 16-1 SAFE MODE OPTIONS

SAFE MODE OPTION	DESCRIPTION
Safe Mode	Starts Windows 2000 using only basic files and drivers (mouse, except serial mice; monitor; keyboard; mass storage; base video; default system services; and no network connections). If your computer does not start successfully using safe mode, you may need to use the Emergency Repair Disk (ERD) feature to repair your system.
Safe Mode with Networking	Starts Windows 2000 using only basic files and drivers, plus network connections.
Safe Mode with Command Prompt	Starts Windows 2000 using only basic files and drivers. After logging on, the command prompt is displayed instead of the Windows desktop, Start menu, and Taskbar.
Enable Boot Logging	Starts Windows 2000 while logging all of the drivers and services that were loaded (or not loaded) by the system to a file. This file is called **ntbtlog.txt,** and it is located in the **%windir%** directory. Safe Mode, Safe Mode with Networking, and Safe Mode with Command Prompt add to the boot log a list of all of the drivers and services that are loaded. The boot log is useful in determining the exact cause of system startup problems.
Enable VGA Mode	Starts Windows 2000 using the basic VGA driver. This mode is useful when you have installed a new driver for your video card that is causing Windows 2000 not to start properly. The basic video driver is always used when you start Windows 2000 in Safe Mode (either Safe Mode, Safe Mode with Networking, or Safe Mode with Command Prompt).
Last Known Good Configuration	Starts Windows 2000 using the registry information that Windows saved at the last shutdown. Use only in cases of incorrect configuration. Last known good configuration does not solve problems caused by corrupted or missing drivers or files. Also, any changes made since the last successful startup will be lost.
Directory Service Restore Mode	Not applicable for Windows 2000 Professional. This is for the Windows 2000 Server operating system and is only used in restoring the SYSVOL directory and the Active Directory directory service on a domain controller.
Debugging Mode	Starts Windows 2000 while sending debug information through a serial cable to another computer.
	If you are using or have used Remote Install Services to install Windows 2000 on your computer, you may see additional options related to restoring or recovering your system using Remote Install Services.

16.1

Using Safe Mode

To perform this exercise, you will need:

■ Access to a Windows 2000 computer

1. Log on as administrator.

2. Click the Start button.

3. Select **Shut Down.**

   ■ The Shut Down Windows dialog box appears.

4. Use the pull-down list to select **Restart.**

5. Click **OK.**

6. When you see the message **For troubleshooting and advanced start up options, press F8,** press F8.

7. Use the arrow keys on the numeric keypad to highlight the appropriate safe mode option, and then press **Enter.**

   ■ Note: NUM LOCK must be off in order for the arrow keys on the numeric keypad to function.

8. Use the arrow keys to highlight an operating system, and then press **Enter.**

   ■ The computer should start in safe mode. You will see the words "Safe Mode" in the cor-

MICROSOFT EXAM OBJECTIVE

Troubleshoot system restoration by starting in safe mode.

ners of the desktop when running in safe mode.

   ■ If the computer does not start, refer to the Recovery Console and Emergency Repair Disks described below.

9. If the cause of the problem was a change in display settings:

   ■ Right-click the desktop and select Properties from the context-menu.

   ■ Click the Settings tab and adjust settings as necessary.

   ■ Click OK and follow the instructions on the screen.

10. If the cause of the problem was a driver change:

   ■ Launch Device Manager and install the appropriate driver.

11. If the cause of the problem was an invalid registry entry:

   ■ Launch the Registry Editor and edit the entry or restore the Registry from backup media.

12. After completing the adjustments, use the shutdown menu to restart the computer.

- If the edits repaired the problem, the system should boot normally.

- If the problem still exists, start the system in safe mode again

and repeat this exercise, making appropriate changes to your previous procedure.

- If the problem still exists, refer to the Recovery Console and Emergency Repair Disks sections described below.

Recovery Console

An option to consider if safe mode does not help is the Recovery Console. The Recovery Console is a command-line interface that can be used to perform both simple and complex tasks that include the following: start and stop services, read and write data on a local drive (including drives formatted with the NTFS file system), copy data from a floppy disk or CD, format drives, fix the boot sector or master boot record, and perform other administrative tasks. The Recovery Console is particularly useful if you need to repair your system by copying a file from a floppy disk or CD-ROM to your hard drive, or if you need to reconfigure a service that is preventing your computer from starting properly. For example, the Recovery Console could be used to replace an overwritten or corrupted driver file with a good copy from a floppy disk.

By default, the Recovery Console is not installed. The console can be installed from the Windows 2000 Server CD-ROM or from the setup disks. Exercise 16.2 lists the installation steps. After installation and rebooting, the Recovery Console will appear as a menu option in the boot menu.

EXERCISE

16.2 Install the Recovery Console as a Start Up Option

• •

To perform this exercise you will need:

- Access to a Windows 2000 computer

- The Windows 2000 Server CD-ROM

- Network policy settings that allow you to complete this procedure

1. Log on as administrator.

2. With Windows running, insert the Windows 2000 Professional or Server CD.

3. Click **No** when prompted to upgrade to Windows 2000.

4. Launch the command prompt (Start, Programs, Accessories, Command Prompt).

5. Type the letter of your CD-ROM drive, followed by a colon and press Enter.

6. Type the following command: **\i386\winnt32.exe /cmdcons.**

   ■ A dialog box appears indicating the purpose of the Recovery Console and how to launch the console if the hard drive is unavailable.

7. Click **Yes** to install the Recovery Console.

   ■ The Setup program installs the Recovery Console files.

   ■ A dialog box appears indicating that you must restart your computer and select Recovery Console from the startup menu.

8. Click **OK.**

See Exercise 16.10 for an example of how to use the Recovery Console to recover system files.

Emergency Repair Disk

You can use the Windows 2000 Emergency Repair Disk (ERD) to fix problems preventing you from starting a computer.

By preparing an ERD when a computer is functioning well, it can be used to repair system files when the computer is not functioning. (In this situation, to start a computer that needs repair, you use the Windows 2000 Setup CD or floppy disks you created from the CD.) The repairs possible with this method are limited to basic system files, the partition boot sector, and the startup environment, and the repair process does not recover the registry. To replace registry files, use the Recovery Console. The Emergency Repair Disk does not back up data or programs, and is not a replacement for regularly backing up your system.

EXERCISE

16.3   Create an Emergency Repair Disk

• •

To perform this exercise, you will need:

■ Access to a Windows 2000 computer

■ One blank, formatted, 3.5-inch, high-density floppy disk

1. Log on as administrator.

2. Click the Start button.

3. Point to **Programs.**

4. Point to **Accessories.**

5. Point to **System Tools.**

6. Select **Backup.**

   ■ The Backup window opens and displays the following three options:

      ■ Backup wizard

      ■ Restore wizard

      ■ Emergency Repair Disk

7. Click the **Emergency Repair Disk** button.

   ■ The Emergency Repair Diskette dialog box prompts you to insert a floppy disk.

   ■ The checkbox allows you to also copy information that will save current registry files in a folder within your *system-root*/repair folder. This is useful if you need to recover a system in the event that the hard disk has failed.

8. Put a checkmark in the **backup registry** option.

9. Insert a high-density, 3.5-inch floppy disk in drive A:.

   ■ Be sure that the floppy disk is empty or there will not be enough room to copy all of the repair files. If the disk is not empty and does not contain important files, use Windows Explorer to format the diskette. (You do not have to close down this procedure in order to launch Windows Explorer.)

10. Click **OK** to begin the copy process.

    ■ System data are copied to the floppy.

    ■ When the process is complete, a message prompts you to label the disk with the date and "Emergency Repair Disk." We also suggest you write the computer name on the disk label as well. (ERDs are computer-specific.)

    ■ Place the diskette in a safe place in case you need it. A disaster is really a disaster if you cannot find your most recent ERD.

11. Click **OK** to close the dialog box.

12. Exit Backup.

Because the emergency repair process is quite powerful, Microsoft recommends it for use only by advanced users or administrators. The next exercise describes how to use the ERD to repair a Windows 2000 computer system. Your instructor will indicate if you should perform this exercise or not.

16.4

Use the Emergency Repair Disk for System Repair

To perform this exercise, you will need:

- Access to a Windows 2000 computer

- The most recently created Emergency Repair Disk for this computer (Exercise 16.3)

1. Insert the Windows 2000 Setup CD or the first floppy disk you created from the CD (see Exercise 16.3) in the appropriate drive.

   - For systems that cannot start (boot) from the CD drive, you must use a boot floppy disk (see Exercise 16.3).

   - For systems that can start (boot) from the CD drive, you can use either the CD or a boot floppy disk.

2. Restart the computer; if you are using floppy disks, respond to the prompts that request each floppy disk in turn.

3. When the text-based part of Setup begins, follow the prompts; choose the **repair or recover** option by pressing **R.**

4. When prompted, insert the Windows 2000 Setup CD in the appropriate drive.

5. When prompted, choose the **emergency repair process** by pressing **R.**

6. When prompted, choose between the following:

   - **Manual Repair** (press **M**): *This should be used only by advanced users or administrators.* Use this option to choose whether you want to repair system files, partition boot sector problems, or startup environment problems.

   - **Fast Repair** (press **F**): This option does not require user input and will attempt to repair problems related to system files, the partition boot sector on the system disk, and the startup environment (for example, if you have a dual-boot or multiple-boot system).

7. Follow the instructions on the screen; when prompted, insert the Emergency Repair Disk in the appropriate drive.

   - During the repair process, missing or corrupted files are replaced with files from the Windows 2000 CD or from the *systemroot*\repair folder on the system partition.

   - Replacement files from either of these sources will not reflect any configuration changes made after setup.

8. Follow the instructions on the screen.

■ You might want to write down the names of files that are detected as faulty or incorrect to help you diagnose how the system was damaged.

9. If the repair was successful, allow the process to complete.

■ The computer should restart. (The restarting of the computer indicates that replacement files were successfully copied to the hard disk.)

As indicated in step 1 of Exercise 16.4, some CD-ROM drives are not bootable. This means that you cannot insert the Windows 2000 Server CD-ROM disk and have the computer be able to retrieve the files it needs from the CD for booting the computer. If this is the case, you will want to create a set of setup disks that contain those files and that will also make the CD-ROM drive accessible for completing the repair process. Exercise 16.5 demonstrates how to create the setup disks.

> **TIP**
>
> Consider creating setup disks even if the CD-ROM drive is bootable. In a worst-case scenario, the CD-ROM drive could decide not to function in addition to the hard drive failure.

E X E R C I S E

16.5 Create Setup Disks

To perform this exercise, you will need:

■ Access to a Windows 2000 computer

■ Disks created from the Windows 2000 Professional CD cannot be used with Windows 2000 Server and vice-versa.

■ A Windows 2000 CD-ROM (that matches the installed operating system)

■ Four blank, 3.5-inch, high-density floppy disks labeled **Setup Disk One, Setup Disk Two, Setup Disk Three,** and **Setup Disk Four**

1. Insert a blank, formatted, 3.5-inch, 1.44 MB disk into the floppy disk drive.

2. Insert the Windows 2000 CD-ROM into the CD-ROM drive.

3. Click the Start button.

4. Select **Run.**

5. In the **Open** box, type **d:\bootdisk\makeboot a:** (where **d:** is the drive letter assigned to the CD-ROM drive).

6. Press **Enter,** or click **OK.**

7. Follow the screen prompts (you will be prompted to insert the next floppy disk once its predecessor has been created).

Lesson 16.2 Explore Backup and Restore Options

To help you understand the importance of backing up your data, consider the following scenario.

Molly is working on the final page of her college thesis when the hard drive suddenly fails. Her initial shock turns to despair as she realizes that she has no other copies of those files. Imagine how she will feel once a new hard drive is installed and she must start on page 1 of a blank document. The moral of the story is that you must take time to make backups.

A backup is simply a copy. If information only exists on a single hard drive, disaster is at your doorstep. Although the system is not fault-tolerant, many options exist for ensuring there are secondary copies of original files, including mirror sets, network drives, tape drives, writable CD-ROMs, Zip drives, floppy disks, and backup programs. In this lesson, we will focus on the backup program that is included with Windows 2000, which is a new and improved version from Windows NT 4.0.

> **MICROSOFT EXAM OBJECTIVE**
>
> Recover systems and user data. Recover systems and user data by using Windows Backup.

Use the Backup Utility

The Backup utility assists in protecting data from accidental loss due to hardware or storage media failure. Using Backup you can do the following:

- Back up selected files and folders on a hard disk

- Restore the backed up files and folders to a hard disk or any other accessible disk

- Create an Emergency Repair Disk (ERD), which will repair system files in the event they get corrupted or are accidentally erased

- Make a copy of any Remote Storage data and any data stored in mounted drives

- Make a copy of the computer's **System State,** which includes such things as the registry, the boot files, and the system files

- Back up services on servers and domain controllers, including such things as the Active Directory directory service database, the Certificate Services database, and the File Replication service SYSVOL directory

- Schedule regular backups to keep backed up data up to date

Backup can be used to back up and restore data on either FAT or NTFS volumes. However, if you have backed up data from an NTFS volume used in Windows 2000, it is recommended that you restore the data to an NTFS volume used in Windows 2000 or you could lose data as well as some file and folder features. For example, permissions, encrypting file system (EFS) settings, disk quota information, mounted drive information, and Remote Storage information will be lost if you back up data from an NTFS volume used in Windows 2000 and then restore it to a FAT volume or an NTFS volume used in Windows NT 4.0.

Backup Types

The Backup wizard provides five backup types that allow for greater flexibility in determining which data are backup up. Some of the backup types rely on the use of backup **markers,** also known as archive attributes or archive bits. When the contents of a file are changed, the archive attribute on the file is set to indicate that the file needs to be backed up. The five backup types are normal, copy, incremental, differential, and daily.

- **Normal:** During a normal backup, all selected files are backed up whether or not their marker is set. After the backup is complete, the markers are all cleared, indicating that the files have been backed up.

- **Copy:** A copy backup is the same as a normal backup except that the markers are not cleared. This type of backup is most useful for taking a snapshot of the system. It does not alter the system in any way.

- **Incremental:** During an incremental backup, only selected files that have the marker set are backed up. After the backup is complete, the markers are cleared. A normal backup usually precedes an incremental backup. During a restoration process, the normal backup is restored and then each incremental backup is restored in sequence. This backup type speeds up the backup process because less information is backed up each time.

- **Differential:** A differential copy is the same as an incremental copy except that the markers are not cleared. During a restoration process, the normal backup is restored and then only the most recent differential copy is restored. This backup type speeds up the restore process because you do not have to restore multiple files in sequence.

- **Daily:** During a daily backup, all selected files that have the current date are backed up. This backup type does not depend on the markers; rather it depends on the time/date stamp of the file. When a file is altered, the time/date stamp is changed to the current day. With a daily backup, the markers are not cleared.

16.6 Use the Backup Wizard to Back Up Selected Files

To perform this exercise, you will need:

- Access to a Windows 2000 computer
- Media to receive the backup data

1. Log on as administrator.

2. Click the Start button.

3. Point to **Programs.**

4. Point to **Accessories.**

5. Point to **System Tools.**

6. Select **Backup.**

7. Click the **Backup wizard** button.

   - The Backup wizard welcome screen appears.

8. Click **Next.**

   - The What to Back Up page appears with three options.

     - Back up everything on my computer.

     - Back up selected drives, files, or network data.

     - Only back up the System State Data.

9. Select **Back Up selected drives, files, or network data.**

10. Click **Next.**

   - The Items to Back Up page appears (see Figure 16-1).

11. Place a checkmark next to a folder if you want to back up the folder and its contents, or expand the tree structure and click on a folder name to place a checkmark next to individual files in the right pane.

12. Click **Next.**

   - The Where to Store Backup page appears.

13. Select the media location by entering the path or by using the **Browse** button.

14. Click **Next.**

   - A summary page is displayed indicating the choices you made.

15. Click the **Advanced** button or click the **Finish** button to start the backup.

   - The **Advanced** button allows the following additional backup configuration options on these pages (click **Next** to advance to the next page):

     - **Type of Backup:** Normal, Copy, Incremental, Daily, Remote

     - **How to Back Up:** Verification of integrity and/or with file compression

FIGURE 16-1
The Items to Back Up Page of the Backup Wizard

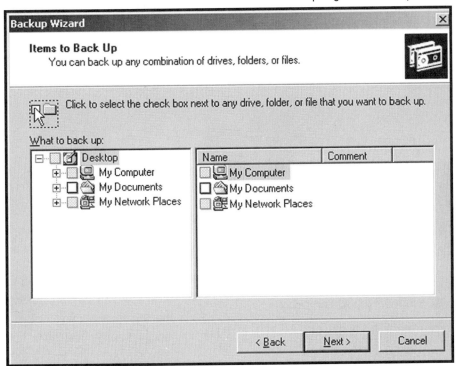

FIGURE 16-1
The Items to Back Up Page of the Backup Wizard

- **Media Options:** Append or replace existing data on the media

- **Backup Label:** Allows you to enter text that describes the backup, such as "Set created on 4-28-01 at 12:41 PM for WKS01"

- **When to Back Up:** Now or Later (enter date and time for the backup to occur)

- The Summary page is displayed again and reflects any additional changes.

16. Click **Finish.**

   - A Backup Progress screen is displayed describing how many bytes have been duplicated, source, destination, and so on.

   - When the backup is complete, a results screen is displayed with the option to view a text-file report detailing the events of the backup.

17. Click **Close.**

18. Exit Backup.

Backing Up System State Data

The Backup wizard can be used to make a copy of the computer's **System State**, which includes such things such as the registry, the boot files, and the system files.

MICROSOFT EXAM OBJECTIVE

Manage and optimize availability of System State data and user data.

EXERCISE

16.7

Make a Copy of System State Data

To perform this exercise you will need:

- Access to a Windows 2000 computer
- Media to receive the backup data

1. Log on as administrator.

2. Launch **Backup.**

3. Click the **Backup wizard** button.

   - The Backup wizard welcome screen appears.

4. Click **Next.**

   - The What to Backup page appears.

5. Select **Only backup the System State Data.**

6. Click **Next.**

   - The Where to Store Backup page appears.

7. Select the media location by entering the path or use the Browse button.

- System state data can be larger than 1.4 MB, which means that the information will not fit on a single floppy. You may have to consider an alternative backup media.

8. Click **Next.**

   - A summary page is displayed indicating the choices you made.

9. Click **Finish.**

   - A Backup Progress screen is displayed describing how many bytes have been duplicated, source, destination, etc.

   - When the backup is complete, a results screen is displayed with the option to view a text-file report detailing the events of the backup.

10. Click **Close.**

11. **Exit** Backup.

RESTORE FILES

If disaster strikes and files are lost, performing a restore procedure from within the Backup utility may get the system to where it was before the disaster occurred. The frequency of the backup procedure will determine the level of recovery. If, for example, the hard drive was backed up yesterday, very little will be lost. If the hard drive was backed up six months ago, six months of data and system configurations will be lost. One task of an administrator is to determine and manage a backup schedule that will minimize loss. It would be challenging to backup every minute of every day, so no matter when the disaster strikes, some data may be lost. Daily backups performed late at night when fewer users are on the system are common. Some organizations, however, do not experience much change on a daily basis, so a weekly backup might be sufficient. Analyze your company's needs and plan accordingly.

EXERCISE

16.8 Use the Restore Wizard to Restore Selected Files

To perform this exercise, you will need:

- Access to a Windows 2000 computer
- Media on which the backup files were stored (Exercise 16.6)

1. Open **Backup.**

2. Click the **Restore wizard** button.

   - The welcome page of the Restore wizard appears.

3. Click **Next.**

   - The What to Restore page appears.

4. Click the **Import File** button.

5. Indicate the location of the backup file.

6. Click **OK.**

- The file is loaded from the media, and its name appears in the right pane.

7. In the What to Restore: pane, navigate through the structure and place a checkmark next to the file(s) you want to restore.

8. Click **Next.**

9. Click the **Advanced** button, or click the **Finish** button (if you do not want to adjust the default advanced settings).

   - The **Advanced** button allows additional backup configuration options on these pages (click **Next** to advance to the next page):

- **Where to Restore:** Original location, Alternate location, Single folder

- **How to Restore:** Do not replace the file on the hard drive, Replace only if the file hard drive file is older, Always replace the files

- **Advanced Restore Options:** Restore security, Restore removable storage database, Restore junction points and not the folders and file data they reference

- The Summary page is displayed again and reflects any changes.

10. Click **Finish.**

- The Restore process begins.

- A Restore Progress screen is displayed describing how many bytes have been copied, source, destination, and so on.

- When the restore is complete, a results screen is displayed with the option to view a text-file report detailing the events of the restore.

11. Click **Close.**

12. Exit Backup.

> ### TIP
>
> Once you become familiar with backups and restores, you could click on the **Backup** and **Restore** tabs. The tabs allow you to use the interface directly instead of being "led" by the Backup wizard or the Restore wizard.

Restore the Registry and System State Data

It is important to have current, reliable backup copies of the registry. You should back up the registry as part of your regular backup routine and before you edit the registry. In Windows 2000, if you click the **System State data** button in Backup, the registry is automatically backed up.

Backup can also be used to restore System State data. To do this, the system must be stable enough for Backup to be launched.

> **MICROSOFT EXAM OBJECTIVE**
>
> Recover System State data by using Windows Backup.

EXERCISE

16.9 Use Backup to Restore System State Data

To perform this exercise you will need:

■ Access to a Windows 2000 computer

■ To have made a backup of System State data

1. Log on as an administrator or backup operator.

2. Start Backup.

3. Click the **Restore** tab, and then select the check box for any drive, folder, or file that you want to restore.

4. Click the box next to **System State** to restore the system state data along with any other data you have selected for the current restore operation.

5. Complete the restore process as described in Exercise 16.8.

You will receive a warning from the system about restoring system state files over existing system state files. Unless the system is dysfunctional, or unless no changes have been made to the system state, restoring over existing files is dangerous and could result in corruption of the system.

You can also use Backup to restore lost data to the registry. The system must be stable enough for you to open Backup. One drawback about using Backup is that it does not allow you to restore only the registry files. If Backup is used to restore lost data to the registry, all system state data is replaced.

Another way to restore the system state is by using the Recovery Console. Many of the commands used in the Recovery Console function like MS-DOS commands. Familiarity with DOS can be beneficial to system administrators.

> **MICROSOFT EXAM OBJECTIVE**
>
> Recover System State data by using the Recovery Console.

16.10

Use the Recovery Console to Restore System State Data

To perform this exercise you will need:

- Access to a Windows 2000 computer
- To have installed the Recovery Console
- To have backed up System State data

1. Insert the Windows 2000 Setup CD-ROM or (if the CD-ROM drive is not bootable) the first floppy disk you created from the CD, in the appropriate drive.

2. Restart the computer, and if using floppy disks, respond to the prompts that request each floppy disk in turn.

3. When the text-based part of Setup begins, follow the prompts; choose the repair or recover option by pressing **R.**

4. When prompted, choose the Recovery Console by pressing **C.**

5. Follow the instructions on the screen for reinserting one or more of the floppy disks you created for starting the system.

6. If you have a dual-boot or multiple-boot system, choose the Windows 2000 installation that you need to access from the Recovery Console.

7. When prompted, type the Administrator password.

   - A system prompt window will appear.
   - Recovery Console commands can now be entered.

8. Type **help** for a list of commands, or **help** *commandname* for help on a specific command.

   - When the system state data is backed up, a copy of the registry files is also saved in %SystemRoot%\Repair\Regback.
   - %SystemRoot% is the path where the Windows 2000 Server files were installed. The default systemroot is C:\WINNT.
   - If registry files become corrupted or are accidentally erased, these files can be used to repair the registry without performing a full restore of the system state data.

CAUTION: Performing the next step may cause your system to become corrupt. Try this on a non-critical computer. It should be used as a last resort when a system is down due to registry edits and when normal backup procedures cannot be performed.

9. To use the copy command to repair the registry, type the following command: copy c:\winnt\repair\regback c:\winnt\system32\config

   ◾ Step 9 copies all the files in the regback folder to the config folder. Two of the files, ntuser.dat and usrclass.dat are files specific to a user. Search the Windows 2000 volume for each of the above filenames and then use the copy command to replace the original files with the files in the regback folder.

10. To exit the Recovery Console and restart the computer, type **exit.**

If you cannot fix the problem with the registry by performing the Emergency Repair Process or by selecting **Last Known Good Configuration** from the **Windows 2000 Advanced Options** menu, it might be necessary to reinstall the operating system and device drivers and to reconfigure the system before data can be restored.

Lesson 16.3 Encrypt Data

Consider the following scenario. Jason has always been curious about the contents of other users' files. One day when Denise was out of the office, he reinstalled the operating system and was able to access the files she stored locally (which she did not appreciate). The administrator then installed Windows 2000 on all of the computers. Although Jason tried to read Michal's files, Michal had encrypted his files using the **Encrypting File System (EFS),** which allows users to store their on-disk data in encrypted format. Jason's efforts were thwarted because EFS was protecting the files in addition to the operating system permissions.

> **MICROSOFT EXAM OBJECTIVE**
>
> Encrypt data on a hard disk by using Encrypting File System (EFS).

    Encryption is the process of converting data into a format that cannot be read by another user. Windows 2000 encrypts data by using a **key algorithm,** which renders it unreadable without the knowledge of the key. Encryption is like locking something valuable into a strong box and only the person with the key can open the lock to get what is inside. **Decryption** is the process of converting data from encrypted format back to the original format. Administrators can decrypt data that was encrypted by another user. This ensures that data are accessible if the user that encrypted the data is no longer available or has lost his or her private key.

Users encrypt a file or folder by setting the encryption property for files and folders just as they would set any other attribute, such as read-only, compressed, or hidden. When a folder is encrypted, the folder itself is not actually encrypted, but all files and subfolders created in or added to the encrypted folder are automatically encrypted. Microsoft recommends that users encrypt at the folder level. Compressed files, system files, and files stored on a non-NTFS volume cannot be encrypted.

EXERCISE

16.11 Encrypt a Data File

To perform this exercise you will need:

- Access to a Windows 2000 computer
- Access to a data file on an NTFS volume

1. Open **Windows Explorer.**

2. Navigate the folder structure to locate the file to be encrypted.

3. Right-click the file.

4. Select **Properties** from the context menu.

5. Click the **General** tab.

6. Click the **Advanced** button.

7. Place a checkmark in the **Encrypt contents to secure data** checkbox.

8. Click **OK** to close the Advanced dialog box.

9. Click **OK** to close the Properties dialog box.

   - The Encryption Warning message appears prompting you to indicate if you want to encrypt this one file only or if you want to also encrypt the parent file (and all of the files it contains).

10. Click the radio button for the action you desire.

11. Click **OK.**

Accessing Encrypted Data

When a user accesses an encrypted file that is stored on disk, the user is able to read the contents of the file in the normal way. When the user stores the file on disk again, EFS transparently encrypts the file again. Only the user that encrypted a file can access it later. If another user tries to access an encrypted file, that user receives an **Access Denied** message.

Decrypting a File

To decrypt a file, clear the Encryption checkbox in the file's Properties dialog box. Decryption is not necessary as long as the user is the only one that needs to access the file. The only reason a user might need to decrypt a file is when the user wants to share the file with another user or make the file available to users across the network.

EFS Recommendations

The following practices are recommended for users when encrypting or decrypting files:

- Users should encrypt the **My Documents** folder if this is where they save most of their documents. This ensures that their personal documents are encrypted by default.

- Users should encrypt their **Temp** folder so that any temporary files created by programs are automatically encrypted.

- Users should encrypt folders instead of individual files so that if a program creates temporary files during editing, these will be encrypted as well.

Summary

Few people think about a disaster before it strikes. After it strikes, people cannot think of much else. If you are prepared, the disasters you experience will be short-lived. Before you begin the recovery process, evaluate what caused the disaster. The cause will lead you to the cure. If, for example, you installed a new video driver and now the screen is black, you would know to start the computer in safe mode so that you could reinstall the original video driver. Running in safe mode does not do any good if the registry is corrupt, however. The Backup utility will help in many cases, especially when the disaster involves lost or damaged files. Lastly, you learned about how encryption helps users protect their files from unauthorized access.

REVIEW EXERCISE

These questions will help you determine if you have learned enough to move on to the next chapter. If the graphic next to the option is a square (❏), there can be more than one answer for that question. If the graphic is a circle (○), there is only one correct answer. Color in the shape(s) to indicate your answer(s).

1. In what recovery option will Windows 2000 use default settings, including a VGA video driver, Microsoft mouse driver, no network connections, and the minimum device drivers required to start Windows?

   a. ○ Recovery mode

   b. ○ Safe mode

   c. ○ Emergency Repair mode

   d. ○ A la mode

2. Lindsey suspects that someone is reading her personal data files that are stored on the server. What options does she have to make sure this does not happen?

   a. ❏ Ask the administrator to check who has permissions to access her files and have the permissions changed.

   b. ❏ She could encrypt the folder that contains her personal data files.

   c. ❏ Shut down her PC whenever she leaves her desk.

   d. ❏ She has no options for keeping this from happening.

3. Phil's task is to make several sets of setup disks for a Windows 2000 Server computer. He inserts the Windows 2000 Server CD in drive E:, clicks Start, selects Run, and types

   a. ○ d:\setupdisk\makesetup a:

   b. ○ d:\setupdisk\makedisk c:

   c. ○ e:\bootdisk\makeboot a:

   d. ○ e:\bootdisk\makeboot c:

4. One of the computers on the network has a corrupted registry. David is the only administrator on duty, and the user is insisting the problem be fixed immediately. What options does David have to get the computer back to normal?

   a. ❏ Run the computer in Safe Mode.

   b. ❏ Use the computer's ERD.

   c. ❏ Use the Restore wizard in the Backup utility.

   d. ❏ Use the Recovery Console.

5. Which of the following statements are true regarding the **Last Known Good Configuration?**

   a. ❑ It is accessed from the Administrative Tools menu.

   b. ❑ It starts Windows 2000 using the registry information that Windows saved at the last shutdown.

   c. ❑ It solves problems caused by corrupted or missing drivers or files.

   d. ❑ Any changes made since the last successful startup will be lost.

▼PERFORMANCE CHALLENGES

■ Document a feature in the Backup utility that was not discussed in the text.

■ Write the step-by-step instructions for launching a Windows 2000 computer using the Setup disks.

■ Run an experiment to discover what happens to encryption when an encrypted file is copied to a folder that is not encrypted, and when it is copied to a folder that is encrypted. Do the same experiment for when an encrypted file is moved. Document your results.

TROUBLESHOOT THE ENVIRONMENT

OBJECTIVES

After completing this chapter, you should be able to:

- Define troubleshooting

- Employ troubleshooting techniques

- Solve common computer problems

- Make resources available to users

- Describe how to solve network problems

- Use the Security Configuration and Analysis Snap-in

- Perform a search for information in Windows 2000 Help

- Identify additional resources for Windows 2000 Server

OUTLINE

Lesson 17.1 Troubleshooting Techniques

Lesson 17.2 Troubleshoot Computers

Lesson 17.3 Troubleshoot Access to Resources

Lesson 17.4 Troubleshoot Hardware Devices

Lesson 17.5 Troubleshoot Storage Use

    Exercise 17.1—Replace a Disk Region in a RAID-5 Volume
    Exercise 17.2—Editing the Boot.ini File

Lesson 17.6 Troubleshoot Network Connections

Lesson 17.7 Use Security Configuration and Analysis

    Exercise 17.3—Set a Working Security Database
    Exercise 17.4—Analyze System Security

Introduction

In a perfect world, there would be no problems with the network or its computers; no components would fail and everything would keep running as it was designed to run . . . forever. It is not a matter of *if* something will fail; it is a matter of *when.* When the network or a computer on the network experiences failure, intermittent problems, or has a drop in performance, it is time to start **troubleshooting.** Troubleshooting is the methodical process of eliminating faults from a system. In this chapter, you will learn good troubleshooting techniques as well as some examples of potential problems with various network components. You will also be given a list of additional resources for assisting in troubleshooting when all else fails.

Lesson 17.1 Troubleshooting Techniques

If you use the following troubleshooting techniques, you should be able to focus your efforts in order to discover what is causing the fault. Troubleshooting a computer involves changing the hardware or software configuration of different components and then testing to see whether the configuration change has eliminated the fault. If hardware caused the fault, find and replace the failed component. If software caused the fault, reconfigure your system to eliminate the fault.

Focus Is Important

Imagine going to a doctor with a stomachache. Instead of asking you your symptoms or making an initial analysis, she simply pulls out a needle, fills it with some medicine, and approaches you. Would you let her give you the shot? Probably not. She could be giving you something that would make you *really* sick.

It is the same with computers. Making random changes in hopes that something will work is not only a waste of time, but it also can potentially create more problems. Repeat the following three steps as often as necessary:

1. Focus on a specific component.

2. Test the component thoroughly.

3. If you are unable to correct the fault, restore the system to its original configuration before moving on to another component.

Troubleshooting Guidelines

Document Your Efforts.   Troubleshooting is not usually an instantaneous event. Some problems may take days or weeks to solve. Write down the symptoms as well as your plan for systematically eliminating the fault. Keep an accurate chronological log of your efforts to correct the fault(s). These lists will be very helpful if the process is extended or if you need to bring in additional help.

Know the System.   Your doctor went to school for many years in order to learn everything he or she could about the human body. In his or her practice, the doctor learns about and documents the peculiarities about each person. As an administrator, you must be diligent to know not only general computing and networking functions but also the peculiarities of the particular system on which you are working.

Be Patient.   Jumping to conclusions can lead you down the wrong path. Be thorough in your research before performing any corrective measures. If one approach does not work, do not give up. Try again.

Isolate the Fault.   Focus on specific components and eliminate from your troubleshooting plan the ones that are working properly. Perform the three steps listed earlier until the fault is located.

Check the Most Recent Change.   If the system was working great and then someone installed a network card just before network performance slowed to a crawl, it is easy to guess which component is the most likely culprit. Ask yourself, "What changed?" The answer to that question is often the source of the problem.

Check Things That Have Failed Before.   Once a component begins to experience problems, it may have recurring problems. Logs are especially helpful in this situation. If you are not able to remember which cable segment had the most recent problem, the log could be a reminder.

Perform Easy Tests First.   You receive a call from a user who says his computer is not working. Sure enough, the entire unit is dead. When you open the case and begin to pull the hard drive, you notice that the power cord had become disconnected. This is one time it pays to be a little lazy. Start with the easiest repair options first, and then progress to the more difficult ones.

Change Only One Setting at a Time.   Partial success in correcting a fault indicates a complex failure involving two or more faults. If this is the case, you will need to focus on one fault before moving on to the next one. In some cases, a problem that appears to relate to a single component may be the result of bottlenecks involving multiple components. For this reason, it is important to address problems individually. Making multiple changes simultaneously may make it impossible to assess the impact of each individual change.

After Every Change, Monitor the System. This is important for understanding the effect of the change and to determine whether additional changes are required. Proceed methodically, making one change to the identified resource at a time and then testing the effects of the changes on performance.

Try to Make Transient Failures Repeatable. If the faults seem to be random or transient (moving from one system to another), try to make the fault occur when *you* want it to. Once you do this, you will be able to combat the fault wherever it occurs.

Resort to Permanent Changes Last. Replacing a hard drive is a permanent change and involves a multitude of steps in order to bring the system back to its original state. Make temporary changes whenever possible until the fault is identified. Otherwise, you may never know what actually caused the fault. In addition, a permanent change is usually the most expensive option.

Lesson 17.2 Troubleshoot Computers

Poor response time on a workstation is most likely a result of memory and processor problems. Servers are more susceptible to disk and network problems.

Memory Problems

Insufficient memory is by far the most common cause of serious performance problems in computer systems. Even if you suspect the cause of the fault to be another problem, check memory counters first to rule out a memory shortage.

If you are experiencing memory problems, you can do the following:

- Install additional RAM, especially if it is at the minimum.

- Create multiple paging files.

- Increase the paging file size.

- Ensure that memory settings are properly configured.

- Run memory-intensive programs on the highest-performing computers or when system workload is light.

Disk Problems

Hard drives are the most common failure point in a computer. Whenever a component has moving parts, those moving parts will eventually wear out. Hard drive technology advances quickly, so upgrading the disk will usually result in higher capacity and faster access speeds.

If you are experiencing disk problems, you can do the following:

- Upgrade to a higher speed disk, or add disks. When you do this, upgrade the disk controller and the bus.

- On servers, use Disk Management to create striped volumes on multiple physical disks.

- Distribute programs among servers. Distributed File System (Dfs) can be used to balance workload.

- Isolate tasks that heavily utilize disk I/O on separate physical disks or disk controllers.

- Use Disk Defragmenter to optimize disk space.

- If you want to improve the efficiency of disk access, consider installing the latest driver software for the host adapters. Contact the adapter manufacturer for information.

Processor Problems

The CPU is the brain of your computer. If the brain cannot keep up with the demands being placed upon it, performance suffers. As with hard disks, processor technologies are advancing at a rapid pace and upgrading often solves the fault. The motherboard configuration will determine your options regarding processor replacement. For example, not all motherboards can accommodate multiple processors.

If you are experiencing processor problems, you can do the following:

- Add a processor (especially for multithreaded programs).

- Upgrade to a faster processor.

- Run processor-intensive programs on the server (thin client concept).

Lesson 17.3 Troubleshoot Access to Resources

Proper planning of file structures, Active Directory organization, and assignment of permissions should circumvent most resource access problems. Networks tend, however, to be living entities that change over time through expansion or contraction. The interrelationships of groups can become complicated, which can cause resource access dilemmas.

If you are experiencing resource access dilemmas, you can do the following:

■ If a user cannot access a program that he or she knows is there or can see, usually he or she does not have sufficient permissions.

■ Log on as the administrator and try the same operation. If successful, the problem is a security problem.

■ The administrator can take ownership of any resource and then reassign permissions as necessary.

■ Examine the user's group memberships for conflicting share and file permissions. Remember that if a file permission and a share permission are set on the same resource, the most restrictive permission takes precedence.

■ Check the status of the resource. If a hard drive fails, the files that are stored on that hard drive are no longer available. If the printer is unplugged or offline, print jobs will not be printed.

■ Check the status of the network. Data flows through the network through connectors, cabling, and NIC cards. Failure of these components can cause resources to be unavailable.

Troubleshooting Printers and Print Devices

One of the most common problems in a network environment involves print devices. These machines must produce high volumes of printed output and, because of their many moving parts, are susceptible to problems. In Microsoft terminology, a printer is the software construct and the print device is the hardware. Most users are not aware of this difference, so you will usually refer to a print device as a "printer." Table 17-1 describes common problems with printing and potential solutions.

Lesson 17.4 Troubleshoot Hardware Devices

When deciding whether the fault is because of hardware or software, always check the hardware before making changes to the software. If the hardware is indeed at fault, no amount of software configuration will completely solve the fault.

TABLE 17-1 COMMON PRINTING PROBLEMS

PROBLEM	POTENTIAL SOLUTION
The print device is not turned on	This may sound simplistic, but a print device will not function without power. The first question to ask a user with printing problems is "Is the printer turned on?"
The print device is not online	When a print device is online, it is ready to receive information. When a print device is offline, it will not accept information. Have the user push the button labeled "Online." Usually a light indicates the print device is now online.
The print device is out of supplies, such as ink, toner, or paper	Take the print device offline while you replenish the supplies. Put the print device back online when done.
The paper jams	Occasionally, a piece of paper will not travel through the print device properly. This could result in a paper jam. Most print devices will display a message indicating the error. Refer to the owner's manual for procedures on clearing a paper jam.
A print job does not print	Check the items listed above first. Instruct the user to refrain from sending the print job repeatedly until the problem is resolved. If the user has access to other network resources: ■ Ensure that the user has the appropriate permissions for accessing the printer. ■ Verify the proper installation and configuration of the printer on the user's computer. Look for appropriate settings for IP addresses, URL designations, printer name, and so on. Try adding a new printer. If the new setting works, remove the old printer. ■ Open the printer dialog box on the print server to check the status of all print jobs. When a paper jam occurs, for example, you will have to fix the print device and then delete the first document in the print queue. Other documents will then be able to print. If the user does not have access to other network resources: ■ Check connectivity to the network such as network card and cabling.
A user can access all print devices except for one	If other users can access the print device, ensure that the user has permission to access the print device. If other users cannot access the print device, check the print device for hardware and/or connectivity problems.

You can do the following to troubleshoot hardware devices:

- Check the following components in order; this will progressively narrow your search for a hardware fault:

  - Power
  - Motherboard
  - Processor
  - RAM
  - Video
  - BIOS configuration
  - Hardware conflicts
  - Hard disk controllers and drives

    - Power or connection problems
    - Hardware configuration problems
    - Incorrect BIOS information
    - Failed mechanisms
    - Failed hard disk controllers
    - Bad sectors
    - Corrupted boot sectors
    - Corrupted file systems
    - Viruses

- Use Device Manager to identify the device driver and to see if it needs to be updated.
- Use the Add/Remove Hardware wizard if the component is Plug and Play compatible.

Lesson 17.5 Troubleshoot Storage Use

Even though you diligently follow the steps for how to alleviate problems with hard disks given in Lesson 17.2, your hard drive still can fail. True recovery from a disk failure involves the implementation of fault-tolerant systems such as mirror sets, RAID, and backups.

Recovering a Mirror Set

When you have configured a mirror set, there is no down time because the operating system is able to use the hard drive that did not fail. The files on both drives "mirrored" each other. You would remove the failed hard drive, install the new hard drive, and reconfigure a mirror between the existing hard drive and the new hard drive.

Recovering a Failed Drive in a RAID Configuration

With a RAID configuration, data are stored across an array of disks. It is important to replace the failed hard drive as soon as possible because there is no fault tolerance until the failed drive is repaired. Few RAID implementations can withstand two simultaneous failures. Once the failed disk is replaced, the data can be regenerated by using the redundant information. When data regeneration is complete, all of the data are current and again are protected against disk failure. The following exercise demonstrates how to reestablish the RAID set after a disk failure. You will not be able to perform the exercise unless you have (or can simulate) a hard drive failure in a RAID.

EXERCISE

17.1 Replace a Disk Region in a RAID-5 Volume

To perform this exercise, you will need:

■ Access to a Windows 2000 computer with a failed hard disk that was configured to be part of a RAID-5 volume

■ A dynamic disk with unallocated space that is at least as large as the region to repair

1. Replace the failed drive.

2. Log on as an administrator.

3. Open **Disk Management.**

4. Right-click the portion of the RAID-5 volume that was located on the failed disk.

5. Click **Repair Volume.**

   ■ If you do not have a dynamic disk with enough unallocated space, the **Repair Volume** command is unavailable.

6. Follow the instructions on the screen.

Use Backups

To recover from a failed hard drive using the Backup utility, you would have had to back up the entire hard drive previous to the failure. Keep in mind that any changes made between the time of the backup and the restore would be lost. After installation of the new hard drive, use the Backup utility to restore the files from the failed drive to the new drive. When indicating the location for the restored files, you would click the **Alternate Location** button and browse to the computer where the new hard drive is located. Log on as an administrator to avoid permission restrictions.

Editing the Boot.ini File

If the hard drive that has failed is the drive from which the operating system boots, you may have to make alterations to the Boot.ini file. This would most likely be the case if a mirror set fails. When Windows 2000 Server is installed, the Setup program saves the Boot.ini file in the active partition. On a system with multiple operating systems, the contents of the boot menu are determined by entries in the boot.ini file.

The Boot.ini file has two sections, [boot loader] and [operating systems]. The file also contains Advanced RISC Computing (ARC) paths pointing to the computer's boot partition. The following is an example of an ARC path:

TIP

RISC stands for Reduced Instruction Set Computing, a design of microprocessors that uses a small set of simple instructions for faster execution.

```
multi(0)disk(0)rdisk(1)partitions(1)
```

- **Multi** refers to the adapter/disk controller. The number in parentheses indicates the load order of the hardware adapter. If the controller is a SCSI controller without SCSI BIOS enabled, the line would say scsi instead of multi. If you had two SCSI adapters in a computer, the first to load receives number 0 on its line, and the next one receives number 1 on its line.

- **Disk** is the SCSI ID for when successive disks are on one controller. For multi, this value is always 0.

- **Rdisk** is a number that identifies the disk (only used with multi and ignored for SCSI controllers)

- **Partition** is a number that identifies the partition.

Below is an example of a Boot.ini file that demonstrates ARC paths:

```
[boot loader]
timeout =30
default=multi(0)disk(0)rdisk(1)partition(2)\ WINNT
```

TABLE 17-2 OPTIONAL BOOT.INI SWITCHES

SWITCH	DESCRIPTION
/basevideo	Uses the standard VGA video driver when the computer boots. This is helpful when a new video driver is not working properly.
/fastdetect=[comx | comx,y,z,]	Disables serial mouse detection. The italicized letters are the port numbers. If a port is not specified, this switch disables port detection on all COM ports. By default, this switch is included in every entry in the Boot.ini file.
/maxmem:n	Specifies the amount of RAM that Windows 2000 uses. Helpful when a memory chip is bad.
/noguiboot	GUI stands for Graphical User Interface. Use this switch if you want to boot the computer without displaying the graphical boot status screen.
/sos	Device driver names will be displayed as they load. Use this switch when startup fails while loading drivers. You may be able to discover which driver is causing the failure.

```
[operating systems]
multi(0)disk(0)rdisk(1)partition(2)\ WINNT="Microsoft
    Windows 2000 Server"
multi(0)disk(0)rdisk(1)partition(1)\ WINNT="Windows NT
    Server 4.0 [VGA Mode]" /basevideo /sos
C:\ = "Previous Operating System on C:"
```

SWITCHES FOR THE BOOT.INI FILE

The Boot.ini file has switches that alter the way a particular line functions. Table 17-2 lists the switches.

EDITING THE BOOT.INI FILE

The Boot.ini file is a text file and can be edited by any text editor. By default, the Boot.ini file is hidden and read-only, so before edits can be made, hidden files would need to be displayed and the read-only attribute would need to be cleared. Exercise 17.2 displays hidden files, clears the attribute, and opens the Boot.ini file.

17.2

Editing the Boot.ini File

To perform this exercise you will need:

■ Access to a Windows 2000 computer

1. Log on as an administrator.

2. Launch **Windows Explorer.**

3. From the **Tools** menu, select **Folder Options.**

4. Click the **View** tab.

5. Under **Hidden Files and Folders,** select **Show Hidden Files and Folders.**

6. Click **OK.**

7. From the **View** menu, select **Refresh.**

8. Click on the volume that contains the Boot.ini file.

9. Right-click Boot.ini.

10. From the context-menu, select **Properties.**

■ The General tab of the file's properties dialog box is displayed.

11. Under **Attributes,** clear the Read-only check box.

12. Click **OK.**

13. Right-click on Boot.ini and select **Open** from the context-menu.

■ Notepad is launched and the contents of the Boot.ini file are displayed.

14. **Exit** Notepad and **DO NOT** save changes.

If a mirror set fails, you would edit the Boot.ini file to indicate that the functional hard drive is the hard drive to be booted from.

Lesson 17.6 Troubleshoot Network Connections

Most network problems are due to the failure of a single component. To see whether network components are playing a part in performance problems, compare the performance of programs that run over the network with programs that are run locally.

To troubleshoot network connections, you can do the following:

- Configure the network so that systems shared by the same group of people are on the same subnet.

- Unbind infrequently used network adapters.

- If you are using more than one protocol, you can set the order in which the workstation and NetBIOS software bind to each protocol.

- Install a high-performance network adapter in the server. If the server uses a 16-bit adapter, replacing it with a high-performance 32-bit adapter can significantly increase performance.

- Use multiple network adapters. Windows 2000 supports multiple adapters for a given protocol and multiple protocols for a given adapter. Although this configuration can create distinct networks that cannot communicate with one another, it is a way to increase file-sharing throughput.

Client Problems

The network problem is a client problem when only a single station is affected. If you are experiencing client problems, you can do the following:

- Make sure that the cable and the connector are in good condition and are functional.

- Make sure that the NIC is installed correctly and that there are no conflicts.

- Make sure that the correct driver is installed and configured.

- Make sure that the proper transport protocols are installed and that the settings are correct.

- Make sure that the client software was properly installed and configured (name and domain membership).

- Use the ping utility on TCP/IP networks.

Server Problems

The network problem is a server problem when the one computer everyone is trying to interact with is not responding properly. To troubleshoot server problems, you can do the following:

- Complete the client checklist provided in the previous section for the server.

- Change two client computers to the same workgroup and share a resource from one to the other. If it does not work, see data link troubleshooting in the following section.

- Verify that clients can attach to another server (if available). If not, see data link troubleshooting in the following section.

- Check the server's hardware for malfunctions or failures.

- Replace the network adapter with an adapter of a different manufacturer.

- Create an Emergency Repair Disk and reinstall Windows 2000 Server using the Repair option.

Data Link Problems

Data link problems occur when a physical or logical device that connects the network fails. This is common, especially in large networks that have many data link devices. When a data link problem occurs, it usually affects entire subnetworks and can deny the network access or access to other subnetworks.

If you are experiencing data link problems, you can do the following:

- Attach a client directly to the server with a single cable (this is called **co-located**). Try to log on.

- Take each hub in the affected areas and verify with the co-located client and server that you can attach to the server through each port of the hub.

- If two subnetworks cannot connect to each other, replace the bridge between them.

- Reboot the router.

Cable Problems

Cable problems are very common in networks. The solution is to fix or replace the portion of the cable that is bad. To troubleshoot cable problems, you can do the following:

- Before replacing cables, exhaust all other possibilities, such as the list for clients given previously. If you do not, you could spend the money for new cable and still have the problem.

- Use network analysis devices that can detect cabling problems.

- Check the connectors by substituting connectors known to be good.

- Perform a systematic search and analyze resource accessibility to locate the problem area.

- Ensure that you have not exceeded the maximum length in the cable's specifications.

- Ensure that the cable was properly installed and that it is not exposed (such as someone being able to roll a chair over the cable under a desk).

General Network Protocol and Connectivity Problems

To resolve problems with network protocols and connectivity, consider these options:

1. Make sure that all system requirements were met.

2. Make sure that the right access numbers are being used and that they are being entered appropriately.

3. Verify that the users understand that dialing properties are applied only to numbers selected from a phone book. If a number is typed or edited by the user, the user must then type all dialing information, including information such as long-distance and external access numbers.

4. Access the Connection Manager troubleshooter Help, and verify the path that the users have taken through the troubleshooter Help.

5. Check the appropriate readme file (including CMAKRead.htm) to determine if the problem is a known issue.

6. Look for common mistakes. Make sure that:

   - The modem is on.

   - Any calling card number on the Dialing Properties page does not exceed 36 characters. This often causes a General Protection Fault error. (To display the Dialing Properties page, in the **Properties** dialog box, on the **General** tab, click **Dialing Rules.**)

   - The appropriate version of Connection Manager is installed.

   - The latest version of Network and Dial-Up Connections is installed.

   - The latest service pack is installed.

   - The proxy settings are correct.

   - All required network protocols, including TCP/IP, IPX, and Net-BEUI (as appropriate), are installed and configured correctly on the user's computer. (If the user can get to the network, but can't reach any services, a protocol on the user's computer may be corrupted.)

   - The required Network and Dial-Up Connections entry is available on the user's computer.

   - If a user has installed remote access, did the user reinstall any service pack previously installed on their system (required after installing remote access).

7. Users have received all workarounds and solutions, as appropriate.

For information on remote access or Network and Dial-Up Connections problems, search the Knowledge Base articles on the Microsoft Developer Network (MSDN) Web site (http://msdn.microsoft.com/developer/default.htm).

Lesson 17.7 Use Security Configuration and Analysis

As a network grows, flaws in the security can develop. **Security Configuration and Analysis** is a tool for analyzing and configuring local system security.

Security Configuration and Analysis allows quick review of security analysis results. The tool gives recommendations for elements you could consider reconfiguring, along with current system settings. Icons or remarks are used to highlight any areas where the current settings do not match the proposed level of security. Security Configuration and Analysis also allows you to resolve any discrepancies the analysis revealed.

MICROSOFT EXAM OBJECTIVE

Implement, configure, manage, and troubleshoot security by using the Security Configuration Tool Set.

EXERCISE

17.3 Set a Working Security Database

To perform this exercise, you will need:

- Access to a domain controller

1. Log on as an administrator.

2. Create a **new console** (see Exercise 11.3).

3. Add the **Security Configuration and Analysis** snap-in to the console (see Exercise 11.5).

4. Right-click **Security Configuration and Analysis** in the tree pane.

5. Select **Open database** from the Context menu.

   - The Open Database dialog box appears.

FIGURE 17-1
The Import Template Dialog Box

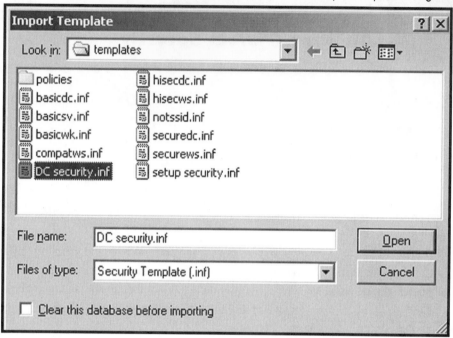

6. Type a file name (keep the extension the same).

   ■ This creates a new personal database.

   ■ In the future, you could choose an existing personal database at this point.

7. Click **Open.**

   ■ The Import Template dialog box appears (see Figure 17-1).

8. Select the **DC Security** template.

   ■ In the future, you could select the security template you want to load into your database.

9. Click **Open.**

   ■ The database is loaded and ready to be used for configuration of the system.

17.4

Analyze System Security

To perform this exercise, you will need:

- Access to a domain controller
- To have performed Exercise 17.3

1. Log on as an administrator.

2. Open the console you created in Exercise 17.3.

3. Right-click **Security Configuration and Analysis.**

4. Select **Analyze System Now** from the Context menu.

   - The Enter Log path dialog box appears.

5. Click **OK** to use the default analysis log path, or enter a file name and valid path.

   - The Analyzing System Security screen appears.

   - The display changes as the various security items are analyzed.

   - When the analysis is complete, the console displays the results of the analysis (see Figure 17-2).

6. Explore the results by navigating the structure in the tree pane.

FIGURE 17-2
Results of a Security Analysis

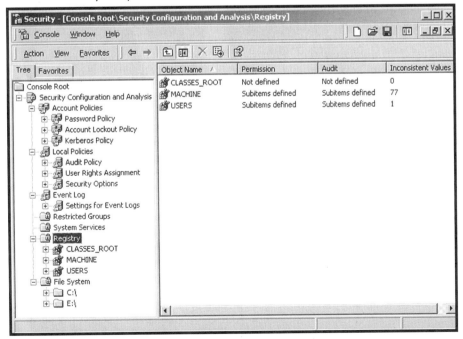

Lesson 17.8 Identify Windows 2000 Troubleshooters

The Windows 2000 troubleshooters are utilities within Windows Help that assist in diagnosing and solving technical problems that are occurring with a computer. When a troubleshooter is started, you must answer a series of questions about the problem. These answers will help Windows 2000 find a solution to the problem. There are several different troubleshooters, each one designed to solve a different type of problem. Table 17-3 lists the troubleshooters that are available in Windows 2000 Server. See Exercise 17.6 for how to access the troubleshooters via Windows Help.

Lesson 17.9 Resources for Troubleshooting

After you have tried everything you can think of and have used the diagnostic utilities provided by Microsoft, you will need to turn to other resources for help.

Windows Help Files

The help files included with Windows 2000 Server are extensive and are based on Microsoft's experience with customer support.

EXERCISE

17.5 Launching Windows Help

To perform this exercise, you will need:

- Access to a domain controller (all Windows 2000 computers have help files, but the files on a server are more extensive)

1. Click the Start button.

2. Select **Help.**

- The Windows Help window opens (see Figure 17-3).

TABLE 17-3 WINDOWS 2000 TROUBLESHOOTERS

PROGRAM	IDENTIFIES AND RESOLVES PROBLEMS RELATED TO
Client Service for Netware	Client Service for Netware, including accessing Netware servers and Novell Directory Services (NDS) objects, printing to Netware printers, using Netware login scripts, and logging onto an NDS tree.
DHCP	Configuring the Dynamic Host Configuration Protocol (DHCP) service on a server, including related error messages and events that appear in the event log.
Display	Video cards and display adapters, including your computer screen, outdated or incompatible video drivers, and incorrect settings for your video hardware.
Group Policy and Active Directory	Group Policy and configuring Active Directory on a server, including related error messages and events that appear in the event log.
Domain Name System	Configuring Domain Name System (DNS) on a server, including related error messages and events that appear in the event log.
Hardware	Cameras, CD-ROM drives, game controllers, hard drives, keyboards, mouse devices, network adapters, and scanners. If you are having problems with a sound card, a modem, or a display or video adapter, see the individual troubleshooters for those devices.
Internet connections	Connecting and logging on to your Internet Service Provider (ISP).
Modem	Modem connections, setup, configuration, and detection.
MS-DOS programs	Running MS-DOS programs on Windows 2000.
Multimedia and games	Installing and configuring Direct X drivers and games.
Networking (TCP/IP)	Internet and intranet connections (client side only) that use Transmission Control Protocol/Internet Protocol (TCP/IP).
Print	Network or local printers and plotters, including outdated or corrupted printer drivers, network and local printer connections, and printer configuration.
Routing and Remote Access	Dial-up networking connections that use a telephone to connect your computer to another computer.
Remote Installation Services	Installing Windows 2000 using Remote Installation Services.
Sound	Sound cards and speakers.
Startup and shutdown	Choosing an operating system at startup, corrupted Ntldr and Ntdetect files, and startup errors related to floppy drives, SCSI host adapters, video, and hard drives.
Stop errors	System startup errors, including Stop errors that occur on Windows 2000 Server.
System setup	Installing and setting up Windows 2000.
Server management	Configuring and managing the Windows 2000 Server.
Windows 3.x programs	Running 16-bit Windows programs on Windows 2000. If you are having problems running an MS-DOS program, see the MS-DOS troubleshooter.
WINS	Configuring Windows Internet Name Service (WINS) on a server, including related error messages and events that appear in the event log.

FIGURE 17-3
The Windows Help Window with the Search Tab Active

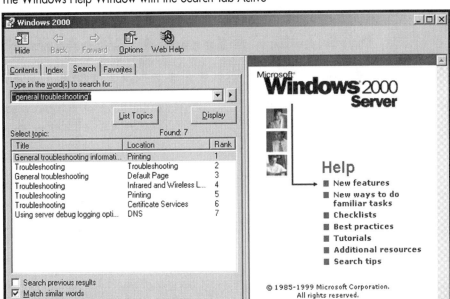

Windows 2000 Help has the following four tabs:

■ **Contents:** Displays the help topics by subject in book-like format. Navigate through the books by double-clicking them. When the icon looks like a paper (rather than a book), double-clicking will result in the presentation of information.

■ **Index:** Similar to the index of a book. Information is arranged alphabetically by topic.

■ **Search:** Allows you to enter a term or phrase that will return a list of topics relating to your entry (see Exercise 17.6).

■ **Favorites:** When a topic is selected that you use frequently, you can click the **Favorites** tab, then click the **Add** button. That topic will appear in the Favorites list for easy access.

17.6 Performing a Search in Windows Help

To perform this exercise, you will need:

- Access to a Windows 2000 computer

1. Click the Start button.

2. Select **Help.**

   - The Windows Help window opens (see Figure 17-3).

3. Click the **Search** tab.

4. In the **Type in the word(s) to search for** text box, enter the word for which you want to search.

   - If you want to search for a phrase, put the phrase in quotations.

5. Press **Enter,** or click **List Topics.**

   - The matching topics are listed, ranked according to how well they match your word or phrase.

6. Double-click on a topic to see its contents in the left pane, or click the **Display** button.

TIP

Search for the phrase "General Troubleshooting" in Windows 2000 Server Help to see a glossary-type format of troubleshooting tips. Search for the word "Glossary" to see a comprehensive glossary of Windows 2000 and networking terms.

17.7 Use Windows Help to Launch a Troubleshooter

To perform this exercise, you will need:

- Access to a domain controller

1. Click the Start button.

2. Select **Help.**

   - The Windows Help window opens (see Figure 17-3).

3. Click the **Search** tab.

4. In the **Type in the word(s) to search for** text box, type "Windows 2000 Troubleshooting" (include the quotations).

5. Press **Enter,** or click **List Topics.**

   ■ The matching topics are listed.

6. Double-click on **Troubleshooter Overview.**

7. In the left pane, click on the **Related Topics** link.

8. From the pull-down list, select **Troubleshooters.**

   ■ A table listing the Windows 2000 troubleshooters appears.

9. Click on the appropriate link to launch the troubleshooter for that topic.

TechNet

TechNet is a resource of information contained on CD-ROM. Microsoft distributes TechNet on a monthly basis to technology (IT) professionals who subscribe to the service. TechNet files contain white papers and articles written by support professionals at Microsoft, career and industry information, discussion groups, technical feedback, and software. For more information about TechNet, see the Microsoft Web site (http://www.microsoft.com/). TechNet CDs can also contain service packs, resource kits, and complete texts of training courses. To subscribe call: 1-800-344-2121.

Directory of Windows 2000 Applications

The Directory of Windows 2000 Applications provides the most recent information about compatible and certified applications for the Windows 2000 Server operating system. You can search for information about applications designed for earlier versions of Windows and new applications designed for Windows 2000 Server. For more information, see the Directory of Windows 2000 Applications at the Microsoft Web site.

Windows 2000 Resource Kit

The **Microsoft Windows 2000 Resource Kit** is the official source of technical background information on the Windows 2000 operating system. It contains everything system and network administrators, Webmasters, and advanced users need to know to install, configure, administer, optimize, and troubleshoot Windows 2000 and networks and Web sites based on it. These materials come directly from the Microsoft product-development teams. They provide the most complete technical information and tools available for deploying and supporting the operating system.

Windows 2000 Support Tools, which is provided on the Windows 2000 CD set, includes a subset of the tools and the online Resource Kit books. These online books explain and help you work more effectively with many important new technologies such as Active Directory and the Kerberos authentication protocol.

FULL WINDOWS 2000 RESOURCE KIT

The full version of the Windows 2000 Resource Kit is a complementary product to Windows 2000. It comes with a companion CD that can be installed on a computer running Windows 2000. The full Windows 2000 Resource Kit contains:

- The Resource Kit books in print format, which include:
    - The *Windows 2000 Professional Resource Kit,* which is a separate volume containing core technologies information for Windows 2000
    - The *Windows 2000 Server Resource Kit,* which is volumes two through seven
- The Resource Kit companion CD, which includes:
    - All Resource Kit books in online format
    - The complete set of over 200 Resource Kit tools
    - Documentation for the tools, the registry, error messages, and performance counters

A Web version of the *Windows 2000 Resource Kit,* including the online books, all tools, and the latest updates, can be downloaded by subscription from the Microsoft Web site (http://mspress.microsoft.com/reslink).

Windows 2000 Support Tools and Online Books

The Windows 2000 CD set contains a subset of the *Windows 2000 Resource Kit,* including:

- All Resource Kit books in online format
- Approximately 50 of the Resource Kit tools

To open the following online documentation, you must first install Windows 2000 Support Tools from the Windows 2000 CD.

Hardware Compatibility List

The Windows 2000 Hardware Compatibility List contains a list of computers, system components, and peripherals that are compatible with Windows 2000 Server. To view this list, see the Microsoft Web site (also see Exercise 2.2).

Updated Technical Information

The Microsoft Personal Support Center Web site contains an extensive collection of articles, troubleshooting wizards, items you can download, and other useful information. The articles are in-depth papers written to help you understand more about the features included in Windows 2000. For more information or to begin a search, see the Microsoft Web site (http://www.microsoft.com).

WWW Search Engines

The Internet is a wealth of information where you can find many resources regarding Windows 2000. Use the various search engines to search for the phrase "Windows 2000," and you will be amazed at the results. You will find on-line magazines, user groups, newsgroups, and businesses—all about Windows 2000. You can also search for "Windows NT," and many of the resulting links will lead you to Windows 2000 upgrade information.

Summary

You are not alone in the Windows 2000 world. A plethora of information and tools are available to assist you in assimilating and implementing Windows 2000 Server on a network. Thorough planning and diligent maintenance should help circumvent most troubleshooting adventures. The troubleshooting techniques work for networks and for real life. Hopefully this book has inspired you to learn more about Windows 2000 Server, for there is much to learn about this powerful operating system. Since Microsoft is already working on the next generation of operating systems, it will benefit you to conquer this material quickly. Many businesses will be looking for people like you who know Windows 2000. Make the most of your opportunities and keep learning.

REVIEW EXERCISE

If the graphic next to the option is a square (❑), there can be more than one answer for that question. If the graphic is a circle (○), there is only one correct answer. Color in the shape(s) to indicate your answer(s).

1. Jay's computer is not working. What is the first thing he should check?

   a. ○ Power connection

   b. ○ Network connection

   c. ○ Server connection

   d. ○ French connection

2. Jay's computer still is not working. Jay's network administrator, Tom, discovers that Jay's computer is the only one that cannot connect to the server. With which network component does the problem lie?

   a. ○ The client computer

   b. ○ The server

   c. ○ The network

   d. ○ The printer

3. Jay's computer is working, but now he cannot access a particular file on the server. What could Tom do to determine why Jay does not have access to the file?

   a. ❏ Delete the file and reformat the hard drive on the server.

   b ❏ Check the permissions on the file.

   c. ❏ Log on as an administrator and try to access the file.

   d. ❏ Check Jay's group memberships and their associated permissions to access the file.

4. Jenny is trying to install Windows 2000 Server but is experiencing problems. Which of the following resources could she use to troubleshoot the situation?

   a. ❏ Windows Help

   b. ❏ Windows 2000 Troubleshooter

   c. ❏ Windows 2000 Resource Kit

   d. ❏ TechNet

5. Tim, Jon, and Casey each have workstations on the network. Jon has access to the server, but Tim and Casey do not. Which of the following items could be causing the fault?

   a. ❏ A network cable

   b. ❏ NIC

   c. ❏ Hub

   d. ❏ Permissions

PERFORMANCE CHALLENGES

■ Choose two topics from this chapter and search the Windows Help for additional information. Discover how to print the topics and do so.

■ Choose two of the troubleshooters and answer all of the questions in each. Document the troubleshooter's conclusions.

■ For each of the troubleshooting guidelines, give one more reason why that guideline is valid. Enter your contribution in a word processing document.

G

Gateway Service for NetWare,
354–356
Gigabytes, 19
Global Catalog Server, 157
Global groups, 189–190, 193
Globally Unique Identifier (GUID), 140
gov, 112
Groups, 43, 187–203, 300–304
adjusting membership in,
196–198, 301–303
built-in, 199–201
configuring, 244–246
creating, 194–196
local, 192–194
properties dialog box, 300–301
scopes, 188–192
determining the best,
191–192
domain local, 190, 193, 200
global, 189–190, 193, 199
purposes of, 191
universal, 189–190, 193
types of, 188–189
GUID. *See* Globally Unique
Identifier

H

Hard disks, 24
See also Disks
Hard drive terminology, 333–334
Hardware, 18–33
64–bit very large memory (VLM)
support, 21
bus, 21–23
CD-ROM drives, 24–25
central processing unit (CPU),
18–19
controllers, 23
drivers, 25
expansion cards, 21
floppy disks, 23–24
hard disks, 24
interrupt request lines (IRQs),
26–28
measurements, 18–19
memory, 19–20
minimum requirements, 62–63
motherboard, 18
plug and play, 28

ports and connectors, 21
tape drives, 25
troubleshooting, 454–456
universal serial bus (USB), 22–23
Hardware Compatibility List (HCL),
29–31, 63–64, 472
HCL. *See* Hardware Compatibility List
Help files, 467, 469–471
Hierarchical structure, 110
Hierarchy, of organizational units, 166
Home folders, 326–328
Host names, 113
Hot-swapping, 23
Hub, 7

I

Improving access speed for remote
locations, 115
Incremental backup, 435
Installation, 36, 77–107
answer file, 102–104
with CD-ROM, 79–82
completing, 93–94
file systems, 86–87
Found New Hardware Wizard, 94
introduction to, 78–79
licensing agreement, 84, 89
network, 82–83
new, 67
partitioning, 85–86, 87–88
searching for other operating
systems, 84
server settings, 87–92
service packs, 95–96
setup wizard, 83–84
troubleshooting failed, 105
unattended, 96–104
Windows 2000 system
components, 90–91, 93–94
See also Setup Manager; Setup
Wizard; Unattended
installation
Installation preparation, 61–75
checklist for, 72–73
hardware, 62–64
joining domains or workgroups,
70–71
medial options, 69–70
multiple OS booting options,
67–69
upgrading vs. new installation,
64–67

int, 11
Intel Corporation, 18
IntelliMirror, 12
Interfaces, 23
Internet Information Server, 5.0, 12
Internet Information Services (IIS),
372–376
software requirements, 373
and web sites, 374–376
Interoperability, 353–356
Interrupt request lines (IRQs), 26–28
common lines, 28
IP addresses, 48, 115
and ping, 111
IPX, 309, 310
IRQs. *See* Interrupt request lines

K

Kerberos, 12
Kerberos policy, 224
Key algorithm, 443
Kilobytes, 19

L

L2TP. *See* Layer two tunneling
protocol
LAN. *See* Local area network
Layer two tunneling protocol
(L2TP), 310
LDAP. *See* Lightweight Directory
Access Protocol
Licensing, 36–39, 84, 89
terminal services, 358–360
Lightweight Directory Access Protocol
(LDAP), 140
Local, 35
Local area network (LAN), 5
Local groups. *See* Groups
Local policies. *See* Policies
Local security database, 52
Local user profile, 286, 288
Location, 55
Logical drive, 334
Logon, 53–54
setting hours, 283–284
Logon events, 227
Logon rights, 231
Logon scripts, 328
Lookup queries, 115